Collected Poems

of

ROBERT SERVICE

Books of Poetry by

ROBERT SERVICE

≡

THE SPELL OF THE YUKON

BALLADS OF A CHEECHAKO

RHYMES OF A ROLLING STONE

RHYMES OF A RED CROSS MAN

BALLADS OF A BOHEMIAN

BAR-ROOM BALLADS

COLLECTED POEMS

SONGS OF A SUN-LOVER

RHYMES OF A ROUGHNECK

LYRICS OF A LOW BROW

RHYMES OF A REBEL

Collected Poems
of
ROBERT SERVICE

DODD, MEAD & COMPANY
New York

TO

C. M.

PRINTED IN THE UNITED STATES OF AMERICA
BY THE VAIL-BALLOU PRESS, INC., BINGHAMTON, N. Y.

CONTENTS

BOOK ONE

THE SPELL OF THE YUKON
AND OTHER VERSES

	Page
THE LAND GOD FORGOT	xviii
THE SPELL OF THE YUKON	3
THE HEART OF THE SOURDOUGH	6
THE THREE VOICES	8
THE LAW OF THE YUKON	10
THE PARSON'S SON	14
THE CALL OF THE WILD	17
THE LONE TRAIL	19
THE PINES	21
THE LURE OF LITTLE VOICES	23
THE SONG OF THE WAGE-SLAVE	25
GRIN	27
THE SHOOTING OF DAN MCGREW	29
THE CREMATION OF SAM MCGEE	33
MY MADONNA	37
UNFORGOTTEN	38
THE RECKONING	39
QUATRAINS	40
THE MEN THAT DON'T FIT IN	42
MUSIC IN THE BUSH	44
THE RHYME OF THE REMITTANCE MAN	46
THE LOW-DOWN WHITE	48
THE LITTLE OLD LOG CABIN	50
THE YOUNGER SON	52
THE MARCH OF THE DEAD	54
"FIGHTING MAC"	57
THE WOMAN AND THE ANGEL	60
THE RHYME OF THE RESTLESS ONES	62

	Page
NEW YEAR'S EVE	64
COMFORT	67
THE HARPY	68
PREMONITION	70
THE TRAMPS	71
L'ENVOI	72

BOOK TWO

BALLADS OF A CHEECHAKO

TO THE MAN OF THE HIGH NORTH	77
MEN OF THE HIGH NORTH	78
THE BALLAD OF THE NORTHERN LIGHTS	80
THE BALLAD OF THE BLACK FOX SKIN	91
THE BALLAD OF PIOUS PETE	98
THE BALLAD OF BLASPHEMOUS BILL	103
THE BALLAD OF ONE-EYED MIKE	107
THE BALLAD OF THE BRAND	111
THE BALLAD OF HARD-LUCK HENRY	117
THE MAN FROM ELDORADO	120
MY FRIENDS	125
THE PROSPECTOR	128
THE BLACK SHEEP	132
THE TELEGRAPH OPERATOR	135
THE WOOD-CUTTER	138
THE SONG OF THE MOUTH-ORGAN	141
THE TRAIL OF NINETY-EIGHT	144
THE BALLAD OF GUM-BOOT BEN	150
CLANCY OF THE MOUNTED POLICE	153
LOST	159
L'ENVOI	163

BOOK THREE

RHYMES OF A ROLLING STONE

Page

PRELUDE 167
A ROLLING STONE 168
THE SOLDIER OF FORTUNE 171
THE GRAMOPHONE AT FOND-DU-LAC 174
THE LAND OF BEYOND 177
SUNSHINE 178
THE IDEALIST 186
ATHABASKA DICK 187
CHEER 191
THE RETURN 192
THE JUNIOR GOD 193
THE NOSTOMANIAC 195
AMBITION 198
TO SUNNYDALE 199
THE BLIND AND THE DEAD 200
THE ATAVIST 202
THE SCEPTIC 205
THE ROVER 206
BARB-WIRE BILL 208
"?" 212
JUST THINK! 213
THE LUNGER 214
THE MOUNTAIN AND THE LAKE 217
THE HEADLINER AND THE BREADLINER 218
DEATH IN THE ARCTIC 219
DREAMS ARE BEST 226
THE QUITTER 228
THE COW-JUICE CURE 229
WHILE THE BANNOCK BAKES 232
THE LOST MASTER 236
LITTLE MOCCASINS 237
THE WANDERLUST 239
THE TRAPPER'S CHRISTMAS EVE 242
THE WORLD'S ALL RIGHT 244

CONTENTS

Page

THE BALDNESS OF CHEWED-EAR 247
THE MOTHER 251
THE DREAMER 252
AT THIRTY-FIVE 256
THE SQUAW MAN 258
HOME AND LOVE 261
I'M SCARED OF IT ALL 262
A SONG OF SUCCESS 265
THE SONG OF THE CAMP-FIRE 266
HER LETTER 270
THE MAN WHO KNEW 271
THE LOGGER 272
THE PASSING OF THE YEAR 274
THE GHOSTS 276
GOOD-BYE, LITTLE CABIN 282
HEART O' THE NORTH 284
THE SCRIBE'S PRAYER 285

BOOK FOUR

RHYMES OF A RED CROSS MAN

FOREWORD 291
THE CALL 293
THE FOOL 295
THE VOLUNTEER 297
THE CONVALESCENT 299
THE MAN FROM ATHABASKA 300
THE RED RETREAT 303
THE HAGGIS OF PRIVATE MC PHEE 306
THE LARK 310
THE ODYSSEY OF 'ERBERT 'IGGINS 311
A SONG OF WINTER WEATHER 316
TIPPERARY DAYS 318
FLEURETTE 320
FUNK 324
OUR HERO 326

CONTENTS

Page

MY MATE 328

MILKING TIME 330

YOUNG FELLOW MY LAD 332

A SONG OF THE SANDBAGS 334

ON THE WIRE 336

BILL'S GRAVE 339

JEAN DESPREZ 341

GOING HOME 345

COCOTTE 346

MY BAY'NIT 349

CARRY ON! 351

OVER THE PARAPET 353

THE BALLAD OF SOULFUL SAM 356

ONLY A BOCHE 359

PILGRIMS 362

MY PRISONER 364

TRI-COLOUR 367

A POT OF TEA 369

THE REVELATION 370

GRAND-PÈRE 373

SON 374

THE BLACK DUDEEN 376

THE LITTLE PIOU-PIOU 379

BILL THE BOMBER 381

THE WHISTLE OF SANDY MC GRAW 385

THE STRETCHER-BEARER 389

WOUNDED 390

FAITH 394

THE COWARD 395

MISSIS MORIARTY'S BOY 398

MY FOE 400

MY JOB 404

THE SONG OF THE PACIFIST 405

THE TWINS 407

THE SONG OF THE SOLDIER-BORN 408

AFTERNOON TEA 410

THE MOURNERS 415

L'ENVOI 417

BOOK FIVE

BALLADS OF A BOHEMIAN

Page

PRELUDE 421

BOOK ONE · SPRING

I

MY GARRET 425
JULOT THE *Apache* 426

II

L'ESCARGOT D'OR 430
IT IS LATER THAN YOU THINK 432
NOCTAMBULE 435

III

INSOMNIA 438
MOON SONG 440
THE SEWING-GIRL 441

IV

LUCILLE 444
ON THE BOULEVARD 449
FACILITY 452

V

GOLDEN DAYS 454
THE JOY OF LITTLE THINGS 455
THE ABSINTHE DRINKERS 456

BOOK TWO · EARLY SUMMER

I

THE RELEASE 463
THE WEE SHOP 464
THE PHILISTINE AND THE BOHEMIAN 467

CONTENTS

Page

II

THE BOHEMIAN DREAMS 470
A DOMESTIC TRAGEDY 472
THE PENCIL SELLER 474

III

FI-FI IN BED 479
GODS IN THE GUTTER 480
THE DEATH OF MARIE TORO 481

IV

THE BOHEMIAN 484
THE AUCTION SALE 486
THE JOY OF BEING POOR 489

V

MY NEIGHBORS 491
  ROOM 4: THE PAINTER CHAP 492
  ROOM 6: THE LITTLE WORKGIRL 494
  ROOM 5: THE CONCERT SINGER 496
  ROOM 7: THE COCO-FIEND 498

BOOK THREE · LATE SUMMER

I

THE PHILANDERER 507
THE *Petit Vieux* 508
MY MASTERPIECE 509
MY BOOK 510
MY HOUR 512

II

A SONG OF SIXTY-FIVE 515
TEDDY BEAR 517
THE OUTLAW 519
THE WALKERS 521

III

POOR PETER 523
THE WISTFUL ONE 524

CONTENTS

	Page
IF YOU HAD A FRIEND	525
THE CONTENTED MAN	526
THE SPIRIT OF THE UNBORN BABE	527

IV

FINISTÈRE	530
OLD DAVID SMAIL	532
THE WONDERER	533
OH, IT IS GOOD	536

V

I HAVE SOME FRIENDS	537
THE QUEST	538
THE COMFORTER	540
THE OTHER ONE	540
CATASTROPHE	542

BOOK FOUR · WINTER

I

PRISCILLA	549
A CASUALTY	552
THE BLOOD-RED *Fourragère*	554
JIM	556

II

KELLY OF THE LEGION	559
THE THREE TOMMIES	562
THE TWA JOCKS	565

III

HIS BOYS	568
THE BOOBY-TRAP	570
BONEHEAD BILL	572

IV

A LAPSE OF TIME AND A WORD OF EXPLANATION	575
MICHAEL	575
THE WIFE	577
VICTORY STUFF	579
WAS IT YOU?	580

CONTENTS

Page

v

Les Grands Mutiles 582
   THE SIGHTLESS MAN 583
   THE LEGLESS MAN 586
   THE FACELESS MAN 589
L'ENVOI 594

BOOK SIX

BAR-ROOM BALLADS

PRELUDE 601
THE BALLAD OF SALVATION BILL 602
EACH DAY A LIFE 606
DOLLS 607
THE BALLAD OF HOW MACPHERSON HELD THE FLOOR . . 610
GIPSY 616
THE BALLAD OF HANK THE FINN 618
SHEILA 622
THE BALLAD OF TOUCH-THE-BUTTON NELL 623
ATOLL 628
THE BALLAD OF THE ICE-WORM COCKTAIL 630
GRANDAD 636
THE BALLAD OF THE LEATHER MEDAL 638
COURAGE 643
A SOURDOUGH STORY 645
ALLOUETTE 648
THE BALLAD OF LENIN'S TOMB 650
MAIDS IN MAY 655
THE BALLAD OF CASEY'S BILLY-GOAT 657
THE SMOKING FROG 662
MADAME LA MARQUISE 664
BEACHCOMBER 668
JOBSON OF THE *Star* 670
BASTARD 673

CONTENTS

Page

BESSIE'S BOIL 675
FIVE-PER-CENT 678
SECURITY 680
LONGEVITY 683
RESIGNATION 685
PRIVACY 686
MATERNITY 688
VIRGINITY 689
SENSIBILITY 691
INFIDELITY 694
LAUGHTER 697
LAZINESS 698
ACCORDION 699
TREES AGAINST THE SKY 701
MOON-LOVER 703
LITTLE PUDDLETON 706
BOOKSHELF 708
FIVE FRIVOLOUS SONGS:—
   YOU CAN'T CAN LOVE 713
   LIP-STICK LIZ 715
   THE BREAD-KNIFE BALLAD 717
   THE BOOLA-BOOLA MAID 718
   THE SONG OF A SARDINE 720
WARSAW 722
ENEMY CONSCRIPT 723
DON'T CHEER 725
L'ENVOI 727

INDEX TO FIRST LINES 729

THE LAND GOD FORGOT

The lonely sunsets flare forlorn
   Down valleys dreadly desolate;
The lordly mountains soar in scorn
   As still as death, as stern as fate.

    The lonely sunsets flame and die;
      The giant valleys gulp the night;
    The monster mountains scrape the sky,
      Where eager stars are diamond-bright.

So gaunt against the gibbous moon,
   Piercing the silence velvet-piled,
A lone wolf howls his ancient rune—
   The fell arch-spirit of the Wild.

    O outcast land! O leper land!
      Let the lone wolf-cry all express
    The hate insensate of thy hand,
      Thy heart's abysmal loneliness.

Book One

THE SPELL OF THE YUKON
AND OTHER VERSES

I have no doubt at all the Devil grins,
As seas of ink I spatter.
Ye gods, forgive my "literary" sins—
The other kind don't matter.

THE SPELL OF THE YUKON

I WANTED the gold, and I sought it;
   I scrabbled and mucked like a slave.
Was it famine or scurvy—I fought it;
   I hurled my youth into a grave.
I wanted the gold, and I got it—
   Came out with a fortune last fall,—
Yet somehow life's not what I thought it,
   And somehow the gold isn't all.

No! There's the land. (Have you seen it?)
   It's the cussedest land that I know,
From the big, dizzy mountains that screen it
   To the deep, deathlike valleys below.
Some say God was tired when He made it;
   Some say it's a fine land to shun;
Maybe; but there's some as would trade it
   For no land on earth—and I'm one.

You come to get rich (damned good reason);
   You feel like an exile at first;
You hate it like hell for a season,
   And then you are worse than the worst.
It grips you like some kinds of sinning;
   It twists you from foe to a friend;
It seems it's been since the beginning;
   It seems it will be to the end.

I've stood in some mighty-mouthed hollow
   That's plumb-full of hush to the brim;

I've watched the big, husky sun wallow
   In crimson and gold, and grow dim,
Till the moon set the pearly peaks gleaming,
   And the stars tumbled out, neck and crop;
And I've thought that I surely was dreaming,
   With the peace o' the world piled on top.

The summer—no sweeter was ever;
   The sunshiny woods all athrill;
The grayling aleap in the river,
   The bighorn asleep on the hill.
The strong life that never knows harness;
   The wilds where the caribou call;
The freshness, the freedom, the farness—
   O God! how I'm stuck on it all.

The winter! the brightness that blinds you,
   The white land locked tight as a drum,
The cold fear that follows and finds you,
   The silence that bludgeons you dumb.
The snows that are older than history,
   The woods where the weird shadows slant;
The stillness, the moonlight, the mystery,
   I've bade 'em good-by—but I can't.

There's a land where the mountains are nameless,
   And the rivers all run God knows where;
There are lives that are erring and aimless,
   And deaths that just hang by a hair;
There are hardships that nobody reckons;
   There are valleys unpeopled and still;
There's a land—oh, it beckons and beckons,
   And I want to go back—and I will.

They're making my money diminish;
   I'm sick of the taste of champagne.
Thank God! when I'm skinned to a finish
   I'll pike to the Yukon again.
I'll fight—and you bet it's no sham-fight;
   It's hell!—but I've been there before;
And it's better than this by a damsite—
   So me for the Yukon once more.

There's gold, and it's haunting and haunting;
   It's luring me on as of old;
Yet it isn't the gold that I'm wanting
   So much as just finding the gold.
It's the great, big, broad land 'way up yonder,
   It's the forests where silence has lease;
It's the beauty that thrills me with wonder,
   It's the stillness that fills me with peace.

THE HEART OF THE SOURDOUGH

THERE where the mighty mountains bare their fangs unto the
moon,
There where the sullen sun-dogs glare in the snow-bright,
bitter noon,
And the glacier-glutted streams sweep down at the clarion call
of June.

There where the livid tundras keep their tryst with the tran-
quil snows;
There where the silences are spawned, and the light of hell-fire
flows
Into the bowl of the midnight sky, violet, amber and rose.

There where the rapids churn and roar, and the ice-floes bel-
lowing run;
Where the tortured, twisted rivers of blood rush to the setting
sun—
I've packed my kit and I'm going, boys, ere another day is
done.

*　　*　　*　　*　　*　　*　　*　　*　　*

I knew it would call, or soon or late, as it calls the whirring
wings;
It's the olden lure, it's the golden lure, it's the lure of the time-
less things,
And to-night, oh, God of the trails untrod, how it whines in
my heart-strings!

6

I'm sick to death of your well-groomed gods, your make-
believe and your show;
I long for a whiff of bacon and beans, a snug shakedown in
the snow;
A trail to break, and a life at stake, and another bout with
the foe.

With the raw-ribbed Wild that abhors all life, the Wild that
would crush and rend,
I have clinched and closed with the naked North, I have
learned to defy and defend;
Shoulder to shoulder we have fought it out—yet the Wild
must win in the end.

I have flouted the Wild. I have followed its lure, fearless,
familiar, alone;
By all that the battle means and makes I claim that land for
mine own;
Yet the Wild must win, and a day will come when I shall be
overthrown.

Then when as wolf-dogs fight we've fought, the lean wolf-
land and I;
Fought and bled till the snows are red under the reeling sky;
Even as lean wolf-dog goes down will I go down and die.

THE THREE VOICES

The waves have a story to tell me,
  As I lie on the lonely beach;
Chanting aloft in the pine-tops,
  The wind has a lesson to teach;
But the stars sing an anthem of glory
  I cannot put into speech.

The waves tell of ocean spaces,
  Of hearts that are wild and brave,
Of populous city places,
  Of desolate shores they lave,
Of men who sally in quest of gold
  To sink in an ocean grave.

The wind is a mighty roamer;
  He bids me keep me free,
Clean from the taint of the gold-lust,
  Hardy and pure as he;
Cling with my love to nature,
  As a child to the mother-knee.

But the stars throng out in their glory,
  And they sing of the God in man;
They sing of the Mighty Master,
  Of the loom his fingers span,
Where a star or a soul is a part of the whole,
  And weft in the wondrous plan.

8

Here by the camp-fire's flicker,
  Deep in my blanket curled,
I long for the peace of the pine-gloom,
  When the scroll of the Lord is unfurled,
And the wind and the wave are silent,
  And world is singing to world.

THE LAW OF THE YUKON

This is the law of the Yukon, and ever she makes it plain:
"Send not your foolish and feeble; send me your strong and
    your sane—
Strong for the red rage of battle; sane, for I harry them sore;
Send me men girt for the combat, men who are grit to the core;
Swift as the panther in triumph, fierce as the bear in defeat,
Sired of a bulldog parent, steeled in the furnace heat.
Send me the best of your breeding, lend me your chosen ones;
Them will I take to my bosom, them will I call my sons;
Them will I gild with my treasure, them will I glut with my
    meat;
But the others—the misfits, the failures—I trample under my
    feet.
Dissolute, damned and despairful, crippled and palsied and
    slain,
Ye would send me the spawn of your gutters— Go! take back
    your spawn again.

"Wild and wide are my borders, stern as death is my sway;
From my ruthless throne I have ruled alone for a million years
    and a day;
Hugging my mighty treasure, waiting for man to come,
Till he swept like a turbid torrent, and after him swept—the
    scum.
The pallid pimp of the dead-line, the enervate of the pen,
One by one I weeded them out, for all that I sought was—
    Men.

One by one I dismayed them, frighting them sore with my
  glooms;
One by one I betrayed them unto my manifold dooms.
Drowned them like rats in my rivers, starved them like curs on
  my plains,
Rotted the flesh that was left them, poisoned the blood in their
  veins;
Burst with my winter upon them, searing forever their sight,
Lashed them with fungus-white faces, whimpering wild in the
  night;

"Staggering blind through the storm-whirl, stumbling mad
  through the snow,
Frozen stiff in the ice-pack, brittle and bent like a bow;
Featureless, formless, forsaken, scented by wolves in their
  flight,
Left for the wind to make music through ribs that are glitter-
  ing white;
Gnawing the black crust of failure, searching the pit of despair,
Crooking the toe in the trigger, trying to patter a prayer;
Going outside with an escort, raving with lips all afoam,
Writing a cheque for a million, driveling feebly of home;
Lost like a louse in the burning . . . or else in the tented town
Seeking a drunkard's solace, sinking and sinking down;
Steeped in the slime at the bottom, dead to a decent world,
Lost 'mid the human flotsam, far on the frontier hurled;
In the camp at the bend of the river, with its dozen saloons
  aglare,
Its gambling dens ariot, its gramophones all ablare;
Crimped with the crimes of a city, sin-ridden and bridled with
  lies,
In the hush of my mountained vastness, in the flush of my mid-
  night skies.

Plague-spots, yet tools of my purpose, so natheless I suffer them thrive,

Crushing my Weak in their clutches, that only my Strong may survive.

"But the others, the men of my mettle, the men who would 'stablish my fame
Unto its ultimate issue, winning me honor, not shame;
Searching my uttermost valleys, fighting each step as they go,
Shooting the wrath of my rapids, scaling my ramparts of snow;
Ripping the guts of my mountains, looting the beds of my creeks,
Them will I take to my bosom, and speak as a mother speaks.
I am the land that listens, I am the land that broods;
Steeped in eternal beauty, crystalline waters and woods.
Long have I waited lonely, shunned as a thing accurst,
Monstrous, moody, pathetic, the last of the lands and the first;
Visioning camp-fires at twilight, sad with a longing forlorn,
Feeling my womb o'er-pregnant with the seed of cities unborn.
Wild and wide are my borders, stern as death is my sway,
And I wait for the men who will win me—and I will not be won in a day;
And I will not be won by weaklings, subtle, suave and mild,
But by men with the hearts of vikings, and the simple faith of a child;
Desperate, strong and resistless, unthrottled by fear or defeat,
Them will I gild with my treasure, them will I glut with my meat.

"Lofty I stand from each sister land, patient and wearily wise,
With the weight of a world of sadness in my quiet, passionless eyes;

Dreaming alone of a people, dreaming alone of a day,
When men shall not rape my riches, and curse me and go away;
Making a bawd of my bounty, fouling the hand that gave—
Till I rise in my wrath and I sweep on their path and I stamp
    them into a grave.
Dreaming of men who will bless me, of women esteeming me
    good,
Of children born in my borders of radiant motherhood,
Of cities leaping to stature, of fame like a flag unfurled,
As I pour the tide of my riches in the eager lap of the world."

This is the Law of the Yukon, that only the Strong shall thrive;
That surely the Weak shall perish, and only the Fit survive.
Dissolute, damned and despairful, crippled and palsied and slain,
This is the Will of the Yukon,— Lo, how she makes it plain!

THE PARSON'S SON

*This is the song of the parson's son, as he squats in his shack
  alone,*
*On the wild, weird nights, when the Northern Lights shoot up
  from the frozen zone,*
*And it's sixty below, and couched in the snow the hungry
  huskies moan:*

"I'm one of the Arctic brotherhood, I'm an old-time pioneer.
I came with the first—O God! how I've cursed this Yukon—
  but still I'm here.
I've sweated athirst in its summer heat, I've frozen and starved
  in its cold;
I've followed my dreams by its thousand streams, I've toiled and
  moiled for its gold.

"Look at my eyes—been snow-blind twice; look where my
  foot's half gone;
And that gruesome scar on my left cheek, where the frost-fiend
  bit to the bone.
Each one a brand of this devil's land, where I've played and
  . I've lost the game,
A broken wreck with a craze for 'hooch,' and never a cent to
  my name.

"This mining is only a gamble; the worst is as good as the best;
I was in with the bunch and I might have come out right on
  top with the rest;

With Cormack, Ladue and Macdonald— O God! but it's hell to
  think
Of the thousands and thousands I've squandered on cards and
  women and drink.

"In the early days we were just a few, and we hunted and fished
  around,
Nor dreamt by our lonely camp-fires of the wealth that lay
  under the ground.
We traded in skins and whiskey, and I've often slept under the
  shade
Of that lone birch tree on Bonanza, where the first big find
  was made.

"We were just like a great big family, and every man had his
  squaw,
And we lived such a wild, free, fearless life beyond the pale of
  the law;
Till sudden there came a whisper, and it maddened us every man,
And I got in on Bonanza before the big rush began.

"Oh, those Dawson days, and the sin and the blaze, and the town
  all open wide!
(If God made me in His likeness, sure He let the devil inside.)
But we all were mad, both the good and the bad, and as for the
  women, well—
No spot on the map in so short a space has hustled more souls
  to hell.

"Money was just like dirt there, easy to get and to spend.
I was all caked in on a dance-hall jade, but she shook me in the
  end.

It put me queer, and for near a year I never drew sober breath,
Till I found myself in the bughouse ward with a claim staked
out on death.

"Twenty years in the Yukon, struggling along its creeks;
Roaming its giant valleys, scaling its god-like peaks;
Bathed in its fiery sunsets, fighting its fiendish cold—
Twenty years in the Yukon . . . twenty years—and I'm old.

"Old and weak, but no matter, there's 'hooch' in the bottle still.
I'll hitch up the dogs to-morrow, and mush down the trail to Bill.
It's so long dark, and I'm lonesome—I'll just lay down on the
bed;
To-morrow I'll go . . . to-morrow . . . I guess I'll play on the
red.

". . . Come, Kit, your pony is saddled. I'm waiting, dear, in
the court . . .
. . . Minnie, you devil, I'll kill you if you skip with that flossy
sport . . .
. . . How much does it go to the pan, Bill? . . . play up,
School, and play the game . . .
. . Our Father, which art in heaven, hallowed be Thy
name . . ."

This was the song of the parson's son, as he lay in his bunk alone,
Ere the fire went out and the cold crept in, and his blue lips
ceased to moan,
And the hunger-maddened malamutes had torn him flesh from
bone.

THE CALL OF THE WILD

Have you gazed on naked grandeur where there's nothing else
    to gaze on,
  Set pieces and drop-curtain scenes galore,
Big mountains heaved to heaven, which the blinding sunsets
    blazon,
  Black canyons where the rapids rip and roar?
Have you swept the visioned valley with the green stream streak-
    ing through it,
  Searched the Vastness for a something you have lost?
Have you strung your soul to silence? Then for God's sake go
    and do it;
  Hear the challenge, learn the lesson, pay the cost.

Have you wandered in the wilderness, the sagebrush desolation,
  The bunch-grass levels where the cattle graze?
Have you whistled bits of rag-time at the end of all creation,
  And learned to know the desert's little ways?
Have you camped upon the foothills, have you galloped o'er the
    ranges,
  Have you roamed the arid sun-lands through and through?
Have you chummed up with the mesa? Do you know its moods
    and changes?
  Then listen to the Wild—it's calling you.

Have you known the Great White Silence, not a snow-gemmed
    twig aquiver?
  (Eternal truths that shame our soothing lies.)

Have you broken trail on snowshoes? mushed your huskies up
    the river,
  Dared the unknown, led the way, and clutched the prize?
Have you marked the map's void spaces, mingled with the mon-
    grel races,
  Felt the savage strength of brute in every thew?
And though grim as hell the worst is, can you round it off with
    curses?
  Then hearken to the Wild—it's wanting you.

Have you suffered, starved and triumphed, groveled down, yet
    grasped at glory,
  Grown bigger in the bigness of the whole?
"Done things" just for the doing, letting babblers tell the story,
  Seeing through the nice veneer the naked soul?
Have you seen God in His splendors, heard the text that nature
    renders?
  (You'll never hear it in the family pew.)
The simple things, the true things, the silent men who do
    things—
  Then listen to the Wild—it's calling you.

They have cradled you in custom, they have primed you with
    their preaching,
  They have soaked you in convention through and through;
They have put you in a showcase; you're a credit to their teach-
    ing—
  But can't you hear the Wild?—it's calling you.
Let us probe the silent places, let us seek what luck betide us;
  Let us journey to a lonely land I know.
There's a whisper on the night-wind, there's a star agleam to
    guide us,
  And the Wild is calling, calling . . . let us go.

THE LONE TRAIL

Ye who know the Lone Trail fain would follow it,
Though it lead to glory or the darkness of the pit.
Ye who take the Lone Trail, bid your love good-by;
The Lone Trail, the Lone Trail follow till you die.

The trails of the world be countless, and most of the trails be
  tried;
You tread on the heels of the many, till you come where the
  ways divide;
And one lies safe in the sunlight, and the other is dreary and wan,
Yet you look aslant at the Lone Trail, and the Lone Trail lures
  you on.
And somehow you're sick of the highway, with its noise and its
  easy needs,
And you seek the risk of the by-way, and you reck not where
  it leads.
And sometimes it leads to the desert, and the tongue swells out
  of the mouth,
And you stagger blind to the mirage, to die in the mocking
  drouth.
And sometimes it leads to the mountain, to the light of the lone
  camp-fire,
And you gnaw your belt in the anguish of hunger-goaded desire.
And sometimes it leads to the Southland, to the swamp where
  the orchid glows,
And you rave to your grave with the fever, and they rob the
  corpse for its clothes.

And sometimes it leads to the Northland, and the scurvy softens
    your bones,
And your flesh dints in like putty, and you spit out your teeth
    like stones.
And sometimes it leads to a coral reef in the wash of a weedy
    sea,
And you sit and stare at the empty glare where the gulls wait
    greedily.
And sometimes it leads to an Arctic trail, and the snows where
    your torn feet freeze,
And you whittle away the useless clay, and crawl on your hands
    and knees.
Often it leads to the dead-pit; always it leads to pain;
By the bones of your brothers ye know it, but oh, to follow
    you're fain.
By your bones they will follow behind you, till the ways of the
    world are made plain.

Bid good-by to sweetheart, bid good-by to friend;
The Lone Trail, the Lone Trail follow to the end.
Tarry not, and fear not, chosen of the true;
Lover of the Lone Trail, the Lone Trail waits for you.

THE PINES

WE sleep in the sleep of ages, the bleak, barbarian pines;
The gray moss drapes us like sages, and closer we lock our lines,
And deeper we clutch through the gelid gloom where never a
    sunbeam shines.

On the flanks of the storm-gored ridges are our black battalions
    massed;
We surge in a host to the sullen coast, and we sing in the ocean
    blast;
From empire of sea to empire of snow we grip our empire fast.

To the niggard lands were we driven, 'twixt desert and floes are
    we penned;
To us was the Northland given, ours to stronghold and defend;
Ours till the world be riven in the crash of the utter end;

Ours from the bleak beginning, through the æons of death-like
    sleep;
Ours from the shock when the naked rock was hurled from the
    hissing deep;
Ours through the twilight ages of weary glacier creep.

Wind of the East, Wind of the West, wandering to and fro,
Chant your songs in our topmost boughs, that the sons of men
    may know
The peerless pine was the first to come, and the pine will be
    last to go!

We pillar the halls of perfumed gloom; we plume where the
    eagles soar;
The North-wind swoops from the brooding Pole, and our an-
    cients crash and roar;
But where one falls from the crumbling walls shoots up a hardy
    score.

We spring from the gloom of the canyon's womb; in the valley's
    lap we lie;
From the white foam-fringe, where the breakers cringe, to the
    peaks that tusk the sky,
We climb, and we peer in the crag-locked mere that gleams like
    a golden eye.

Gain to the verge of the hog-back ridge where the vision ranges
    free:
Pines and pines and the shadow of pines as far as the eye can see;
A steadfast legion of stalwart knights in dominant empery.

Sun, moon and stars give answer; shall we not staunchly stand,
Even as now, forever, wards of the wilder strand,
Sentinels of the stillness, lords of the last, lone land?

THE LURE OF LITTLE VOICES

THERE'S a cry from out the loneliness—oh, listen, Honey, listen!
　Do you hear it, do you fear it, you're a-holding of me so?
You're a-sobbing in your sleep, dear, and your lashes, how they
　　glisten—
　Do you hear the Little Voices all a-begging me to go?

All a-begging me to leave you. Day and night they're pleading,
　　praying,
　On the North-wind, on the West-wind, from the peak and
　　from the plain;
Night and day they never leave me—do you know what they
　　are saying?
　"He was ours before you got him, and we want him once
　　again."

Yes, they're wanting me, they're haunting me, the awful lonely
　　places;
　They're whining and they're whimpering as if each had a
　　soul;
They're calling from the wilderness, the vast and God-like
　　spaces,
　The stark and sullen solitudes that sentinel the Pole.

They miss my little camp-fires, ever brightly, bravely gleaming
　In the womb of desolation, where was never man before;
As comradeless I sought them, lion-hearted, loving, dreaming,
　And they hailed me as a comrade, and they loved me evermore.

And now they're all a-crying, and it's no use me denying;
    The spell of them is on me and I'm helpless as a child;
My heart is aching, aching, but I hear them, sleeping, waking;
    It's the Lure of Little Voices, it's the mandate of the Wild.

I'm afraid to tell you, Honey, I can take no bitter leaving;
    But softly in the sleep-time from your love I'll steal away.
Oh, it's cruel, dearie, cruel, and it's God knows how I'm grieving;
    But His loneliness is calling, and He knows I must obey.

THE SONG OF THE WAGE-SLAVE

When the long, long day is over, and the Big Boss gives me my
　pay,
I hope that it won't be hell-fire, as some of the parsons say.
And I hope that it won't be heaven, with some of the parsons
　I've met—
All I want is just quiet, just to rest and forget.
Look at my face, toil-furrowed; look at my calloused hands;
Master, I've done Thy bidding, wrought in Thy many lands—
Wrought for the little masters, big-bellied they be, and rich;
I've done their desire for a daily hire, and I die like a dog in a
　ditch.
I have used the strength Thou hast given, Thou knowest I did
　not shirk;
Threescore years of labor—Thine be the long day's work.
And now, Big Master, I'm broken and bent and twisted and
　scarred,
But I've held my job, and Thou knowest, and Thou will not
　judge me hard.
Thou knowest my sins are many, and often I've played the
　fool—
Whiskey and cards and women, they made me the devil's tool.
I was just like a child with money; I flung it away with a curse,
Feasting a fawning parasite, or glutting a harlot's purse;
Then back to the woods repentant, back to the mill or the mine,
I, the worker of workers, everything in my line.
Everything hard but headwork (I'd no more brains than a kid),
A brute with brute strength to labor, doing as I was bid;
Living in camps with men-folk, a lonely and loveless life;

Never knew kiss of sweetheart, never caress of wife.
A brute with brute strength to labor, and they were so far
above—
Yet I'd gladly have gone to the gallows for one little look of
Love.
I, with the strength of two men, savage and shy and wild—
Yet how I'd ha' treasured a woman, and the sweet, warm kiss of
a child!
Well, 'tis Thy world, and Thou knowest. I blaspheme and my
ways be rude;
But I've lived my life as I found it, and I've done my best to be
good;
I, the primitive toiler, half naked and grimed to the eyes,
Sweating it deep in their ditches, swining it stark in their sties;
Hurling down forests before me, spanning tumultuous streams;
Down in the ditch building o'er me palaces fairer than dreams;
Boring the rock to the ore-bed, driving the road through the fen,
Resolute, dumb, uncomplaining, a man in a world of men.
Master, I've filled my contract, wrought in Thy many lands;
Not by my sins wilt Thou judge me, but by the work of my
hands.
Master, I've done Thy bidding, and the light is low in the west,
And the long, long shift is over . . . Master, I've earned it—
Rest.

GRIN

If you're up against a bruiser and you're getting knocked
about—
>> Grin.

If you're feeling pretty groggy, and you're licked beyond a
doubt—
>> Grin.

Don't let him see you're funking, let him know with every clout,
Though your face is battered to a pulp, your blooming heart is
stout;
Just stand upon your pins until the beggar knocks you out—
>> And grin.

This life's a bally battle, and the same advice holds true
>> Of grin.

If you're up against it badly, then it's only one on you,
>> So grin.

If the future's black as thunder, don't let people see you're blue;
Just cultivate a cast-iron smile of joy the whole day through;
If they call you "Little Sunshine," wish that *they'd* no troubles,
too—
>> You may—grin.

Rise up in the morning with the will that, smooth or rough,
>> You'll grin.

Sink to sleep at midnight, and although you're feeling tough,
>> Yet grin.

There's nothing gained by whining, and you're not that kind of
stuff;
You're a fighter from away back, and you *won't* take a rebuff;

27

Your trouble is that you don't know when you have had
     enough—
                       Don't give in.
If Fate should down you, just get up and take another cuff;
You may bank on it that there is no philosophy like bluff,
                      And grin.

THE SHOOTING OF DAN McGREW

A BUNCH of the boys were whooping it up in the Malamute
    saloon;
The kid that handles the music-box was hitting a jag-time tune;
Back of the bar, in a solo game, sat Dangerous Dan McGrew,
And watching his luck was his light-o'-love, the lady that's
    known as Lou.

When out of the night, which was fifty below, and into the din
    and the glare,
There stumbled a miner fresh from the creeks, dog-dirty, and
    loaded for bear.
He looked like a man with a foot in the grave and scarcely the
    strength of a louse,
Yet he tilted a poke of dust on the bar, and he called for drinks
    for the house.
There was none could place the stranger's face, though we
    searched ourselves for a clue;
But we drank his health, and the last to drink was Dangerous
    Dan McGrew.

There's men that somehow just grip your eyes, and hold them
    hard like a spell;
And such was he, and he looked to me like a man who had lived
    in hell;
With a face most hair, and the dreary stare of a dog whose day
    is done,
As he watered the green stuff in his glass, and the drops fell one
    by one.

Then I got to figgering who he was, and wondering what he'd
do,
And I turned my head—and there watching him was the lady
that's known as Lou.

His eyes went rubbering round the room, and he seemed in a
kind of daze,
Till at last that old piano fell in the way of his wandering gaze.
The rag-time kid was having a drink; there was no one else on
the stool,
So the stranger stumbles across the room, and flops down there
like a fool.
In a buckskin shirt that was glazed with dirt he sat, and I saw
him sway;
Then he clutched the keys with his talon hands—my God! but
that man could play.

Were you ever out in the Great Alone, when the moon was
awful clear,
And the icy mountains hemmed you in with a silence you most
could *hear;*
With only the howl of a timber wolf, and you camped there
in the cold,
A half-dead thing in a stark, dead world, clean mad for the
muck called gold;
While high overhead, green, yellow and red, the North Lights
swept in bars?—
Then you've a hunch what the music meant . . . hunger and
night and the stars.

And hunger not of the belly kind, that's banished with bacon
and beans,

But the gnawing hunger of lonely men for a home and all that
    it means;
For a fireside far from the cares that are, four walls and a roof
    above;
But oh! so cramful of cosy joy, and crowned with a woman's
    love—
A woman dearer than all the world, and true as Heaven is true—
(God! how ghastly she looks through her rouge,—the lady
    that's known as Lou.)

Then on a sudden the music changed, so soft that you scarce
    could hear;
But you felt that your life had been looted clean of all that it
    once held dear;
That someone had stolen the woman you loved; that her love
    was a devil's lie;
That your guts were gone, and the best for you was to crawl
    away and die.
'Twas the crowning cry of a heart's despair, and it thrilled you
    through and through—
"I guess I'll make it a spread misere," said Dangerous Dan
    McGrew.

The music almost died away . . . then it burst like a pent-up
    flood;
And it seemed to say, "Repay, repay," and my eyes were blind
    with blood.
The thought came back of an ancient wrong, and it stung like a
    frozen lash,
And the lust awoke to kill, to kill . . . then the music stopped
    with a crash,
And the stranger turned, and his eyes they burned in a most
    peculiar way;

In a buckskin shirt that was glazed with dirt he sat, and I saw
    him sway;
Then his lips went in in a kind of grin, and he spoke, and his
    voice was calm,
And "Boys," says he, "you don't know me, and none of you
    care a damn;
But I want to state, and my words are straight, and I'll bet my
    poke they're true,
That one of you is a hound of hell . . . and that one is Dan
    McGrew."

Then I ducked my head, and the lights went out, and two guns
    blazed in the dark,
And a woman screamed, and the lights went up, and two men
    lay stiff and stark.
Pitched on his head, and pumped full of lead, was Dangerous
    Dan McGrew,
While the man from the creeks lay clutched to the breast of the
    lady that's known as Lou.

These are the simple facts of the case, and I guess I ought to
    know.
They say that the stranger was crazed with "hooch," and I'm
    not denying it's so.
I'm not so wise as the lawyer guys, but strictly between us
    two—
The woman that kissed him and—pinched his poke—was the
    lady that's known as Lou.

THE CREMATION OF SAM McGEE

There are strange things done in the midnight sun
  By the men who moil for gold;
The Arctic trails have their secret tales
  That would make your blood run cold;
The Northern Lights have seen queer sights,
  But the queerest they ever did see
Was that night on the marge of Lake Lebarge
  I cremated Sam McGee.

Now Sam McGee was from Tennessee, where the cotton blooms
  and blows.
Why he left his home in the South to roam 'round the Pole,
  God only knows.
He was always cold, but the land of gold seemed to hold him like
  a spell;
Though he'd often say in his homely way that "he'd sooner live
  in hell."

On a Christmas Day we were mushing our way over the Daw-
  son trail.
Talk of your cold! through the parka's fold it stabbed like a
  driven nail.
If our eyes we'd close, then the lashes froze till sometimes we
  couldn't see;
It wasn't much fun, but the only one to whimper was Sam
  McGee.

And that very night, as we lay packed tight in our robes be-
  neath the snow,

And the dogs were fed, and the stars o'erhead were dancing heel and toe,
He turned to me, and "Cap," says he, "I'll cash in this trip, I guess;
And if I do, I'm asking that you won't refuse my last request."

Well, he seemed so low that I couldn't say no; then he says with a sort of moan:
"It's the cursèd cold, and it's got right hold till I'm chilled clean through to the bone.
Yet 'tain't being dead—it's my awful dread of the icy grave that pains;
So I want you to swear that, foul or fair, you'll cremate my last remains."

A pal's last need is a thing to heed, so I swore I would not fail;
And we started on at the streak of dawn; but God! he looked ghastly pale.
He crouched on the sleigh, and he raved all day of his home in Tennessee;
And before nightfall a corpse was all that was left of Sam McGee.

There wasn't a breath in that land of death, and I hurried, horror-driven,
With a corpse half hid that I couldn't get rid, because of a promise given;
It was lashed to the sleigh, and it seemed to say: "You may tax your brawn and brains,
But you promised true, and it's up to you to cremate those last remains."

Now a promise made is a debt unpaid, and the trail has its own stern code.

In the days to come, though my lips were dumb, in my heart
how I cursed that load.
In the long, long night, by the lone firelight, while the huskies,
round in a ring,
Howled out their woes to the homeless snows— O God! how
I loathed the thing.

And every day that quiet clay seemed to heavy and heavier
grow;
And on I went, though the dogs were spent and the grub was
getting low;
The trail was bad, and I felt half mad, but I swore I would not
give in;
And I'd often sing to the hateful thing, and it hearkened with
a grin.

Till I came to the marge of Lake Lebarge, and a derelict there
lay;
It was jammed in the ice, but I saw in a trice it was called the
"Alice May."
And I looked at it, and I thought a bit, and I looked at my frozen
chum;
Then "Here," said I, with a sudden cry, "is my cre-ma-tor-eum."

Some planks I tore from the cabin floor, and I lit the boiler
fire;
Some coal I found that was lying around, and I heaped the fuel
higher;
The flames just soared, and the furnace roared—such a blaze you
seldom see;
And I burrowed a hole in the glowing coal, and I stuffed in
Sam McGee.

Then I made a hike, for I didn't like to hear him sizzle so;
And the heavens scowled, and the huskies howled, and the wind
began to blow.
It was icy cold, but the hot sweat rolled down my cheeks, and I
don't know why;
And the greasy smoke in an inky cloak went streaking down
the sky.

I do not know how long in the snow I wrestled with grisly fear;
But the stars came out and they danced about ere again I ven-
tured near;
I was sick with dread, but I bravely said: "I'll just take a peep
inside.
I guess he's cooked, and it's time I looked"; . . . then the door
I opened wide.

And there sat Sam, looking cool and calm, in the heart of the
furnace roar;
And he wore a smile you could see a mile, and he said: "Please
close that door.
It's fine in here, but I greatly fear you'll let in the cold and
storm—
Since I left Plumtree, down in Tennessee, it's the first time I've
been warm."

> *There are strange things done in the midnight sun*
> *By the men who moil for gold;*
> *The Arctic trails have their secret tales*
> *That would make your blood run cold;*
> *The Northern Lights have seen queer sights,*
> *But the queerest they ever did see*
> *Was that night on the marge of Lake Lebarge*
> *I cremated Sam McGee.*

MY MADONNA

I HALED me a woman from the street,
  Shameless, but, oh, so fair!
I bade her sit in the model's seat
  And I painted her sitting there.

I hid all trace of her heart unclean;
  I painted a babe at her breast;
I painted her as she might have been
  If the Worst had been the Best.

She laughed at my picture and went away.
  Then came, with a knowing nod,
A connoisseur, and I heard him say;
  " 'Tis Mary, the Mother of God."

So I painted a halo round her hair,
  | And I sold her and took my fee,
And she hangs in the church of Saint Hillaire,
  Where you and all may see.

UNFORGOTTEN

I KNOW a garden where the lilies gleam,
    And one who lingers in the sunshine there;
    She is than white-stoled lily far more fair,
And oh, her eyes are heaven-lit with dream!

I know a garret, cold and dark and drear,
    And one who toils and toils with tireless pen,
    Until his brave, sad eyes grow weary—then
He seeks the stars, pale, silent as a seer.

And ah, it's strange; for, desolate and dim,
    Between these two there rolls an ocean wide;
    Yet he is in the garden by her side
And she is in the garret there with him.

THE RECKONING

It's fine to have a blow-out in a fancy restaurant,
With terrapin and canvas-back and all the wine you want;
To enjoy the flowers and music, watch the pretty women pass,
Smoke a choice cigar, and sip the wealthy water in your glass.
It's bully in a high-toned joint to eat and drink your fill,
But it's quite another matter when you
                                        Pay the bill.

It's great to go out every night on fun or pleasure bent;
To wear your glad rags always and to never save a cent;
To drift along regardless, have a good time every trip;
To hit the high spots sometimes, and to let your chances slip;
To know you're acting foolish, yet to go on fooling still,
Till Nature calls a show-down, and you
                                        Pay the bill.

Time has got a little bill—get wise while yet you may,
For the debit side's increasing in a most alarming way;
The things you had no right to do, the things you should have
     done,
They're all put down; it's up to you to pay for every one.
So eat, drink and be merry, have a good time if you will,
But God help you when the time comes, and you
                                        Foot the bill.

QUATRAINS

ONE said: Thy life is thine to make or mar,
To flicker feebly, or to soar, a star;
   It lies with thee—the choice is thine, is thine,
To hit the ties or drive thy auto-car.

I answered Her: The choice is mine—ah, no!
We all were made or marred long, long ago.
   The parts are written; hear the super wail:
"Who is stage-managing this cosmic show?"

Blind fools of fate and slaves of circumstance,
Life is a fiddler, and we all must dance.
   From gloom where mocks that will-o'-wisp, Free-will
I heard a voice cry: "Say, give us a chance."

Chance! Oh, there is no chance! The scene is set.
Up with the curtain! Man, the marionette,
   Resumes his part. The gods will work the wires.
They've got it all down fine, you bet, you bet!

It's all decreed—the mighty earthquake crash;
The countless constellations' wheel and flash;
   The rise and fall of empires, war's red tide;
The composition of your dinner hash.

There's no haphazard in this world of ours.
Cause and effect are grim, relentless powers.
   They rule the world. (A king was shot last night;
Last night I held the joker and both bowers.)

From out the mesh of fate our heads we thrust.
We can't do what we would, but what we must.
   Heredity has got us in a cinch—
(Consoling thought when you've been on a "bust.")

Hark to the song where spheral voices blend:
"There's no beginning, never will be end."
   It makes us nutty; hang the astral chimes!
The table's spread; come, let us dine, my friend.

THE MEN THAT DON'T FIT IN

THERE'S a race of men that don't fit in,
  A race that can't stay still;
So they break the hearts of kith and kin,
  And they roam the world at will.
They range the field and they rove the flood,
  And they climb the mountain's crest;
Theirs is the curse of the gypsy blood,
  And they don't know how to rest.

If they just went straight they might go far;
  They are strong and brave and true;
But they're always tired of the things that are,
  And they want the strange and new.
They say: "Could I find my proper groove,
  What a deep mark I would make!"
So they chop and change, and each fresh move
  Is only a fresh mistake.

And each forgets, as he strips and runs
  With a brilliant, fitful pace,
It's the steady, quiet, plodding ones
  Who win in the lifelong race.
And each forgets that his youth has fled,
  Forgets that his prime is past,
Till he stands one day, with a hope that's dead,
  In the glare of the truth at last.

He has failed, he has failed; he has missed his chance;
  He has just done things by half.

Life's been a jolly good joke on him,
   And now is the time to laugh.
Ha, ha! He is one of the Legion Lost;
   He was never meant to win;
He's a rolling stone, and it's bred in the bone;
   He's a man who won't fit in.

MUSIC IN THE BUSH

O'ER the dark pines she sees the silver moon,
  And in the west, all tremulous, a star;
And soothing sweet she hears the mellow tune
  Of cow-bells jangled in the fields afar.

Quite listless, for her daily stent is done,
  She stands, sad exile, at her rose-wreathed door,
And sends her love eternal with the sun
  That goes to gild the land she'll see no more.

The grave, gaunt pines imprison her sad gaze,
  All still the sky and darkling drearily;
She feels the chilly breath of dear, dead days
  Come sifting through the alders eerily.

Oh, how the roses riot in their bloom!
  The curtains stir as with an ancient pain;
Her old piano gleams from out the gloom
  And waits and waits her tender touch in vain

But now her hands like moonlight brush the keys
  With velvet grace—melodious delight;
And now a sad refrain from over seas
  Goes sobbing on the bosom of the night;

And now she sings. (O! singer in the gloom,
  Voicing a sorrow we can ne'er express,
Here in the Farness where we few have room
  Unshamed to show our love and tenderness,

Our hearts will echo, till they beat no more,
That song of sadness and of motherland;
And, stretched in deathless love to England's shore,
Some day she'll hearken and she'll understand.)

A prima-donna in the shining past,
But now a mother growing old and gray,
She thinks of how she held a people fast
In thrall, and gleaned the triumphs of a day.

She sees a sea of faces like a dream;
She sees herself a queen of song once more;
She sees lips part in rapture, eyes agleam;
She sings as never once she sang before.

She sings a wild, sweet song that throbs with pain,
The added pain of life that transcends art—
A song of home, a deep, celestial strain,
The glorious swan-song of a dying heart.

A lame tramp comes along the railway track,
A grizzled dog whose day is nearly done:
He passes, pauses, then comes slowly back
And listens there—an audience of one.

She sings—her golden voice is passion-fraught,
As when she charmed a thousand eager ears;
He listens trembling, and she knows it not,
And down his hollow cheeks roll bitter tears.

She ceases and is still, as if to pray;
There is no sound, the stars are all alight—
Only a wretch who stumbles on his way,
Only a vagrant sobbing in the night.

THE RHYME OF THE REMITTANCE MAN

THERE'S a four-pronged buck a-swinging in the shadow of my
    cabin,
  And it roamed the velvet valley till to-day;
But I tracked it by the river, and I trailed it in the cover,
  And I killed it on the mountain miles away.
Now I've had my lazy supper, and the level sun is gleaming
  On the water where the silver salmon play;
And I light my little corn-cob, and I linger, softly dreaming,
  In the twilight, of a land that's far away.

Far away, so faint and far, is flaming London, fevered Paris,
  That I fancy I have gained another star;
Far away the din and hurry, far away the sin and worry,
  Far away—God knows they cannot be too far.
Gilded galley-slaves of Mammon—how my purse-proud broth-
    ers taunt me!
  I might have been as well-to-do as they
Had I clutched like them my chances, learned their wisdom,
    crushed my fancies,
  Starved my soul and gone to business every day.

Well, the cherry bends with blossom and the vivid grass is
    springing,
  And the star-like lily nestles in the green;
And the frogs their joys are singing, and my heart in tune is
    ringing,
  And it doesn't matter what I might have been.
While above the scented pine-gloom, piling heights of golden
    glory,

The sun-god paints his canvas in the west,
I can couch me deep in clover, I can listen to the story
  Of the lazy, lapping water—it is best.

While the trout leaps in the river, and the blue grouse thrills the
        cover,
  And the frozen snow betrays the panther's track,
And the robin greets the dayspring with the rapture of a lover,
  I am happy, and I'll nevermore go back.
For I know I'd just be longing for the little old log cabin,
  With the morning-glory clinging to the door,
Till I loathed the city places, cursed the care on all the faces,
  Turned my back on lazar London evermore.

So send me far from Lombard Street, and write me down a
        failure;
  Put a little in my purse and leave me free.
Say: "He turned from Fortune's offering to follow up a pale
        lure,
  He is one of us no longer—let him be."
I am one of you no longer; by the trails my feet have broken,
  The dizzy peaks I've scaled, the camp-fire's glow;
By the lonely seas I've sailed in—yea, the final word is spoken,
  I am signed and sealed to nature. Be it so.

THE LOW-DOWN WHITE

This is the pay-day up at the mines, when the bearded brutes
    come down;
There's money to burn in the streets to-night, so I've sent my
    klooch to town,
With a haggard face and a ribband of red entwined in her hair
    of brown.

And I know at the dawn she'll come reeling home with the
    bottles, one, two, three—
One for herself, to drown her shame, and two big bottles for me,
To make me forget the thing I am and the man I used to be.

To make me forget the brand of the dog, as I crouch in this
    hideous place;
To make me forget once I kindled the light of love in a lady's
    face,
Where even the squalid Siwash now holds me a black disgrace.

Oh, I have guarded my secret well! And who would dream as I
    speak
In a tribal tongue like a rogue unhung, 'mid the ranch-house
    filth and reek,
I could roll to bed with a Latin phrase and rise with a verse of
    Greek?

Yet I was a senior prizeman once, and the pride of a college
    eight;
Called to the bar—my friends were true! but they could not
    keep me straight;

Then came the divorce, and I went abroad and "died" on the
    River Plate.

But I'm not dead yet; though with half a lung there isn't time
    to spare,
And I hope that the year will see me out, and, thank God, no one
    will care—
Save maybe the little slim Siwash girl with the rose of shame in
    her hair.

She will come with the dawn, and the dawn is near; I can see its
    evil glow,
Like a corpse-light seen through a frosty pane in a night of want
    and woe;
And yonder she comes by the bleak bull-pines, swift staggering
    through the snow.

THE LITTLE OLD LOG CABIN

When a man gits on his uppers in a hard-pan sort of town,
 An' he ain't got nothin' comin' an' he can't afford ter eat,
An' he's in a fix for lodgin' an' he wanders up an' down,
  An' you'd fancy he'd been boozin', he's so locoed 'bout the
   feet;
When he's feelin' sneakin' sorry an' his belt is hangin' slack,
 An' his face is peaked an' gray-like an' his heart gits down an'
  whines,
Then he's apt ter git a-thinkin' an' a-wishin' he was back
 In the little ol' log cabin in the shadder of the pines.

When he's on the blazin' desert an' his canteen's sprung a leak,
 An' he's all alone an' crazy an' he's crawlin' like a snail,
An' his tongue's so black an' swollen that it hurts him fer to
  speak,
 An' he gouges down fer water an' the raven's on his trail;
When he's done with care and cursin' an' he feels more like to
  cry,
 An' he sees ol' Death a-grinnin' an' he thinks upon his crimes,
Then he's like ter hev' a vision, as he settles down ter die,
 Of the little ol' log cabin an' the roses an' the vines.

Oh, the little ol' log cabin, it's a solemn shinin' mark,
 When a feller gits ter sinnin' an' a-goin' ter the wall,
An' folks don't understand him an' he's gropin' in the dark,
 An' he's sick of bein' cursed at an' he's longin' fer his call!
When the sun of life's a-sinkin' you can see it 'way above,
 On the hill from out the shadder in a glory 'gin the sky,

An' your mother's voice is callin', an' her arms are stretched in
    love,
  An' somehow you're glad you're goin', an' you ain't a-scared
    to die;
When you'll be like a kid again an' nestle to her breast,
An' never leave its shelter, an' forget, an' love, an' rest.

THE YOUNGER SON

If you leave the gloom of London and you seek a glowing land,
  Where all except the flag is strange and new,
There's a bronzed and stalwart fellow who will grip you by
    the hand,
  And greet you with a welcome warm and true;
For he's your younger brother, the one you sent away
  Because there wasn't room for him at home;
And now he's quite contented, and he's glad he didn't stay,
  And he's building Britain's greatness o'er the foam.

When the giant herd is moving at the rising of the sun,
  And the prairie is lit with rose and gold,
And the camp is all abustle, and the busy day's begun,
  He leaps into the saddle sure and bold.
Through the round of heat and hurry, through the racket and
    the rout,
  He rattles at a pace that nothing mars;
And when the night-winds whisper and camp-fires flicker out,
  He is sleeping like a child beneath the stars.

When the wattle-blooms are drooping in the sombre shed-oak
    glade,
  And the breathless land is lying in a swoon,
He leaves his work a moment, leaning lightly on his spade,
  And he hears the bell-bird chime the Austral noon.
The parrakeets are silent in the gum-tree by the creek;
  The ferny grove is sunshine-steeped and still;
But the dew will gem the myrtle in the twilight ere he seek
  His little lonely cabin on the hill.

Around the purple, vine-clad slope the argent river dreams;
  The roses almost hide the house from view;
A snow-peak of the Winterberg in crimson splendor gleams;
  The shadow deepens down on the karroo.
He seeks the lily-scented dusk beneath the orange tree;
  His pipe in silence glows and fades and glows;
And then two little maids come out and climb upon his knee,
  And one is like the lily, one the rose.

He sees his white sheep dapple o'er the green New Zealand
    plain,
  And where Vancouver's shaggy ramparts frown,
When the sunlight threads the pine-gloom he is fighting might
    and main
  To clinch the rivets of an Empire down.
You will find him toiling, toiling, in the south or in the west,
  . A child of nature, fearless, frank and free;
And the warmest heart that beats for you is beating in his breast,
  And he sends you loyal greeting o'er the sea.

You've a brother in the army, you've another in the Church;
  One of you is a diplomatic swell;
You've had the pick of everything and left him in the lurch,
  And yet I think he's doing very well.
I'm sure his life is happy, and he doesn't envy yours;
  I know he loves the land his pluck has won;
And I fancy in the years unborn, while England's fame endures,
  She will come to bless with pride—The Younger Son.

THE MARCH OF THE DEAD

THE cruel war was over—oh, the triumph was so sweet!
  We watched the troops returning, through our tears;
There was triumph, triumph, triumph down the scarlet glitter-
    ing street,
  And you scarce could hear the music for the cheers.
And you scarce could see the house-tops for the flags that flew
    between;
  The bells were pealing madly to the sky;
And everyone was shouting for the Soldiers of the Queen,
  And the glory of an age was passing by.

And then there came a shadow, swift and sudden, dark and
    drear;
  The bells were silent, not an echo stirred.
The flags were drooping sullenly, the men forgot to cheer;
  We waited, and we never spoke a word.
The sky grew darker, darker, till from out the gloomy rack
  There came a voice that checked the heart with dread:
"Tear down, tear down your bunting now, and hang up sable
    black;
  They are coming—it's the Army of the Dead."

They were coming, they were coming, gaunt and ghastly, sad
    and slow;
  They were coming, all the crimson wrecks of pride;
With faces seared, and cheeks red smeared, and haunting eyes of
    woe,
  And clotted holes the khaki couldn't hide.

Oh, the clammy brow of anguish! the livid, foam-flecked lips!
   The reeling ranks of ruin swept along!
The limb that trailed, the hand that failed, the bloody finger tips!
   And oh, the dreary rhythm of their song!

"They left us on the veldt-side, but we felt we couldn't stop
   On this, our England's crowning festal day;
We're the men of Magersfontein, we're the men of Spion Kop,
   Colenso—we're the men who had to pay.
We're the men who paid the blood-price. Shall the grave be all
     our gain?
   You owe us. Long and heavy is the score.
Then cheer us for our glory now, and cheer us for our pain,
   And cheer us as ye never cheered before."

The folks were white and stricken, and each tongue seemed
     weighted with lead;
   Each heart was clutched in hollow hand of ice;
And every eye was staring at the horror of the dead,
   The pity of the men who paid the price.
They were come, were come to mock us, in the first flush of our
     peace;
   Through writhing lips their teeth were all agleam;
They were coming in their thousands—oh, would they never
     cease!
   I closed my eyes, and then—it was a dream.

There was triumph, triumph, triumph down the scarlet gleam-
     ing street;
   The town was mad; a man was like a boy.
A thousand flags were flaming where the sky and city meet;
   A thousand bells were thundering the joy.

There was music, mirth and sunshine; but some eyes shone with
    regret;
  And while we stun with cheers our homing braves,
O God, in Thy great mercy, let us nevermore forget
  The graves they left behind, the bitter graves.

"FIGHTING MAC"

A LIFE TRAGEDY

A PISTOL shot rings round and round the world;
  In pitiful defeat a warrior lies.
A last defiance to dark Death is hurled,
  A last wild challenge shocks the sunlit skies.
  Alone he falls, with wide, wan, woeful eyes:
Eyes that could smile at death—could not face shame.

Alone, alone he paced his narrow room,
  In the bright sunshine of that Paris day;
Saw in his thought the awful hand of doom;
  Saw in his dream his glory pass away;
  Tried in his heart, his weary heart, to pray:
"O God! who made me, give me strength to face
The spectre of this bitter, black disgrace."

    *   *   *   *   *   *   *

The burn brawls darkly down the shaggy glen;
  The bee-kissed heather blooms around the door;
He sees himself a barefoot boy again,
  Bending o'er page of legendary lore.
  He hears the pibroch, grips the red claymore,
Runs with the Fiery Cross, a clansman true,
Sworn kinsman of Rob Roy and Roderick Dhu.

Eating his heart out with a wild desire,
  One day, behind his counter trim and neat,
He hears a sound that sets his brain afire—

The Highlanders are marching down the street.
  Oh, how the pipes shrill out, the mad drums beat!
"On to the gates of Hell, my Gordons gay!"
He flings his hated yardstick away.

He sees the sullen pass, high-crowned with snow,
  Where Afghans cower with eyes of gleaming hate.
He hurls himself against the hidden foe.
  They try to rally—ah, too late, too late!
  Again, defenseless, with fierce eyes that wait
For death, he stands, like baited bull at bay,
And flouts the Boers, that mad Majuba day.

He sees again the murderous Soudan,
  Blood-slaked and rapine-swept. He seems to stand
Upon the gory plain of Omdurman.
  Then Magersfontein, and supreme command
  Over his Highlanders. To shake his hand
A King is proud, and princes call him friend.
And glory crowns his life—and now the end,

The awful end. His eyes are dark with doom;
  He hears the shrapnel shrieking overhead;
He sees the ravaged ranks, the flame-stabbed gloom.
  Oh, to have fallen!—the battle-field his bed,
  With Wauchope and his glorious brother-dead.
Why was he saved for this, for this? And now
He raises the revolver to his brow.

     *   *   *   *   *   *   *   *

In many a Highland home, framed with rude art,
  You'll find his portrait, rough-hewn, stern and square;
It's graven in the Fuyam fellah's heart;

The Ghurka reads it at his evening prayer;
　The raw lands know it, where the fierce suns glare;
The Dervish fears it. Honor to his name
Who holds aloft the shield of England's fame.

Mourn for our hero, men of Northern race!
　We do not know his sin; we only know
His sword was keen. He laughed death in the face,
　And struck, for Empire's sake, a giant blow.
　His arm was strong. Ah! well they learnt, the foe.
The echo of his deeds is ringing yet—
Will ring for aye. All else . . . let us forget.

THE WOMAN AND THE ANGEL

An angel was tired of heaven, as he lounged in the golden street;
His halo was tilted sideways, and his harp lay mute at his feet;
So the Master stooped in His pity, and gave him a pass to go,
For the space of a moon, to the earth-world, to mix with the men
  below.

He doffed his celestial garments, scarce waiting to lay them
  straight;
He bade good-by to Peter, who stood by the golden gate;
The sexless singers of heaven chanted a fond farewell,
And the imps looked up as they pattered on the red-hot flags
  of hell.

Never was seen such an angel—eyes of heavenly blue,
Features that shamed Apollo, hair of a golden hue;
The women simply adored him; his lips were like Cupid's bow;
But he never ventured to use them—and so they voted him slow.

Till at last there came One Woman, a marvel of loveliness,
And she whispered to him: "Do you love me?" And he answered
  that woman, "Yes."
And she said: "Put your arms around me, and kiss me, and hold
  me—so—"
But fiercely he drew back, saying: "This thing is wrong, and I
  know."

Then sweetly she mocked his scruples, and softly she him be-
  guiled:
"You, who are verily man among men, speak with the tongue of
  a child.

We have outlived the old standards; we have burst, like an over-
   tight thong,
The ancient, outworn, Puritanic traditions of Right and
   Wrong."

Then the Master feared for His angel, and called him again to
   His side,
For oh, the woman was wondrous, and oh, the angel was tried!
And deep in his hell sang the Devil, and this was the strain of his
   song:
"The ancient, outworn, Puritanic traditions of Right and
   Wrong."

THE RHYME OF THE RESTLESS ONES

WE couldn't sit and study for the law;
 The stagnation of a bank we couldn't stand;
For our riot blood was surging, and we didn't need much urging
 To excitements and excesses that are banned.
So we took to wine and drink and other things,
 And the devil in us struggled to be free;
Till our friends rose up in wrath, and they pointed out the path,
 And they paid our debts and packed us o'er the sea.

Oh, they shook us off and shipped us o'er the foam,
To the larger lands that lure a man to roam;
 And we took the chance they gave
 Of a far and foreign grave,
And we bade good-by for evermore to home.

And some of us are climbing on the peak,
 And some of us are camping on the plain;
By pine and palm you'll find us, with never claim to bind us,
 By track and trail you'll meet us once again.

We are fated serfs to freedom—sky and sea;
 We have failed where slummy cities overflow;
But the stranger ways of earth know our pride and know our
 worth,
 And we go into the dark as fighters go.

Yes, we go into the night as brave men go,
Though our faces they be often streaked with woe;

Yet we're hard as cats to kill,
And our hearts are reckless still,
And we've danced with death a dozen times or so.

And you'll find us in Alaska after gold,
And you'll find us herding cattle in the South.
We like strong drink and fun, and, when the race is run,
We often die with curses in our mouth.
We are wild as colts unbroke, but never mean.
Of our sins we've shoulders broad to bear the blame;
But we'll never stay in town and we'll never settle down,
And we'll never have an object or an aim.

No, there's that in us that time can never tame;
And life will always seem a careless game;
And they'd better far forget—
Those who say they love us yet—
Forget, blot out with bitterness our name.

NEW YEAR'S EVE

It's cruel cold on the water-front, silent and dark and drear;
    Only the black tide weltering, only the hissing snow;
And I, alone, like a storm-tossed wreck, on this night of the glad
    New Year,
    Shuffling along in the icy wind, ghastly and gaunt and slow.

They're playing a tune in McGuffy's saloon, and it's cheery and
    bright in there
    (God! but I'm weak—since the bitter dawn, and never a bite
    of food);
I'll just go over and slip inside—I mustn't give way to despair—
    Perhaps I can bum a little booze if the boys are feeling good.

They'll jeer at me, and they'll sneer at me, and they'll call me a
    whiskey soak;
    ("Have a drink? Well, thankee kindly, sir, I don't mind if I
    do.")
A drivelling, dirty, gin-joint fiend, the butt of the bar-room
    joke;
    Sunk and sodden and hopeless—"Another? Well, here's to
    you!"

McGuffy is showing a bunch of the boys how Bob Fitzsimmons
    hit;
    The barman is talking of Tammany Hall, and why the ward
    boss got fired.
I'll just sneak into a corner and they'll let me alone a bit;

The room is reeling round and round . . . O God! but I'm
  tired, I'm tired. . . .

*   *   *   *   *   *   *   *   *

Roses she wore on her breast that night. Oh, but their scent was
  sweet!
  Alone we sat on the balcony, and the fan-palms arched above;
The witching strain of a waltz by Strauss came up to our cool
  retreat,
    And I prisoned her little hand in mine, and I whispered my
    plea of love.

Then sudden the laughter died on her lips, and lowly she bent
  her head;
And oh, there came in the deep, dark eyes a look that was heaven
  to see;
And the moments went, and I waited there, and never a word
  was said,
    And she plucked from her bosom a rose of red and shyly gave
    it to me.

Then the music swelled to a crash of joy, and the lights blazed
  up like day,
    And I held her fast to my throbbing heart, and I kissed her
    bonny brow.
"She is mine, she is mine for evermore!" the violins seemed to
  say,
    And the bells were ringing the New Year in— O God! I can
    hear them now.

Don't you remember that long, last waltz, with its sobbing, sad
  refrain?
    Don't you remember that last good-by, and the dear eyes dim
    with tears?

Don't you remember that golden dream, with never a hint of
     pain,
  Of lives that would blend like an angel-song in the bliss of the
     coming years?

Oh, what have I lost! What have I lost! Ethel, forgive, forgive!
  The red, red rose is faded now, and it's fifty years ago.
'Twere better to die a thousand deaths than live each day as I
     live!
  I have sinned, I have sunk to the lowest depths—but oh, I have
     suffered so!

Hark! Oh, hark! I can hear the bells! . . . Look! I can see her
     there,
  Fair as a dream . . . but it fades . . . And now—I can hear
     the dreadful hum
Of the crowded court . . . See! the Judge looks down . . .
     NOT GUILTY, my Lord, I swear . . .
  The bells—I can hear the bells again! . . . Ethel, I come, I
     come! . . .

     *   *   *   *   *   *   *   *   *

"Rouse up, old man, it's twelve o'clock. You can't sleep here,
     you know.
  Say! ain't you got no sentiment? Lift up your muddled head;
Have a drink to the glad New Year, a drop before you go—
  You darned old dirty hobo . . . My God! Here, boys! He's
     DEAD!"

COMFORT

Say! You've struck a heap of trouble—
　　Bust in business, lost your wife;
No one cares a cent about you,
　　You don't care a cent for life;
Hard luck has of hope bereft you,
　　Health is failing, wish you'd die—
Why, you've still the sunshine left you
　　And the big, blue sky.

Sky so blue it makes you wonder
　　If it's heaven shining through;
Earth so smiling 'way out yonder,
　　Sun so bright it dazzles you;
Birds a-singing, flowers a-flinging
　　All their fragrance on the breeze;
Dancing shadows, green, still meadows—
　　Don't you mope, you've still got these.

These, and none can take them from you;
　　These, and none can weigh their worth.
What! you're tired and broke and beaten?—
　　Why, you're rich—you've got the earth!
Yes, if you're a tramp in tatters,
　　While the blue sky bends above
You've got nearly all that matters—
　　You've got God, and God is love.

THE HARPY

There was a woman, and she was wise; woefully wise was she;
She was old, so old, yet her years all told were but a score and
    three;
And she knew by heart, from finish to start, the Book of In-
    iquity.

There is no hope for such as I on earth, nor yet in Heaven;
Unloved I live, unloved I die, unpitied, unforgiven;
A loathèd jade, I ply my trade, unhallowed and unshriven.

I paint my cheeks, for they are white, and cheeks of chalk men
    hate;
Mine eyes with wine I make them shine, that man may seek and
    sate;
With overhead a lamp of red I sit me down and wait

Until they come, the nightly scum, with drunken eyes aflame;
Your sweethearts, sons, ye scornful ones—'tis I who know their
    shame.
The gods, ye see, are brutes to me—and so I play my game.

For life is not the thing we thought, and not the thing we plan;
And Woman in a bitter world must do the best she can—
Must yield the stroke, and bear the yoke, and serve the will of
    man;

Must serve his need and ever feed the flame of his desire,
Though be she loved for love alone, or be she loved for hire;
For every man since life began is tainted with the mire.

And though you know he love you so and set you on love's
    throne;
Yet let your eyes but mock his sighs, and let your heart be stone,
Lest you be left (as I was left) attainted and alone.

From love's close kiss to hell's abyss is one sheer flight, I trow,
And wedding ring and bridal bell are will-o'-wisps of woe,
And 'tis not wise to love too well, and this all women know.

Wherefore, the wolf-pack having gorged upon the lamb, their
    prey,
With siren smile and serpent guile I make the wolf-pack pay—
With velvet paws and flensing claws, a tigress roused to slay.

One who in youth sought truest truth and found a devil's lies;
A symbol of the sin of man, a human sacrifice.
Yet shall I blame on man the shame? Could it be otherwise?

Was I not born to walk in scorn where others walk in pride?
The Maker marred, and, evil-starred, I drift upon His tide;
And He alone shall judge His own, so I His judgment bide.

Fate has written a tragedy; its name is "The Human Heart."
The Theatre is the House of Life, Woman the mummer's part;
The Devil enters the prompter's box and the play is ready to
    start.

PREMONITION

'Twas a year ago and the moon was bright
  (Oh, I remember so well, so well);
I walked with my love in a sea of light,
  And the voice of my sweet was a silver bell.
    And sudden the moon grew strangely dull,
      And sudden my love had taken wing;
    I looked on the face of a grinning skull,
      I strained to my heart a ghastly thing.

'Twas but fantasy, for my love lay still
  In my arms, with her tender eyes aglow,
And she wondered why my lips were chill,
  Why I was silent and kissed her so.
    A year has gone and the moon is bright,
      A gibbous moon, like a ghost of woe;
    I sit by a new-made grave to-night,
      And my heart is broken—it's strange, you know.

THE TRAMPS

Can you recall, dear comrade, when we tramped God's land
together,
And we sang the old, old Earth-song, for our youth was very
sweet;
When we drank and fought and lusted, as we mocked at tie and
tether,
Along the road to Anywhere, the wide world at our feet—

Along the road to Anywhere, when each day had its story;
When time was yet our vassal, and life's jest was still unstale;
When peace unfathomed filled our hearts as, bathed in amber
glory,
Along the road to Anywhere we watched the sunsets pale?

Alas! the road to Anywhere is pitfalled with disaster;
There's hunger, want, and weariness, yet O we loved it so!
As on we tramped exultantly, and no man was our master,
And no man guessed what dreams were ours, as, swinging heel
and toe,
We tramped the road to Anywhere, the magic road to Any-
where,
The tragic road to Anywhere, such dear, dim years ago.

L'ENVOI

You who have lived in the land,
*   You who have trusted the trail,*
You who are strong to withstand,
*   You who are swift to assail:*
*   Songs have I sung to beguile,*
*   Vintage of desperate years*
*   Hard as a harlot's smile,*
*   Bitter as unshed tears.*

Little of joy or mirth,
*   Little of ease I sing;*
Sagas of men of earth
*   Humanly suffering,*
*   Such as you all have done;*
*   Savagely faring forth,*
*   Sons of the midnight sun,*
*   Argonauts of the North.*

Far in the land God forgot
*   Glimmers the lure of your trail;*
Still in your lust are you taught
*   Even to win is to fail.*
*   Still you must follow and fight*
*   Under the vampire wing;*
*   There in the long, long night*
*   Hoping and vanquishing.*

Husbandman of the Wild,
*   Reaping a barren gain;*

Scourged by desire, reconciled
  Unto disaster and pain;
    These, my songs, are for you,
      You who are seared with the brand.
    God knows I have tried to be true;
      Please God you will understand.

Book Two

BALLADS OF A CHEECHAKO

TO THE MAN OF THE HIGH NORTH

My rhymes are rough, and often in my rhyming
  I've drifted, silver-sailed, on seas of dream,
Hearing afar the bells of Elfland chiming,
  Seeing the groves of Arcadie agleam.

I was the thrall of Beauty that rejoices
  From peak snow-diademed to regal star;
Yet to mine aerie ever pierced the voices,
  The pregnant voices of the Things That Are.

The Here, the Now, the vast Forlorn around us;
  The gold-delirium, the ferine strife;
The lusts that lure us on, the hates that hound us;
  Our red rags in the patch-work quilt of Life.

The nameless men who nameless rivers travel,
  And in strange valleys greet strange deaths alone;
The grim, intrepid ones who would unravel
  The mysteries that shroud the Polar Zone.

These will I sing, and if one of you linger
  Over my pages in the Long, Long Night,
And on some lone line lay a calloused finger,
  Saying: "It's human-true—it hits me right";
Then will I count this loving toil well spent;
Then will I dream awhile—content, content.

MEN OF THE HIGH NORTH

Men of the High North, the wild sky is blazing,
  Islands of opal float on silver seas;
Swift splendors kindle, barbaric, amazing;
  Pale ports of amber, golden argosies.
Ringed all around us the proud peaks are glowing;
  Fierce chiefs in council, their wigwam the sky;
Far, far below us the big Yukon flowing,
  Like threaded quicksilver, gleams to the eye.

Men of the High North, you who have known it;
  You in whose hearts its splendors have abode;
Can you renounce it, can you disown it?
  Can you forget it, its glory and its goad?
Where is the hardship, where is the pain of it?
  Lost in the limbo of things you've forgot;
Only remain the guerdon and gain of it;
  Zest of the foray, and God, how you fought!

You who have made good, you foreign faring;
  You money magic to far lands has whirled;
Can you forget those days of vast daring,
  There with your soul on the Top o' the World?
Nights when no peril could keep you awake on
  Spruce boughs you spread for your couch in the snow;
Taste all your feasts like the beans and the bacon
  Fried at the camp-fire at forty below?

Can you remember your huskies all going,
  Barking with joy and their brushes in air;

You in your parka, glad-eyed and glowing,
　Monarch, your subjects the wolf and the bear?
Monarch, your kingdom unravisht and gleaming;
　Mountains your throne, and a river your car;
Crash of a bull moose to rouse you from dreaming;
　Forest your couch, and your candle a star.

You who this faint day the High North is luring
　Unto her vastness, taintlessly sweet;
You who are steel-braced, straight-lipped, enduring,
　Dreadless in danger and dire in defeat:
Honor the High North ever and ever,
　Whether she crown you, or whether she slay;
Suffer her fury, cherish and love her—
　He who would rule he must learn to obey.

Men of the High North, fierce mountains love you,
　Proud rivers leap when you ride on their breast.
See, the austere sky, pensive above you,
　Dons all her jewels to smile on your rest.
Children of Freedom, scornful of frontiers,
　We who are weaklings honor your worth.
Lords of the wilderness, Princes of Pioneers,
　Let's have a rouse that will ring round the earth.

THE BALLAD OF THE NORTHERN LIGHTS

ONE of the Down and Out—that's me. Stare at me well, ay, stare!
Stare and shrink—say! you wouldn't think that I was a millionaire.
Look at my face, it's crimped and gouged—one of them death-mask things;
Don't seem the sort of man, do I, as might be the pal of kings?
Slouching along in smelly rags, a bleary-eyed, no-good bum;
A knight of the hollow needle, pard, spewed from the sodden slum.
Look me all over from head to foot; how much would you think I was worth?
A dollar? a dime? a nickel? Why, *I'm the wealthiest man on earth.*

No, don't you think that I'm off my base. You'll sing a different tune
If only you'll let me spin my yarn. Come over to this saloon;
Wet my throat—it's as dry as chalk, and seeing as how it's you,
I'll tell the tale of a Northern trail, and so help me God, it's true.
I'll tell of the howling wilderness and the haggard Arctic heights,
Of a reckless vow that I made, and how *I staked the Northern Lights.*

Remember the year of the Big Stampede and the trail of Ninety-eight,
When the eyes of the world were turned to the North, and the hearts of men elate;

Hearts of the old dare-devil breed thrilled at the wondrous strike,

And to every man who could hold a pan came the message, "Up and hike."

Well, I was there with the best of them, and I knew I would not fail.

You wouldn't believe it to see me now; but wait till you've heard my tale.

You've read of the trail of Ninety-eight, but its woe no man may tell;

It was all of a piece and a whole yard wide, and the name of the brand was "Hell."

We heard the call and we staked our all; we were plungers playing blind,

And no man cared how his neighbor fared, and no man looked behind;

For a ruthless greed was born of need, and the weakling went to the wall,

And a curse might avail where a prayer would fail, and the gold lust crazed us all.

Bold were we, and they called us three the "Unholy Trinity";

There was Ole Olson, the Sailor Swede, and the Dago Kid and me.

We were the discards of the pack, the foreloopers of Unrest,

Reckless spirits of fierce revolt in the ferment of the West.

We were bound to win and we revelled in the hardships of the way.

We staked our ground and our hopes were crowned, and we hoisted out the pay.

We were rich in a day beyond our dreams, it was gold from the grass-roots down;

But we weren't used to such sudden wealth, and there was
the siren town.

We were crude and careless frontiersmen, with much in us of
the beast;

We could bear the famine worthily, but we lost our heads at
the feast.

The town looked mighty bright to us, with a bunch of dust to
spend,

And nothing was half too good them days, and everyone was
our friend.

Wining meant more than mining then, and life was a dizzy
whirl,

Gambling and dropping chunks of gold down the neck of a
dance-hall girl;

Till we went clean mad, it seems to me, and we squandered our
last poke,

And we sold our claim, and we found ourselves one bitter morn-
ing—broke.

The Dago Kid he dreamed a dream of his mother's aunt who
died—

In the dawn-light dim she came to him, and she stood by his
bedside,

And she said: "Go forth to the highest North till a lonely trail
ye find;

Follow it far and trust your star, and fortune will be kind."

But I jeered at him, and then there came the Sailor Swede to
me,

And he said: "I dreamed of my sister's son, who croaked at the
age of three.

From the herded dead he sneaked and said: 'Seek you an Arctic
trail;

'Tis pale and grim by the Polar rim, but seek and ye shall not
    fail.' "
And lo! that night I too did dream of my mother's sister's son,
And he said to me: "By the Arctic Sea there's a treasure to be
    won.
Follow and follow a lone moose trail, till you come to a valley
    grim,
On the slope of the lonely watershed that borders the Polar
    brim."
Then I woke my pals, and soft we swore by the mystic Silver
    Flail,
'Twas the hand of Fate, and to-morrow straight we would seek
    the lone moose trail.

We watched the groaning ice wrench free, crash on with a hol-
    low din;
Men of the wilderness were we, freed from the taint of sin.
The mighty river snatched us up and it bore us swift along;
The days were bright, and the morning light was sweet with
    jewelled song.
We poled and lined up nameless streams, portaged o'er hill and
    plain;
We burnt our boat to save the nails, and built our boat again;
We guessed and groped, North, ever North, with many a twist
    and turn;
We saw ablaze in the deathless days the splendid sunsets burn.
O'er soundless lakes where the grayling makes a rush at the
    clumsy fly;
By bluffs so steep that the hard-hit sheep falls sheer from out the
    sky;
By lilied pools where the bull moose cools and wallows in huge
    content;

By rocky lairs where the pig-eyed bears peered at our tiny tent.
Through the black canyon's angry foam we hurled to dreamy
    bars,
And round in a ring the dog-nosed peaks bayed to the mocking
    stars.
Spring and summer and autumn went; the sky had a tallow
    gleam,
Yet North and ever North we pressed to the land of our Golden
    Dream.

So we came at last to a tundra vast and dark and grim and lone;
And there was the little lone moose trail, and we knew it for our
    own.
By muskeg hollow and nigger-head it wandered endlessly;
Sorry of heart and sore of foot, weary men were we.
The short-lived sun had a leaden glare and the darkness came
    too soon,
And stationed there with a solemn stare was the pinched, anaemic
    moon.
Silence and silvern solitude till it made you dumbly shrink,
And you thought to hear with an outward ear the things you
    ought to think.

Oh, it was wild and weird and wan, and ever in camp o' nights
We would watch and watch the silver dance of the mystic
    Northern Lights.
And soft they danced from the Polar sky and swept in primrose
    haze;
And swift they pranced with their silver feet, and pierced with a
    blinding blaze.
They danced a cotillion in the sky; they were rose and silver
    shod;

It was not good for the eyes of man—'twas a sight for the eyes
    of God.
It made us mad and strange and sad, and the gold whereof we
    dreamed
Was all forgot, and our only thought was of the lights that
    gleamed.

Oh, the tundra sponge it was golden brown, and some was a
    bright blood-red;
And the reindeer moss gleamed here and there like the tomb-
    stones of the dead.
And in and out and around about the little trail ran clear,
And we hated it with a deadly hate and we feared with a deadly
    fear.
And the skies of night were alive with light, with a throbbing,
    thrilling flame;
Amber and rose and violet, opal and gold it came.
It swept the sky like a giant scythe, it quivered back to a wedge;
Argently bright, it cleft the night with a wavy golden edge.
Pennants of silver waved and streamed, lazy banners unfurled;
Sudden splendors of sabres gleamed, lightning javelins were
    hurled.
There in our awe we crouched and saw with our wild, uplifted
    eyes
Charge and retire the hosts of fire in the battlefield of the skies.

But all things come to an end at last, and the muskeg melted
    away,
And frowning down to bar our path a muddle of mountains lay.
And a gorge sheered up in granite walls, and the moose trail
    crept betwixt;
'Twas as if the earth had gaped too far and her stony jaws were
    fixt.

Then the winter fell with a sudden swoop, and the heavy clouds
  sagged low,
And earth and sky were blotted out in a whirl of driving snow.

We were climbing up a glacier in the neck of a mountain pass,
When the Dago Kid slipped down and fell into a deep crevasse.
When we got him out one leg hung limp, and his brow was
  wreathed with pain,
And he says: " 'Tis badly broken, boys, and I'll never walk
  again.
It's death for all if ye linger here, and that's no cursèd lie;
Go on, go on while the trail is good, and leave me down to die."
He raved and swore, but we tended him with our uncouth,
  clumsy care.
The camp-fire gleamed and he gazed and dreamed with a fixed
  and curious stare.
Then all at once he grabbed my gun and he put it to his head,
And he says: "I'll fix it for you, boys"—them are the words he
  said.

So we sewed him up in a canvas sack and we slung him to a tree;
And the stars like needles stabbed our eyes, and woeful men
  were we.
And on we went on our woeful way, wrapped in a daze of
  dream,
And the Northern Lights in the crystal nights came forth with
  a mystic gleam.
They danced and they danced the devil-dance over the naked
  snow;
And soft they rolled like a tide upshoaled with a ceaseless ebb
  and flow.
They rippled green with a wondrous sheen, they fluttered out
  like a fan;

They spread with a blaze of rose-pink rays never yet seen of
man.

They writhed like a brood of angry snakes, hissing and sulphur
pale;

Then swift they changed to a dragon vast, lashing a cloven tail.

It seemed to us, as we gazed aloft with an everlasting stare,

The sky was a pit of bale and dread, and a monster revelled
there.

We climbed the rise of a hog-back range that was desolate and
drear,

When the Sailor Swede had a crazy fit, and he got to talking
queer.

He talked of his home in Oregon and the peach trees all in bloom,

And the fern head-high, and the topaz sky, and the forest's
scented gloom.

He talked of the sins of his misspent life, and then he seemed to
brood,

And I watched him there like a fox a hare, for I knew it was
not good.

And sure enough in the dim dawn-light I missed him from the
tent,

And a fresh trail broke through the crusted snow, and I knew
not where it went.

But I followed it o'er the seamless waste, and I found him at
shut of day,

Naked there as a new-born babe—so I left him where he lay.

Day after day was sinister, and I fought fierce-eyed despair,

And I clung to life, and I struggled on, I knew not why nor
where.

I packed my grub in short relays, and I cowered down in my
tent,

And the world around was purged of sound like a frozen continent.
Day after day was dark as death, but ever and ever at nights,
With a brilliancy that grew and grew, blazed up the Northern Lights.

They rolled around with a soundless sound like softly bruiséd silk;
They poured into the bowl of the sky with the gentle flow of milk.
In eager, pulsing violet their wheeling chariots came,
Or they poised above the Polar rim like a coronal of flame.
From depths of darkness fathomless their lancing rays were hurled,
Like the all-combining search-lights of the navies of the world.
There on the roof-pole of the world as one bewitched I gazed,
And howled and grovelled like a beast as the awful splendors blazed.
My eyes were seared, yet thralled I peered through the parka hood nigh blind;
But I staggered on to the lights that shone, and never I looked behind.

There is a mountain round and low that lies by the Polar rim,
And I climbed its height in a whirl of light, and I peered o'er its jaggèd brim;
And there in a crater deep and vast, ungained, unguessed of men,
The mystery of the Arctic world was flashed into my ken.
For there these poor dim eyes of mine beheld the sight of sights—
That hollow ring was the source and spring of the mystic Northern Lights.

Then I staked that place from crown to base, and I hit the
homeward trail.
Ah, God! it was good, though my eyes were blurred, and I
crawled like a sickly snail.
In that vast white world where the silent sky communes with
the silent snow,
In hunger and cold and misery I wandered to and fro.
But the Lord took pity on my pain, and He led me to the sea,
And some ice-bound whalers heard my moan, and they fed and
sheltered me.
They fed the feeble scarecrow thing that stumbled out of the
wild
With the ravaged face of a mask of death and the wandering
wits of a child—
A craven, cowering bag of bones that once had been a man.
They tended me and they brought me back to the world, and
here I am.

Some say that the Northern Lights are the glare of the Arctic
ice and snow;
And some that it's electricity, and nobody seems to know.
But I'll tell you now—and if I lie, may my lips be stricken
dumb—
It's a *mine*, a mine of the precious stuff that men call radium.
It's a million dollars a pound, they say, and there's tons and
tons in sight.
You can see it gleam in a golden stream in the solitudes of
night.
And it's mine, all mine—and say! if you have a hundred plunks
to spare,
I'll let you have the chance of your life, I'll sell you a quarter
share.

You turn it down? Well, I'll make it ten seeing as you are my
    friend.
Nothing doing? Say! don't be hard—have you got a dollar to
    lend?
Just a dollar to help me out, I know you'll treat me white;
I'll do as much for you some day . . . God bless you, sir; good-
    night.

THE BALLAD OF THE BLACK FOX SKIN

I

THERE was Claw-fingered Kitty and Windy Ike living the life
of shame,
When unto them in the Long, Long Night came the man-who-
had-no-name;
Bearing his prize of a black fox pelt, out of the Wild he came.

His cheeks were blanched as the flume-head foam when the
brown spring freshets flow;
Deep in their dark, sin-calcined pits were his sombre eyes aglow;
They knew him far for the fitful man who spat forth blood on
the snow.

"Did ever you see such a skin?" quoth he; "there's nought in the
world so fine—
Such fullness of fur as black as the night, such lustre, such size,
such shine;
It's life to a one-lunged man like me; it's London, it's women,
it's wine.

"The Moose-hides called it the devil-fox, and swore that no man
could kill;
That he who hunted it, soon or late, must surely suffer some ill;
But I laughed at them and their old squaw-tales. Ha! Ha! I'm
laughing still.

"For look ye, the skin—it's as smooth as sin, and black as the
core of the Pit.
By gun or by trap, whatever the hap, I swore I would capture it;
By star and by star afield and afar, I hunted and would not quit.

91

"For the devil-fox, it was swift and sly, and it seemed to fleer
   at me;
I would wake in fright by the camp-fire light hearing its evil
   glee;
Into my dream its eyes would gleam, and its shadow would I see.

"It sniffed and ran from the ptarmigan I had poisoned to excess;
Unharmed it sped from my wrathful lead ('twas as if I shot by
   guess);
Yet it came by night in the stark moonlight to mock at my
   weariness.

"I tracked it up where the mountains hunch like the vertebrae
   of the world;
I tracked it down to the death-still pits where the avalanche is
   hurled;
From the glooms to the sacerdotal snows, where the carded
   clouds are curled.

"From the vastitudes where the world protrudes through clouds
   like seas up-shoaled,
I held its track till it led me back to the land I had left of old—
The land I had looted many moons. I was weary and sick and
   cold.

"I was sick, soul-sick, of the futile chase, and there and then I
   swore
The foul fiend fox might scathless go, for I would hunt no more;
Then I rubbed mine eyes in a vast surprise—it stood by my
   cabin door.

"A rifle raised in the wraith-like gloom, and a vengeful shot
   that sped;

A howl that would thrill a cream-faced corpse—and the demon
fox lay dead. . . .
Yet there was never a sign of wound, and never a drop he bled.

"So that was the end of the great black fox, and here is the prize
I've won;
And now for a drink to cheer me up—I've mushed since the
early sun;
We'll drink a toast to the sorry ghost of the fox whose race is
run."

II

Now Claw-fingered Kitty and Windy Ike, bad as the worst
were they;
In their road-house down by the river-trail they waited and
watched for prey;
With wine and song they joyed night long, and they slept like
swine by day.

For things were done in the Midnight Sun that no tongue will
ever tell;
And men there be who walk earth-free, but whose names are
writ in hell—
Are writ in flames with the guilty names of Fournier and Labelle.

Put not your trust in a poke of dust would ye sleep the sleep
of sin;
For there be those who would rob your clothes ere yet the dawn
comes in;
And a prize likewise in a woman's eyes is a peerless black fox
skin.

Put your faith in the mountain cat if you lie within his lair;
Trust the fangs of the mother-wolf, and the claws of the lead-
    ripped bear;
But oh, of the wiles and the gold-tooth smiles of a dance-hall
    wench beware!

Wherefore it was beyond all laws that lusts of man restrain,
A man drank deep and sank to sleep never to wake again;
And the Yukon swallowed through a hole the cold corpse of
    the slain.

III

The black fox skin a shadow cast from the roof nigh to the floor;
And sleek it seemed and soft it gleamed, and the woman stroked
    it o'er;
And the man stood by with a brooding eye, and gnashed his
    teeth and swore.

When thieves and thugs fall out and fight there's fell arrears to
    pay;
And soon or late sin meets its fate, and so it fell one day
That Claw-fingered Kitty and Windy Ike fanged up like dogs
    at bay.

"The skin is mine, all mine," she cried; "I did the deed alone."
"It's share and share with a guilt-yoked pair," he hissed in a
    pregnant tone;
And so they snarled like malamutes over a mildewed bone.

And so they fought, by fear untaught, till haply it befell
One dawn of day she slipped away to Dawson town to sell
The fruit of sin, this black fox skin that had made their lives a
    hell.

She slipped away as still he lay, she clutched the wondrous fur;
Her pulses beat, her foot was fleet, her fear was as a spur;
She laughed with glee, she did not see him rise and follow her.

The bluffs uprear and grimly peer far over Dawson town;
They see its lights a blaze o' nights and harshly they look down;
They mock the plan and plot of man with grim, ironic frown.

The trail was steep; 'twas at the time when swiftly sinks the
    snow;
All honey-combed, the river ice was rotting down below;
The river chafed beneath its rind with many a mighty throe.

And up the swift and oozy drift a woman climbed in fear,
Clutching to her a black fox fur as if she held it dear;
And hard she pressed it to her breast—then Windy Ike drew
    near.

She made no moan—her heart was stone—she read his smiling
    face,
And like a dream flashed all her life's dark horror and disgrace;
A moment only—with a snarl he hurled her into space.

She rolled for nigh an hundred feet; she bounded like a ball;
From crag to crag she caromed down through snow and timber
    fall; . . .
A hole gaped in the river ice; the spray flashed—that was all.

A bird sang for the joy of spring, so piercing sweet and frail;
And blinding bright the land was dight in gay and glittering
    mail;
And with a wondrous black fox skin a man slid down the trail.

IV

A wedge-faced man there was who ran along the river bank,
Who stumbled through each drift and slough, and ever slipped
    and sank,
And ever cursed his Maker's name, and ever "hooch" he drank.

He travelled like a hunted thing, hard harried, sore distrest;
The old grandmother moon crept out from her cloud-quilted
    nest;
The aged mountains mocked at him in their primeval rest.

Grim shadows diapered the snow; the air was strangely mild;
The valley's girth was dumb with mirth, the laughter of the
    wild;
The still sardonic laughter of an ogre o'er a child.

The river writhed beneath the ice; it groaned like one in pain,
And yawning chasms opened wide, and closed and yawned
    again;
And sheets of silver heaved on high until they split in twain.

From out the road-house by the trail they saw a man afar
Make for the narrow river-reach where the swift cross-currents
    are;
Where, frail and worn, the ice is torn and the angry waters jar.

But they did not see him crash and sink into the icy flow;
They did not see him clinging there, gripped by the undertow,
Clawing with bleeding finger-nails at the jagged ice and snow.

They found a note beside the hole where he had stumbled in:
"Here met his fate by evil luck a man who lived in sin,
And to the one who loves me least I leave this black fox skin."

And strange it is; for, though they searched the river all around,
No trace or sign of black fox skin was ever after found;
Though one man said he saw the tread of *hoofs* deep in the
   ground.

THE BALLAD OF PIOUS PETE

"The North has got him."—Yukonism.

I TRIED to refine that neighbor of mine, honest to God, I did.
I grieved for his fate, and early and late I watched over him like
    a kid.
I gave him excuse, I bore his abuse in every way that I could;
I swore to prevail; I camped on his trail; I plotted and planned
    for his good.
By day and by night I strove in men's sight to gather him into
    the fold,
With precept and prayer, with hope and despair, in hunger and
    hardship and cold.
I followed him into Gehennas of sin, I sat where the sirens sit;
In the shade of the Pole, for the sake of his soul, I strove with
    the powers of the Pit.
I shadowed him down to the scrofulous town; I dragged him
    from dissolute brawls;
But I killed the galoot when he started to shoot electricity into
    my walls.

God knows what I did he should seek to be rid of one who
    would save him from shame.
God knows what I bore that night when he swore and bade me
    make tracks from his claim.
I started to tell of the horrors of hell, when sudden his eyes lit
    like coals;
And "Chuck it," says he, "don't persecute me with your cant
    and your saving of souls."

I'll swear I was mild as I'd be with a child, but he called me the
    son of a slut;
And, grabbing his gun with a leap and a run, he threatened my
    face with the butt.
So what could I do (I leave it to you)? With curses he harried
    me forth;
Then he was alone, and I was alone, and over us menaced the
    North.

Our cabins were near; I could see, I could hear; but between us
    there rippled the creek;
And all summer through, with a rancor that grew, he would pass
    me and never would speak.
Then a shuddery breath like the coming of Death crept down
    from the peaks far away;
The water was still; the twilight was chill; the sky was a tatter
    of gray.
Swift came the Big Cold, and opal and gold the lights of the
    witches arose;
The frost-tyrant clinched, and the valley was cinched by the
    stark and cadaverous snows.
The trees were like lace where the star-beams could chase, each
    leaf was a jewel agleam.
The soft white hush lapped the Northland and wrapped us
    round in a crystalline dream;
So still I could hear quite loud in my ear the swish of the pinions
    of time;
So bright I could see, as plain as could be, the wings of God's
    angels ashine.

As I read in the Book I would oftentimes look to that cabin just
    over the creek.

Ah me, it was sad and evil and bad, two neighbors who never
    would speak!
I knew that full well like a devil in hell he was hatching out,
    early and late,
A system to bear through the frost-spangled air the warm,
    crimson waves of his hate.
I only could peer and shudder and fear—'twas ever so ghastly
    and still;
But I knew over there in his lonely despair he was plotting me
    terrible ill.
I knew that he nursed a malice accurst, like the blast of a win-
    nowing flame;
I pleaded aloud for a shield, for a shroud— Oh, God! then
    calamity came.

Mad! If I'm mad then you too are mad; but it's all in the point
    of view.
If you'd looked at them things gallivantin' on wings, all purple
    and green and blue;
If you'd noticed them twist, as they mounted and hissed like
    scorpions dim in the dark;
If you'd seen them rebound with a horrible sound, and spitefully
    spitting a spark;
If you'd watched *It* with dread, as it hissed by your bed, that
    thing with the feelers that crawls—
You'd have settled the brute that attempted to shoot electricity
    into your walls.

Oh, some they were blue, and they slithered right through; they
    were silent and squashy and round;
And some they were green; they were wriggly and lean; they
    writhed with so hateful a sound.

My blood seemed to freeze; I fell on my knees; my face was a
  white splash of dread.
Oh, the Green and the Blue, they were gruesome to view; but
  the worst of them all were the Red.
They came through the door, they came through the floor, they
  came through the moss-creviced logs.
They were savage and dire; they were whiskered with fire; they
  bickered like malamute dogs.
They ravined in rings like iniquitous things; they gulped down
  the Green and the Blue.
I crinkled with fear whene'er they drew near, and nearer and
  nearer they drew.

And then came the crown of Horror's grim crown, the monster
  so loathsomely red.
Each eye was a pin that shot out and in, as, squidlike, it oozed
  to my bed;
So softly it crept with feelers that swept and quivered like fine
  copper wire;
Its belly was white with a sulphurous light, its jaws were a-drool-
  ing with fire.
It came and it came; I could breathe of its flame, but never a
  wink could I look.
I thrust in its maw the Fount of the Law; I fended it off with
  the Book.
I was weak—oh, so weak—but I thrilled at its shriek, as wildly
  it fled in the night;
And deathlike I lay till the dawn of the day. (Was ever so wel-
  come the light?)

I loaded my gun at the rise of the sun; to his cabin so softly I
  slunk.

My neighbor was there in the frost-freighted air, all wrapped in a robe in his bunk.

It muffled his moans; it outlined his bones, as feebly he twisted about;

His gums were so black, and his lips seemed to crack, and his teeth all were loosening out.

'Twas a death's head that peered through the tangle of beard; 'twas a face I will never forget;

Sunk eyes full of woe, and they troubled me so with their pleadings and anguish, and yet

As I rested my gaze in a misty amaze on the scurvy-degenerate wreck,

I thought of the Things with the dragon-fly wings, then laid I my gun on his neck.

He gave out a cry that was faint as a sigh, like a perishing malamute,

And he says unto me, "I'm converted," says he; "for Christ's sake, Peter, don't shoot!"

*   *   *   *   *   *   *   *   *

They're taking me out with an escort about, and under a sergeant's care;

I am humbled indeed, for I'm 'cuffed to a Swede that thinks he's a millionaire.

But it's all Gospel true what I'm telling to you—up there where the Shadow falls—

That I settled Sam Noot when he started to shoot electricity into my walls.

THE BALLAD OF BLASPHEMOUS BILL

I took a contract to bury the body of blasphemous Bill MacKie,
Whenever, wherever or whatsoever the manner of death he
die—
Whether he die in the light o' day or under the peak-faced
moon;
In cabin or dance-hall, camp or dive, mucklucks or patent shoon;
On velvet tundra or virgin peak, by glacier, drift or draw;
In muskeg hollow or canyon gloom, by avalanche, fang or claw;
By battle, murder or sudden wealth, by pestilence, hooch or
lead—
I swore on the Book I would follow and look till I found my
tombless dead.

For Bill was a dainty kind of cuss, and his mind was mighty sot
On a dinky patch with flowers and grass in a civilized bone-
yard lot.
And where he died or how he died, it didn't matter a damn
So long as he had a grave with frills and a tombstone "epigram."
So I promised him, and he paid the price in good cheechako coin
(Which the same I blowed in that very night down in the
Tenderloin).
Then I painted a three-foot slab of pine: "Here lies poor Bill
MacKie,"
And I hung it up on my cabin wall and I waited for Bill to die.

Years passed away, and at last one day came a squaw with a
story strange,
Of a long-deserted line of traps 'way back of the Bighorn range;

Of a little hut by the great divide, and a white man stiff and still,
Lying there by his lonesome self, and I figured it must be Bill.
So I thought of the contract I'd made with him, and I took down
   from the shelf
The swell black box with the silver plate he'd picked out for
   hisself;
And I packed it full of grub and "hooch," and I slung it on the
   sleigh;
Then I harnessed up my team of dogs and was off at dawn of day.

You know what it's like in the Yukon wild when it's sixty-nine.
   below;
When the ice-worms wriggle their purple heads through the
   crust of the pale blue snow;
When the pine-trees crack like little guns in the silence of the
   wood,
And the icicles hang down like tusks under the parka hood;
When the stove-pipe smoke breaks sudden off, and the sky is
   weirdly lit,
And the careless feel of a bit of steel burns like a red-hot spit;
When the mercury is a frozen ball, and the frost-fiend stalks to
   kill—
Well, it was just like that that day when I set out to look for Bill.

Oh, the awful hush that seemed to crush me down on every
   hand,
As I blundered blind with a trail to find through that blank and
   bitter land;
Half dazed, half crazed in the winter wild, with its grim heart-
   breaking woes,
And the ruthless strife for a grip on life that only the sourdough
   knows!
North by the compass, North I pressed; river and peak and plain

Passed like a dream I slept to lose and I waked to dream again.

River and plain and mighty peak—and who could stand un-
    awed?
As their summits blazed, he could stand undazed at the foot of
    the throne of God.
North, aye, North, through a land accurst, shunned by the
    scouring brutes,
And all I heard was my own harsh word and the whine of the
    malamutes,
Till at last I came to a cabin squat, built in the side of a hill,
And I burst in the door, and there on the floor, frozen to death,
    lay Bill.

Ice, white ice, like a winding-sheet, sheathing each smoke-
    grimed wall;
Ice on the stove-pipe, ice on the bed, ice gleaming over all;
Sparkling ice on the dead man's chest, glittering ice in his hair,
Ice on his fingers, ice in his heart, ice in his glassy stare;
Hard as a log and trussed like a frog, with his arms and legs
    outspread.
I gazed at the coffin I'd brought for him, and I gazed at the
    gruesome dead,
And at last I spoke: "Bill liked his joke; but still, goldarn his eyes,
A man had ought to consider his mates in the way he goes and
    dies."

Have you ever stood in an Arctic hut in the shadow of the Pole,
With a little coffin six by three and a grief you can't control?
Have you ever sat by a frozen corpse that looks at you with a
    grin,
And that seems to say: "You may try all day, but you'll never
    jam me in"?

I'm not a man of the quitting kind, but I never felt so blue
As I sat there gazing at that stiff and studying what I'd do.
Then I rose and I kicked off the husky dogs that were nosing
    round about,
And I lit a roaring fire in the stove, and I started to thaw Bill out.

Well, I thawed and thawed for thirteen days, but it didn't seem
    no good;
His arms and legs stuck out like pegs, as if they was made of
    wood.
Till at last I said: "It ain't no use—he's froze too hard to thaw;
He's obstinate, and he won't lie straight, so I guess I got to—
    saw."
So I sawed off poor Bill's arms and legs, and I laid him snug and
    straight
In the little coffin he picked hisself, with the dinky silver plate,
And I came nigh near to shedding a tear as I nailed him safely
    down;
Then I stowed him away in my Yukon sleigh, and I started back
    to town.

So I buried him as the contract was in a narrow grave and deep,
And there he's waiting the Great Clean-up, when the Judgment
    sluice-heads sweep;
And I smoke my pipe and I meditate in the light of the Midnight
    Sun,
And sometimes I wonder if they *was*, the awful things I done.
And as I sit and the parson talks, expounding of the Law,
I often think of poor old Bill—*and how hard he was to saw.*

THE BALLAD OF ONE-EYED MIKE

*This is the tale that was told to me by the man with the crystal
eye,*
*As I smoked my pipe in the camp-fire light, and the Glories
swept the sky;*
*As the Northlights gleamed and curved and streamed, and the
bottle of "hooch" was dry.*

A man once aimed that my life be shamed, and wrought me a
deathly wrong;
I vowed one day I would well repay, but the heft of his hate
was strong.
He thonged me East and he thonged me West; he harried me
back and forth,
Till I fled in fright from his peerless spite to the bleak, bald-
headed North.

And there I lay, and for many a day I hatched plan after plan,
For a golden haul of the wherewithal to crush and to kill my
man;
And there I strove, and there I clove through the drift of icy
streams;
And there I fought, and there I sought for the pay-streak of my
dreams.

So twenty years, with their hopes and fears and smiles and tears
and such,
Went by and left me long bereft of hope of the Midas touch;
About as fat as a chancel rat, and lo! despite my will,

In the weary fight I had clean lost sight of the man I sought to
    kill.

'Twas so far away, that evil day when I prayed the Prince of
    Gloom
For the savage strength and the sullen length of life to work his
    doom.
Nor sign nor word had I seen or heard, and it happed so long
    ago;
My youth was gone and my memory wan, and I willed it even so.

It fell one night in the waning light by the Yukon's oily flow,
I smoked and sat as I marvelled at the sky's port-winey glow;
Till it paled away to an absinthe gray, and the river seemed to
    shrink,
All wobbly flakes and wriggling snakes and goblin eyes a-wink.

'Twas weird to see and it 'wildered me in a queer, hypnotic
    dream,
Till I saw a spot like an inky blot come floating down the stream;
It bobbed and swung; it sheered and hung; it romped round in
    a ring;
It seemed to play in a tricksome way; it sure was a merry thing.

In freakish flights strange oily lights came fluttering round its
    head,
Like butterflies of a monster size—then I knew it for the Dead.
Its face was rubbed and slicked and scrubbed as smooth as a
    shaven pate;
In the silver snakes that the water makes it gleamed like a dinner-
    plate.

It gurgled near, and clear and clear and large and large it grew;
It stood upright in a ring of light and it looked me through and
 through.
It weltered round with a woozy sound, and ere I could retreat,
With the witless roll of a sodden soul it wantoned to my feet.

And here I swear by this Cross I wear, I heard that "floater" say:
"I am the man from whom you ran, the man you sought to slay.
That you may note and gaze and gloat, and say 'Revenge is
 sweet,'
In the grit and grime of the river's slime I am rotting at your feet.

"The ill we rue we must e'en undo, though it rive us bone from
 bone;
So it came about that I sought you out, for I prayed I might
 atone.
I did you wrong, and for long and long I sought where you
 might live;
And now you're found, though I'm dead and drowned, I beg
 you to forgive."

So sad it seemed, and its cheek-bones gleamed, and its fingers
 flicked the shore;
And it lapped and lay in a weary way, and its hands met to
 implore;
That I gently said: "Poor, restless dead, I would never work you
 woe;
Though the wrong you rue you can ne'er undo, I forgave you
 long ago."

Then, wonder-wise, I rubbed my eyes and I woke from a horrid
 dream.

The moon rode high in the naked sky, and something bobbed
    in the stream.
It held my sight in a patch of light, and then it sheered from the
    shore;
It dipped and sank by a hollow bank, and I never saw it more.

This was the tale he told to me, that man so warped and gray,
Ere he slept and dreamed, and the camp-fire gleamed in his eye
    in a wolfish way—
That crystal eye that raked the sky in the weird Auroral ray.

THE BALLAD OF THE BRAND

'Twas up in a land long famed for gold, where women were
    far and rare,
Tellus, the smith, had taken to wife a maiden amazingly fair;
Tellus, the brawny worker in iron, hairy and heavy of hand,
Saw her and loved her and bore her away from the tribe of a
    Southern land;
Deeming her worthy to queen his home and mother him little
    ones,
That the name of Tellus, the master smith, might live in his
    stalwart sons.

Now there was little of law in the land, and evil doings were rife,
And every man who joyed in his home guarded the fame of his
    wife.
For there were those of the silver tongue and the honeyed art
    to beguile,
Who would cozen the heart from a woman's breast and damn
    her soul with a smile.
And there were women too quick to heed a look or a whispered
    word,
And once in a while a man was slain, and the ire of the King was
    stirred;
So far and wide he proclaimed his wrath, and this was the law he
    willed:
"That whosoever killeth a man, even shall he be killed."

Now Tellus, the smith, he trusted his wife; his heart was empty
    of fear.

High on the hill was the gleam of their hearth, a beacon of love
    and cheer.
High on the hill they builded their bower, where the broom and
    the bracken meet;
Under a grave of oaks it was, hushed and drowsily sweet.
Here he enshrined her, his dearest saint, his idol, the light of his
    eye;
Her kisses rested upon his lips as brushes a butterfly.
The weight of her arms around his neck was light as the thistle
    down;
And sweetly she studied to win his smile, and gently she mocked
    his frown.
And when at the close of the dusty day his clangorous toil was
    done,
She hastened to meet him down the way all lit by the amber sun.

Their dove-cot gleamed in the golden light, a temple of stainless
    love;
Like the hanging cup of a big blue flower was the topaz sky
    above.
The roses and lilies yearned to her, as swift through their throng
    she pressed;
A little white, fragile, fluttering thing that lay like a child on
    his breast.
Then the heart of Tellus, the smith, was proud, and sang for the
    joy of life,
And there in the bronzing summertide he thanked the gods for
    his wife.

Now there was one called Philo, a scribe, a man of exquisite
    grace,
Carved like the god Apollo in limb, fair as Adonis in face:

Eager and winning of manner, full of such radiant charm,
Womenkind fought for his favor and loved to their uttermost
    harm.
Such was his craft and his knowledge, such was his skill at the
    game,
Never was woman could flout him, so be he plotted her shame.
And so he drank deep of pleasure, and then it fell on a day
He gazed on the wife of Tellus and marked her out for his prey.

Tellus, the smith, was merry, and the time of the year it was
    June,
So he said to his stalwart helpers: "Shut down the forge at noon.
Go ye and joy in the sunshine, rest in the coolth of the grove,
Drift on the dreamy river, every man with his love."
Then to himself: "Oh, Beloved, sweet will be your surprise;
To-day will we sport like children, laugh in each other's eyes;
Weave gay garlands of poppies, crown each other with flowers,
Pull plump carp from the lilies, rifle the ferny bowers.
To-day with feasting and gladness the wine of Cyprus will flow;
To-day is the day we were wedded only a twelve-month ago."

The larks trilled high in the heavens; his heart was lyric with joy;
He plucked a posy of lilies; he sped like a love-sick boy.
He stole up the velvety pathway—his cottage was sunsteeped
    and still;
Vines honeysuckled the window; softly he peeped o'er the sill.
The lilies dropped from his fingers; devils were choking his
    breath;
Rigid with horror, he stiffened; ghastly his face was as death.
Like a nun whose faith in the Virgin is met with a prurient jibe,
He shrank—'twas the wife of his bosom in the arms of Philo, the
    scribe.

Tellus went back to his smithy; he reeled like a drunken man:
His heart was riven with anguish; his brain was brooding a plan.
Straight to his anvil he hurried; started his furnace aglow;
Heated his iron and shaped it with savage and masterful blow.
Sparks showered over and round him; swiftly under his hand
There at last it was finished—a hideous and infamous Brand.

That night the wife of his bosom, the light of joy in her eyes,
Kissed him with words of rapture; but he knew that her words
    were lies.
Never was she so beguiling, never so merry of speech
(For passion ripens a woman as the sunshine ripens a peach).
He clenched his teeth into silence; he yielded up to her lure,
Though he knew that her breasts were heaving from the fire of
    her paramour.
"To-morrow," he said, "to-morrow"—he wove her hair in a
    strand,
Twisted it round his fingers and smiled as he thought of the
    Brand.

The morrow was come, and Tellus swiftly stole up the hill.
Butterflies drowsed in the noon-heat; coverts were sunsteeped
    and still.
Softly he padded the pathway unto the porch, and within
Heard he the low laugh of dalliance, heard he the rapture of sin.
Knew he her eyes were mystic with light that no man should see,
No man kindle and joy in, no man on earth save he.
And never for him would it kindle. The bloodlust surged in his
    brain;
Through the senseless stone could he see them, wanton and
    warily fain.
Horrible! Heaven he sought for, gained it and gloried and fell—
Oh, it was sudden—headlong into the nethermost hell. . . .

Was this he, Tellus, this marble? Tellus . . . not dreaming a
 dream?
Ah! sharp-edged as a javelin, was that woman's scream?
Was it a door that shattered, shell-like, under his blow?
Was it his saint, that strumpet, dishevelled and cowering low?
Was it her lover, that wild thing, that twisted and gouged and
 tore?
Was it a man he was crushing, whose head he beat on the floor?
Laughing the while at its weakness, till sudden he stayed his
 hand—
Through the red ring of his madness flamed the thought of the
 Brand.

Then bound he the naked Philo with thongs that cut in the flesh,
And the wife of his bosom, fear-frantic, he gagged with a silken
 mesh,
Choking her screams into silence; bound her down by the hair;
Dragged her lover unto her under her frenzied stare.
In the heat of the hearth-fire embers he heated the hideous
 Brand;
Twisting her fingers open, he forced its haft in her hand.
He pressed it downward and downward; she felt the living
 flesh sear;
She saw the throe of her lover; she heard the scream of his fear.
Once, twice and thrice he forced her, heedless of prayer and
 shriek—
Once on the forehead of Philo, twice in the soft of his cheek.
Then (for the thing was finished) he said to the woman: "See
How you have branded your lover! Now will I let him go free."
He severed the thongs that bound him, laughing: "Revenge is
 sweet,"
And Philo, sobbing in anguish, feebly rose to his feet.

The man who was fair as Apollo, god-like in woman's sight,
Hideous now as a satyr, fled to the pity of night.

*Then came they before the Judgment Seat, and thus spoke the
   Lord of the Land:*
*"He who seeketh his neighbor's wife shall suffer the doom of
   the Brand.*
*Brutish and bold on his brow be it stamped, deep in his cheek let
   it sear,*
*That every man may look on his shame, and shudder and sicken
   and fear.*
*He shall hear their mock in the market-place, their fleering jibe
   at the feast;*
*He shall seek the caves and the shroud of night, and the fellow-
   ship of the beast.*
Outcast forever from homes of men, far and far shall he roam.
*Such be the doom, sadder than death, of him who shameth a
   home."*

THE BALLAD OF HARD-LUCK HENRY

Now wouldn't you expect to find a man an awful crank
That's staked out nigh three hundred claims, and every one a
    blank;
That's followed every fool stampede, and seen the rise and fall
Of camps where men got gold in chunks and he got none at all;
That's prospected a bit of ground and sold it for a song
To see it yield a fortune to some fool that came along;
That's sunk a dozen bed-rock holes, and not a speck in sight,
Yet sees them take a million from the claims to left and right?
Now aren't things like that enough to drive a man to booze?
But Hard-Luck Smith was hoodoo-proof—he knew the way to
    lose.

'Twas in the fall of nineteen four—leap-year I've heard them
    say—
When Hard-Luck came to Hunker Creek and took a hillside lay.
And lo! as if to make amends for all the futile past,
Late in the year he struck it rich, the real pay-streak at last.
The riffles of his sluicing-box were choked with speckled earth,
And night and day he worked that lay for all that he was worth.
And when in chill December's gloom his lucky lease expired,
He found that he had made a stake as big as he desired.

One day while meditating on the waywardness of fate,
He felt the ache of lonely man to find a fitting mate;
A petticoated pard to cheer his solitary life,
A woman with soft, soothing ways, a confident, a wife,
And while he cooked his supper on his little Yukon stove,

He wished that he had staked a claim in Love's rich treasure-
    trove:
When suddenly he paused and held aloft a Yukon egg,
For there in pencilled letters was the magic name of Peg.

You know these Yukon eggs of ours—some pink, some green,
    some blue—
A dollar per, assorted tints, assorted flavors too.
The supercilious cheechako might designate them high,
But one acquires a taste for them and likes them by-and-by.
Well, Hard-Luck Henry took this egg and held it to the light,
And there was more faint pencilling that sorely taxed his sight.
At last he made it out, and then the legend ran like this—
"Will Klondike miner write to Peg, Plumhollow, Squashville,
    Wis.?"

That night he got to thinking of this far-off, unknown fair;
It seemed so sort of opportune, an answer to his prayer.
She flitted sweetly through his dreams, she haunted him by day,
She smiled through clouds of nicotine, she cheered his weary
    way.
At last he yielded to the spell; his course of love he set—
Wisconsin his objective point; his object, Margaret.

With every mile of sea and land his longing grew and grew.
He practised all his pretty words, and these, I fear, were few.
At last, one frosty evening, with a cold chill down his spine,
He found himself before her house, the threshold of the shrine.
His courage flickered to a spark, then glowed with sudden
    flame—
He knocked; he heard a welcome word; she came—his goddess
    came.
Oh, she was fair as any flower, and huskily he spoke:

"I'm all the way from Klondike, with a mighty heavy poke.
I'm looking for a lassie, one whose Christian name is Peg,
Who sought a Klondike miner, and who wrote it on an egg."

The lassie gazed at him a space, her cheeks grew rosy red;
She gazed at him with tear-bright eyes, then tenderly she said:
"Yes, lonely Klondike miner, it is true my name is Peg.
It's also true I longed for you and wrote it on an egg.
My heart went out to someone in that land of night and cold;
But oh, I fear that Yukon egg must have been mighty old.
I waited long, I hoped and feared; you should have come before;
I've been a wedded woman now for eighteen months or more.
I'm sorry, since you've come so far, you ain't the one that wins;
But won't you take a step inside—*I'll let you see the twins.*"

THE MAN FROM ELDORADO

I

He's the man from Eldorado, and he's just arrived in town,
  In moccasins and oily buckskin shirt.
He's gaunt as any Indian, and pretty nigh as brown;
  He's greasy, and he smells of sweat and dirt.
He sports a crop of whiskers that would shame a healthy hog;
  Hard work has racked his joints and stooped his back;
He slops along the sidewalk followed by his yellow dog,
  But he's got a bunch of gold-dust in his sack.

He seems a little wistful as he blinks at all the lights,
  And maybe he is thinking of his claim
And the dark and dwarfish cabin where he lay and dreamed at
    nights,
  (Thank God, he'll never see the place again!)
Where he lived on tinned tomatoes, beef embalmed and sour-
    dough bread,
  On rusty beans and bacon furred with mould;
His stomach's out of kilter and his system full of lead,
  But it's over, and his poke is full of gold.

He has panted at the windlass, he has loaded in the drift,
  He has pounded at the face of oozy clay;
He has taxed himself to sickness, dark and damp and double
    shift,
  He has labored like a demon night and day.
And now, praise God, it's over, and he seems to breathe again
  Of new-mown hay, the warm, wet, friendly loam;
He sees a snowy orchard in a green and dimpling plain,
  And a little vine-clad cottage, and it's—Home.

II

He's the man from Eldorado, and he's had a bite and sup,
  And he's met in with a drouthy friend or two;
He's cached away his gold-dust, but he's sort of bucking up,
  So he's kept enough to-night to see him through.
His eye is bright and genial, his tongue no longer lags;
  His heart is brimming o'er with joy and mirth;
He may be far from savory, he may be clad in rags,
  But to-night he feels as if he owns the earth.

Says he: "Boys, here is where the shaggy North and I will shake;
  I thought I'd never manage to get free.
I kept on making misses; but at last I've got my stake;
  There's no more thawing frozen muck for me.
I am going to God's Country, where I'll live the simple life;
  I'll buy a bit of land and make a start;
I'll carve a little homestead, and I'll win a little wife,
  And raise ten little kids to cheer my heart."

They signified their sympathy by crowding to the bar;
  They bellied up three deep and drank his health.
He shed a radiant smile around and smoked a rank cigar;
  They wished him honor, happiness and wealth.
They drank unto his wife to be—that unsuspecting maid;
  They drank unto his children half a score;
And when they got through drinking very tenderly they laid
  The man from Eldorado on the floor.

III

He's the man from Eldorado, and he's only starting in
  To cultivate a thousand-dollar jag.

His poke is full of gold-dust and his heart is full of sin,
   And he's dancing with a girl called Muckluck Mag.
She's as light as any fairy; she's as pretty as a peach;
   She's mistress of the witchcraft to beguile;
There's sunshine in her manner, there is music in her speech,
   And there's concentrated honey in her smile.

Oh, the fever of the dance-hall and the glitter and the shine,
   The beauty, and the jewels, and the whirl,
The madness of the music, the rapture of the wine,
   The languorous allurement of a girl!
She is like a lost madonna; he is gaunt, unkempt and grim;
   But she fondles him and gazes in his eyes;
Her kisses seek his heavy lips, and soon it seems to him
   He has staked a little claim in Paradise.

"Who's for a juicy two-step?" cries the master of the floor;
   The music throbs with soft, seductive beat.
There's glitter, gilt and gladness; there are pretty girls galore;
   There's a woolly man with moccasins on feet.
They know they've got him going; he is buying wine for all;
   They crowd around as buzzards at a feast,
Then when his poke is empty they boost him from the hall,
   And spurn him in the gutter like a beast.

He's the man from Eldorado, and he's painting red the town;
   Behind he leaves a trail of yellow dust;
In a whirl of senseless riot he is ramping up and down;
   There's nothing checks his madness and his lust.
And soon the word is passed around—it travels like a flame;
   They fight to clutch his hand and call him friend,
The chevaliers of lost repute, the dames of sorry fame;
   Then comes the grim awakening—the end.

IV

He's the man from Eldorado, and he gives a grand affair;
  There's feasting, dancing, wine without restraint.
The smooth Beau Brummels of the bar, the faro men, are there;
  The tinhorns and purveyors of red paint;
The sleek and painted women, their predacious eyes aglow—
  Sure Klondike City never saw the like;
Then Muckluck Mag proposed the toast, "The giver of the
    show,
  The livest sport that ever hit the pike."

The "live one" rises to his feet; he stammers to reply—
  And then there comes before his muddled brain
A vision of green vastitudes beneath an April sky,
  And clover pastures drenched with silver rain.
He knows that it can never be, that he is down and out;
  Life leers at him with foul and fetid breath;
And then amid the revelry, the song and cheer and shout,
  He suddenly grows grim and cold as death.

He grips the table tensely, and he says: "Dear friends of mine,
  I've let you dip your fingers in my purse;
I've crammed you at my table, and I've drowned you in my
    wine,
  And I've little left to give you but—my curse.
I've failed supremely in my plans; it's rather late to whine;
  My poke is mighty wizened up and small.
I thank you each for coming here; the happiness is mine—
  And now, you thieves and harlots, take it all."

He twists the thong from off his poke; he swings it o'er his head;
  The nuggets fall around their feet like grain.

They rattle over roof and wall; they scatter, roll and spread;
  The dust is like a shower of golden rain.
The guests a moment stand aghast, then grovel on the floor;
  They fight, and snarl, and claw, like beasts of prey;
And then, as everybody grabbed and everybody swore,
  The man from Eldorado slipped away.

v

He's the man from Eldorado, and they found him stiff and dead,
  Half covered by the freezing ooze and dirt.
A clotted Colt was in his hand, a hole was in his head,
  And he wore an old and oily buckskin shirt.
His eyes were fixed and horrible, as one who hails the end;
  The frost had set him rigid as a log;
And there, half lying on his breast, his last and only friend,
  There crouched and whined a mangy yellow dog.

MY FRIENDS

THE man above was a murderer, the man below was a thief,
And I lay there in the bunk between, ailing beyond belief,
A weary armful of skin and bone, wasted with pain and grief.

My feet were froze, and the lifeless toes were purple and green
    and gray;
The little flesh that clung to my bones, you could punch it in
    holes like clay;
The skin on my gums was a sullen black, and slowly peeling
    away.

I was sure enough in a direful fix, and often I wondered why
They did not take the chance that was left and leave me alone
    to die,
Or finish me off with a dose of dope—so utterly lost was I.

But no; they brewed me the green-spruce tea, and nursed me
    there like a child;
And the homicide he was good to me, and bathed my sores and
    smiled;
And the thief he starved that I might be fed, and his eyes were
    kind and mild.

Yet they were woefully wicked men, and often at night in pain
I heard the murderer speak of his deed and dream it over again;
I heard the poor thief sorrowing for the dead self he had slain.

I'll never forget that bitter dawn, so evil, askew and gray,
When they wrapped me round in the skins of beasts and they
    bore me to a sleigh,
And we started out with the nearest post an hundred miles away.

I'll never forget the trail they broke, with its tense, unuttered
    woe;
And the crunch, crunch, crunch as their snowshoes sank through
    the crust of the hollow snow;
And my breath would fail, and every beat of my heart was like
    a blow.

And oftentimes I would die the death, yet wake up to life anew;
The sun would be all ablaze on the waste, and the sky a blighting
    blue,
And the tears would rise in my snow-blind eyes and furrow my
    cheeks like dew.

And the camps we made when their strength outplayed and the
    day was pinched and wan;
And oh, the joy of that blessed halt, and how I did dread the
    dawn;
And how I hated the weary men who rose and dragged me on.

And oh, how I begged to rest, to rest—the snow was so sweet a
    shroud;
And oh, how I cried when they urged me on, cried and cursed
    them aloud;
Yet on they strained, all racked and pained, and sorely their
    backs were bowed.

And then it was all like a lurid dream, and I prayed for a swift
    release

From the ruthless ones who would not leave me to die alone
    in peace;
Till I wakened up and I found myself at the post of the Mounted
    Police.

And there was my friend the murderer, and there was my friend
    the thief,
With bracelets of steel around their wrists, and wicked beyond
    belief:
But when they come to God's judgment seat—may I be allowed
    the brief.

THE PROSPECTOR

I STROLLED up old Bonanza, where I staked in ninety-eight,
  A-purpose to revisit the old claim.
I kept thinking mighty sadly of the funny ways of Fate,
  And the lads who once were with me in the game.
Poor boys, they're down-and-outers, and there's scarcely one
      to-day
  Can show a dozen colors in his poke;
And me, I'm still prospecting, old and battered, gaunt and gray,
  And I'm looking for a grub-stake, and I'm broke.

I strolled up old Bonanza. The same old moon looked down;
  The same old landmarks seemed to yearn to me;
But the cabins all were silent, and the flat, once like a town,
  Was mighty still and lonesome-like to see.
There were piles and piles of tailings where we toiled with pick
      and pan,
  And turning round a bend I heard a roar,
And there a giant gold-ship of the very newest plan
  Was tearing chunks of pay-dirt from the shore.

It wallowed in its water-bed; it burrowed, heaved and swung;
  It gnawed its way ahead with grunts and sighs;
Its bill of fare was rock and sand; the tailings were its dung;
  It glared around with fierce electric eyes.
Full fifty buckets crammed its maw; it bellowed out for more;
  It looked like some great monster in the gloom.
With two to feed its sateless greed, it worked for seven score,
  And I sighed: "Ah, old-time miner, here's your doom!"

The idle windlass turns to rust; the sagging sluice-box falls;
   The holes you digged are water to the brim;
Your little sod-roofed cabins with the snugly moss-chinked
      walls
   Are deathly now and mouldering and dim.
The battle-field is silent where of old you fought it out;
   The claims you fiercely won are lost and sold.
But there's a little army that they'll never put to rout—
   The men who simply live to seek the gold.

The men who can't remember when they learned to swing a
      pack,
   Or in what lawless land the quest began;
The solitary seeker with his grub-stake on his back,
   The restless buccaneer of pick and pan.
On the mesas of the Southland, on the tundras of the North,
   You will find us, changed in face but still the same;
And it isn't need, it isn't greed that sends us faring forth—
   It's the fever, it's the glory of the game.

For once you've panned the speckled sand and seen the bonny
      dust,
   Its peerless brightness blinds you like a spell;
It's little else you care about; you go because you must,
   And you feel that you could follow it to hell.
You'd follow it in hunger, and you'd follow it in cold;
   You'd follow it in solitude and pain;
And when you're stiff and battened down let someone whisper
      "Gold,"
   You're lief to rise and follow it again.

Yet look you, if I find the stuff it's just like so much dirt;
   I fling it to the four winds like a child.

It's wine and painted women and the things that do me hurt,
  Till I crawl back, beggared, broken, to the Wild.
Till I crawl back, sapped and sodden, to my grub-stake and my
      tent—
  There's a city, there's an army (hear them shout).
There's the gold in millions, millions, but I haven't got a cent;
  And oh, it's me, it's me that found it out.

It was my dream that made it good, my dream that made me go
  To lands of dread and death disprized of man;
But oh, I've known a glory that their hearts will never know,
  When I picked the first big nugget from my pan.
It's still my dream, my dauntless dream, that drives me forth
      once more
  To seek and starve and suffer in the Vast;
That heaps my heart with eager hope, that glimmers on before—
  My dream that will uplift me to the last.

Perhaps I am stark crazy, but there's none of you too sane;
  It's just a little matter of degree.
My hobby is to hunt out gold; it's fortressed in my brain;
  It's life and love and wife and home to me.
And I'll strike it, yes, I'll strike it; I've a hunch I cannot fail;
  I've a vision, I've a prompting, I've a call;
I hear the hoarse stampeding of an army on my trail,
  To the last, the greatest gold camp of them all.

Beyond the shark-tooth ranges sawing savage at the sky
  There's a lowering land no white man ever struck;
There's gold, there's gold in millions, and I'll find it if I die,
  And I'm going there once more to try my luck.
Maybe I'll fail—what matter? It's a mandate, it's a vow;
  And when in lands of dreariness and dread

You seek the last lone frontier, far beyond your frontiers now,
  You will find the old prospector, silent, dead.

You will find a tattered tent-pole with a ragged robe below it;
  You will find a rusted gold-pan on the sod;
You will find the claim I'm seeking, with my bones as stakes to
      show it;
    But I've sought the last Recorder, and He's—God.

THE BLACK SHEEP

"The aristocratic ne'er-do-well in Canada frequently finds his way into the ranks of the Royal North-West Mounted Police."—
Extract.

Hark to the ewe that bore him:
"What has muddied the strain?
Never his brothers before him
Showed the hint of a stain."
Hark to the tups and wethers;
Hark to the old gray ram:
"We're all of us white, but he's black as night,
And he'll never be worth a damn."

I'm up on the bally wood-pile at the back of the barracks yard;
"A damned disgrace to the force, sir," with a comrade standing
   guard;
Making the bluff I'm busy, doing my six months hard.

"Six months hard and dismissed, sir." Isn't that rather hell?
And all because of the liquor laws and the wiles of a native
   belle—
Some "hooch" I gave to a siwash brave who swore that he
   wouldn't tell.

At least they *say* that I did it. It's so in the town report.
All that I can recall is a night of revel and sport,
When I woke with a "head" in the guard-room, and they
   dragged me sick into court.

And the O. C. said: "You are guilty," and I said never a word;
For, hang it, you see I couldn't—I didn't know *what* had oc-
    curred,
And, under the circumstances, denial would be absurd.

But the one that cooked my bacon was Grubbe, of the City
    Patrol.
He fagged for my room at Eton, and didn't I devil his soul!
And now he is getting even, landing me down in the hole.

Plugging away on the wood-pile, doing chores round the square.
There goes an officer's lady—gives me a haughty stare—
Me that's an earl's own nephew—that is the hardest to bear.

To think of the poor old mater awaiting her prodigal son.
Tho' I broke her heart with my folly, I was always the white-
    haired one.
(That fatted calf that they're cooking will surely be overdone.)

I'll go back and yarn to the Bishop; I'll dance with the village
    belle;
I'll hand round tea to the ladies, and everything will be well.
Where I have been won't matter; what I have seen I won't tell.

I'll soar to their ken like a comet. They'll see me with never a
    stain;
But will they reform me?—far from it. We pay for our pleasure
    with pain;
But the dog will return to his vomit, the hog to his wallow again.

I've chewed on the rind of creation, and bitter I've tasted the
    same;

Stacked up against hell and damnation, I've managed to stay in
the game;
I've had my moments of sorrow; I've had my seasons of shame.

That's past; when one's nature's a cracked one, it's too jolly hard
to mend.
So long as the road is level, so long as I've cash to spend,
I'm bound to go to the devil, and it's all the same in the end.

The bugle is sounding for stables; the men troop off through
the gloom;
An orderly laying the tables sings in the bright mess-room.
(I'll wash in the prison bucket, and brush with the prison
broom.)

I'll lie in my cell and listen; I'll wish that I couldn't hear
The laugh and the chaff of the fellows swigging the canteen
beer;
The nasal tone of the gramophone playing "The Bandolier."

And it seems to me, though it's misty, that night of the flowing
bowl,
That the man who potlatched the whiskey and landed me into
the hole
*Was Grubbe, that unmerciful bounder, Grubbe, of the City
Patrol.*

THE TELEGRAPH OPERATOR

I will not wash my face;
   I will not brush my hair;
I "pig" around the place—
   There's nobody to care.
Nothing but rock and tree;
   Nothing but wood and stone,
Oh, God, it's hell to be
   Alone, alone, alone!

Snow-peaks and deep-gashed draws
   Corral me in a ring.
I feel as if I was
   The only living thing
On all this blighted earth;
   And so I frowst and shrink,
And crouching by my hearth
   I hear the thoughts I think.

I think of all I miss—
   The boys I used to know;
The girls I used to kiss;
   The coin I used to blow;
The bars I used to haunt;
   The racket and the row;
The beers I didn't want
   (I wish I had 'em now).

Day after day the same,
   Only a little worse;

No one to grouch or blame—
   Oh, for a loving curse!
Oh, in the night I fear,
   Haunted by nameless things,
Just for a voice to cheer,
   Just for a hand that clings!

Faintly as from a star
   Voices come o'er the line;
Voices of ghosts afar,
   Not in this world of mine;
Lives in whose loom I grope;
   Words in whose weft I hear
Eager the thrill of hope,
   Awful the chill of fear.

I'm thinking out aloud;
   I reckon that is bad:
(The snow is like a shroud)—
   Maybe I'm going mad.
Say! wouldn't that be tough?
   This awful hush that hugs
And chokes one is enough
   To make a man go "bugs."

There's not a thing to do;
   I cannot sleep at night;
No wonder I'm so blue;
   Oh, for a friendly fight!
The din and rush of strife;
   A music-hall aglow;
A crowd, a city, life—
   Dear God, I miss it so!

Here, you have moped enough!
  Brace up and play the game!
But say, it's awful tough—
  Day after day the same
(I've said that twice, I bet).
  Well, there's not much to say.
I wish I had a pet,
  Or something I could play.

Cheer up! don't get so glum
  And sick of everything;
The worst is yet to come;
  God help you till the Spring.
God shield you from the Fear;
  Teach you to laugh, not moan.
Ha! ha! it sounds so queer—
  Alone, alone, alone!

THE WOOD-CUTTER

The sky is like an envelope,
  One of those blue official things;
And, sealing it, to mock our hope,
  The moon, a silver wafer, clings.
What shall we find when death gives leave
To read—our sentence or reprieve?

I'm holding it down on God's scrap-pile, up on the fag-end of
    earth;
  O'er me a menace of mountains, a river that grits at my feet;
Face to face with my soul-self, weighing my life at its worth;
  Wondering what I was made for, here in my last retreat.

Last! Ah, yes, it's the finish. Have ever you heard a man cry?
  (Sobs that rake him and rend him, right from the base of the
    chest.)
That's how I've cried, oh, so often; and now that my tears are
    dry,
  I sit in the desolate quiet and wait for the infinite Rest.

Rest! Well, it's restful around me; it's quiet clean to the core.
  The mountains pose in their ermine, in golden the hills are
    clad;
The big, blue, silt-freighted Yukon seethes by my cabin door,
  And I think it's only the river that keeps me from going mad.

By day it's a ruthless monster, a callous, insatiate thing,
  With oily bubble and eddy, with sudden swirling of breast;
By night it's a writhing Titan, sullenly murmuring,
  Ever and ever goaded, and ever crying for rest.

It cries for its human tribute, but me it will never drown.
  I've learned the lore of my river; my river obeys me well.
I hew and I launch my cordwood, and raft it to Dawson town,
  Where wood means wine and women, and, incidentally, hell.

Hell and the anguish thereafter. Here as I sit alone
  I'd give the life I have left me to lighten some load of care:
(The bitterest part of the bitter is being denied to atone;
  Lips that have mocked at Heaven lend themselves ill to
    prayer.)

Impotent as a beetle pierced on the needle of Fate;
  A wretch in a cosmic death-cell, peaks for my prison bars;
'Whelmed by a world stupendous, lonely and listless I wait,
  Drowned in a sea of silence, strewn with confetti of stars.

See! from far up the valley a rapier pierces the night,
  The white search-ray of a steamer. Swiftly, serenely it nears;
A proud, white, alien presence, a glittering galley of light,
  Confident-poised, triumphant, freighted with hopes and
    fears.

I look as one looks on a vision; I see it pulsating by;
  I glimpse joy-radiant faces; I hear the thresh of the wheel.
Hoof-like my heart beats a moment; then silence swoops from
    the sky.
  Darkness is piled upon darkness. God only knows how I feel.

Maybe you've seen me sometimes; maybe you've pitied me
    then—
  The lonely waif of the wood-camp, here by my cabin door.
Some day you'll look and see not; futile and outcast of men,
  I shall be far from your pity, resting forevermore.

My life was a problem in ciphers, a weary and profitless sum.
   Slipshod and stupid I worked it, dazed by negation and doubt.
Ciphers the total confronts me. Oh, Death, with thy moistened
       thumb,
   Stoop like a petulant schoolboy, wipe me forever out!

THE SONG OF THE MOUTH-ORGAN

(With apologies to the singer of the "Song of the Banjo.")

I'M a homely little bit of tin and bone;
    I'm beloved by the Legion of the Lost;
I haven't got a "vox humana" tone,
    And a dime or two will satisfy my cost.
I don't attempt your high-falutin' flights;
    I am more or less uncertain on the key;
But I tell you, boys, there's lots and lots of nights
    When you've taken mighty comfort out of me.

I weigh an ounce or two, and I'm so small
    You can pack me in the pocket of your vest;
And when at night so wearily you crawl
    Into your bunk and stretch your limbs to rest,
You take me out and play me soft and low,
    The simple songs that trouble your heartstrings:
The tunes you used to fancy long ago,
    Before you made a rotten mess of things.

Then a dreamy look will come into your eyes,
    And you break off in the middle of a note;
And then, with just the dreariest of sighs,
    You drop me in the pocket of your coat.
But somehow I have bucked you up a bit;
    And, as you turn around and face the wall,
You don't feel quite so spineless and unfit—
    You're not so bad a fellow after all.

Do you recollect the bitter Arctic night;
  Your camp beside the canyon on the trail;
Your tent a tiny square of orange light;
  The moon above consumptive-like and pale;
Your supper cooked, your little stove aglow;
  You tired, but snug and happy as a child?
Then 'twas "Turkey in the Straw" till your lips were nearly
    raw,
  And you hurled your bold defiance at the Wild.

Do you recollect the flashing, lashing pain;
  The gulf of humid blackness overhead;
The lightning making rapiers of the rain;
  The cattle-horns like candles of the dead;
You sitting on your bronco there alone,
  In your slicker, saddle-sore and sick with cold?
Do you think the silent herd did not hear "The Mocking Bird,"
  Or relish "Silver Threads among the Gold"?

Do you recollect the wild Magellan coast;
  The head-winds and the icy, roaring seas;
The nights you thought that everything was lost;
  The days you toiled in water to your knees;
The frozen ratlines shrieking in the gale;
  The hissing steeps and gulfs of livid foam:
When you cheered your messmates nine with "Ben Bolt" and
    "Clementine,"
  And "Dixie Land" and "Seeing Nellie Home"?

Let the jammy banjo voice the Younger Son,
  Who waits for his remittance to arrive;
I represent the grimy, gritty one,
  Who sweats his bones to keep himself alive;

Who's up against the real thing from his birth;
  Whose heritage is hard and bitter toil;
I voice the weary, smeary ones of earth,
  The helots of the sea and of the soil.

I'm the Steinway of strange mischief and mischance;
  I'm the Stradivarius of blank defeat;
In the down-world, when the devil leads the dance,
  I am simply and symbolically meet;
I'm the irrepressive spirit of mankind;
  I'm the small boy playing knuckle down with Death;
At the end of all things known, where God's rubbish-heap is
        thrown,
  I shrill impudent triumph at a breath.

I'm a humble little bit of tin and horn;
  I'm a byword, I'm a plaything, I'm a jest;
The virtuoso looks on me with scorn;
  But there's times when I am better than the best
Ask the stoker and the sailor of the sea;
  Ask the mucker and the hewer of the pine;
Ask the herder of the plain, ask the gleaner of the grain—
  There's a lowly, loving kingdom—and it's mine.

THE TRAIL OF NINETY-EIGHT

I

Gold! We leapt from our benches. Gold! We sprang from our
stools.
Gold! We wheeled in the furrow, fired with the faith of fools.
Fearless, unfound, unfitted, far from the night and the cold,
Heard we the clarion summons, followed the master-lure—
Gold!

Men from the sands of the Sunland; men from the woods of the
West;
Men from the farms and the cities, into the Northland we
pressed.
Graybeards and striplings and women, good men and bad men
and bold,
Leaving our homes and our loved ones, crying exultantly—
"Gold!"

Never was seen such an army, pitiful, futile, unfit;
Never was seen such a spirit, manifold courage and grit.
Never has been such a cohort under one banner unrolled
As surged to the ragged-edged Arctic, urged by the arch-
tempter—Gold.

"Farewell!" we cried to our dearests; little we cared for their
tears.
"Farewell!" we cried to the humdrum and the yoke of the hire-
ling years;

Just like a pack of school-boys, and the big crowd cheered us
  good-bye.
Never were hearts so uplifted, never were hopes so high.

The spectral shores flitted past us, and every whirl of the screw
Hurled us nearer to fortune, and ever we planned what we'd
  do—
Do with the gold when we got it—big, shiny nuggets like plums,
There in the sand of the river, gouging it out with our thumbs.

And one man wanted a castle, another a racing stud;
A third would cruise in a palace yacht like a red-necked prince
  of blood.
And so we dreamed and we vaunted, millionaires to a man,
Leaping to wealth in our visions long ere the trail began.

II

We landed in wind-swept Skagway. We joined the weltering
  mass,
Clamoring over their outfits, waiting to climb the Pass.
We tightened our girths and our pack-straps; we linked on the
  Human Chain,
Struggling up to the summit, where every step was a pain.

Gone was the joy of our faces, grim and haggard and pale;
The heedless mirth of the shipboard was changed to the care of
  the trail.
We flung ourselves in the struggle, packing our grub in relays,
Step by step to the summit in the bale of the winter days.

Floundering deep in the sump-holes, stumbling out again;
Crying with cold and weakness, crazy with fear and pain.

Then from the depths of our travail, ere our spirits were broke,
Grim, tenacious and savage, the lust of the trail awoke.

"Klondike or bust!" rang the slogan; every man for his own.
Oh, how we flogged the horses, staggering skin and bone!
Oh, how we cursed their weakness, anguish they could not tell,
Breaking their hearts in our passion, lashing them on till they
　　fell!

For grub meant gold to our thinking, and all that could walk
　　must pack;
The sheep for the shambles stumbled, each with a load on its
　　back;
And even the swine were burdened, and grunted and squealed
　　and rolled,
And men went mad in the moment, huskily clamoring "Gold!"

Oh, we were brutes and devils, goaded by lust and fear!
Our eyes were strained to the summit; the weaklings dropped
　　to the rear,
Falling in heaps by the trail-side, heart-broken, limp and wan;
But the gaps closed up in an instant, and heedless the chain went
　　on.

Never will I forget it, there on the mountain face,
Antlike, men with their burdens, clinging in icy space;
Dogged, determined and dauntless, cruel and callous and cold,
Cursing, blaspheming, reviling, and ever that battle-cry—
　　"Gold!"

Thus toiled we, the army of fortune, in hunger and hope and
　　despair,
Till glacier, mountain and forest vanished, and, radiantly fair,

There at our feet lay Lake Bennett, and down to its welcome we
    ran:
The trail of the land was over, the trail of the water began.

III

We built our boats and we launched them. Never has been such
    a fleet;
A packing-case for a bottom, a mackinaw for a sheet.
Shapeless, grotesque, lopsided, flimsy, makeshift and crude,
Each man after his fashion builded as best he could.

Each man worked like a demon, as prow to rudder we raced;
The winds of the Wild cried "Hurry!" the voice of the waters,
    "Haste!"
We hated those driving before us; we dreaded those pressing
    behind;
We cursed the slow current that bore us; we prayed to the God
    of the wind.

Spring! and the hillsides flourished, vivid in jewelled green;
Spring! and our hearts' blood nourished envy and hatred and
    spleen.
Little cared we for the Spring-birth; much cared we to get on—
Stake in the Great White Channel, stake ere the best be gone.

The greed of the gold possessed us; pity and love were forgot;
Covetous visions obsessed us; brother with brother fought.
Partner with partner wrangled, each one claiming his due;
Wrangled and halved their outfits, sawing their boats in two.

Thuswise we voyaged Lake Bennett, Tagish, then Windy Arm,
Sinister, savage and baleful, boding us hate and harm.

Many a scow was shattered there on that iron shore;
Many a heart was broken straining at sweep and oar.

We roused Lake Marsh with a chorus, we drifted many a mile;
There was the canyon before us—cave-like its dark defile;
The shores swept faster and faster; the river narrowed to wrath;
Waters that hissed disaster reared upright in our path.

Beneath us the green tumult churning, above us the cavernous
    gloom;
Around us, swift twisting and turning, the black, sullen walls of
    a tomb.
We spun like a chip in a mill-race; our hearts hammered under
    the test;
Then—oh, the relief on each chill face!—we soared into sun-
    light and rest.

Hand sought for hand on the instant. Cried we, "Our troubles
    are o'er!"
Then, like a rumble of thunder, heard we a canorous roar.
Leaping and boiling and seething, saw we a cauldron afume;
There was the rage of the rapids, there was the menace of doom.

The river springs like a racer, sweeps through a gash in the
    rock;
Butts at the boulder-ribbed bottom, staggers and rears at the
    shock;
Leaps like a terrified monster, writhes in its fury and pain;
Then with the crash of a demon springs to the onset again.

Dared we that ravening terror; heard we its din in our ears;
Called on the Gods of our fathers, juggled forlorn with our
    fears;

Sank to our waists in its fury, tossed to the sky like a fleece;
Then, when our dread was the greatest, crashed into safety and
    peace.

But what of the others that followed, losing their boats by the
    score?
Well could we see them and hear them, strung down that deso-
    late shore.
What of the poor souls that perished? Little of them shall be
    said—
On to the Golden Valley, pause not to bury the dead.

Then there were days of drifting, breezes soft as a sigh;
Night trailed her robe of jewels over the floor of the sky.
The moonlit stream was a python, silver, sinuous, vast,
That writhed on a shroud of velvet—well, it was done at last.

There were the tents of Dawson, there the scar of the slide;
Swiftly we poled o'er the shallows, swiftly leapt o'er the side.
Fires fringed the mouth of Bonanza; sunset gilded the dome;
The test of the trail was over—thank God, thank God, we were
    Home!

THE BALLAD OF GUM-BOOT BEN

He was an old prospector with a vision bleared and dim.
He asked me for a grubstake, and the same I gave to him.
He hinted of a hidden trove, and when I made so bold
To question his veracity, this is the tale he told.

"I do not seek the copper streak, nor yet the yellow dust.
I am not fain for sake of gain to irk the frozen crust;
Let fellows gross find gilded dross, far other is my mark;
Oh, gentle youth, this is the truth—I go to seek the Ark.

"I prospected the Pelly bed, I prospected the White;
The Nordenscold for love of gold I piked from morn till night;
Afar and near for many a year I led the wild stampede,
Until I guessed that all my quest was vanity and greed.

"Then came I to a land I knew no man had ever seen,
A haggard land, forlornly spanned by mountains lank and lean;
The nitchies said 'twas full of dread, of smoke and fiery breath,
And no man dare put foot in there for fear of pain and death.

"But I was made all unafraid, so, careless and alone,
Day after day I made my way into that land unknown;
Night after night by camp-fire light I crouched in lonely
    thought;
Oh, gentle youth, this is the truth—I knew not what I sought.

"I rose at dawn; I wandered on. 'Tis somewhat fine and grand
To be alone and hold your own in God's vast awesome land;

Come woe or weal, 'tis fine to feel a hundred miles between
The trails you dare and pathways where the feet of men have
    been.

"And so it fell on me a spell of wander-lust was cast.
The land was still and strange and chill, and cavernous and vast;
And sad and dead, and dull as lead, the valleys sought the snows;
And far and wide on every side the ashen peaks arose.

"The moon was like a silent spike that pierced the sky right
    through;
The small stars popped and winked and hopped in vastitudes of
    blue;
And unto me for company came creatures of the shade,
And formed in rings and whispered things that made me half
    afraid.

"And strange though be, 'twas borne on me that land had lived
    of old,
And men had crept and slain and slept where now they toiled
    for gold;
Through jungles dim the mammoth grim had sought the oozy
    fen,
And on his track, all bent of back, had crawled the hairy men.

"And furthermore, strange deeds of yore in this dead place
    were done.
They haunted me, as wild and free I roamed from sun to sun;
Until I came where sudden flame uplit a terraced height,
A regnant peak that seemed to seek the coronal of night.

"I scaled the peak; my heart was weak, yet on and on I pressed.
Skyward I strained until I gained its dazzling silver crest;

And there I found, with all around a world supine and stark,
Swept clean of snow, a flat plateau, and on it lay—the Ark.

"Yes, there, I knew, by two and two the beasts did disembark,
And so in haste I ran and traced in letters on the Ark
My human name—Ben Smith's the same. And now I want to
    float
A syndicate to haul and freight to town that noble boat."

> *I met him later in a bar and made a gay remark*
> *Anent an ancient miner and an option on the Ark.*
> *He gazed at me reproachfully, as only topers can;*
> *But what he said I can't repeat—he was a bad old man.*

CLANCY OF THE MOUNTED POLICE

In the little Crimson Manual it's written plain and clear
That who would wear the scarlet coat shall say good-bye to
   fear;
Shall be a guardian of the right, a sleuth-hound of the trail—
In the little Crimson Manual there's no such word as "fail"—
Shall follow on though heavens fall, or hell's top-turrets freeze,
Half round the world, if need there be, on bleeding hands and
   knees.
It's duty, duty, first and last, the Crimson Manual saith;
The Scarlet Rider makes reply: "It's duty—to the death."
And so they sweep the solitudes, free men from all the earth;
And so they sentinel the woods, the wilds that know their
   worth;
And so they scour the startled plains and mock at hurt and pain,
And read their Crimson Manual, and find their duty plain.
Knights of the lists of unrenown, born of the frontier's need,
Disdainful of the spoken word, exultant in the deed;
Unconscious heroes of the waste, proud players of the game,
Props of the power behind the throne, upholders of the name:
For thus the Great White Chief hath said, "In all my lands be
   peace,"
And to maintain his word he gave his West the Scarlet Police.

Livid-lipped was the valley, still as the grave of God;
   Misty shadows of mountain thinned into mists of cloud;
Corpselike and stark was the land, with a quiet that crushed and
   awed,
   And the stars of the weird sub-arctic glimmered over its
   shroud.

Deep in the trench of the valley two men stationed the Post,
 Seymour and Clancy the reckless, fresh from the long patrol;
Seymour, the sergeant, and Clancy—Clancy who made his boast
 He could cinch like a bronco the Northland, and cling to the
  prongs of the Pole.

Two lone men on detachment, standing for law on the trail;
 Undismayed in the vastness, wise with the wisdom of old—
Out of the night hailed a half-breed telling a pitiful tale,
 "White man starving and crazy on the banks of the Norden-
  scold."

Up sprang the red-haired Clancy, lean and eager of eye;
 Loaded the long toboggan, strapped each dog at its post;
Whirled his lash at the leader; then, with a whoop and a cry,
 Into the Great White Silence faded away like a ghost.

The clouds were a misty shadow, the hills were a shadowy mist;
 Sunless, voiceless and pulseless, the day was a dream of woe;
Through the ice-rifts the river smoked and bubbled and hissed;
 Behind was a trail fresh broken, in front the untrodden snow.

Ahead of the dogs ploughed Clancy, haloed by steaming breath;
 Through peril of open water, through ache of insensate cold;
Up rivers wantonly winding in a land affianced to death,
 Till he came to a cowering cabin on the banks of the Norden-
  scold.

Then Clancy loosed his revolver, and he strode through the
 open door;
 And there was the man he sought for, crouching beside the
  fire;

The hair of his beard was singeing, the frost on his back was
　　hoar,
　　And ever he crooned and chanted as if he never would tire:—

*"I panned and I panned in the shiny sand, and I sniped on the
　　river bar;*
*But I know, I know, that it's down below that the golden treas-
　　ures are;*
*So I'll wait and wait till the floods abate, and I'll sink a shaft once
　　more,*
*And I'd like to bet that I'll go home yet with a brass band play-
　　ing before."*

He was nigh as thin as a sliver, and he whined like a Moose-hide
　　cur;
　　So Clancy clothed him and nursed him as a mother nurses a
　　child;
Lifted him on the toboggan, wrapped him in robes of fur,
　　Then with the dogs sore straining started to face the Wild.

Said the Wild, "I will crush this Clancy, so fearless and insolent;
　　For him will I loose my fury, and blind and buffet and beat;
Pile up my snows to stay him; then when his strength is spent,
　　Leap on him from my ambush and crush him under my feet.

"Him will I ring with my silence, compass him with my cold;
　　Closer and closer clutch him unto mine icy breast;
Buffet him with my blizzards, deep in my snows enfold,
　　Claiming his life as my tribute, giving my wolves the rest."

Clancy crawled through the vastness; o'er him the hate of the
　　Wild;
　　Full on his face fell the blizzard; cheering his huskies he ran;

Fighting, fierce-hearted and tireless, snows that drifted and
   piled,
With ever and ever behind him singing the crazy man.

> *"Sing hey, sing ho, for the ice and snow,*
>   *And a heart that's ever merry;*
> *Let us trim and square with a lover's care*
> *(For why should a man be sorry?)*
> *A grave deep, deep, with the moon a-peep,*
>   *A grave in the frozen mould.*
> *Sing hey, sing ho, for the winds that blow,*
> *And a grave deep down in the ice and snow,*
>   *A grave in the land of gold."*

Day after day of darkness, the whirl of the seething snows;
   Day after day of blindness, the swoop of the stinging blast;
On through a blur of fury the swing of staggering blows;
   On through a world of turmoil, empty, inane and vast.

Night with its writhing storm-whirl, night despairingly black;
   Night with its hours of terror, numb and endlessly long;
Night with its weary waiting, fighting the shadows back.
   And ever the crouching madman singing his crazy song.

Cold with its creeping terror, cold with its sudden clinch;
   Cold so utter you wonder if 'twill ever again be warm;
Clancy grinned as he shuddered, "Surely it isn't a cinch
   Being wet-nurse to a loony in the teeth of an arctic storm."

The blizzard passed and the dawn broke, knife-edged and crys-
   tal clear;
   The sky was a blue-domed iceberg, sunshine outlawed away;

Ever by snowslide and ice-rip haunted and hovered the Fear;
  Ever the Wild malignant poised and panted to slay.

The lead-dog freezes in harness—cut him out of the team!
  The lung of the wheel-dog's bleeding—shoot him and let
    him lie!
On and on with the others—lash them until they scream!
  "Pull for your lives, you devils! On! To halt is to die."

There in the frozen vastness Clancy fought with his foes;
  The ache of the stiffened fingers, the cut of the snowshoe
    thong;
Cheeks black-raw through the hood-flap, eyes that tingled and
  closed,
  And ever to urge and cheer him quavered the madman's song.

Colder it grew and colder, till the last heat left the earth,
  And there in the great stark stillness the balefires glinted and
    gleamed,
And the Wild all around exulted and shook with a devilish mirth,
  And life was far and forgotten, the ghost of a joy once
    dreamed.

Death! And one who defied it, a man of the Mounted Police;
  Fought it there to a standstill long after hope was gone;
Grinned through his bitter anguish, fought without let or cease,
  Suffering, straining, striving, stumbling, struggling on.

Till the dogs lay down in their traces, and rose and staggered
  and fell;
  Till the eyes of him dimmed with shadows, and the trail was
    so hard to see;

Till the Wild howled out triumphant, and the world was a
    frozen hell—
  Then said Constable Clancy: "I guess that it's up to me."

Far down the trail they saw him, and his hands they were
    blanched like bone;
  His face was a blackened horror, from his eyelids the salt
    rheum ran;
His feet he was lifting strangely, as if they were made of stone,
  But safe in his arms and sleeping he carried the crazy man.

So Clancy got into Barracks, and the boys made rather a scene;
  And the O. C. called him a hero, and was nice as a man
    could be;
But Clancy gazed down his trousers at the place where his toes
    had been,
  And then he howled like a husky, and sang in a shaky key.

"When I go back to the old love that's true to the finger-tips,
I'll say: 'Here's bushels of gold, love,' and I'll kiss my girl on the
    lips;
'It's yours to have and to hold, love.' It's the proud, proud boy
    I'll be,
When I go back to the old love that's waited so long for me."

LOST

"Black is the sky, but the land is white—
(O the wind, the snow and the storm!)—
Father, where is our boy to-night?
Pray to God he is safe and warm."

"Mother, mother, why should you fear?
Safe is he, and the Arctic moon
Over his cabin shines so clear—
Rest and sleep, 'twill be morning soon."

"It's getting dark awful sudden. Say, this is mighty queer!
  Where in the world have I got to? It's still and black as a
      tomb.
I reckoned the camp was yonder, I figured the trail was here—
  Nothing! Just draw and valley packed with quiet and gloom:
Snow that comes down like feathers, thick and gobby and gray;
Night that looks spiteful ugly—seems that I've lost my way.

"The cold's got an edge like a jackknife—it must be forty below;
  Leastways that's what it seems like—it cuts so fierce to the
      bone.
The wind's getting real ferocious; it's heaving and whirling the
      snow;
  It shrieks with a howl of fury, it dies away to a moan;
Its arms sweep round like a banshee's, swift and icily white,
And buffet and blind and beat me. Lord! it's a hell of a night.

"I'm all tangled up in a blizzard. There's only one thing to do—
  Keep on moving and moving; it's death, it's death if I rest.

Oh, God! if I see the morning, if only I struggle through,
  I'll say the prayers I've forgotten since I lay on my mother's
    breast.
I seem going round in a circle; maybe the camp is near.
  Say! did somebody holler? Was it a light I saw?
Or was it only a notion? I'll shout, and maybe they'll hear—
  No! the wind only drowns me—shout till my throat is raw.

"The boys are all round the camp-fire wondering when I'll be
    back.
  They'll soon be starting to seek me; they'll scarcely wait for
    the light.
What will they find, I wonder, when they come to the end of
    my track—
  A hand stuck out of a snowdrift, frozen and stiff and white.
That's what they'll strike, I reckon; that's how they'll find their
    pard,
  A pie-faced corpse in a snowbank—curse you, don't be a fool!
Play the game to the finish; bet on your very last card;
  Nerve yourself for the struggle. Oh, you coward, keep cool!

"I'm going to lick this blizzard; I'm going to live the night.
  It can't down me with its bluster—I'm not the kind to be beat.
On hands and knees will I buck it; with every breath will I fight;
  It's life, it's life that I fight for—never it seemed so sweet.
I know that my face is frozen; my hands are numblike and dead;
  But oh, my feet keep a-moving, heavy and hard and slow;
They're trying to kill me, kill me, the night that's black over-
    head,
  The wind that cuts like a razor, the whipcord lash of the snow.
Keep a-moving, a-moving; don't, don't stumble, you fool!
  Curse this snow that's a-piling a-purpose to block my way.
It's heavy as gold in the rocker, it's white and fleecy as wool;

It's soft as a bed of feathers, it's warm as a stack of hay.
Curse on my feet that slip so, my poor tired, stumbling feet—
  I guess they're a job for the surgeon, they feel so queerlike
    to lift—
I'll rest them just for a moment—oh, but to rest is sweet!
  The awful wind cannot get me, deep, deep down in the drift."

"Father, a bitter cry I heard,
  Out of the night so dark and wild.
Why is my heart so strangely stirred?
  'Twas like the voice of our erring child."

"Mother, mother, you only heard
  A waterfowl in the locked lagoon—
Out of the night a wounded bird—
  Rest and sleep, 'twill be morning soon."

Who is it talks of sleeping? I'll swear that somebody shook
  Me hard by the arm for a moment, but how on earth could
    it be?
See how my feet are moving—awfully funny they look—
  Moving as if they belonged to a someone that wasn't me.
The wind down the night's long alley bowls me down like a pin;
  I stagger and fall and stagger, crawl arm-deep in the snow,
Beaten back to my corner, how can I hope to win?
  And there is the blizzard waiting to give me the knockout
    blow.

Oh, I'm so warm and sleepy! No more hunger and pain.
  Just to rest for a moment; was ever rest such a joy?
Ha! what was that? I'll swear it, somebody shook me again;
  Somebody seemed to whisper: "Fight to the last, my boy."
Fight! That's right, I must struggle. I know that to rest means
  death;

Death, but then what does death mean?—ease from a world
    of strife.
Life has been none too pleasant; yet with my failing breath
    Still and still must I struggle, fight for the gift of life.

    *   *   *   *   *   *   *   *   *

Seems that I must be dreaming! Here is the old home trail;
    Yonder a light is gleaming; oh, I know it so well!
The air is scented with clover; the cattle wait by the rail;
    Father is through with the milking; there goes the supper-bell.

    *   *   *   *   *   *   *   *   *

Mother, your boy is crying, out in the night and cold;
    Let me in and forgive me, I'll never be bad any more:
I'm, oh, so sick and so sorry: please, dear mother, don't scold—
    It's just your boy, and he wants you. . . . Mother, open the
    door. . . .

> *"Father, father, I saw a face*
>   *Pressed just now to the window-pane!*
> *Oh, it gazed for a moment's space,*
>   *Wild and wan, and was gone again!"*

> *"Mother, mother, you saw the snow*
>   *Drifted down from the maple tree*
> *(Oh, the wind that is sobbing so!*
>   *Weary and worn and old are we)—*
> *Only the snow and a wounded loon—*
> *Rest and sleep, 'twill be morning soon."*

L'ENVOI

We talked of yesteryears, of trails and treasure,
  Of men who played the game and lost or won;
Of mad stampedes, of toil beyond all measure,
  Of camp-fire comfort when the day was done.
We talked of sullen nights by moon-dogs haunted,
  Of bird and beast and tree, of rod and gun;
Of boat and tent, of hunting-trip enchanted
  Beneath the wonder of the midnight sun;
Of bloody-footed dogs that gnawed the traces,
  Of prisoned seas, wind-lashed and winter-locked;
The ice-gray dawn was pale upon our faces,
  Yet still we filled the cup and still we talked.

The city street was dimmed. We saw the glitter
  Of moon-picked brilliants on the virgin snow,
And down the drifted canyon heard the bitter,
  Relentless slogan of the winds of woe.
The city was forgot, and, parka-skirted,
  We trod that leagueless land that once we knew;
We saw stream past, down valleys glacier-girted,
  The wolf-worn legions of the caribou.
We smoked our pipes, o'er scenes of triumph dwelling,
  Of deeds of daring, dire defeats, we talked;
And other tales that lost not in the telling,
  Ere to our beds uncertainly we walked.

And so, dear friends, in gentler valleys roaming,
  Perhaps, when on my printed page you look,
Your fancies by the firelight may go homing

To that lone land that haply you forsook.
And if perchance you hear the silence calling,
   The frozen music of star-yearning heights,
Or, dreaming, see the seines of silver trawling
   Across the sky's abyss on vasty nights,
You may recall that sweep of savage splendor,
   That land that measures each man at his worth.
And feel in memory, half fierce, half tender,
   The brotherhood of men that know the North.

Book Three

RHYMES OF A ROLLING STONE

PRELUDE

I sing no idle songs of dalliance days,
No dreams Elysian inspire my rhyming;
I have no Celia to enchant my lays,
No pipes of Pan have set my heart to chiming.
I am no wordsmith dripping gems divine
Into the golden chalice of a sonnet;
If love songs witch you, close this book of mine,
   Waste no time on it.

Yet bring I to my work an eager joy,
A lusty love of life and all things human;
Still in me leaps the wonder of the boy,
A pride in man, a deathless faith in woman.
Still red blood calls, still rings the valiant fray;
Adventure beacons through the summer gloaming:
Oh long and long and long will be the day
   Ere I come homing!

This earth is ours to love: lute, brush and pen,
They are but tongues to tell of life sincerely;
The thaumaturgic Day, the might of men,
O God of Scribes, grant us to grave them clearly!
Grant heart that homes in heart, then all is well.
Honey is honey-sweet, howe'er the hiving.
Each to his work, his wage at evening bell
   The strength of striving.

A ROLLING STONE

There's sunshine in the heart of me,
My blood sings in the breeze;
The mountains are a part of me,
I'm fellow to the trees.
My golden youth I'm squandering,
Sun-libertine am I;
A-wandering, a-wandering,
Until the day I die.

I was once, I declare, a Stone-Age man,
    And I roomed in the cool of a cave;
I have known, I will swear, in a new life-span
    The fret and the sweat of a slave:
For far over all that folks hold worth,
    There lives and there leaps in me
A love of the lowly things of earth,
    And a passion to be free.

To pitch my tent with no prosy plan,
    To range and to change at will;
To mock at the mastership of man,
    To seek Adventure's thrill.
Carefree to be, as a bird that sings;
    To go my own sweet way;
To reck not at all what may befall,
    But to live and to love each day.

To make my body a temple pure
    Wherein I dwell serene;

To care for the things that shall endure,
    The simple, sweet and clean.
To oust out envy and hate and rage,
    To breathe with no alarm;
For Nature shall be my anchorage,
    And none shall do me harm.

To shun all lures that debauch the soul,
    The orgied rites of the rich;
To eat my crust as a rover must
    With the rough-neck down in the ditch.
To trudge by his side whate'er betide;
    To share his fire at night;
To call him friend to the long trail-end,
    And to read his heart aright.

To scorn all strife, and to view all life
    With the curious eyes of a child;
From the plangent sea to the prairie,
    From the slum to the heart of the Wild.
From the red-rimmed star to the speck of sand,
    From the vast to the greatly small;
For I know that the whole for good is planned,
    And I want to see it all.

To see it all, the wide world-way,
    From the fig-leaf belt to the Pole;
With never a one to say me nay,
    And none to cramp my soul.
In belly-pinch I will pay the price,
    But God! let me be free;
For once I know in the long ago,
    They made a slave of me.

In a flannel shirt from earth's clean dirt,
    Here, pal, is my calloused hand!
Oh, I love each day as a rover may,
    Nor seek to understand.
To *enjoy* is good enough for me;
    The gipsy of God am I;
Then here's a hail to each flaring dawn!
And here's a cheer to the night that's gone!
And may I go a-roaming on
    Until the day I die!

    Then every star shall sing to me
    Its song of liberty;
    And every morn shall bring to me
    Its mandate to be free.
    In every throbbing vein of me
    I'll feel the vast Earth-call;
    O body, heart and brain of me
    Praise Him who made it all!

THE SOLDIER OF FORTUNE

"Deny your God!" they ringed me with their spears;
Blood-crazed were they, and reeking from the strife;
Hell-hot their hate, and venom-fanged their sneers,
And one man spat on me and nursed a knife.
And there was I, sore wounded and alone,
I, the last living of my slaughtered band.
Oh sinister the sky, and cold as stone!
In one red laugh of horror reeled the land.
And dazed and desperate I faced their spears,
And like a flame out-leaped that naked knife,
And like a serpent stung their bitter jeers:
"Deny your God, and we will give you life."

Deny my God! Oh life was very sweet!
And it is hard in youth and hope to die;
And there my comrades dear lay at my feet,
And in that blear of blood soon must I lie.
And yet . . . I almost laughed—it seemed so odd,
For long and long had I not vainly tried
To reason out and body forth my God,
And prayed for light, and doubted—and *denied:*
Denied the Being I could not conceive,
Denied a life-to-be beyond the grave. . . .
And now they ask me, who do not believe,
Just to deny, to voice my doubt, to save
This life of mine that sings so in the sun,
The bloom of youth yet red upon my cheek,
My only life!—O fools! 'tis easy done,
I will deny . . . and yet I do not speak.

"Deny your God!" their spears are all agleam,
And I can see their eyes with blood-lust shine;
Their snarling voices shrill into a scream,
And, mad to slay, they quiver for the sign.
Deny my God, yes, I could do it well;
Yet if I did, what of my race, my name?
How they would spit on me, these dogs of hell!
Spurn me, and put on me the brand of shame.
A white man's honour! what of that, I say?
Shall these black curs cry "Coward" in my face?
They who would perish for their gods of clay—
Shall I defile my country and my race?
My country! what's my country to me now?
Soldier of Fortune, free and far I roam;
All men are brothers in my heart, I vow;
The wide and wondrous world is all my home.
My country! reverent of her splendid Dead,
Her heroes proud, her martyrs pierced with pain:
For me her puissant blood was vainly shed;
For me her drums of battle beat in vain,
And free I fare, half-heedless of her fate:
No faith, no flag I owe—then why not seek
This last loop-hole of life? Why hesitate?
I will deny . . . and yet I do not speak.

"Deny your God!" their spears are poised on high,
And tense and terrible they wait the word;
And dark and darker glooms the dreary sky,
And in that hush of horror no thing stirred.
Then, through the ringing terror and sheer hate
Leaped there a vision to me— Oh, how far!
A face, Her face . . . through all my stormy fate
A joy, a strength, a glory and a star.

Beneath the pines, where lonely camp-fires gleam,
In seas forlorn, amid the deserts drear,
How I had gladdened to that face of dream!
And never, never had it seemed so dear.
O silken hair that veils the sunny brow!
O eyes of grey, so tender and so true!
O lips of smiling sweetness! must I now
For ever and for ever go from you?
Ah, yes, I must . . . for if I do this thing,
How can I look into your face again?
Knowing you think me more than half a king,
I with my craven heart, my honour slain.

No! no! my mind's made up. I gaze above,
Into that sky insensate as a stone;
Not for my creed, my country, but my Love
Will I stand up and meet my death alone.
Then though it be to utter dark I sink,
The God that dwells in me is not denied;
"Best" triumphs over "Beast,"—and so I think
Humanity itself is glorified. . . .

"And now, my butchers, I embrace my fate.
"Come! let my heart's blood slake the thirsty sod.
"Curst be the life you offer! Glut your hate!
"Strike! Strike, you dogs! I'll *not* deny my God."

I saw the spears that seemed a-leap to slay,
All quiver earthward at the headman's nod;
And in a daze of dream I heard him say:
"Go, set him free who serves so well his God!"

THE GRAMOPHONE AT FOND-DU-LAC

Now Eddie Malone got a swell grammyfone to draw all the
   trade to his store;
An' sez he: "Come along for a season of song, which the like ye
   had niver before."
Then Dogrib, an' Slave, an' Yellow-knife brave, an' Cree in his
   dinky canoe,
Confluated near, to see an' to hear Ed's grammyfone make its
   dayboo.

Then Ed turned the crank, an' there on the bank they squatted
   like bumps on a log.
For acres around there wasn't a sound, not even the howl of a
   dog.
When out of the horn there sudden was born such a marvellous
   elegant tone;
An' then like a spell on that auddyence fell the voice of its first
   grammyfone.

"*Bad medicine!*" cried Old Tom, the One-eyed, an' made for to
   jump in the lake;
But no one gave heed to his little stampede, so he guessed he had
   made a mistake.
Then Roll-in-the-Mud, a chief of the blood, observed in choice
   Chippewayan:
"You've brought us canned beef, an' it's now my belief that this
   here's a case of '*canned man.*' "

Well, though I'm not strong on the Dago in song, that sure got
   me goin' for fair.

There was Crusoe an' Scotty, an' Ma'am Shoeman Hank, an'
    Melber an' Bonchy was there.
'Twas silver an' gold, an' sweetness untold to hear all them big
    guinneys sing;
An' thick all around an' inhalin' the sound, them Indians formed
    in a ring.

So solemn they sat, an' they smoked an' they spat, but their eyes
    sort o' glistened an' shone;
Yet niver a word of approvin' occurred till that guy Harry
    Lauder came on.
Then hunter of moose, an' squaw an' papoose jest laughed till
    their stummicks was sore;
Six times Eddie set back that record an' yet they hollered an'
    hollered for more.

I'll never forget that frame-up, you bet; them caverns of sunset
    agleam;
Them still peaks aglow, them shadders below, an' the lake like a
    petrified dream;
The teepees that stood by the edge of the wood; the evenin' star
    blinkin' alone;
The peace an' the rest, an' final an' best, the music of Ed's
    grammyfone.

Then sudden an' clear there rang on my ear a song mighty simple
    an' old;
Heart-hungry an' high it thrilled to the sky, all about "silver
    threads in the gold."
'Twas tender to tears, an' it brung back the years, the mem'ries
    that hallow an' yearn;
'Twas home-love an' joy, 'twas the thought of my boy . . . an'
    right there I vowed I'd return.

Big Four-finger Jack was right at my back, an' I saw with a
 kind o' surprise,
He gazed at the lake with a heartful of ache, an' the tears irrigated
 his eyes.
An' sez he: "Cuss me, pard! but that there hits me hard; I've a
 mother does nuthin' but wait.
"She's turned eighty-three, an' she's only got me, an' I'm scared
 it'll soon be too late."

* * * * * * * * *

On Fond-du-lac's shore I'm hearin' once more that blessed old
 grammyfone play.
The summer's all gone, an' I'm still livin' on in the same old
 haphazardous way.
Oh, I cut out the booze, an' with muscles an' thews I corralled
 all the coin to go back;
But it wasn't to be: he'd a mother, you see, so I—*slipped it to
 Four-finger Jack.*

THE LAND OF BEYOND

Have ever you heard of the Land of Beyond,
    That dreams at the gates of the day?
Alluring it lies at the skirts of the skies,
    And ever so far away;
Alluring it calls: O ye the yoke galls,
    And ye of the trail overfond,
With saddle and pack, by paddle and track,
    Let's go to the Land of Beyond!

Have ever you stood where the silences brood,
    And vast the horizons begin,
At the dawn of the day to behold far away
    The goal you would strive for and win?
Yet ah! in the night when you gain to the height,
    With the vast pool of heaven star-spawned,
Afar and agleam, like a valley of dream,
    Still mocks you a Land of Beyond.

Thank God! there is always a Land of Beyond
    For us who are true to the trail;
A vision to seek, a beckoning peak,
    A fairness that never will fail;
A pride in our soul that mocks at a goal,
    A manhood that irks at a bond,
And try how we will, unattainable still,
    Behold it, our Land of Beyond!

SUNSHINE

I

F<small>LAT</small> as a drum-head stretch the haggard snows;
The mighty skies are palisades of light;
The stars are blurred; the silence grows and grows;
Vaster and vaster vaults the icy night.
Here in my sleeping-bag I cower and pray:
"Silence and night, have pity! stoop and slay."

I have not slept for many, many days.
I close my eyes with weariness—that's all.
I still have strength to feed the drift-wood blaze,
That flickers weirdly on the icy wall.
I still have strength to pray: "God rest her soul,
Here in the awful shadow of the Pole."

There in the cabin's alcove low she lies,
Still candles gleaming at her head and feet;
All snow-drop white, ash-cold, with closéd eyes,
Lips smiling, hands at rest— O God, how sweet!
How all unutterably sweet she seems. . . .
Not dead, not dead indeed—she dreams, she dreams.

II

"Sunshine," I called her, and she brought, I vow,
God's blessed sunshine to this life of mine.
I was a rover, of the breed who plough
Life's furrow in a far-flung, lonely line;

The wilderness my home, my fortune cast
In a wild land of dearth, barbaric, vast.

When did I see her first? Long had I lain
Groping my way to life through fevered gloom.
Sudden the cloud of darkness left my brain;
A velvet bar of sunshine pierced the room,
And in that mellow glory aureoled
She stood, she stood, all golden in its gold.

Sunshine! O miracle! the earth grew glad;
Radiant each blade of grass, each living thing.
What a huge strength, high hope, proud will I had!
All the wide world with rapture seemed to ring.
Would she but wed me? *Yes:* then fared we forth
Into the vast, unvintageable North.

III

In Muskrat Land the conies leap,
The wavies linger in their flight;
The jewelled, snakelike rivers creep;
The sun, sad rogue, is out all night;
The great wood bison paws the sand,
In Muskrat Land, in Muskrat Land.

In Muskrat Land dim streams divide
The tundras belted by the sky.
How sweet in slim canoe to glide,
And dream, and let the world go by!
Build gay camp-fires on greening strand!
In Muskrat Land, in Muskrat Land.

IV

And so we dreamed and drifted, she and I;
And how she loved that free, unfathomed life!
There in the peach-bloom of the midnight sky,
The silence welded us, true man and wife.
Then North and North invincibly we pressed
Beyond the Circle, to the world's white crest.

And on the wind-flailed Arctic waste we stayed,
Dwelt with the Huskies by the Polar sea.
Fur had they, white fox, marten, mink to trade,
And we had food-stuff, bacon, flour and tea.
So we made snug, chummed up with all the band:
Sudden the Winter swooped on Husky Land.

V

What was that ill so sinister and dread,
Smiting the tribe with sickness to the bone?
So that we waked one morn to find them fled;
So that we stood and stared, alone, alone.
Bravely she smiled and looked into my eyes;
Laughed at their troubled, stern, foreboding pain;
Gaily she mocked the menace of the skies,
Turned to our cheery cabin once again,
Saying: " 'Twill soon be over, dearest one,
The long, long night: then O the sun, the sun!"

VI

God made a heart of gold, of gold,
Shining and sweet and true;

Gave it a home of fairest mould,
Blest it, and called it—You.

God gave the rose its grace of glow,
And the lark its radiant glee;
But, better than all, I know, I know
God gave you, Heart, to me.

VII

She was all sunshine in those dubious days;
Our cabin beaconed with defiant light;
We chattered by the friendly drift-wood blaze;
Closer and closer cowered the hag-like night.
A wolf-howl would have been a welcome sound,
And there was none in all that stricken land;
Yet with such silence, darkness, death around,
Learned we to love as few can understand.
Spirit with spirit fused, and soul with soul,
There in the sullen shadow of the Pole.

VIII

What was that haunting horror of the night?
Brave was she; buoyant, full of sunny cheer.
Why was her face so small, so strangely white?
Then did I turn from her, heart-sick with fear;
Sought in my agony the outcast snows;
Prayed in my pain to that insensate sky;
Grovelled and sobbed and cursed, and then arose:
"Sunshine! O heart of gold! to die! to die!"

IX

She died on Christmas day—it seems so sad
That one you love should die on Christmas day.
Head-bowed I knelt by her; O God! I had
No tears to shed, no moan, no prayer to pray.
I heard her whisper: "Call me, will you, dear?
They say Death parts, but I won't go away.
I will be with you in the cabin here;
Oh I will plead with God to let me stay!
Stay till the Night is gone, till Spring is nigh,
Till sunshine comes . . . be brave . . . I'm tired . . .
          good-bye. . . ."

X

For weeks, for months I have not seen the sun;
The minatory dawns are leprous pale;
The felon days malinger one by one;
How like a dream Life is! how vain! how stale!
I, too, am faint; that vampire-like disease
Has fallen on me; weak and cold am I,
Hugging a tiny fire in fear I freeze:
The cabin must be cold, and so I try
To bear the frost, the frost that fights decay,
The frost that keeps her beautiful alway.

XI

She lies within an icy vault;
It glitters like a cave of salt.
All marble-pure and angel-sweet

With candles at her head and feet,
Under an ermine robe she lies.
I kiss her hands, I kiss her eyes:
"Come back, come back, O Love, I pray,
Into this house, this house of clay!
Answer my kisses soft and warm;
Nestle again within my arm.
Come! for I know that you are near;
Open your eyes and look, my dear.
Just for a moment break the mesh;
Back from the spirit leap to flesh.
Weary I wait; the night is black;
Love of my life, come back, come back!"

XII

Last night maybe I was a little mad,
For as I prayed despairful by her side,
Such a strange, antic visioning I had:
Lo! it did seem *her eyes were open wide.*
Surely I must have dreamed! I stared once more. . . .
No, 'twas a candle's trick, a shadow cast.
There were her lashes locking as before.
(Oh, but it filled me with a joy so vast!)
No, 'twas a freak, a fancy of the brain,
(Oh, but to-night I'll try again, again!)

XIII

It was no dream; now do I know that Love
Leapt from the starry battlements of Death;
For in my vigil as I bent above,
Calling her name with eager, burning breath,

Sudden there came a change: again I saw
The radiance of the rose-leaf stain her cheek;
Rivers of rapture thrilled in sunny thaw;
Cleft were her coral lips as if to speak;
Curved were her tender arms as if to cling;
Open the flower-like eyes of lucent blue,
Looking at me with love so pitying
That I could fancy Heaven shining through.
"Sunshine," I faltered, "stay with me, oh, stay!"
Yet ere I finished, in a moment's flight,
There in her angel purity she lay—
Ah! but I know she'll come again to-night.
Even as radiant sword leaps from the sheath,
Soul from the body leaps—we call it Death.

XIV

Even as this line I write,
Do I know that she is near;
Happy am I, every night
Comes she back to bid me cheer;
Kissing her, I hold her fast;
Win her into life at last.

Did I dream that yesterday
On yon mountain ridge a glow
Soft as moonstone paled away,
Leaving less forlorn the snow?
Could it be the sun? Oh, fain
Would I see the sun again!

Oh, to see a coral dawn
Gladden to a crocus glow!

Day's a spectre dim and wan,
Dancing on the furtive snow;
Night's a cloud upon my brain:
Oh, to see the sun again!

You who find us in this place,
Have you pity in your breast;
Let us in our last embrace,
Under earth sun-hallowed rest.
Night's a claw upon my brain:
Oh, to see the sun again!

xv

The Sun! at last the Sun! I write these lines,
Here on my knees, with feeble, fumbling hand.
Look! in yon mountain cleft a radiance shines,
Gleam of a primrose—see it thrill, expand,
Grow glorious. Dear God be praised! it streams
Into the cabin in a gush of gold.
Look! there she stands, the angel of my dreams,
All in the radiant shimmer aureoled;
First as I saw her from my bed of pain;
First as I loved her when the darkness passed.
Now do I know that Life is not in vain;
Now do I know God cares, at last, at last!
Light outlives dark, joy grief, and Love's the sum:
Heart of my heart! Sunshine! I come . . . I come. . . .

THE IDEALIST

Oн you who have daring deeds to tell!
  And you who have felt Ambition's spell!
Have you heard of the louse who longed to dwell
  In the golden hair of a queen?
He sighed all day and he sighed all night,
  And no one could understand it quite,
For the head of a slut is a louse's delight,
  But he pined for the head of a queen.

So he left his kinsfolk in merry play,
  And off by his lonesome he stole away,
From the home of his youth so bright and gay,
  And gloriously unclean.
And at last he came to the palace gate,
  And he made his way in a manner straight
(For a louse may go where a man must wait)
  To the tiring-room of the queen.

The queen she spake to her tiring-maid:
  "There's something the matter, I'm afraid.
To-night ere for sleep my hair ye braid,
  Just see what may be seen."
And lo, when they combed that shining hair
  They found him alone in his glory there,
And he cried: "I die, but I do not care,
  For I've lived in the head of a queen!"

ATHABASKA DICK

When the boys come out from Lac Labiche in the lure of the
early Spring,
To take the pay of the "Hudson's Bay," as their fathers did
before,
They are all a-glee for the jamboree, and they make the Landing
ring
With a whoop and a whirl, and a "Grab your girl," and a rip
and a skip and a roar.
For the spree of Spring is a sacred thing, and the boys must have
their fun;
Packer and tracker and half-breed Cree, from the boat to the
bar they leap;
And then when the long flotilla goes, and the last of their pay
is done,
The boys from the banks of Lac Labiche swing to the heavy
sweep.
And oh, how they sigh! and their throats are dry, and sorry are
they and sick:
Yet there's none so cursed with a lime-kiln thirst as that Atha-
baska Dick.

He was long and slim and lean of limb, but strong as a stripling
bear;
And by the right of his skill and might he guided the Long
Brigade.
All water-wise were his laughing eyes, and he steered with a
careless care,
And he shunned the shock of foam and rock, till they came to
the Big Cascade.

And here they must make the long *portăge*, and the boys sweat
in the sun;
And they heft and pack, and they haul and track, and each must
do his trick;
But their thoughts are far in the Landing bar, where the founts
of nectar run:
And no man thinks of such gorgeous drinks as that Athabaska
Dick.

'Twas the close of day and his long boat lay just over the Big
Cascade,
When there came to him one Jack-pot Jim, with a wild light in
his eye;
And he softly laughed, and he led Dick aft, all eager, yet half
afraid,
And snugly stowed in his coat he showed a pilfered flask of
"rye."
And in haste he slipped, or in fear he tripped, but—Dick in
warning roared—
And there rang a yell, and it befell that Jim was overboard.

Oh, I heard a splash, and quick as a flash I knew he could not
swim.
I saw him whirl in the river swirl, and thresh his arms about.
In a queer, strained way I heard Dick say: "I'm going after him,"
Throw off his coat, leap down the boat—and then I gave a shout:
"Boys, grab him, quick! You're crazy, Dick! Far better one
than two!
"Hell, man! You know you've got no show! It's sure and certain
death. . . ."
And there we hung, and there we clung, with beef and brawn
and thew,

And sinews cracked and joints were racked, and panting came
  our breath;
And there we swayed and there we prayed, till strength and
  hope were spent—
Then Dick, he threw us off like rats, and after Jim he went.

With mighty urge amid the surge of river-rage he leapt,
And gripped his mate and desperate he fought to gain the shore;
With teeth a-gleam he bucked the stream, yet swift and sure he
  swept
To meet the mighty cataract that waited all a-roar.
And there we stood like carven wood, our faces sickly white,
And watched him as he beat the foam, and inch by inch he lost;
And nearer, nearer drew the fall, and fiercer grew the fight,
Till on the very cascade crest a last farewell he tossed.
Then down and down and down they plunged into that pit of
  dread;
And mad we tore along the shore to claim our bitter dead.

And from that hell of frenzied foam, that crashed and fumed
  and boiled,
Two little bodies bubbled up, and they were heedless then;
And oh, they lay like senseless clay! and bitter hard we toiled,
Yet never, never gleam of hope, and we were weary men.
And moments mounted into hours, and black was our despair;
And faint were we, and we were fain to give them up as dead,
When suddenly I thrilled with hope: "Back, boys! and give
  him air;
"I feel the flutter of his heart. . . ." And, as the word I said,
Dick gave a sigh, and gazed around, and saw our breathless
  band;
And saw the sky's blue floor above, all strewn with golden
  fleece;

And saw his comrade Jack-pot Jim, and touched him with his
    hand:
And then there came into his eyes a look of perfect peace.
And as there, at his very feet, the thwarted river raved,
I heard him murmur low and deep:
       "Thank God! the *whiskey's* saved."

CHEER

It's a mighty good world, so it is, dear lass,
　　When even the worst is said.
There's a smile and a tear, a sigh and a cheer,
　　But better be living than dead;
A joy and a pain, a loss and a gain;
　　There's honey and may be some gall:
Yet still I declare, foul weather or fair,
　　It's a mighty good world after all.

For look, lass! at night when I break from the fight,
　　My Kingdom's awaiting for me;
There's comfort and rest, and the warmth of your breast,
　　And little ones climbing my knee.
There's fire-light and song— Oh, the world may be wrong!
　　Its empires may topple and fall:
My home is my care—if gladness be there,
　　It's a mighty good world after all.

O heart of pure gold! I have made you a fold,
　　It's sheltered, sun-fondled and warm.
O little ones, rest! I have fashioned a nest;
　　Sleep on! you are safe from the storm.
For there's no foe like fear, and there's no friend like cheer,
　　And sunshine will flash at our call;
So crown Love as King, and let us all sing—
　　"It's a mighty good world after all."

THE RETURN

They turned him loose; he bowed his head,
    A felon, bent and grey.
His face was even as the Dead,
    He had no word to say.

He sought the home of his old love,
    To look on her once more;
And where her roses breathed above,
    He cowered beside the door.

She sat there in the shining room;
    Her hair was silver grey.
He stared and stared from out the gloom;
    He turned to go away.

Her roses rustled overhead.
    She saw, with sudden start.
"I knew that you would come," she said,
    And held him to her heart.

Her face was rapt and angel-sweet;
    She touched his hair of grey;

       .   .   .   .

But he, sob-shaken, at her feet,
    Could only pray and pray.

THE JUNIOR GOD

THE Junior God looked from his place
    In the conning towers of heaven,
And he saw the world through the span of space
    Like a giant golf-ball driven.
And because he was bored, as some gods are,
    With high celestial mirth,
He clutched the reins of a shooting star,
    And he steered it down to earth.

The Junior God, 'mid leaf and bud,
    Passed on with a weary air,
Till lo! he came to a pool of mud,
    And some hogs were rolling there.
Then in he plunged with gleeful cries,
    And down he lay supine;
For they had no mud in paradise,
    And they likewise had no swine.

The Junior God forgot himself;
    He squelched mud through his toes;
With the careless joy of a wanton boy
    His reckless laughter rose.
Till, tired at last, in a brook close by,
    He washed off every stain;
Then softly up to the radiant sky
    He rose, a god again.

The Junior God now heads the roll
    In the list of heaven's peers;
He sits in the House of High Control,
    And he regulates the spheres.
Yet does he wonder, do you suppose,
    If, even in gods divine,
The best and wisest may not be those
    Who have wallowed awhile with the swine?

THE NOSTOMANIAC

On the ragged edge of the world I'll roam,
And the home of the wolf shall be my home,
And a bunch of bones on the boundless snows
The end of my trail . . . who knows, who knows!

I'm dreaming to-night in the fire-glow, alone in my study tower,
My books battalioned around me, my Kipling flat on my knee;
But I'm not in the mood for reading, I haven't moved for an
    hour;
Body and brain I'm weary, weary the heart of me;
Weary of crushing a longing it's little I understand,
For I thought that my trail was ended, I thought I had earned
    my rest;
But oh, it's stronger than life is, the call of the heartless land!
And I turn to the North in my trouble, as a child to the mother-
    breast.

Here in my den it's quiet; the sea-wind taps on the pane;
There's comfort and ease and plenty, the smile of the South is
    sweet.
All that a man might long for, fight for and seek in vain,
Pictures and books and music, pleasure my last retreat.
Peace! I thought I had gained it, I swore that my tale was told;
By my hair that is grey I swore it, by my eyes that are slow to
    see;
Yet what does it all avail me? to-night, to-night as of old,
Out of the dark I hear it—the Northland calling to me.

And I'm daring a rampageous river that runs the devil knows
    where;
My hand is athrill on the paddle, the birch-bark bounds like a
    bird.
Hark to the rumble of rapids! Here in my morris chair
Eager and tense I'm straining—isn't it most absurd?
Now in the churn and the lather, foam that hisses and stings,
Leap I, keyed for the struggle, fury and fume and roar;
Rocks are spitting like hell-cats— Oh, it's a sport for kings,
Life on a twist of the paddle . . . there's my "Kim" on the floor.

How I thrill and I vision! Then my camp of a night;
Red and gold of the fire-glow, net afloat in the stream;
Scent of the pines and silence, little "pal" pipe alight,
Body a-purr with pleasure, sleep untroubled of dream:
Banquet of paystreak bacon! moment of joy divine,
When the bannock is hot and gluey, and the teapot's nearing the
    boil!
Never was wolf so hungry, stomach cleaving to spine. . . .
Ha! there's my servant calling, says that dinner will spoil.

What do I want with dinner? Can I eat any more?
Can I sleep as I used to? . . . Oh, I abhor this life!
Give me the Great Uncertain, the Barren Land for a floor,
The Milky Way for a roof-beam, splendour and space and strife:
Something to fight and die for—the limpid Lake of the Bear,
The Empire of Empty Bellies, the dunes where the Dogribs
    dwell;
Big things, real things, live things . . . here on my morris chair
How I ache for the Northland! "Dinner and servants"—Hell!!

Am I too old, I wonder? Can I take one trip more?
Go to the granite-ribbed valleys, flooded with sunset wine,

Peaks that pierce the aurora, rivers I must explore,
Lakes of a thousand islands, millioning hordes of the Pine?
Do they not miss me, I wonder, valley and peak and plain?
Whispering each to the other: "Many a moon has passed . . .
"Where has he gone, our lover? Will he come back again?
"Star with his fires our tundra, leave us his bones at last?"

Yes, I'll go back to the Northland, back to the way of the bear,
Back to the muskeg and mountain, back to the ice-leaguered sea.
Old am I! what does it matter? Nothing I would not dare;
Give me a trail to conquer— Oh, it is "meat" to me!
I will go back to the Northland, feeble and blind and lame;
Sup with the sunny-eyed Husky, eat moose-nose with the Cree;
Play with the Yellow-knife bastards, boasting my blood and my
        name:
I will go back to the Northland, for the Northland is calling
        to me.

Then give to me paddle and whiplash, and give to me tumpline
        and gun;
Give to me salt and tobacco, flour and a gunny of tea;
Take me up over the Circle, under the flamboyant sun;
Turn me foot-loose like a savage—that is the finish of me.
I know the trail I am seeking, it's up by the Lake of the Bear:
It's down by the Arctic Barrens, it's over to Hudson's Bay;
Maybe I'll get there,—maybe: death is set by a hair. . . .
Hark! it's the Northland calling! now must I go away. . . .

> *Go to the Wild that waits for me;*
> *Go where the moose and the musk-ox be;*
> *Go to the wolf and the secret snows;*
> *Go to my fate . . . who knows, who knows!*

AMBITION

THEY brought the mighty chief to town;
They showed him strange, unwonted sights;
Yet as he wandered up and down,
He seemed to scorn their vain delights.
His face was grim, his eye lacked fire,
As one who mourns a glory dead;
And when they sought his heart's desire:
"Me like'um tooth same gold," he said.

A dental place they quickly found.
He neither moaned nor moved his head.
They pulled his teeth so white and sound;
They put in teeth of gold instead.
Oh, never saw I man so gay!
His very being seemed to swell:
"Ha! ha!" he cried, "Now Injun say
Me heap big chief, *me look like hell*."

TO SUNNYDALE

THERE lies the trail to Sunnydale,
Amid the lure of laughter.
Oh, how can we unhappy be
Beneath its leafy rafter!
Each perfect hour is like a flower,
Each day is like a posy.
How can you say the skies are grey?
You're wrong, my friend, they're rosy.

With right good will let's climb the hill,
And leave behind all sorrow.
Oh, we'll be gay! a bright to-day
Will make a bright to-morrow.
Oh, we'll be strong! the way is long
That never has a turning;
The hill is high, but there's the sky,
And how the West is burning!

And if through chance of circumstance
We have to go bare-foot, sir,
We'll not repine—a friend of mine
Has got no feet to boot, sir.
This Happiness a habit is,
And Life is what we make it:
See! there's the trail to Sunnydale!
Up, friend! and let us take it.

THE BLIND AND THE DEAD

She lay like a saint on her copper couch;
    Like an angel asleep she lay,
In the stare of the ghoulish folks that slouch
    Past the Dead and sneak away.

Then came old Jules of the sightless gaze,
    Who begged in the streets for bread.
Each day he had come for a year of days,
    And groped his way to the Dead.

"What's the Devil's Harvest to-day?" he cried;
    "A wanton with eyes of blue!
I've known too many a such," he sighed;
    "Maybe I know this . . . mon Dieu!"

He raised the head of the heedless Dead;
    He fingered the frozen face. . . .
Then a deathly spell on the watchers fell—
    God! it was still, that place!

He raised the head of the careless Dead;
    He fumbled a vagrant curl;
And then with his sightless smile he said:
    "It's only my little girl."

"Dear, my dear, did they hurt you so!
    Come to your daddy's heart. . . ."
Aye, and he held so tight, you know,
    They were hard to force apart.

No! Paris isn't always gay;
    And the morgue has its stories too:
You are a writer of tales, you say—
    Then there is a tale for you.

THE ATAVIST

What are you doing here, Tom Thorne, on the white top-knot
    o' the world,
Where the wind has the cut of a naked knife and the stars are
    rapier keen?
Hugging a smudgy willow fire, deep in a lynx robe curled,
You that's a lord's own son, Tom Thorne—what does your
    madness mean?

Go home, go home to your clubs, Tom Thorne! home to your
    evening dress!
Home to your place of power and pride, and the feast that waits
    for you!
Why do you linger all alone in the splendid emptiness,
Scouring the Land of the Little Sticks on the trail of the caribou?

Why did you fall off the Earth, Tom Thorne, out of our social
    ken?
What did your deep damnation prove? What was your dark
    despair?
Oh with the width of a world between, and years to the count
    of ten,
If they cut out your heart to-night, Tom Thorne, *Her* name
    would be graven there!

And you fled afar for the thing called Peace, and you thought
    you would find it here,
In the purple tundras vastly spread, and the mountains whitely
    piled;

It's a weary quest and a dreary quest, but I think that the end
    is near;
For they say that the Lord has hidden it in the secret heart of
    the Wild.

And you know that heart as few men know, and your eyes are
    fey and deep,
With a "something lost" come welling back from the raw, red
    dawn of life:
With woe and pain have you greatly lain, till out of abysmal
    sleep
The soul of the Stone Age leaps in you, alert for the ancient
    strife.

And if you came to our feast again, with its pomp and glee and
    glow,
I think you would sit stone-still, Tom Thorne, and see in a daze
    of dream,
A mad sun goading to frenzied flame the glittering gems of the
    snow,
And a monster musk-ox bulking black against the blood-red
    gleam.

I think you would see berg-battling shores, and stammer and halt
    and stare,
With a sudden sense of the frozen void, serene and vast and still;
And the aching gleam and the hush of dream, and the track of
    a great white bear,
And the primal lust that surged in you as you sprang to make
    your kill.

I think you would hear the bull-moose call, and the glutted river
    roar;

And spy the hosts of the caribou shadow the shining plain;
And feel the pulse of the Silences, and stand elate once more
On the verge of the yawning vastitudes that call to you in vain.

For I think you are one with the stars and the sun, and the wind
    and the wave and the dew;
And the peaks untrod that yearn to God, and the valleys unde-
    filed;
Men soar with wings, and they bridle kings, but what is it all to
    you,
Wise in the ways of the wilderness, and strong with the strength
    of the Wild?

You have spent your life, you have waged your strife where
    never we play a part;
You have held the throne of the Great Unknown, you have
    ruled a kingdom vast:

    .   .   .   .

But to-night there's a strange, new trail for you, and you go, O
    weary heart!
To the peace and rest of the Great Unguessed . . . at last, Tom
    Thorne, at last.

THE SCEPTIC

My Father Christmas passed away
When I was barely seven.
At twenty-one, alack-a-day,
I lost my hope of heaven.

Yet not in either lies the curse:
The hell of it's because
I don't know which loss hurt the worse—
My God or Santa Claus.

THE ROVER

I

Oh, how good it is to be
Foot-loose and heart-free!
Just my dog and pipe and I, underneath the vast sky;
Trail to try and goal to win, white road and cool inn;
Fields to lure a lad afar, clear spring and still star;
Lilting feet that never tire, green dingle, fagot fire;
None to hurry, none to hold, heather hill and hushed fold;
Nature like a picture book, laughing leaf and bright brook;
Every day a jewel bright, set serenely in the night;
Every night a holy shrine, radiant for a day divine.

Weathered cheek and kindly eye, let the wanderer go by.
Woman-love and wistful heart, let the gipsy one depart.
For the farness and the road are his glory and his goad.
Oh, the lilt of youth and Spring! Eyes laugh and lips sing.
Yea, but it is good to be
Foot-loose and heart-free!

II

Yet how good it is to come
Home at last, home, home!
On the clover swings the bee, overhead's the hale tree;
Sky of turquoise gleams through, yonder glints the lake's blue.
In a hammock let's swing, weary of wandering;
Tired of wild, uncertain lands, strange faces, faint hands.

Has the wondrous world gone cold? Am I growing old, old?
Grey and weary . . . let me dream, glide on the tranquil stream.
Oh, what joyous days I've had, full, fervid, gay, glad!
Yet there comes a subtile change, let the stripling rove, range.
From sweet roving comes sweet rest, after all, home's best.
And if there's a little bit of woman-love with it,
I will count my life content, God-blest and well spent. . . .

>Oh but it is good to be
>Foot-loose and heart-free!
>Yet how good it is to come
>Home at last, home, home!

BARB-WIRE BILL

AT dawn of day the white land lay all gruesome-like and grim,
When Bill Mc'Gee he says to me: "We've *got* to do it, Jim.
"We've got to make Fort Liard quick. I know the river's bad,
"But, oh! the little woman's sick . . . why! don't you savvy,
    lad?"
And me! Well, yes, I must confess it wasn't hard to see
Their little family group of two would soon be one of three.
And so I answered, careless-like: "Why, Bill! you don't suppose
"I'm scared of that there 'babbling brook'? Whatever you say—
    goes."

A real live man was Barb-wire Bill, with insides copperlined;
For "barb-wire" was the brand of "hooch" to which he most
    inclined.
They knew him far; his igloos are on Kittiegazuit strand
They knew him well, the tribes who dwell within the Barren
    Land.
From Koyokuk to Kuskoquim his fame was everywhere;
And he did love, all life above, that little Julie Claire,
The lithe, white slave-girl he had bought for seven hundred
    skins,
And taken to his wickiup to make his moccasins.

We crawled down to the river bank and feeble folk were we,
That Julie Claire from God-knows-where, and Barb-wire Bill
    and me.
From shore to shore we heard the roar the heaving ice-floes
    make,

And loud we laughed, and launched our raft, and followed in
their wake.
The river swept and seethed and leapt, and caught us in its
stride;
And on we hurled amid a world that crashed on every side.
With sullen din the banks caved in; the shore-ice lanced the
stream;
The naked floes like spooks arose, all jiggling and agleam.
Black anchor-ice of strange device shot upward from its bed,
As night and day we cleft our way, and arrow-like we sped.

But "Faster still!" cried Barb-wire Bill, and looked the live-long
day
In dull despair at Julie Claire, as white like death she lay.
And sometimes he would seem to pray and sometimes seem to
curse,
And bent above, with eyes of love, yet ever she grew worse.
And as we plunged and leapt and lunged, her face was plucked
with pain,
And I could feel his nerves of steel a-quiver at the strain.
And in the night he gripped me tight as I lay fast asleep:
"The river's kicking like a steer . . . run out the forward
sweep!
"That's Hell-gate Canyon right ahead; I know of old its roar,
"And . . . I'll be damned! *the ice is jammed!* We've *got* to
make the shore."

With one wild leap I gripped the sweep. The night was black
as sin.
The float-ice crashed and ripped and smashed, and stunned us
with its din.
And near and near, and clear and clear I heard the canyon boom;
And swift and strong we swept along to meet our awful doom.

And as with dread I glimpsed ahead the death that waited there,
My only thought was of the girl, the little Julie Claire;
And so, like demon mad with fear, I panted at the oar,
And foot by foot, and inch by inch, we worked the raft ashore.

The bank was staked with grinding ice, and as we scraped and
    crashed,
I only knew one thing to do, and through my mind it flashed:
Yet while I groped to find the rope, I heard Bill's savage cry:
"That's my job, lad! It's me that jumps. I'll snub this raft or die!"
I saw him leap, I saw him creep, I saw him gain the land;
I saw him crawl, I saw him fall, then run with rope in hand.
And then the darkness gulped him up, and down we dashed once
    more,
And nearer, nearer drew the jam, and thunder-like its roar.

Oh God! all's lost . . . from Julie Claire there came a wail of
    pain,
And then—the rope grew sudden taut, and quivered at the strain;
It slacked and slipped, it whined and gripped, and oh, I held my
    breath!
And there we hung and there we swung right in the jaws of
    death.

A little strand of hempen rope, and how I watched it there,
With all around a hell of sound, and darkness and despair;
A little strand of hempen rope, I watched it all alone,
And somewhere in the dark behind I heard a woman moan;
And somewhere in the dark ahead I heard a man cry out,
Then silence, silence, silence fell, and mocked my hollow shout.
And yet once more from out the shore I heard that cry of pain,
A moan of mortal agony, then all was still again.

That night was hell with all the frills, and when the dawn broke
  dim,
I saw a lean and level land, but never sign of him.
I saw a flat and frozen shore of hideous device,
I saw a long-drawn strand of rope that vanished through the ice.
And on that treeless, rockless shore I found my partner—dead.
No place was there to snub the raft, so—*he had served instead;*
And with the rope lashed round his waist, in last defiant fight,
He'd thrown himself beneath the ice, that closed and gripped
  him tight;
And there he'd held us back from death, as fast in death he
  lay. . . .
Say, boys! I'm not the pious brand, but—I just tried to pray.
And then I looked to Julie Claire, and sore abashed was I,
For from the robes that covered her, *I—heard—a—baby—
  cry.* . . .

Thus was Love conqueror of death, and life for life was given;
And though no saint on earth, d'ye think—Bill's squared hisself
  with Heaven?

"?"

IF you had the choice of the two women to wed,
(Though of course the idea is quite absurd)
And the first from her heels to her dainty head
Was charming in every sense of the word:
And yet in the past (I grieve to state),
She never had been exactly "straight."

And the second—she was beyond all cavil,
A model of virtue, I must confess;
And yet, alas! she was dull as the devil,
And rather a dowd in the way of dress;
Though what she was lacking in wit and beauty,
She more than made up for in "sense of duty."

Now, suppose you must wed, and make no blunder,
And either would love you, and let you win her—
Which of the two would you choose, I wonder,
The stolid saint or the sparkling sinner?

JUST THINK!

Just think! some night the stars will gleam
 Upon a cold, grey stone,
And trace a name with silver beam,
 And lo! 'twill be your own.

That night is speeding on to greet
 Your epitaphic rhyme.
You life is but a little beat
 Within the heart of Time.

A little gain, a little pain,
 A laugh, lest you may moan;
A little blame, a little fame,
 A star-gleam on a stone.

THE LUNGER

JACK would laugh an' joke all day;
Never saw a lad so gay;
Singin' like a medder lark,
Loaded to the Plimsoll mark
With God's sunshine was that boy;
Had a strangle-holt on Joy.
Held his head 'way up in air,
Left no callin' cards on Care;
Breezy, buoyant, brave and true;
Sent his sunshine out to you;
Cheerfulest when clouds was black—
　　Happy Jack! Oh, Happy Jack!

Sittin' in my shack alone
I could hear him in his own,
Singin' far into the night,
Till it didn't seem just right
One man should corral the fun,
Live his life so in the sun;
Didn't seem quite natural
Not to have a grouch at all;
Not a trouble, not a lack—
　　Happy Jack! Oh, Happy Jack!

He was plumbful of good cheer
Till he struck that low-down year;
Got so thin, so little to him,
You could most see day-light through him.

Never was his eye so bright,
Never was his cheek so white.
Seemed as if somethin' was wrong,
Sort o' quaver in his song.
Same old smile, same hearty voice:
"Bless you, boys! let's all rejoice!"
But old Doctor shook his head:
"Half a lung," was all he said.
Yet that half was surely right,
For I heard him every night,
Singin', singin' in his shack—
    Happy Jack! Oh, Happy Jack!

Then one day a letter came
Endin' with a female name;
Seemed to get him in the neck,
Sort o' pile-driver effect;
Paled his lip and plucked his breath,
Left him starin' still as death.
Somethin' had gone awful wrong,
Yet that night he sang his song.
Oh, but it was good to hear!
For there clutched my heart a fear,
So that I quaked listenin'
Every night to hear him sing.
But each day he laughed with me,
An' his smile was full of glee.
Nothin' seemed to set him back—
    Happy Jack! Oh, Happy Jack!

Then one night the singin' stopped . . .
Seemed as if my heart just flopped;
For I'd learned to love the boy

With his gilt-edged line of joy,
With his glorious gift of bluff,
With his splendid fightin' stuff.
Sing on, lad, and play the game!
O dear God! . . . no singin' came,
But there surged to me instead—
Silence, silence, deep and dread;
Till I shuddered, tried to pray.
Said: "He's maybe gone away."

Oh, yes, he had gone away,
Gone forever and a day.
But he'd left behind him there,
In his cabin, pinched and bare,
His poor body, skin and bone,
His sharp face, cold as a stone.
An' his stiffened fingers pressed
Somethin' bright upon his breast:
Locket with a silken curl,
Poor, sweet portrait of a girl.
Yet I reckon at the last
How defiant-like he passed;
For there sat upon his lips
Smile that death could not eclipse;
An' within his eyes lived still
Joy that dyin' could not kill.

An' now when the nights are long,
How I miss his cheery song!
How I sigh an' wish him back!
    Happy Jack! Oh, Happy Jack!

THE MOUNTAIN AND THE LAKE

I KNOW a mountain thrilling to the stars,
Peerless and pure, and pinnacled with snow;
Glimpsing the golden dawn o'er coral bars,
Flaunting the vanisht sunset's garnet glow;
Proudly patrician, passionless, serene;
Soaring in silvered steeps where cloud-surfs break;
Virgin and vestal— Oh, a very Queen!
And at her feet there dreams a quiet lake.

My lake adores my mountain—well I know,
For I have watched it from its dawn-dream start,
Stilling its mirror to her splendid snow,
Framing her image in its trembling heart;
Glassing her graciousness of greening wood,
Kissing her throne, melodiously mad,
Thrilling responsive to her every mood,
Gloomed with her sadness, gay when she is glad.

My lake has dreamed and loved since time was born;
Will love and dream till time shall cease to be;
Gazing to Her in worship half forlorn,
Who looks towards the stars and will not see—
My peerless mountain, splendid in her scorn. . . .
Alas! poor little lake! Alas! poor me!

THE HEADLINER AND THE BREADLINER

Moкo, the Educated Ape is here,
The pet of vaudeville, so the posters say,
    And every night the gaping people pay
To see him in his panoply appear;
To see him pad his paunch with dainty cheer,
    Puff his perfecto, swill champagne, and sway
    Just like a gentleman, yet all in play,
Then bow himself off stage with brutish leer.

And as to-night, with noble knowledge crammed,
    I 'mid this human compost take my place,
I, once a poet, now so dead and damned,
    The woeful tears half freezing on my face:
"O God!" I cry, "let me but take his shape,
    Moko's, the Blest, the Educated Ape."

DEATH IN THE ARCTIC

I

I TOOK the clock down from the shelf;
"At eight," said I, "I shoot myself."
It lacked a *minute* of the hour,
And as I waited all a-cower,
A skinful of black, boding pain,
Bits of my life came back again. . . .

"*Mother, there's nothing more to eat—*
Why don't you go out on the street?
Always you sit and cry and cry;
Here at my play I wonder why.
Mother, when you dress up at night,
Red are your cheeks, your eyes are bright:
Twining a ribband in your hair,
Kissing good-bye you go down-stair
Then I'm as lonely as can be.
Oh, how I wish you were with me!
Yet when you go out on the street,
Mother, there's always lots to eat. . . ."

II

For days the igloo has been dark;
But now the rag wick sends a spark
That glitters in the icy air,
And wakes frost sapphires everywhere;
Bright, bitter flames, that adder-like

Dart here and there, yet fear to strike
The gruesome gloom wherein *they* lie,
My comrades, oh, so keen to die!
And I, the last—well, here I wait
The clock to strike the hour of eight. . . .

"*Boy, it is bitter to be hurled*
Nameless and naked on the world;
Frozen by night and starved by day,
Curses and kicks and clouts your pay.
But you must fight! Boy, look on me!
Anarch of all earth-misery;
Beggar and tramp and shameless sot;
Emblem of ill, in rags that rot.
Would you be foul and base as I?
Oh, it is better far to die!
Swear to me now you'll fight and fight,
Boy, or I'll kill you here to-night. . . ."

III

Curse this silence soft and black!
Sting, little light, the shadows back!
Dance, little flame, with freakish glee!
Twinkle with brilliant mockery!
Glitter on ice-robed roof and floor!
Jewel the bear-skin of the door!
Gleam in my beard, illume my breath,
Blanch the clock face that times my death!
But do not pierce that murk so deep,
Where in their sleeping-bags they sleep!
But do not linger where they lie,
They who had all the luck to die! . . .

"There is nothing more to say;
Let us part and go our way.
Since it seems we can't agree,
I will go across the sea.
Proud of heart and strong am I;
Not for woman will I sigh;
Hold my head up gay and glad:
You can find another lad. . . ."

IV

Above the igloo piteous flies
Our frayed flag to the frozen skies.
Oh, would you know how earth can be
A hell—go north of Eighty-three!
Go, scan the snows day after day,
And hope for help, and pray and pray;
Have seal-hide and sea-lice to eat;
Melt water with your body's heat;
Sleep all the fell, black winter through
Beside the dear, dead men you knew.
(The walrus blubber flares and gleams—
O. God! how long a minute seems!) . . .

"Mary, many a day has passed,
Since that morn of hot-head youth.
Come I back at last, at last,
Crushed with knowing of the truth;
How through bitter, barren years
You loved me, and me alone;
Waited, wearied, wept your tears—
Oh, could I atone, atone,
I would pay a million-fold!

Pay you for the love you gave.
Mary, look down as of old—
I am kneeling by your grave." . . .

V

Olaf, the Blonde, was first to go;
Bitten his eyes were by the snow;
Sightless and sealed his eyes of blue,
So that he died before I knew.
Here in those poor weak arms he died:
"Wolves will not get you, lad," I lied;
"For I will watch till Spring come round;
Slumber you shall beneath the ground."
Oh, how I lied! I scarce can wait:
Strike, little clock, the hour of eight! . . .

"Comrade, can you blame me quite?
The horror of the long, long night
Is on me, and I've borne with pain
So long, and hoped for help in vain.
So frail am I, and blind and dazed;
With scurvy sick, with silence crazed.
Beneath the Arctic's heel of hate,
Avid for Death I wait, I wait.
Oh if I falter, fail to fight,
Can you, dear comrade, blame me quite?" . . .

VI

Big Eric gave up months ago.
But seldom do men suffer so.
His feet sloughed off, his fingers died,

His hands shrunk up and mummified.
I had to feed him like a child;
Yet he was valiant, joked and smiled,
Talked of his wife and little one
(Thanks be to God that I have none),
Passed in the night without a moan,
Passed, and I'm here, alone, alone. . . .

"I've got to kill you, Dick.
Your life for mine, you know.
Better to do it quick,
A swift and sudden blow.
See! here's my hand to lick;
A hug before you go—
God! but it makes me sick:
Old dog, I love you so.
Forgive, forgive me, Dick—
A swift and sudden blow. . . ."

VII

Often I start up in the dark,
Thinking the sound of bells to hear.
Often I wake from sleep. "Oh, hark!
Help . . . it is coming . . . near and near."
Blindly I reel toward the door;
There the snow billows bleak and bare;
Blindly I seek my den once more,
Silence and darkness and despair.
Oh, it is all a dreadful dream!
Scurvy and cold and death and dearth;
I will awake to warmth and gleam,
Silvery seas and greening earth.

Life is a dream, its wakening,
Death, gentle shadow of God's wing. . . .

"Tick, little clock, my life away!
Even a second seems a day.
Even a minute seems a year,
Peopled with ghosts, that press and peer
Into my face so charnel white,
Lit by the devilish, dancing light.
Tick, little clock! mete out my fate:
Tortured and tense I wait, I wait. . . ."

VIII

Oh, I have sworn! the hour is nigh:
When it strikes eight, I die, I die.
Raise up the gun—it stings my brow—
When it strikes eight . . . all ready . . . *now—*

*　*　*　*　*　*　*

Down from my hand the weapon dropped;
Wildly I stared. . . .
      THE CLOCK HAD STOPPED.

IX

Phantoms and fears and ghosts have gone.
Peace seems to nestle in my brain.
Lo! the clock stopped, I'm living on;
Heart-sick I was, and less than sane.
Yet do I scorn the thing I planned,
Hearing a voice: "O coward, fight!"
Then the clock stopped . . . whose was the hand?

Maybe 'twas God's—ah well, all's right.
Heap on me darkness, fold on fold!
Pain! wrench and rack me! What care I?
Leap on me, hunger, thirst and cold!
I will await my time to die;
Looking to Heaven that shines above;
Looking to God, and love . . . and love.

x

Hark! what is that? Bells, dogs again!
Is it a dream? I sob and cry.
See! the door opens, fur-clad men
Rush to my rescue; frail am I;
Feeble and dying, dazed and glad.
There is the pistol where it dropped.
"Boys, it was hard—but I'm not mad. . . .
Look at the clock—it stopped, it stopped.
Carry me out. The heavens smile.
See! there's an arch of gold above.
Now, let me rest a little while—
Looking to God and love . . . and love. . . ."

DREAMS ARE BEST

I just think that dreams are best,
    Just to sit and fancy things;
    Give your gold no acid test,
Try not how your silver rings;
Fancy women pure and good,
    Fancy men upright and true:
    Fortressed in your solitude,
Let Life be a dream to you.

For I think that Thought is all;
    Truth's a minion of the mind;
    Love's ideal comes at call;
As ye seek so shall ye find.
But ye must not seek too far;
    Things are never what they seem:
    Let a star be just a star,
And a woman—just a dream.

O you Dreamers, proud and pure,
    You have gleaned the sweet of life!
    Golden truths that shall endure
Over pain and doubt and strife.
    I would rather be a fool
        Living in my Paradise,
        Than the leader of a school,
    Sadly sane and weary wise.

O you Cynics with your sneers,
    Fallen brains and hearts of brass,

Tweak me by my foolish ears,
  Write me down a simple ass!
I'll believe the real "you"
  Is the "you" without a taint;
  I'll believe each woman too,
But a slightly damaged saint.

Yes, I'll smoke my cigarette,
  Vestured in my garb of dreams,
  And I'll borrow no regret;
All is gold that golden gleams.
So I'll charm my solitude
  With the faith that Life is blest,
  Brave and noble, bright and good, . . .
  Oh, I think that dreams are best!

THE QUITTER

When you're lost in the Wild, and you're scared as a child,
  And Death looks you bang in the eye,
And you're sore as a boil, it's according to Hoyle
  To cock your revolver and . . . die.
But the Code of a Man says: "Fight all you can,"
  And self-dissolution is barred.
In hunger and woe, oh, it's easy to blow . . .
  It's the hell-served-for-breakfast that's hard.

"You're sick of the game!" Well, now, that's a shame.
  You're young and you're brave and you're bright.
"You've had a raw deal!" I know—but don't squeal,
  Buck up, do your damnedest, and fight.
It's the plugging away that will win you the day,
  So don't be a piker, old pard!
Just draw on your grit; it's so easy to quit:
  It's the keeping-your-chin-up that's hard.

It's easy to cry that you're beaten—and die;
  It's easy to crawfish and crawl;
But to fight and to fight when hope's out of sight—
  Why, that's the best game of them all!
And though you come out of each gruelling bout,
  All broken and beaten and scarred,
Just have one more try—it's dead easy to die,
  It's the keeping-on-living that's hard.

THE COW-JUICE CURE

THE clover was in blossom, an' the year was at the June,
When Flap-jack Billy hit the town, likewise O'Flynn's saloon.
The frost was on the fodder an' the wind was growin' keen,
When Billy got to seein' snakes in Sullivan's shebeen.

Then in meandered Deep-hole Dan, once comrade of the cup:
"Oh Billy, for the love of Mike, why don't ye sober up?
I've got the gorgus recipay, 'tis smooth an' slick as silk—
Jest quit yer strangle-holt on hooch, an' irrigate with milk.
Lackteeal flooid is the lubrication you require;
Yer nervus frame-up's like a bunch of snarled piano wire.
You want to get it coated up with addypose tishoo,
So's it will work elastic-like, an' milk's the dope for you."

Well, Billy was complyable, an' in a month it's strange.
That cow-juice seemed to oppyrate a most amazin' change.
"Call up the water-wagon, Dan, an' book my seat," sez he.
" 'Tis mighty queer," sez Deep-hole Dan, " 'twas just the same
    with me."
They shanghaied little Tim O'Shane, they cached him safe
    away,
An' though he objurgated some, they "cured" him night an'
    day;
An' pretty soon there came the change amazin' to explain:
"I'll never take another drink," sez Timothy O'Shane.
They tried it out on Spike Muldoon, that toper of renown;
They put it over Grouch McGraw, the terror of the town.

229

They roped in "tanks" from far and near, an' every test was
    sure,
An' like a flame there ran the fame of Deep-hole's Cow-juice
    Cure.

"It's mighty queer," sez Deep-hole Dan, "I'm puzzled through
    and through;
It's only milk from Riley's ranch, no other milk will do."
An' it jest happened on that night with no predictive plan,
He left some milk from Riley's ranch a-settin' in a pan;
An' picture his amazement when he poured that milk next day—
There in the bottom of the pan a dozen "colours" lay.

"Well, what d'ye know 'bout that," sez Dan; "Gosh ding my
    dasted eyes,
We've been an' had the Gold Cure, Bill, an' none of us was wise.
The milk's free-millin' that's a cinch; there's colours every-
    where.
Now, let us figger this thing out—how does the dust git there?
'Gold from the grass-roots down,' they say—why, Bill! we've
    got it cold—
Them cows what nibbles up the grass, jest nibbles up the gold.
We're blasted, bloomin' millionaires; dissemble an' lie low:
We'll follow them gold-bearin' cows, an' prospect where they
    go."

An' so it came to pass, fer weeks them miners might be found
A-sneakin' round on Riley's ranch, an' snipin' at the ground;
Till even Riley stops an' stares, an' presently allows:
"Them boys appear to take a mighty interest in cows."
An' night an' day they shadowed each auriferous bovine,
An' panned the grass-roots on their trail, yet nivver gold they
    seen.

An' all that season, secret-like, they worked an' nothin' found;
An' there was colours in the milk, but none was in the ground
An' mighty desperate was they, an' down upon their luck,
When sudden, inspirationlike, the source of it they struck.
An' where d'ye think they traced it to? it grieves my heart to
    tell—
In the black sand at the bottom of that wicked milkman's *well*.

WHILE THE BANNOCK BAKES

Light up your pipe again, old chum, and sit awhile with me;
I've got to watch the bannock bake—how restful is the air!
You'd little think that we were somewhere north of Sixty-three,
Though where I don't exactly know, and don't precisely care.
The man-size mountains palisade us round on every side;
The river is a-flop with fish, and ripples silver-clear;
The midnight sunshine brims yon cleft—we think it's the Divide;
We'll get there in a month, maybe, or maybe in a year.

It doesn't matter, does it, pal? We're of that breed of men
With whom the world of wine and cards and women disagree;
Your trouble was a roofless game of poker now and then,
And "raising up my elbow," that's what got away with me.
We're merely "Undesirables," artistic more or less;
My horny hands are Chopin-wise; you quote your Browning
well;
And yet we're fooling round for gold in this damned wilderness:
The joke is, if we found it, we would both go straight to hell.

Well, maybe we won't find it—and at least we've got the "life."
We're both as brown as berries, and could wrestle with a bear:
(That bannock's raising nicely, pal; just jab it with your knife.)
Fine specimens of manhood they would reckon us out there
It's the tracking and the packing and the poling in the sun;
It's the sleeping in the open, it's the rugged, unfaked food;
It's the snow-shoe and the paddle, and the camp-fire and the gun,
And when I think of what I was, I know that it is good.

Just think of how we've poled all day up this strange little
    stream;
Since life began no eye of man has seen this place before;
How fearless all the wild things are! the banks with goose-grass
    gleam,
And there's a bronzy musk-rat sitting sniffing at his door.
A mother duck with brood of ten comes squattering along;
The tawny, white-winged ptarmigan are flying all about;
And in that swirly, golden pool, a restless, gleaming throng,
The trout are waiting till we condescend to take them out.

Ah, yes, it's good! I'll bet that there's no doctor like the Wild:
(Just turn that bannock over there; it's getting nicely brown.)
I might be in my grave by now, forgotten and reviled,
Or rotting like a sickly cur in some far, foreign town.
I might be that vile thing I was,—it all seems like a dream;
I owed a man a grudge one time that only life could pay;
And yet it's half-forgotten now—how petty these things seem!
(But that's "another story," pal; I'll tell it you some day.)

How strange two "irresponsibles" should chum away up here!
But round the Arctic Circle friends are few and far between.
We've shared the same camp-fire and tent for nigh on seven
    year,
And never had a word that wasn't cheering and serene.
We've halved the toil and split the spoil, and borne each other's
    packs;
By all the Wild's freemasonry we're brothers, tried and true;
We've swept on danger side by side, and fought it back to back,
And you would die for me, old pal, and I would die for you.

Now there was that time I got lost in Rory Bory Land,
(How quick the blizzards sweep on one across that Polar sea!)

You formed a rescue crew of One, and saw a frozen hand
That stuck out of a drift of snow—and, partner, it was Me.
But I got even, did I not, that day the paddle broke?
White water on the Coppermine—a rock—a split canoe—
Two fellows struggling in the foam (one couldn't swim a
     stroke):
A half-drowned man I dragged ashore . . . and partner, it was
     You.

    *   *   *   *   *   *   *   *   *

In Rory Borealis Land the winter's long and black.
The silence seems a solid thing, shot through with wolfish woe;
And rowelled by the eager stars the skies vault vastly back,
And man seems but a little mite on that weird-lit plateau.
Nothing to do but smoke and yarn of wild and misspent lives,
Beside the camp-fire there we sat—what tales you told to me
Of love and hate, and chance and fate, and temporary wives!
In Rory Borealis Land, beside the Arctic Sea.

One yarn you told me in those days I can remember still;
It seemed as if I visioned it, so sharp you sketched it in;
Bellona was the name, I think; a coast town in Brazil,
Where nobody did anything but serenade and sin.
I saw it all—the jewelled sea, the golden scythe of sand,
The stately pillars of the palms, the feathery bamboo,
The red-roofed houses and the swart, sun-dominated land,
The people ever children, and the heavens ever blue.

You told me of that girl of yours, that blossom of old Spain,
All glamour, grace and witchery, all passion, verve and glow.
How maddening she must have been! You made me see her
     plain,
There by our little camp-fire, in the silence and the snow.

You loved her and she loved you. She'd a husband, too, I think,
A doctor chap, you told me, whom she treated like a dog,
A white man living on the beach, a hopeless slave to drink—
(Just turn that bannock over there, that's propped against the
    log.)

That story seemed to strike me, pal—it happens every day:
You had to go away awhile, then somehow it befell
The doctor chap discovered, gave her up, and disappeared;
You came back, tired of her in time . . . there's nothing more
    to tell.
Hist! see those willows silvering where swamp and river meet!
Just reach me up my rifle quick; that's Mister Moose, I know—
There now, *I've got him dead to rights* . . . but hell! we've lots
    to eat
I don't believe in taking life—we'll let the beggar go.

Heigh ho! I'm tired; the bannock's cooked; it's time we both
    turned in.
The morning mist is coral-kissed, the morning sky is gold.
The camp-fire's a confessional—what funny yarns we spin!
It sort of made me think a bit, that story that you told.
The fig-leaf belt and Rory Bory are such odd extremes,
Yet after all how very small this old world seems to be . . .
Yes, that was quite a yarn, old pal, and yet to me it seems
You missed the point: the point is that the "doctor chap" . . .
    was ME. . . .

THE LOST MASTER

"AND when I come to die," he said,
"Ye shall not lay me out in state,
Nor leave your laurels at my head,
Nor cause your men of speech orate;
No monument your gift shall be,
No column in the Hall of Fame;
But just this line ye grave for me:
      'He played the game.'"

So when his glorious task was done,
It was not of his fame we thought;
It was not of his battles won,
But of the pride with which he fought;
But of his zest, his ringing laugh,
His trenchant scorn of praise or blame:
And so we graved his epitaph,
      "He played the game."

And so we, too, in humbler ways
Went forth to fight the fight anew,
And heeding neither blame nor praise,
We held the course he set us true.
And we, too, find the fighting sweet;
And we, too, fight for fighting's sake;
And though we go down in defeat,
And though our stormy hearts may break,
We will not do our Master shame:
We'll play the game, please God,
      We'll play the game.

LITTLE MOCCASINS

COME out, O Little Moccasins, and frolic on the snow!
Come out, O tiny beaded feet, and twinkle in the light!
I'll play the old Red River reel, you used to love it so:
Awake, O Little Moccasins, and dance for me to-night!

Your hair was all a gleamy gold, your eyes a corn-flower blue;
Your cheeks were pink as tinted shells, you stepped light as a
    fawn;
Your mouth was like a coral bud, with seed pearls peeping
    through;
As gladdening as Spring you were, as radiant as dawn.

Come out, O Little Moccasins! I'll play so soft and low,
The songs you loved, the old heart-songs that in my mem'ry
    ring;
O child, I want to hear you now beside the camp-fire glow!
With all your heart a-throbbing in the simple words you sing.

For there was only you and I, and you were all to me;
And round us were the barren lands, but little did we fear;
Of all God's happy, happy folks the happiest were we. . . .
(Oh, call her, poor old fiddle mine, and maybe she will hear!)

Your mother was a half-breed Cree, but you were white all
    through;
And I, your father was—but well, that's neither here nor there;
I only know, my little Queen, that all my world was you,
And now that world can end to-night, and I will never care.

For there's a tiny wooden cross that pricks up through the snow:
(Poor Little Moccasins! you're tired, and so you lie at rest.)
And there's a grey-haired, weary man beside the camp-fire glow:
(O fiddle mine! the tears to-night are drumming on your breast.)

THE WANDERLUST

THE Wanderlust has lured me to the seven lonely seas,
Has dumped me on the tailing-piles of dearth;
The Wanderlust has haled me from the morris chair of ease,
Has hurled me to the ends of all the earth.
How bitterly I've cursed it, oh, the Painted Desert knows,
The wraithlike heights that hug the pallid plain,
The all-but-fluid silence,—yet the longing grows and grows,
And I've got to glut the Wanderlust again.

Soldier, sailor, in what a plight I've been!
Tinker, tailor, oh what a sight I've seen!
And I'm hitting the trail in the morning, boys,
And you won't see my heels for dust;
For it's "all day" with you
When you answer the cue
Of the Wan-der-lust.

The Wanderlust has got me . . . by the belly-aching fire,
By the fever and the freezing and the pain;
By the darkness that just drowns you, by the wail of home de-
sire,
I've tried to break the spell of it—in vain.
Life might have been a feast for me, now there are only crumbs;
In rags and tatters, beggar-wise I sit;
Yet there's no rest or peace for me, imperious it drums,
The Wanderlust, and I must follow it.

Highway, by-way, many a mile I've done;
Rare way, fair way, many a height I've won;

But I'm pulling my freight in the morning, boys,
And it's over the hills or bust;
For there's never a cure
When you list to the lure
Of the Wan-der-lust.

The Wanderlust has taught me . . . it has whispered to my
heart
Things all you stay-at-homes will never know.
The white man and the savage are but three short days apart,
Three days of cursing, crawling, doubt and woe.
Then it's down to chewing muclucs, to the water you can *eat*,
To fish you bolt with nose held in your hand.
When you get right down to cases, it's King's Grub that rules
the races,
And the Wanderlust will help you understand.

Haunting, taunting, that is the spell of it;
Mocking, baulking, that is the hell of it;
But I'll shoulder my pack in the morning, boys,
And I'm going because I must;
For it's so-long to all
When you answer the call
Of the Wan-der-lust.

The Wanderlust has blest me . . . in a ragged blanket curled,
I've watched the gulf of Heaven foam with stars;
I've walked with eyes wide open to the wonder of the world,
I've seen God's flood of glory burst its bars.
I've seen the gold a-blinding in the riffles of the sky,
Till I fancied me a bloated plutocrat;
But I'm freedom's happy bond-slave, and I will be till I die,
And I've got to thank the Wanderlust for that.

Wild heart, child heart, all of the world your home.
Glad heart, mad heart, what can you do but roam?
Oh, I'll beat it once more in the morning, boys,
With a pinch of tea and a crust;
For you cannot deny
When you hark to the cry
      Of the Wan-der-lust.

The Wanderlust will claim me at the finish for its own.
I'll turn my back on men and face the Pole.
Beyond the Arctic outposts I will venture all alone;
Some Never-never Land will be my goal.
Thank God! there's none will miss me, for I've been a bird of
    flight;
And in my moccasins I'll take my call;
For the Wanderlust has ruled me,
And the Wanderlust has schooled me,
And I'm ready for the darkest trail of all.

Grim land, dim land, oh, how the vastness calls!
Far land, star land, oh, how the stillness falls!
For you never can tell if it's heaven or hell,
And I'm taking the trail on trust;
But I haven't a doubt
That my soul will leap out
      On its Wan-der-lust.

THE TRAPPER'S CHRISTMAS EVE

It's mighty lonesome-like and drear.
Above the Wild the moon rides high,
And shows up sharp and needle-clear
The emptiness of earth and sky;
No happy homes with love a-glow;
No Santa Claus to make believe:
Just snow and snow, and then more snow;
It's Christmas Eve, it's Christmas Eve.

And here am I where all things end,
And Undesirables are hurled;
A poor old man without a friend,
Forgot and dead to all the world;
Clean out of sight and out of mind . . .
Well, maybe it is better so;
We all in life our level find,
And mine, I guess, is pretty low.

Yet as I sit with pipe alight
Beside the cabin-fire, it's queer
This mind of mine must take to-night
The backward trail of fifty year.
The school-house and the Christmas tree;
The children with their cheeks a-glow;
Two bright blue eyes that smile on me . . .
Just half a century ago.

Again (it's maybe forty years),
With faith and trust almost divine,

These same blue eyes, abrim with tears,
Through depths of love look into mine.
A parting, tender, soft and low,
With arms that cling and lips that cleave . . .
Ah me! it's all so long ago,
Yet seems so sweet this Christmas Eve.

Just thirty years ago, again . . .
We say a bitter, *last* good-bye;
Our lips are white with wrath and pain;
Our little children cling and cry.
Whose was the fault? it matters not,
For man and woman both deceive;
It's buried now and all forgot,
Forgiven, too, this Christmas Eve.

And she (God pity me) is dead;
Our children men and women grown.
I like to think that they are wed,
With little children of their own,
That crowd around their Christmas tree . . .
I would not ever have them grieve,
Or shed a single tear for me,
To mar their joy this Christmas Eve.

Stripped to the buff and gaunt and still
Lies all the land in grim distress.
Like lost soul wailing, long and shrill,
A wolf-howl cleaves the emptiness.
Then hushed as Death is everything.
The moon rides haggard and forlorn . . .
"O hark the herald angels sing!"
God bless all men—it's Christmas morn.

THE WORLD'S ALL RIGHT

Be honest, kindly, simple, true;
Seek good in all, scorn but pretence;
Whatever sorrow come to you,
Believe in Life's Beneficence!

The World's all right; serene I sit,
And cease to puzzle over it.
There's much that's mighty strange, no doubt;
But Nature knows what she's about;
And in a million years or so
We'll know more than to-day we know.
Old Evolution's under way—
　　　What ho! the World's all right, I say.

Could things be other than they are?
All's in its place, from mote to star.
The thistledown that flits and flies
Could drift no hair-breadth otherwise.
What is, must be; with rhythmic laws
All Nature chimes, Effect and Cause.
The sand-grain and the sun obey—
　　　What ho! the World's all right, I say.

Just try to get the Cosmic touch,
The sense that "you" don't matter much.
A million stars are in the sky;
A million planets plunge and die;
A million million men are sped;

A million million wait ahead.
Each plays his part and has his day—
    What ho! the World's all right, I say.

Just try to get the Chemic view:
A million million lives made "you."
In lives a million you will be
Immortal down Eternity;
Immortal on this earth to range,
With never death, but ever change.
You always were, and will be aye—
    What ho! the World's all right, I say.

Be glad! And do not blindly grope
For Truth that lies beyond our scope:
A sober plot informeth all
Of Life's uproarious carnival.
Your day is such a little one,
A gnat that lives from sun to sun;
Yet gnat and you have parts to play—
    What ho! the World's all right, I say.

And though it's written from the start,
Just act your best your little part.
Just be as happy as you can,
And serve your kind, and die—a man.
Just live the good that in you lies,
And seek no guerdon of the skies;
Just make your Heaven here, to-day—
    What ho! the World's all right, I say.

Remember! in Creation's swing
The Race and not the man's the thing.

There's battle, murder, sudden death,
And pestilence, with poisoned breath.
Yet quick forgotten are such woes;
On, on the stream of Being flows.
Truth, Beauty, Love uphold their sway—
　　What ho! the World's all right, I say.

The World's all right; serene I sit,
And joy that I am part of it;
And put my trust in Nature's plan,
And try to aid her all I can;
Content to pass, if in my place
I've served the uplift of the Race.
Truth! Beauty! Love! O Radiant Day—
　　What ho! the World's all right, I say.

THE BALDNESS OF CHEWED-EAR

WHEN Chewed-ear Jenkins got hitched up to Guinneyveer
    McGee,
His flowin' locks, ye recollect, wuz frivolous an' free;
But in old Hymen's jack-pot, it's a most amazin' thing,
Them flowin' locks jest disappeared like snow-balls in the
    Spring;
Jest seemed to wilt an' fade away like dead leaves in the Fall,
An' left old Chewed-ear balder than a white-washed cannon
    ball.

Now Missis Chewed-ear Jenkins, that wuz Guinneyveer Mc-
    Gee,
Wuz jest about as fine a draw as ever made a pair;
But when the boys got joshin' an' suggested it was she
That must be inflooenshul for the old man's slump in hair—
Why! Missis Chewed-ear Jenkins jest went clean up in the air.

"To demonstrate," sez she that night, "the lovin' wife I am,
I've bought a dozen bottles of Bink's Anty-Dandruff Balm.
'Twill make yer hair jest sprout an' curl like squash-vines in the
    sun,
An' I'm propose to sling it on till every drop is done."
That hit old Chewed-ear's funny side, so he lays back an' hol-
    lers:
"The day you raise a hair, old girl, you'll git a thousand dollars."

Now, whether 'twas the prize or not 'tis mighty hard to say,
But Chewed-ear didn't seem to have much comfort from that
    day.

With bottles of that dandruff dope she followed at his heels,
An' sprinkled an' massaged him even when he ate his meals.
She waked him from his beauty sleep with tender, lovin' care,
An' rubbed an' scrubbed assiduous, yet never sign of hair.

Well, naturally all the boys soon tumbled to the joke,
An' at the Wow-wow's Social 'twas Cold-deck Davis spoke:
"The little woman's working mighty hard on Chewed-ear's
     crown;
Let's give her for a three-fifth's share a hundred dollars down.
We stand to make five hundred clear—boys, drink in whiskey
     straight.
'The Chewed-ear Jenkins Hirsute Propagation Syndicate.' "

The boys wuz on, an' soon chipped in the necessary dust;
They primed up a committy to negotiate the deal;
Then Missis Jenkins yielded, bein' rather in disgust,
An' all wuz signed an' witnessed, an' invested with a seal.
They rounded up old Chewed-ear, an' they broke it what they'd
     done;
Allowed they'd bought an interest in his chance of raisin' hair;
They yanked his hat off anxiouslike, opinin' one by one
Their magnifyin' glasses showed fine prospects everywhere.
They bought Hairlene, an' Thatchem, an' Jay's Capillery Juice,
An' Seven Something Sisters, an' Macassar an' Bay Rum,
An' everyone insisted on his speshul right to sluice
His speshul line of lotion onto Chewed-ear's cranium.
They only got the merrier the more the old man roared,
An' shares in "Jenkins Hirsute" went sky-highin' on the board.

The Syndicate wuz hopeful that they'd demonstrate the pay,
An' Missis Jenkins laboured in her perseverin' way.

The boys discussed on "surface rights," an' "out-crops" an' so on,
An' planned to have it "crown" surveyed, an' blue prints of it
    drawn.
They ran a base line, sluiced an' yelled, an' everyone wuz glad,
Except the balance of the property, an' he wuz "mad."
"It gives me pain," he interjects, "to squash yer glowin' dream,
But you wuz fools when you got in on this here 'Hirsute'
    scheme.
You'll never raise a hair on me," when lo! that very night,
Preparin' to retire he got a most onpleasant fright:
For on that shinin' dome of his, so prominently bare,
He felt the baby outcrop of a second growth of hair.

A thousand dollars! Sufferin' Cæsar! Well, it must be saved!
He grabbed his razor recklesslike, an' shaved an' shaved an'
    shaved.
An' when his head was smooth again he gives a mighty sigh,
An' sneaks away, an' buys some Hair Destroyer on the sly.
So there wuz Missis Jenkins with "Restorer" wagin' fight,
An' Chewed-ear with "Destroyer" circumventin' her at night.
The battle wuz a mighty one; his nerves wuz on the strain,
An' yet in spite of all he did that hair began to gain.

The situation grew intense, so quietly one day,
He gave his share-holders the slip, an' made his get-a-way.
Jest like a criminal he skipped, an' aimed to defalcate
The Chewed-ear Jenkins Hirsute Propagation Syndicate.
His guilty secret burned him, an' he sought the city's din:
"I've got to get a wig," sez he, "to cover up my sin.
It's growin', growin' night an' day; it's most amazin' hair";
An' when he looked at it that night, he shuddered with despair.
He shuddered an' suppressed a cry at what his optics seen—
For on my word of honour, boys, that hair wuz growin' *green*.

At first he guessed he'd get some dye, an' try to dye it black;
An' then he saw 'twas Nemmysis wuz layin' on his track.
He must jest face the music, an' confess the thing he done,
An' pay the boys an' Guinneyveer the money they had won.
An' then there came a big idee—it thrilled him like a shock.
Why not control the Syndicate by buyin' up the Stock?

An' so next day he hurried back with smoothly shaven pate,
An' for a hundred dollars he bought up the Syndicate.
'Twas mighty frenzied finance an' the boys set up a roar,
But "Hirsutes" from the market wuz withdrawn for evermore.
An' to this day in Nuggetsville they tell the tale how slick
The Syndicate sold out too soon, and Chewed-ear turned the
    trick.

THE MOTHER

THERE will be a singing in your heart,
There will be a rapture in your eyes;
You will be a woman set apart,
You will be so wonderful and wise.
You will sleep, and when from dreams you start,
As of one that wakes in Paradise,
There will be a singing in your heart,
There will be a rapture in your eyes.

There will be a moaning in your heart,
There will be an anguish in your eyes,
You will see your dearest ones depart,
You will hear their quivering good-byes.
Yours will be the heart-ache and the smart,
Tears that scald and lonely sacrifice;
There will be a moaning in your heart,
There will be an anguish in your eyes.

There will come a glory in your eyes,
There will come a peace within your heart;
Sitting 'neath the quiet evening skies,
Time will dry the tear and dull the smart.
You will know that you have played your part;
Yours shall be the love that never dies:
You, with Heaven's peace within your heart,
You, with God's own glory in your eyes.

THE DREAMER

THE lone man gazed and gazed upon his gold,
His sweat, his blood, the wage of weary days;
But now how sweet, how doubly sweet to hold
All gay and gleamy to the camp-fire blaze.
The evening sky was sinister and cold;
The willows shivered, wanly lay the snow;
The uncommiserating land, so old,
So worn, so grey, so niggard in its woe,
Peered through its ragged shroud. The lone man sighed,
Poured back the gaudy dust into its poke,
Gazed at the seething river listless-eyed,
Loaded his corn-cob pipe as if to smoke;
Then crushed with weariness and hardship crept
Into his ragged robe, and swiftly slept.

.　　.　　.　　.　　.　　.　　.

Hour after hour went by; a shadow slipped
From vasts of shadow to the camp-fire flame;
Gripping a rifle with a deadly aim,
A gaunt and hairy man with wolfish eyes . . .

*　　*　　*　　*　　*　　*　　*

The sleeper dreamed, and lo! this was his dream:
He rode a streaming horse across a moor.
Sudden 'mid pit-black night a lightning gleam
Showed him a way-side inn, forlorn and poor.
A sullen host unbarred the creaking door,
And led him to a dim and dreary room;
Wherein he sat and poked the fire a-roar,

So that weird shadows jigged athwart the gloom.
He ordered wine. 'Od's blood! but he was tired.
What matter! Charles was crushed and George was King,
His party high in power; but he aspired!
Red guineas packed his purse, too tight to ring.
The fire-light gleamed upon his silken hose,
His silver buckles and his powdered wig.
What ho! more wine! He drank, he slowly rose.
What made the shadows dance that madcap jig?
He clutched the candle, steered his way to bed,
And in a trice was sleeping like the dead.

.   .   .   .   .   .

Across the room there crept, so shadow soft,
His sullen host, with naked knife a-gleam,
(A gaunt and hairy man with wolfish eyes.) . . ,
And as he lay, the sleeper dreamed a dream.

*   *   *   *   *   *   *

'Twas in a ruder land, a wilder day.
A rival princeling sat upon his throne,
Within a dungeon, dark and foul he lay,
With chains that bit and festered to the bone.
They haled him harshly to a vaulted room,
Where One gazed on him with malignant eye;
And in that devil-face he read his doom,
Knowing that ere the dawn-light he must die.
Well, he was sorrow-glutted; let them bring
Their prize assassins to the bloody work.
His kingdom lost, yet would he die a King,
Fearless and proud, as when he faced the Turk.
Ah God! the glory of that great Crusade!
The bannered pomp, the gleam, the splendid urge!

The crash of reeking combat, blade to blade!
The reeling ranks, blood-avid and a-surge!
For long he thought; then feeling o'er him creep
Vast weariness, he fell into a sleep.

    .   .   .   .

The cell door opened; soft the headsman came,
Within his hand a mighty axe a-gleam,
(A gaunt and hairy man with wolfish eyes,) . . .
And as he lay, the sleeper dreamed a dream.

    *   *   *   *   *   *   *

'Twas in a land unkempt of life's red dawn;
Where in his sanded cave he dwelt alone;
Sleeping by day, or sometimes worked upon
His flint-head arrows and his knives of stone;
By night stole forth and slew the savage boar,
So that he loomed a hunter of loud fame,
And many a skin of wolf and wild-cat wore,
And counted many a flint-head to his name;
Wherefore he walked the envy of the band,
Hated and feared, but matchless in his skill.
Till lo! one night deep in that shaggy land,
He tracked a yearling bear and made his kill;
Then over-worn he rested by a stream,
And sank into a sleep too deep for dream.

    .   .   .   .

Hunting his food a rival caveman crept
Through those dark woods, and marked him where he lay;
Cowered and crawled upon him as he slept,
Poising a mighty stone aloft to slay—
(A gaunt and hairy man with wolfish eyes.) . . .

    *   *   *   *   *   *   *

The great stone crashed. The Dreamer shrieked and woke,
And saw, fear-blinded, in his dripping cell,
A gaunt and hairy man, who with one stroke
Swung a great axe of steel that flashed and fell . . .

So that he woke amid his bedroom gloom,
And saw, hair-poised, a naked, thirsting knife,
A gaunt and hairy man with eyes of doom—
And then the blade plunged down to drink his life . . .
So that he woke, wrenched back his robe, and looked,
And saw beside his dying fire upstart
A gaunt and hairy man with finger crooked—
A rifle rang, a bullet searched his heart . . .

* * * * * * *

The morning sky was sinister and cold.
Grotesque the Dreamer sprawled, and did not rise.
For long and long there gazed upon some gold
A gaunt and hairy man with wolfish eyes.

AT THIRTY-FIVE

THREE score and ten, the psalmist saith,
And half my course is well-nigh run;
I've had my flout at dusty death,
I've had my whack of feast and fun.
I've mocked at those who prate and preach;
I've laughed with any man alive;
But now with sobered heart I reach
The Great Divide of Thirty-five.

And looking back I must confess
I've little cause to feel elate.
I've played the mummer more or less;
I fumbled fortune, flouted fate.
I've vastly dreamed and little done;
I've idly watched my brothers strive:
Oh, I have loitered in the sun
By primrose paths to Thirty-five!

And those who matched me in the race,
Well, some are out and trampled down;
The others jog with sober pace;
Yet one wins delicate renown.
O midnight feast and famished dawn!
O gay, hard life, with hope alive!
O golden youth, forever gone,
How sweet you seem at Thirty-five!

Each of our lives is just a book
As absolute as Holy Writ;

We humbly read, and may not look
Ahead, nor change one word of it.
And here are joys and here are pains;
And here we fail and here we thrive;
O wondrous volume! what remains
When we reach chapter Thirty-five?

The very best, I dare to hope,
Ere Fate writes Finis to the tome;
A wiser head, a wider scope,
And for the gipsy heart, a home;
A songful home, with loved ones near,
With joy, with sunshine all alive:
Watch me grow younger every year—
Old Age! thy name is Thirty-five!

THE SQUAW MAN

THE cow-moose comes to water, and the beaver's overbold,
The net is in the eddy of the stream;
The teepee stars the vivid sward with russet, red and gold,
And in the velvet gloom the fire's a-gleam.
The night is ripe with quiet, rich with incense of the pine;
From sanctuary lake I hear the loon;
The peaks are bright against the blue, and drenched with sunset
    wine,
And like a silver bubble is the moon.

Cloud-high I climbed but yesterday; a hundred miles around
I looked to see a rival fire a-gleam,
As in a crystal lens it lay, a land without a bound,
All lure, and virgin vastitude, and dream.
The great sky soared exultantly, the great earth bared its breast,
All river-veined and patterned with the pine;
The heedless hordes of caribou were streaming to the West,
A land of lustrous mystery—and mine.

Yea, mine to frame my Odyssey: Oh, little do they know
My conquest and the kingdom that I keep!
The meadows of the musk-ox, where the laughing grasses grow,
The rivers where the careless conies leap.
Beyond the silent Circle, where white men are fierce and few,
I lord it, and I mock at man-made law;
Like a flame upon the water is my little light canoe,
And yonder in the fireglow is my squaw.

A squaw man! yes, that's what I am; sneer at me if you will.
I've gone the grilling pace that cannot last;
With bawdry, bridge and brandy— Oh, I've drunk enough to
    kill
A dozen such as you, but that is past.
I've swung round to my senses, found the place where I belong;
The City made a madman out of me;
But here beyond the Circle, where there's neither right or
    wrong,
I leap from life's strait-jacket, and I'm free.

Yet ever in the far forlorn, by trails of lone desire;
Yet ever in the dawn's white leer of hate;
Yet ever by the dripping kill, beside the drowsy fire,
There comes the fierce heart-hunger for a mate.
There comes the mad blood-clamour for a woman's clinging
    hand,
Love-humid eyes, the velvet of a breast;
And so I sought the Bonnet-plumes, and chose from out the
    band
The girl I thought the sweetest and the best.

O wistful women I have loved before my dark disgrace!
O women fair and rare in my home land!
Dear ladies, if I saw you now I'd turn away my face,
Then crawl to kiss your foot-prints in the sand!
And yet—that day the rifle jammed—a wounded moose at
    bay—
A roar, a charge . . . I faced it with my knife:
A shot from out the willow-scrub, and there the monster
    lay. . . .
Yes, little Laughing Eyes, you saved my life.

The man must have the woman, and we're all brutes more or less,
Since first the male ape shinned the family tree;
And yet I think I love her with a husband's tenderness,
And yet I know that she would die for me.
Oh, if I left you, Laughing Eyes, and nevermore came back,
God help you, girl! I know what you would do. . . .
I see the lake wan in the moon, and from the shadow black,
There drifts a little, *empty* birch canoe.

We're here beyond the Circle, where there's never wrong nor
    right;
We aren't spliced according to the law;
But by the gods I hail you on this hushed and holy night
As the mother of my children, and my squaw.
I see your little slender face set in the firelight glow;
I pray that I may never make it sad;
I hear you croon a baby song, all slumber-soft and low—
God bless you, little Laughing Eyes! I'm glad.

HOME AND LOVE

Just Home and Love! the words are small
Four little letters unto each;
And yet you will not find in all
The wide and gracious range of speech
Two more so tenderly complete:
When angels talk in Heaven above,
I'm sure they have no words more sweet
  Than Home and Love.

Just Home and Love! it's hard to guess
Which of the two were best to gain;
Home without Love is bitterness;
Love without Home is often pain.
No! each alone will seldom do;
Somehow they travel hand and glove:
If you win one you must have two,
  Both Home and Love.

And if you've both, well then I'm sure
You ought to sing the whole day long;
It doesn't matter if you're poor
With these to make divine your song.
And so I praisefully repeat,
When angels talk in Heaven above,
There are no words more simply sweet
  Than Home and Love.

I'M SCARED OF IT ALL

I'M scared of it all, God's truth! so I am;
It's too big and brutal for me.
My nerve's on the raw and I don't give a damn
For all the "hoorah" that I see.
I'm pinned between subway and overhead train,
Where automobillies swoop down:
Oh, I want to go back to the timber again—
I'm scared of the terrible town.

I want to go back to my lean, ashen plains;
My rivers that flash into foam;
My ultimate valleys where solitude reigns;
My trail from Fort Churchill to Nome.
My forests packed full of mysterious gloom,
My ice-fields agrind and aglare:
The city is deadfalled with danger and doom—
I know that I'm safer up there.

I watch the wan faces that flash in the street;
All kinds and all classes I see.
Yet never a one in the million I meet,
Has the smile of a comrade for me.
Just jaded and panting like dogs in a pack;
Just tensed and intent on the goal:
O God! but I'm lonesome— I wish I was back,
Up there in the land of the Pole.

I wish I was back on the Hunger Plateaus,
And seeking the lost caribou;

I wish I was up where the Coppermine flows
To the kick of my little canoe.
I'd like to be far on some weariful shore,
In the Land of the Blizzard and Bear;
Oh, I wish I was snug in the Arctic once more,
For I know I am safer up there!

I prowl in the canyons of dismal unrest;
I cringe—I'm so weak and so small.
I can't get my bearings, I'm crushed and oppressed
With the haste and the waste of it all.
The slaves and the madman, the lust and the sweat,
The fear in the faces I see;
The getting, the spending, the fever, the fret—
It's too bleeding cruel for me.

I feel it's all wrong, but I can't tell you why—
The palace, the hovel next door;
The insolent towers that sprawl to the sky,
The crush and the rush and the roar.
I'm trapped like a fox and I fear for my pelt;
I cower in the crash and the glare;
Oh, I want to be back in the avalanche belt,
For I know that it's safer up there!

I'm scared of it all: Oh, afar I can hear
The voice of my solitudes call!
We're nothing but brute with a little veneer,
And nature is best after all.
There's tumult and terror abroad in the street;
There's menace and doom in the air;
I've got to get back to my thousand-mile beat;
The trail where the cougar and silver-tip meet;

The snows and the camp-fire, with wolves at my feet.
Good-bye, for it's safer up there.

To be forming good habits up there;
To be starving on rabbits up there;
In your hunger and woe,
Though it's sixty below,
Oh, I know that it's safer up there!

A SONG OF SUCCESS

Ho! we were strong, we were swift, we were brave.
Youth was a challenge, and Life was a fight.
All that was best in us gladly we gave,
Sprang from the rally, and leapt for the height.
Smiling is Love in a foam of Spring flowers:
Harden our hearts to him—on let us press!
Oh, what a triumph and pride shall be ours!
See where it beacons, the star of success!

Cares seem to crowd on us—so much to do;
New fields to conquer, and time's on the wing.
Grey hairs are showing, a wrinkle or two;
Somehow our footstep is losing its spring.
Pleasure's forsaken us, Love ceased to smile;
Youth has been funeralled; Age travels fast.
Sometimes we wonder: is it worth while?
There! we have gained to the summit at last.

Aye, we have triumphed! Now must we haste,
Revel in victory . . . why! what is wrong?
Life's choicest vintage is flat to the taste—
Are we too late? Have we laboured too long?
Wealth, power, fame we hold . . . ah! but the truth:
Would we not give this vain glory of ours
For one mad, glad year of glorious youth,
Life in the Springtide, and Love in the flowers.

THE SONG OF THE CAMP-FIRE

I

Heed me, feed me, I am hungry, I am red-tongued with desire;
Boughs of balsam, slabs of cedar, gummy fagots of the pine,
Heap them on me, let me hug them to my eager heart of fire,
Roaring, soaring up to heaven as a symbol and a sign.
Bring me knots of sunny maple, silver birch and tamarack;
Leaping, sweeping, I will lap them with my ardent wings of
    flame;
I will kindle them to glory, I will beat the darkness back;
Streaming, gleaming, I will goad them to my glory and my fame.
Bring me gnarly limbs of live-oak, aid me in my frenzied fight;
Strips of iron-wood, scaly blue-gum, writhing redly in my hold;
With my lunge of lurid lances, with my whips that flail the
    night,
They will burgeon into beauty, they will foliate in gold.
Let me star the dim sierras, stab with light the inland seas;
Roaming wind and roaring darkness! seek no mercy at my
    hands;
I will mock the marly heavens, lamp the purple prairies,
I will flaunt my deathless banners down the far, unhouseled
    lands.
In the vast and vaulted pine-gloom where the pillared forests
    frown,
By the sullen, bestial rivers running where God only knows,
On the starlit coral beaches when the combers thunder down,
In the death-spell of the barrens, in the shudder of the snows;
In a blazing belt of triumph from the palm-leaf to the pine,
As a symbol of defiance lo! the wilderness I span;

And my beacons burn exultant as an everlasting sign
Of unending domination, of the mastery of Man;
I, the Life, the fierce Uplifter, I that weaned him from the mire;
I, the angel and the devil; I, the tyrant and the slave;
I, the Spirit of the Struggle; I, the mighty God of Fire;
I, the Maker and Destroyer; I, the Giver and the Grave.

II

Gather round me, boy and grey-beard, frontiersman of every
    kind.
Few are you, and far and lonely, yet an army forms behind:
By your camp-fires shall they know you, ashes scattered to the
    wind.

Peer into my heart of solace, break your bannock at my blaze;
Smoking, stretched in lazy shelter, build your castles as you
    gaze;
Or, it may be, deep in dreaming, think of dim, unhappy days.

Let my warmth and glow caress you, for your trails are grim and
    hard;
Let my arms of comfort press you, hunger-hewn and battle-
    scarred:
O my lovers! how I bless you with your lives so madly marred!

For you seek the silent spaces, and their secret lore you glean:
For you win the savage races, and the brutish Wild you wean;
And I gladden desert places, where camp-fire has never been.

From the Pole unto the Tropics is there trail ye have not dared?
And because you hold death lightly, so by death shall you be
    spared,
(As the sages of the ages in their pages have declared.)

On the roaring Arkilinik in a leaky bark canoe;
Up the cloud of Mount McKinley, where the avalanche leaps
    through;
In the furnace of Death Valley, when the mirage glimmers blue.

Now a smudge of wiry willows on the weary Kuskoquim;
Now a flare of gummy pine-knots where Vancouver's scaur is
    grim;
Now a gleam of sunny ceiba, when the Cuban beaches dim.

Always, always God's Great Open: lo! I burn with keener light
In the corridors of silence, in the vestibules of night;
'Mid the ferns and grasses gleaming, was there ever gem so
    bright?

Not for weaklings, not for women, like my brother of the
    hearth;
Ring your songs of wrath around me, I was made for manful
    mirth,
In the lusty, gusty greatness, on the bald spots of the earth.

Men, my masters! men, my lovers! ye have fought and ye have
    bled;
Gather round my ruddy embers, softly glowing is my bed;
By my heart of solace dreaming, rest ye and be comforted!

III

I am dying, O my masters! by my fitful flame ye sleep;
    My purple plumes of glory droop forlorn.
Grey ashes choke and cloak me, and above the pines there creep
    The stealthy silver moccasins of morn.
There comes a countless army, it's the Legion of the Light;

It tramps in gleaming triumph round the world;
And before its jewelled lances all the shadows of the night
    Back in to abysmal darknesses are hurled.

Leap to life again, my lovers! ye must toil and never tire;
    The day of daring, doing, brightens clear,
When the bed of spicy cedar and the jovial camp-fire
    Must only be a memory of cheer.
There is hope and golden promise in the vast portentous dawn;
    There is glamour in the glad, effluent sky:
Go and leave me; I will dream of you and love you when you're
      gone;
    I have served you, O my masters! let me die.

A little heap of ashes, grey and sodden by the rain,
    Wind-scattered, blurred and blotted by the snow:
Let that be all to tell of me, and glorious again,
    ' Ye things of greening gladness, leap and glow!
A black scar in the sunshine by the palm-leaf or the pine,
    Blind to the night and dead to all desire;
Yet oh, of life and uplift what a symbol and a sign!
Yet oh, of power and conquest what a destiny is mine!
A little heap of ashes— Yea! a miracle divine,
    The foot-print of a god, all-radiant Fire.

HER LETTER

"I'm taking pen in hand this night, and hard it is for me;
My poor old fingers tremble so, my hand is stiff and slow,
And even with my glasses on I'm troubled sore to see. . . .
You'd little know your mother, boy; you'd little, little know.
You mind how brisk and bright I was, how straight and trim and
      smart;
'Tis weariful I am the now, and bent and frail and grey.
I'm waiting at the road's end, lad; and all that's in my heart,
Is just to see my boy again before I'm called away."

"Oh well I mind the sorry day you crossed the gurly sea;
'Twas like the heart was torn from me, a waeful wife was I.
You said that you'd be home again in two years, maybe three;
But nigh a score of years have gone, and still the years go by.
I know it's cruel hard for you, you've bairnies of your own;
I know the siller's hard to win, and folks have used you ill:
But oh, think of your mother, lad, that's waiting by her lone!
And even if you canna come—*just write and say you will.*"

"Aye, even though there's little hope, just promise that you'll
      try.
It's weary, weary waiting, lad; just say you'll come next year.
I'm thinking there will be no 'next'; I'm thinking soon I'll lie
With all the ones I've laid away . . . but oh, the hope will
      cheer!
You know you're all that's left to me, and we are seas apart;
But if you'll only *say* you'll come, then will I hope and pray.
I'm waiting by the grave-side, lad; and all that's in my heart
Is just to see my boy again before I'm called away."

THE MAN WHO KNEW

THE Dreamer visioned Life as it might be,
And from his dream forthright a picture grew,
A painting all the people thronged to see,
And joyed therein—till came the Man Who Knew,
Saying: " 'Tis bad! Why do ye gape, ye fools!
He painteth not according to the schools."

The Dreamer probed Life's mystery of woe,
And in a book he sought to give the clue;
The people read, and saw that it was so,
And read again—then came the Man Who Knew,
Saying: "Ye witless ones! this book is vile:
It hath not got the rudiments of style."

Love smote the Dreamer's lips, and silver clear
He sang a song so sweet, so tender true,
That all the market-place was thrilled to hear,
And listened rapt—till came the Man Who Knew,
Saying: "His technique's wrong; he singeth ill.
Waste not your time." The singer's voice was still.

And then the people roused as if from sleep,
Crying: "What care we if it be not Art!
Hath he not charmed us, made us laugh and weep?
Come, let us crown him where he sits apart."
Then, with his picture spurned, his book unread,
His song unsung, they found their Dreamer—*dead*.

THE LOGGER

In the moonless, misty night, with my little pipe alight,
  I am sitting by the camp-fire's fading cheer;
Oh, the dew is falling chill on the dim, deer-haunted hill,
  And the breakers in the bay are moaning drear.
The toilful hours are sped, the boys are long abed,
  And I alone a weary vigil keep;
In the sightless, sullen sky I can hear the night-hawk cry,
  And the frogs in frenzied chorus from the creek.

And somehow the embers' glow brings me back the long ago,
  The days of merry laughter and light song;
When I sped the hours away with the gayest of the gay
  In the giddy whirl of fashion's festal throng.
Oh, I ran a grilling race and I little recked the pace,
  For the lust of youth ran riot in my blood;
But at last I made a stand in this God-forsaken land
  Of the pine-tree and the mountain and the flood.

And now I've got to stay, with an overdraft to pay,
  For pleasure in the past with future pain;
And I'm not the chap to whine, for if the chance were mine
  I know I'd choose the old life once again.
With its woman's eyes a-shine, and its flood of golden wine,
  Its fever and its frolic and its fun;
The old life with its din, its laughter and its sin—
  And chuck me in the gutter when it's done.

Ah, well! it's past and gone, and the memory is wan,
  That conjures up each old familiar face;

And here by fortune hurled, I am dead to all the world,
    And I've learned to lose my pride and keep my place.
My ways are hard and rough, and my arms are strong and tough,
    And I hew the dizzy pine till darkness falls;
And sometimes I take a dive, just to keep my heart alive,
    Among the gay saloons and dancing halls.

In the distant, dinful town just a little drink to drown
    The cares that crowd and canker in my brain;
Just a little joy to still set my pulses all a-thrill,
    Then back to brutish labour once again.
And things will go on so until one day I shall know
    That Death has got me cinched beyond a doubt;
Then I'll crawl away from sight, and morosely in the night
    My weary, wasted life will peter out.

Then the boys will gather round, and they'll launch me in the
        ground,
    And pile the stones the timber wolf to foil;
And the moaning pine will wave overhead a nameless grave,
    Where the black snake in the sunshine loves to coil.
And they'll leave me there alone, and perhaps with softened tone
    Speak of me sometimes in the camp-fire's glow,
As a played-out, broken chum, who has gone to Kingdom
        Come,
    And who went the pace in England long ago.

THE PASSING OF THE YEAR

My glass is filled, my pipe is lit,
    My den is all a cosy glow;
And snug before the fire I sit,
    And wait to *feel* the old year go.
I dedicate to solemn thought
    Amid my too-unthinking days,
This sober moment, sadly fraught
    With much of blame, with little praise.

Old Year! upon the Stage of Time
    You stand to bow your last adieu;
A moment, and the prompter's chime
    Will ring the curtain down on you.
Your mien is sad, your step is slow;
    You falter as a Sage in pain;
Yet turn, Old Year, before you go,
    And face your audience again.

That sphinx-like face, remote, austere,
    Let us all read, whate'er the cost:
O Maiden! why that bitter tear?
    Is it for dear one you have lost?
Is it for fond illusion gone?
    For trusted lover proved untrue?
O sweet girl-face, so sad, so wan
    What hath the Old Year meant to you?

And you, O neighbour on my right
    So sleek, so prosperously clad!

What see you in that aged wight
   That makes your smile so gay and glad?
What opportunity unmissed?
   What golden gain, what pride of place?
What splendid hope? O Optimist!
   What read you in that withered face?

And You, deep shrinking in the gloom,
   What find you in that filmy gaze?
What menace of a tragic doom?
   What dark, condemning yesterdays?
What urge to crime, what evil done?
   What cold, confronting shape of fear?
O haggard, haunted, hidden One
   What see you in the dying year?

And so from face to face I flit,
   The countless eyes that stare and stare;
Some are with approbation lit,
   And some are shadowed with despair.
Some show a smile and some a frown;
   Some joy and hope, some pain and woe:
Enough! Oh, ring the curtain down!
   Old weary year! it's time to go.

My pipe is out, my glass is dry;
   My fire is almost ashes too;
But once again, before you go,
   And I prepare to meet the New:
Old Year! a parting word that's true,
   For we've been comrades, you and I—
I thank God for each day of you;
   There! bless you now! Old Year, good-bye!

THE GHOSTS

Smith, great writer of stories, drank; found it immortalised his
    pen;
Fused in his brain-pan, else a blank, heavens of glory now and
    then;
Gave him the magical genius touch; God-given power to gouge
    out, fling
Flat in your face a soul-thought— Bing! Twiddle your heart-
    strings in his clutch.
"Bah!" said Smith, "let my body lie stripped to the buff in swin-
    ish shame,
If I can blaze in the radiant sky out of adoring stars my name.
Sober am I nonentitised; drunk am I more than half a god.
Well, let the flesh be sacrificed; spirit shall speak and shame the
    clod.
Who would not gladly, gladly give Life to do one thing that
    will live?"

Smith had a friend, we'll call him Brown; dearer than brothers
    were those two.
When in the wassail Smith would drown, Brown would rescue
    and pull him through.
When Brown was needful Smith would lend; so it fell as the
    years went by,
Each on the other would depend: then at the last Smith came to
    die.

There Brown sat in the sick man's room, still as a stone in his
    despair;
Smith bent on him his eyes of doom, shook back his lion mane
    of hair;

Said, "Is there one in my chosen line, writer of forthright tales,
 my peer?
Look in that little desk of mine; there is a package, bring it
 here.
Story of stories, gem of all; essence and triumph, key and clue;
Tale of a loving woman's fall; soul swept hell-ward, and God!
 it's true.
I was the man— Oh, yes, I've paid, paid with mighty and mor-
 dant pain.
Look! here's the masterpiece I've made out of my sin, my man-
 hood slain.
Art supreme! yet the world would stare, know my mistress and
 blaze my shame.
I have a wife and daughter—there! take it and thrust it in the
 flame."

Brown answered: "Master, you have dipped pen in your heart,
 your phrases sear.
Ruthless, unflinching, you have stripped naked your soul and
 set it here.
Have I not loved you well and true? See! between us the shad-
 ows drift;
This bit of blood and tears means You— Oh, let me have it, a
 parting gift.
Sacred I'll hold it, a trust divine; sacred your honour, her dark
 despair;
Never shall it see printed line: here, by the living God I swear."
Brown on a Bible laid his hand; Smith, great writer of stories,
 sighed:
"Comrade, I trust you, and understand. Keep my secret!" And
 so he died.

Smith was buried—up soared his sales; lured you his books in
every store;
Exquisite, whimsy, heart-wrung tales; men devoured them and
craved for more.
So when it slyly got about Brown had a posthumous manuscript,
Jones, the publisher, sought him out, into his pocket deep he
dipped.
"A thousand dollars?" Brown shook his head. "The story is not
for sale," he said.

Jones went away, then others came. Tempted and taunted,
Brown was true.
Guarded at friendship's shrine the fame of the unpublished story
grew and grew.
It's a long, long lane that has no end, but some lanes end in the
Potter's field;
Smith to Brown had been more than friend: patron, protector,
spur and shield.
Poor, loving-wistful, dreamy Brown, long and lean, with a smile
askew,
Friendless he wandered up and down, gaunt as a wolf, as hungry
too.
Brown with his lilt of saucy rhyme, Brown with his tilt of tender
mirth
Garretless in the gloom and grime, singing his glad, mad songs
of earth:
So at last with a faith divine, down and down to the Hunger-
line.

There as he stood in a woeful plight, tears a-freeze on his sharp
cheek-bones,
Who should chance to behold his plight, but the publisher, the
plethoric Jones;

Peered at him for a little while, held out a bill: "*Now*, will you
    sell?"
Brown scanned it with his twisted smile: "A thousand dollars!
    you go to hell!"

Brown enrolled in the homeless host, sleeping anywhere, any-
    when;
Suffered, strove, became a ghost, slave of the lamp for other
    men;
For What's-his-name and So-and-so in the abyss his soul he
    stripped,
Yet in his want, his worst of woe, held he fast to the manuscript.
Then one day as he chewed his pen, half in hunger and half
    despair,
Creaked the door of his garret den; Dick, his brother, was stand-
    ing there.
Down on the pallet bed he sank, ashen his face, his voice a wail:
"Save me, brother! I've robbed the bank; to-morrow it's ruin,
    capture, gaol.
Yet there's a chance: I could to-day pay back the money, save
    our name;
You have a manuscript, they say, worth a thousand—think,
    man! the shame. . . ."
Brown with his heart pain-pierced the while, with his stern,
    starved face, and his lips stone-pale,
Shuddered and smiled his twisted smile: "Brother, I guess you
    go to gaol."

While poor Brown in the leer of dawn wrestled with God for
    the sacred fire,
Came there a woman weak and wan, out of the mob, the murk,
    the mire;
Frail as a reed, a fellow ghost, weary with woe, with sorrowing;

Two pale souls in the legion lost; lo! Love bent with a tender
   wing,
Taught them a joy so deep, so true, it seemed that the whole-
   world fabric shook,
Thrilled and dissolved in radiant dew; then Brown made him
   a golden book,
Full of the faith that Life is good, that the earth is a dream di-
   vinely fair,
Lauding his gem of womanhood in many a lyric rich and rare;
Took it to Jones, who shook his head: "I will consider it," he
   said.

While he considered, Brown's wife lay clutched in the tentacles
   of pain;
Then came the doctor, grave and grey; spoke of decline, of
   nervous strain;
Hinted Egypt, the South of France—Brown with terror was
   tiger-gripped.
Where was the money? What the chance? Pitiful God! . . .
   the manuscript!
A thousand dollars! his only hope! he gazed and gazed at the
   garret wall. . . .
Reached at last for the envelope, turned to his wife and told her
   all.
Told of his friend, his promise true; told like his very heart
   would break:
"Oh, my dearest! what shall I do? shall I not sell it for your
   sake?"
Ghostlike she lay, as still as doom; turned to the wall her weary
   head;
Icy-cold in the pallid gloom, silent as death . . . at last she said:
"Do! my husband? Keep your vow! Guard his secret and let me
   die. . . .

Oh, my dear, I must tell you now—*the woman he loved and wronged was I;*

Darling! I haven't long to live: I never told you—forgive, forgive!"

For a long, long time Brown did not speak; sat bleak-browed in the wretched room;

Slowly a tear stole down his cheek, and he kissed her hand in the dismal gloom.

To break his oath, to brand her shame; his well-loved friend, his worshipped wife;

To keep his vow, to save her name, yet at the cost of what? Her life!

A moment's space did he hesitate, a moment of pain and dread and doubt,

Then he broke the seals, and, stern as fate, unfolded the sheets and spread them out. . . .

On his knees by her side he limply sank, peering amazed—*each page was blank.*

(For oh, the supremest of our art are the stories we do not dare to tell,

Locked in the silence of the heart, for the awful records of Heav'n and Hell.)

Yet those two in the silence there, seemed less weariful than before.

Hark! a step on the garret stair, a postman knocks at the flimsy door.

"Registered letter!" Brown thrills with fear; opens, and reads, then bends above:

"Glorious tidings! Egypt, dear! The book is accepted—life and love."

GOOD-BYE, LITTLE CABIN

O DEAR little cabin, I've loved you so long,
And now I must bid you good-bye!
I've filled you with laughter, I've thrilled you with song
And sometimes I've wished I could cry.
Your walls they have witnessed a weariful fight,
And rung to a won Waterloo:
But oh, in my triumph I'm dreary to-night—
Good-bye, little cabin, to you!

Your roof is bewhiskered, your floor is a-slant,
Your walls seem to sag and to swing;
I'm trying to find just your faults, but I can't—
You poor, tired, heart-broken old thing!
I've seen when you've been the best friend that I had
Your light like a gem on the snow;
You're sort of a part of me— Gee! but I'm sad;
I hate, little cabin, to go.

Below your cracked window red raspberries climb;
A hornet's nest hangs from a beam;
Your rafters are scribbled with adage and rhyme,
And dimmed with tobacco and dream.
"Each day has its laugh," and "Don't worry, just work."
Such mottoes reproachfully shine.
Old calendars dangle—what memories lurk
About you, dear cabin of mine!

I hear the world-call and the clang of the fight;
I hear the hoarse cry of my kind;

Yet well do I know, as I quit you to-night,
It's Youth that I'm leaving behind.
And often I'll think of you, empty and black,
Moose antlers nailed over your door:
Oh, if I should perish my ghost will come back
To dwell in you, cabin, once more!

How cold, still and lonely, how weary you seem!
A last wistful look and I'll go.
Oh, will you remember the lad with his dream!
The lad that you comforted so.
The shadows enfold you, it's drawing to-night;
The evening star needles the sky:
And huh! but it's stinging and stabbing my sight—
God bless you, old cabin, good-bye!

HEART O' THE NORTH

AND when I come to the dim trail-end,
　　I who have been Life's rover,
This is all I would ask, my friend,
　　Over and over and over:

A little space on a stony hill
　　With never another near me,
Sky o' the North that's vast and still,
　　With a single star to cheer me;

Star that gleams on a moss-grey stone
　　Graven by those who love me—
There would I lie alone, alone,
　　With a single pine above me;

Pine that the north wind whinnys through—
　　Oh, I have been Life's lover!
But there I'd lie and listen to
　　Eternity passing over.

THE SCRIBE'S PRAYER

When from my fumbling hand the tired pen falls,
And in the twilight weary droops my head;
While to my quiet heart a still voice calls,
Calls me to join my kindred of the Dead:
Grant that I may, O Lord, ere rest be mine,
Write to Thy praise one radiant, ringing line.

For all of worth that in this clay abides,
The leaping rapture and the ardent flame,
The hope, the high resolve, the faith that guides:
All, all is Thine, and liveth in Thy name:
Lord, have I dallied with the sacred fire!
Lord, have I trailed Thy glory in the mire!

E'en as a toper from the dram-shop reeling,
Sees in his garret's blackness, dazzling fair,
All that he might have been, and, heart-sick, kneeling,
Sobs in the passion of a vast despair:
So my ideal self haunts me alway—
When the accounting comes, how shall I pay?

For in the dark I grope, nor understand;
And in my heart fight selfishness and sin:
Yet, Lord, I do not seek Thy helping hand;
Rather let me my own salvation win:
Let me through strife and penitential pain
Onward and upward to the heights attain.

Yea, let me live my life, its meaning seek;
Bear myself fitly in the ringing fight;
Strive to be strong that I may aid the weak;
Dare to be true— O God! the Light, the Light!
Cometh the Dark so soon. I've mocked Thy Word;
Yet do I know Thy Love: have mercy, Lord. . . .

Book Four

RHYMES OF A RED CROSS MAN

FOREWORD

I've tinkered at my bits of rhymes
In weary, woeful, waiting times;
In doleful hours of battle-din,
Ere yet they brought the wounded in;
Through vigils of the fateful night,
In lousy barns by candle-light;
In dug-outs, sagging and aflood,
On stretchers stiff and bleared with blood;
By ragged grove, by ruined road,
By hearths accurst where Love abode;
By broken altars, blackened shrines
I've tinkered at my bits of rhymes.

I've solaced me with scraps of song
The desolated ways along:
Through sickly fields all shrapnel-sown,
And meadows reaped by death alone;
By blazing cross and splintered spire,
By headless Virgin in the mire;
By gardens gashed amid their bloom,
By gutted grave, by shattered tomb;
Beside the dying and the dead,
Where rocket green and rocket red,
In trembling pools of poising light,
With flowers of flame festoon the night.
Ah me! by what dark ways of wrong
I've cheered my heart with scraps of song.

So here's my sheaf of war-won verse,
And some is bad, and some is worse.
And if at times I curse a bit,
You needn't read that part of it;
For through it all like horror runs
The red resentment of the guns.
And you yourself would mutter when
You took the things that once were men
And sped them through that zone of hate
To where the dripping surgeons wait;
And wonder too if in God's sight
War ever, ever can be right.

Yet may it not be, crime and war
But effort misdirected are?
And if there's good in war and crime,
There may be in my bits of rhyme,
My songs from out the slaughter mill:
So take or leave them as you will.

THE CALL

(France, August first, 1914)

FAR and near, high and clear,
  Hark to the call of War!
Over the gorse and the golden dells,
Ringing and swinging of clamorous bells,
Praying and saying of wild farewells:
  War! War! War!

High and low, all must go:
  Hark to the shout of War!
Leave to the women the harvest yield;
Gird ye, men, for the sinister field;
A sabre instead of a scythe to wield:
  War! Red War!

Rich and poor, lord and boor,
  Hark to the blast of War!
Tinker and tailor and millionaire,
Actor in triumph and priest in prayer,
Comrades now in the hell out there,
  Sweep to the fire of War!

Prince and page, sot and sage,
  Hark to the roar of War!
Poet, professor and circus clown,
Chimney-sweeper and fop o' the town,
Into the pot and be melted down:
  Into the pot of War!

Women all, hear the call,
 The pitiless call of War!
Look your last on your dearest ones,
Brothers and husbands, fathers, sons:
Swift they go to the ravenous guns,
 The gluttonous guns of War.

 Everywhere thrill the air
 The maniac bells of War.
There will be little of sleeping to-night;
There will be wailing and weeping to-night;
Death's red sickle is reaping to-night:
 War! War! War!

THE FOOL

"BUT it isn't playing the game," he said,
And he slammed his books away;
"The Latin and Greek I've got in my head
Will do for a duller day."
"Rubbish!" I cried; "The bugle's call
Isn't for lads from school."
D'ye think he'd listen? Oh, not at all:
So I called him a fool, a fool.

Now there's his dog by his empty bed,
And the flute he used to play,
And his favourite bat . . . but Dick he's dead,
Somewhere in France, they say:
Dick with his rapture of song and sun,
Dick of the yellow hair,
Dicky whose life had but begun,
Carrion-cold out there.

Look at his prizes all in a row:
Surely a hint of fame.
Now he's finished with,—nothing to show:
Doesn't it seem a shame?
Look from the window! All you see
Was to be his one day:
Forest and furrow, lawn and lea,
And he goes and chucks it away.

Chucks it away to die in the dark:
Somebody saw him fall,

Part of him mud, part of him blood,
The rest of him—not at all.
And yet I'll bet he was never afraid,
And he went as the best of 'em go,
For his hand was clenched on his broken blade,
And his face was turned to the foe.

And I called him a fool . . . oh, how blind was I!
And the cup of my grief's abrim.
Will Glory o' England ever die
So long as we've lads like him?
So long as we've fond and fearless fools,
Who, spurning fortune and fame,
Turn out with the rallying cry of their schools,
Just bent on playing the game.

A fool! Ah no! He was more than wise.
His was the proudest part.
He died with the glory of faith in his eyes,
And the glory of love in his heart.
And though there's never a grave to tell,
Nor a cross to mark his fall,
Thank God! we know that he "batted well"
In the last great Game of all.

THE VOLUNTEER

Sᴇᴢ I: My Country calls? Well, let it call.
I grins perlitely and declines wiv thanks.
Go, let 'em plaster every blighted wall,
'Ere's *one* they don't stampede into the ranks.
Them politicians with their greasy ways;
Them empire-grabbers—fight for 'em? No fear!
I've seen this mess a-comin' from the days
Of Algyserious and Aggydear:

    I've felt me passion rise and swell,
    But . . . wot the 'ell, Bill? Wot the 'ell?

Sez I: My Country? Mine? I likes their cheek.
Me mud-bespattered by the cars they drive,
Wot makes my measly thirty bob a week,
And sweats red blood to keep meself alive!
Fight for the right to slave that they may spend,
Them in their mansions, me 'ere in my slum?
No, let 'em fight wot's something to defend:
But me, I've nothin'—let the Kaiser come.

    And so I cusses 'ard and well,
    But . . . wot the 'ell, Bill? Wot the 'ell?

Sez I: If they would do the decent thing,
And shield the missis and the little 'uns,
Why, even *I* might shout "God save the King,"
And face the chances of them 'ungry guns.
But we've got three, another on the way;
It's that wot makes me snarl and set me jor:

The wife and nippers, wot of 'em, I say,
If I gets knocked out in this blasted war?
　　Gets proper busted by a shell,
　　But . . . wot the 'ell, Bill? Wot the 'ell?

Ay, wot the 'ell's the use of all this talk?
To-day some boys in blue was passin' me,
And some of 'em they 'ad no legs to walk,
And some of 'em they 'ad no eyes to see.
And—well, I couldn't look 'em in the face,
And so I'm goin', goin' to declare
I'm under forty-one and take me place
To face the music with the bunch out there.
　　A fool, you say! Maybe you're right.
　　I'll 'ave no peace unless I fight.
　　I've ceased to think; I only know
　　I've gotta go, Bill, gotta go.

THE CONVALESCENT

. . . So I walked among the willows very quietly all night;
There was no moon at all, at all; no timid star alight;
There was no light at all, at all; I wint from tree to tree,
And I called him as his mother called, but he nivver answered me.

Oh I called him all the night-time, as I walked the wood alone;
And I listened and I listened, but I nivver heard a moan;
Then I found him at the dawnin', when the sorry sky was red:
I was lookin' for the livin', but I only found the dead.

Sure I know that it was Shamus by the silver cross he wore;
But the bugles they were callin', and I heard the cannon roar.
Oh I had no time to tarry, so I said a little prayer,
And I clasped his hands together, and I left him lyin' there.

Now the birds are singin', singin', and I'm home in Donegal,
And it's Springtime, and I'm thinkin' that I only dreamed it all;
I dreamed about that evil wood, all crowded with its dead,
Where I knelt beside me brother when the battle-dawn was red.

Where I prayed beside me brother ere I wint to fight anew:
Such dreams as these are evil dreams; I can't believe it's true.
Where all is love and laughter, sure it's hard to think of loss . . .
But mother's sayin' nothin', and she clasps—*a silver cross*.

THE MAN FROM ATHABASKA

Oh the wife she tried to tell me that 'twas nothing but the
    thrumming
Of a wood-pecker a-rapping on the hollow of a tree;
And she thought that I was fooling when I said it was the
    drumming
Of the mustering of legions, and 'twas calling unto me;
'Twas calling me to pull my freight and hop across the sea.

And a-mending of my fish-nets sure I started up in wonder,
For I heard a savage roaring and 'twas coming from afar;
Oh the wife she tried to tell me that 'twas only summer thunder,
And she laughed a bit sarcastic when I told her it was War;
'Twas the chariots of battle where the mighty armies are.

Then down the lake came Half-breed Tom with russet sail
    a-flying,
And the word he said was "War" again, so what was I to do?
Oh the dogs they took to howling, and the missis took to crying,
As I flung my silver foxes in the little birch canoe:
Yes, the old girl stood a-blubbing till an island hid the view.

Says the factor: "Mike, you're crazy! They have soldier men
    a-plenty.
You're as grizzled as a badger, and you're sixty year or so."
"But I haven't missed a scrap," says I, "since I was one and
    twenty.
And shall I miss the biggest? You can bet your whiskers—no!"
So I sold my furs and started . . . and that's eighteen months
    ago.

For I joined the Foreign Legion, and they put me for a starter
In the trenches of the Argonne with the Boche a step away;
And the partner on my right hand was an *apache* from
    Montmartre;
On my left there was a millionaire from Pittsburgh, U. S. A.
(Poor fellow! They collected him in bits the other day.)

But I'm sprier than a chipmunk, save a touch of the lumbago,
And they calls me Old Methoosalah, and *blagues* me all the day.
I'm their exhibition sniper, and they work me like a Dago,
And laugh to see me plug a Boche a half a mile away.
Oh I hold the highest record in the regiment, they say.

And at night they gather round me, and I tell them of my
    roaming
In the Country of the Crepuscule beside the Frozen Sea,
Where the musk-ox runs unchallenged, and the cariboo goes
    homing;
And they sit like little children, just as quiet as can be:
Men of every crime and colour, how they harken unto me!

And I tell them of the Furland, of the tumpline and the paddle,
Of secret rivers loitering, that no one will explore;
And I tell them of the ranges, of the pack-strap and the saddle,
And they fill their pipes in silence, and their eyes beseech for
    more;
While above the star-shells fizzle and the high explosives roar.

And I tell of lakes fish-haunted, where the big bull moose are
    calling,
And forests still as sepulchres with never trail or track;
And valleys packed with purple gloom, and mountain peaks
    appalling,

And I tell them of my cabin on the shore at Fond du Lac;
And I find myself a-thinking: Sure I wish that I was back.

So I brag of bear and beaver while the batteries are roaring,
And the fellows on the firing steps are blazing at the foe;
And I yarn of fur and feather when the *marmites* are a-soaring,
And they listen to my stories, seven *poilus* in a row,
Seven lean and lousy *poilus* with their cigarettes aglow.

And I tell them when it's over how I'll hike for Athabaska;
And those seven greasy *poilus* they are crazy to go too.
And I'll give the wife the "pickle-tub" I promised, and I'll ask
    her
The price of mink and marten, and the run of cariboo,
And I'll get my traps in order, and I'll start to work anew.

For I've had my fill of fighting, and I've seen a nation scattered,
And an army swung to slaughter, and a river red with gore,
And a city all a-smoulder, and . . . as if it really mattered,
For the lake is yonder dreaming, and my cabin's on the shore;
And the dogs are leaping madly, and the wife is singing gladly,
And I'll rest in Athabaska, and I'll leave it nevermore.

THE RED RETREAT

Tramp, tramp, the grim road, the road from Mons to Wipers
(I've 'ammered out this ditty with me bruised and bleedin' feet);
Tramp, tramp, the dim road—we didn't 'ave no pipers,
And bellies that was 'oller was the drums we 'ad to beat.
Tramp, tramp, the bad road, the bits o' kiddies cryin' there,
The fell birds a-flyin' there, the 'ouses all aflame;
Tramp, tramp, the sad road, the pals I left a-lyin' there,
Red there, and dead there. . . . Oh, blimy, it's a shame!

A-singin' " 'Oo's Yer Lady Friend?" we started out from 'Arver,
A-singin' till our froats was dry—we didn't care a 'ang;
The Frenchies 'ow they lined the way, and slung us their palaver,
And all we knowed to arnser was the one word "vang";
They gave us booze and caporal, and cheered for us like crazy,
And all the pretty gels was out to kiss us as we passed;
And 'ow they all went dotty when we 'owled the Marcelaisey!
Oh, Gawd! Them was the 'appy days, the days too good to last.

We started out for God Knows Where, we started out a-roarin';
We 'ollered: " 'Ere We Are Again," and 'struth! but we was
    dry.
The dust was gummin' up our ears, and 'ow the sweat was
    pourin';
The road was long, the sun was like a brazier in the sky.
We wondered where the 'Uns was—we wasn't long a-
    wonderin',
For down a scruff of 'ill-side they rushes like a flood;
Then oh! 'twas music 'eavenly, our batteries a-thunderin',
And arms and legs went soarin' in the fountain of their blood.

For on they came like bee-swarms, a-hochin' and a-singin';
We pumped the bullets into 'em, we couldn't miss a shot.
But though we mowed 'em down like grass, like grass was they
    a-springin',
And all our 'ands was blistered, for our rifles was so 'ot.
We roared with battle-fury, and we lammed the stuffin' out
    of 'em,
And then we fixed our bay'nets and we spitted 'em like meat.
You should 'ave 'eard the beggars squeal; you should 'ave seen
    the rout of 'em,
And 'ow we cussed and wondered when the word came:
    Retreat!

Retreat! That was the 'ell of it. It fair upset our 'abits,
A-runnin' from them blighters over 'alf the roads of France;
A-scurryin' before 'em like a lot of blurry rabbits,
And knowin' we could smash 'em if we just 'ad 'alf a chance.
Retreat! That was the bitter bit, a-limpin' and a-blunderin';
All day and night a-hoofin' it and sleepin' on our feet;
A-fightin' rear guard actions for a bit o' rest, and wonderin'
If sugar beets or mangels was the 'olesomest to eat.

Ho yus, there isn't many left that started out so cheerily;
There was no bands a-playin' and we 'ad no autmobeels.
Our tummies they was 'oller, and our 'eads was 'angin' wearily,
And if we stopped to light a fag the 'Uns was on our 'eels.
That rotten road! I can't forget the kids and mothers flyin' there,
The bits of barns a-blazin' and the 'orrid sights I sor;
The stiffs that lined the wayside, me own pals a-lyin' there,
Their faces covered over wiv a little 'eap of stror.

Tramp, tramp, the red road, the wicked bullets 'ummin'
(I've panted out this ditty with me 'ot 'ard breath).

Tramp, tramp, the dread road, the Boches all a-comin',
The lootin' and the shootin' and the shrieks o' death.
Tramp, tramp, the fell road, the mad 'orde pursuin' there,
And 'ow we 'urled it back again, them grim, grey waves;
Tramp, tramp, the 'ell road, the 'orror and the ruin there,
The graves of me mateys there, the grim, sour graves.

THE HAGGIS OF PRIVATE McPHEE

"Hae ye heard whit ma auld mither's postit tae me?
It fair maks me hamesick," says Private McPhee.
"And whit did she send ye?" says Private McPhun,
As he cockit his rifle and bleezed at a Hun.
"A haggis! A *Haggis!*" says Private McPhee;
"The brawest big haggis I ever did see.
And think! it's the morn when fond memory turns
Tae haggis and whuskey—the Birthday o' Burns.
We maun find a dram; then we'll ca' in the rest
O' the lads, and we'll hae a Burns' Nicht wi' the best."

"Be ready at sundoon," snapped Sergeant McCole;
"I want you two men for the List'nin' Patrol."
Then Private McPhee looked at Private McPhun:
"I'm thinkin', ma lad, we're confoundedly done."
Then Private McPhun looked at Private McPhee:
"I'm thinkin' auld chap, it's a' aff wi' oor spree."
But up spoke their crony, wee Wullie McNair:
"Jist lea' yer braw haggis for me tae prepare;
And as for the dram, if I search the camp roun',
We maun hae a drappie tae jist haud it doon.
Sae rin, lads, and think, though the nicht it be black,
O' the haggis that's waitin' ye when ye get back."

My! but it wis waesome on Naebuddy's Land,
And the deid they were rottin' on every hand.
And the rockets like corpse candles hauntit the sky,
And the winds o' destruction went shudderin' by.

There wis skelpin' o' bullets and skirlin' o' shells,
And breengin' o' bombs and a thoosand death-knells;
But cooryin' doon in a Jack Johnson hole
Little fashed the twa men o' the List'nin' Patrol.
For sweeter than honey and bricht as a gem
Wis the thocht o' the haggis that waitit for them.

Yet alas! in oor moments o' sunniest cheer
Calamity's aften maist cruelly near.
And while the twa talked o' their puddin' divine
The Boches below them were howkin' a mine.
And while the twa cracked o' the feast they would hae,
The fuse it wis burnin' and burnin' away.
Then sudden a roar like the thunner o' doom,
A hell-leap o' flame . . . then the wheesht o' the tomb.

"Haw, Jock! Are ye hurtit?" says Private McPhun.
"Ay, Geordie, they've got me; I'm fearin' I'm done.
It's ma leg; I'm jist thinkin' it's aff at the knee;
Ye'd best gang and leave me," says Private McPhee.
"Oh leave ye I wunna," says Private McPhun;
"And leave ye I canna, for though I micht run,
It's no faur I wud gang, it's no muckle I'd see:
I'm blindit, and that's whit's the maitter wi' me."
Then Private McPhee sadly shakit his heid:
"If we bide here for lang, we'll be bidin' for deid.
And yet, Geordie lad, I could gang weel content
If I'd tasted that haggis ma auld mither sent."
"That's droll," says McPhun; "ye've jist speakit ma mind.
Oh I ken it's a terrible thing tae be blind;
And yet it's no that that embitters ma lot—
It's missin' that braw muckle haggis ye've got."
For a while they were silent; then up once again

Spoke Private McPhee, though he whussilt wi' pain:
"And why should we miss it? Between you and me
We've legs for tae run, and we've eyes for tae see.
You lend me your shanks and I'll lend you ma sicht,
And we'll baith hae a kyte-fu' o' haggis the nicht."

Oh the sky it wis dourlike and dreepin' a wee,
When Private McPhun gruppit Private McPhee.
Oh the glaur it wis fylin' and crieshin' the grun',
When Private McPhee guidit Private McPhun.
"Keep clear o' them corpses—they're maybe no deid!
Haud on! There's a big muckle crater aheid.
Look oot! There's a sap; we'll be haein' a coup.
A staur-shell! For Godsake! Doun, lad, on yer daup.
Bear aff tae yer richt. . . . Aw yer jist daein' fine:
Before the nicht's feenished on haggis we'll dine."

There wis death and destruction on every hand;
There wis havoc and horror on Naebuddy's Land.
And the shells bickered doun wi' a crump and a glare,
And the hameless wee bullets were dingin' the air.
Yet on they went staggerin', cooryin' doun
When the stutter and cluck o' a Maxim crept roun'.
And the legs o' McPhun they were sturdy and stoot,
And McPhee on his back kept a bonnie look-oot.
"On, on, ma brave lad! We're no faur frae the goal;
I can hear the braw sweerin' o' Sergeant McCole."

But strength has its leemit, and Private McPhun,
Wi' a sab and a curse fell his length on the grun'.
Then Private McPhee shoutit doon in his ear:
"Jist think o' the haggis! I smell it from here.
It's gushin' wi' juice, it's embaumin' the air;

It's steamin' for us, and we're—jist—aboot—there."
Then Private McPhun answers: "Dommit, auld chap!
For the sake o' that haggis I'll gang till I drap."
And he gets on his feet wi' a heave and a strain,
And onward he staggers in passion and pain.
And the flare and the glare and the fury increase,
Till you'd think they'd jist taken a' hell on a lease.
And on they go reelin' in peetifu' plight,
And someone is shoutin' away on their right;
And someone is runnin', and noo they can hear
A sound like a prayer and a sound like a cheer;
And swift through the crash and the flash and the din,
The lads o' the Hielands are bringin' them in.

"They're baith sairly woundit, but is it no droll
Hoo they rave aboot haggis?" says Sergeant McCole.
When hirplin alang comes wee Wullie McNair,
And they a' wonnert why he wis greetin' sae sair.
And he says: "I'd jist liftit it oot o' the pot,
And there it lay steamin' and savoury hot,
When sudden I dooked at the fleech o' a shell,
And it—*drapped on the haggis and dinged it tae hell.*"

And oh but the lads were fair taken aback;
Then sudden the order wis passed tae attack,
And up from the trenches like lions they leapt,
And on through the nicht like a torrent they swept.
On, on, wi' their bayonets thirstin' before!
On, on tae the foe wi' a rush and a roar!
And wild to the welkin their battle-cry rang,
And doon on the Boches like tigers they sprang:
And there wisna a man but had death in his ee,
For he thocht o' the haggis o' Private McPhee.

THE LARK

FROM wrath-red dawn to wrath-red dawn,
The guns have brayed without abate;
And now the sick sun looks upon
The bleared, blood-boltered fields of hate
As if it loathed to rise again.
How strange the hush! Yet sudden, hark!
From yon down-trodden gold of grain,
The leaping rapture of a lark.

A fusillade of melody,
That sprays us from yon trench of sky;
A new amazing enemy
We cannot silence though we try;
A battery on radiant wings,
That from yon gap of golden fleece
Hurls at us hopes of such strange things
As joy and home and love and peace.

Pure heart of song! do you not know
That we are making earth a hell?
Or is it that you try to show
Life still is joy and all is well?
Brave little wings! Ah, not in vain
You beat into that bit of blue:
Lo! we who pant in war's red rain
Lift shining eyes, see Heaven too.

THE ODYSSEY OF 'ERBERT 'IGGINS

ME and Ed and a stretcher
Out on the nootral ground.
(If there's one dead corpse, I'll betcher
There's a 'undred smellin' around.)
Me and Eddie O'Brian,
Both of the R. A. M. C.
"It's a 'ell of a night
For a soul to take flight,"
As Eddie remarks to me.
Me and Ed crawlin' 'omeward,
Thinkin' our job is done,
When sudden and clear,
Wot do we 'ear:
'Owl of a wounded 'Un.

"Got to take 'im," snaps Eddie;
"Got to take all we can.
'E may be a Germ
Wiv the 'eart of a worm,
But, blarst 'im! ain't 'e a man?"
So 'e sloshes out fixin' a dressin'
('E'd always a medical knack),
When that wounded 'Un
'E rolls to 'is gun,
And 'e plugs me pal in the back.

Now what would you do? I arst you.
There was me slaughtered mate.
There was that 'Un

311

(I'd collered 'is gun),
A-snarlin' 'is 'ymn of 'ate.
Wot did I do? 'Ere, whisper . . .
'E'd a shiny bald top to 'is 'ead,
But when I got through,
Between me and you,
It was 'orrid and jaggy and red.

" 'Ang on like a limpet, Eddie.
Thank Gord! you ain't dead after all."
It's slow and it's sure and it's steady
(Which is 'ard, for 'e's big and I'm small).
The rockets are shootin' and shinin',
It's rainin' a perishin' flood,
The bullets are buzzin' and whinin',
And I'm up to me stern in the mud.
There's all kinds of 'owlin' and 'ootin';
It's black as a bucket of tar;
Oh, I'm doin' my bit,
But I'm 'avin' a fit,
And I wish I was 'ome wiv Mar.

"Stick on like a plaster, Eddie.
Old sport, you're a-slackin' your grip."
Gord! But I'm crocky already;
My feet, 'ow they slither and slip!
There goes the biff of a bullet.
The Boches have got us for fair.
Another one—*Whut!*
The son of a slut!
'E managed to miss by a 'air.
'Ow! Wot was it jabbed at me shoulder?
Gave it a dooce of a wrench.

Is it Eddie or me
Wot's a-bleedin' so free?
Crust! but it's long to the trench.
I ain't just as strong as a Sandow,
And Ed ain't a flapper by far;
I'm blamed if I understand 'ow
We've managed to get where we are.
But 'ere's for a bit of a breather.
"Steady there, Ed, 'arf a mo'.
Old pal, it's all right;
It's a 'ell of a fight,
But are we down-'earted? No-o-o."
Now war is a funny thing, ain't it?
It's the rummiest sort of a go.
For when it's most real,
It's then that you feel
You're a-watchin' a cinema show.
'Ere's me wot's a barber's assistant.
Hey, presto! It's somewheres in France,
And I'm 'ere in a pit
Where a coal-box 'as 'it,
And it's all like a giddy romance.
The ruddy quick-firers are spittin',
The 'eavies are bellowin' 'ate,
And 'ere I am cashooly sittin',
And 'oldin' the 'ead of me mate.
Them gharstly green star-shells is beamin',
'Ot shrapnel is poppin' like rain,
And I'm sayin': "Bert 'Iggins, you're dreamin',
And you'll wake up in 'Ampstead again.
You'll wake up and 'ear yourself sayin':
'Would you like, sir, to 'ave a shampoo?'
'Stead of sheddin' yer blood

In the rain and the mud,
Which is some'ow the right thing to do;
Which is some'ow yer 'oary-eyed dooty,
Wot you're doin' the best wot you can,
For 'Ampstead and 'ome and beauty,
And you've been and you've slaughtered a man.
A feller wot punctured your partner;
Oh, you 'ammered 'im 'ard on the 'ead,
And you still see 'is eyes
Starin' bang at the skies,
And you ain't even sorry 'e's dead.
But you wish you was back in your diggin's
Asleep on your mouldy old stror.
Oh, you're doin' yer bit, 'Erbert 'Iggins,
But you ain't just enjoyin' the war."

" 'Ang on like a hoctopus, Eddie.
It's us for the bomb-belt again.
Except for the shrap
Which 'as 'it me a tap,
I'm feelin' as right as the rain.
It's my silly old feet wot are slippin',
It's as dark as a 'ogs'ead o' sin,
But don't be oneasy, my pippin,
I'm goin' to pilot you in.
It's my silly old 'ead wot is reelin'.
The bullets is buzzin' like bees.
Me shoulder's red-'ot,
And I'm bleedin' a lot,
And me legs is on'inged at the knees.
But we're staggerin' nearer and nearer.
Just stick it, old sport, play the game.
I make 'em out clearer and clearer,

Our trenches a-snappin' with flame.
Oh, we're stumblin' closer and closer.
'Ang on there, lad! Just one more try.
Did you say: Put you down? Damn it, no, sir!
I'll carry you in if I die.
By cracky! old feller, they've seen us.
They're sendin' out stretchers for two.
Let's give 'em the hoorah between us
('Anged lucky we aren't booked through).
My flipper is mashed to a jelly.
A bullet 'as tickled your spleen.
We've shed lots of gore
And we're leakin' some more,
But—wot a hoccasion it's been!
Ho! 'Ere comes the rescuin' party.
They're crawlin' out cautious and slow.
Come! Buck up and greet 'em, my 'earty,
Shoulder to shoulder—so.
They mustn't think we was down-'earted.
Old pal, we was never down-'earted.
If they arsts us if we was down-'earted
We'll 'owl in their fyces: 'No-o-o!' "

A SONG OF WINTER WEATHER

It isn't the foe that we fear;
It isn't the bullets that whine;
It isn't the business career
Of a shell, or the bust of a mine;
It isn't the snipers who seek
To nip our young hopes in the bud:
No, it isn't the guns,
And it isn't the Huns—
It's the *mud*,
       mud,
            mud.

     It isn't the *mêlée* we mind.
     That often is rather good fun.
     It isn't the shrapnel we find
     Obtrusive when rained by the ton;
     It isn't the bounce of the bombs
     That gives us a positive pain:
     It's the strafing we get
     When the weather is wet—
     It's the *rain*,
            rain,
                rain.

It isn't because we lack grit
We shrink from the horrors of war.
We don't mind the battle a bit;
In fact that is what we are for;
It isn't the rum-jars and things

Make us wish we were back in the fold:
It's the fingers that freeze
In the boreal breeze—
It's the *cold*,
      cold,
         cold.

Oh, the rain, the mud, and the cold,
The cold, the mud, and the rain;
With weather at zero it's hard for a hero
From language that's rude to refrain.
With porridgy muck to the knees,
With sky that's a-pouring a flood,
Sure the worst of our foes
Are the pains and the woes
Of the *rain*,
      the *cold*,
         and the *mud*.

TIPPERARY DAYS

Oh, weren't they the fine boys! You never saw the beat of them,
Singing all together with their throats bronze-bare;
Fighting-fit and mirth-mad, music in the feet of them,
Swinging on to glory and the wrath out there.
Laughing by and chaffing by, frolic in the smiles of them,
On the road, the white road, all the afternoon;
Strangers in a strange land, miles and miles and miles of them,
Battle-bound and heart-high, and singing this tune:

> *It's a long way to Tipperary,*
> *It's a long way to go;*
> *It's a long way to Tipperary,*
> *And the sweetest girl I know.*
> *Good-bye, Piccadilly,*
> *Farewell, Leicester Square:*
> *It's a long, long way to Tipperary,*
> *But my heart's right there.*

"Come, Yvonne and Juliette! Come, Mimi, and cheer for them!
Throw them flowers and kisses as they pass you by.
Aren't they the lovely lads! Haven't you a tear for them
Going out so gallantly to dare and die?
What is it they're singing so? Some high hymn of Motherland?
Some immortal chanson of their Faith and King?
Marseillaise or Brabançon, anthem of that other land,
Dears, let us remember it, that song they sing:

> *"C'est un chemin long 'to Tepararee,'*
> *C'est un chemin long, c'est vrai;*

C'est un chemin long 'to Tepararee,'
Et la belle fille qu'je connais.
Bonjour, Peekadeely!
Au revoir, Lestaire Squaire!
C'est un chemin long 'to Tepararee,'
Mais mon coeur 'ees zaire.' "

The gallant old "Contemptibles"! There isn't much remains of
    them,
So full of fun and fitness, and a-singing in their pride;
For some are cold as clabber and the corby picks the brains of
    them,
And some are back in Blighty, and a-wishing they had died.
And yet it seems but yesterday, that great, glad sight of them,
Swinging on to battle as the sky grew black and black;
But oh their glee and glory, and the great, grim fight of them!—
Just whistle Tipperary and it all comes back:

    It's a long way to Tipperary
    (Which means " 'ome" anywhere);
    It's a long way to Tipperary
    (And the things wot make you care).
    Good-bye, Piccadilly
    ('Ow I 'opes my folks is well);
    It's a long, long way to Tipperary—
    ('R! Ain't War just 'ell?)

FLEURETTE

(The Wounded Canadian Speaks)

My leg? It's off at the knee.
Do I miss it? Well, some. You see
I've had it since I was born;
And lately a devilish corn.
(I rather chuckle with glee
To think how I've fooled that corn.)

But I'll hobble around all right.
It isn't that, it's my face.
Oh I know I'm a hideous sight,
Hardly a thing in place;
Sort of gargoyle, you'd say.
Nurse won't give me a glass,
But I see the folks as they pass
Shudder and turn away;
Turn away in distress . . .
Mirror enough, I guess.

I'm gay! You bet I *am* gay;
But I wasn't a while ago.
If you'd seen me even to-day,
The darndest picture of woe,
With this Caliban mug of mine,
So ravaged and raw and red,
Turned to the wall—in fine,
Wishing that I was dead. . . .
What has happened since then,

Since I lay with my face to the wall,
The most despairing of men?
Listen! I'll tell you all.

That *poilu* across the way,
With the shrapnel wound in his head,
Has a sister: she came to-day
To sit awhile by his bed.
All morning I heard him fret:
"Oh, when will she come, Fleurette?"

Then sudden, a joyous cry;
The tripping of little feet;
The softest, tenderest sigh;
A voice so fresh and sweet;
Clear as a silver bell,
Fresh as the morning dews:
"C'est toi, c'est toi, Marcel!
Mon frère, comme je suis heureuse!"

So over the blanket's rim
I raised my terrible face,
And I saw—how I envied him!
A girl of such delicate grace;
Sixteen, all laughter and love;
As gay as a linnet, and yet
As tenderly sweet as a dove;
Half woman, half child—Fleurette.

Then I turned to the wall again.
(I was awfully blue, you see,)
And I thought with a bitter pain:
"Such visions are not for me."

So there like a log I lay,
All hidden, I thought, from view,
When sudden I heard her say:
"Ah! Who is that *malheureux?*"
Then briefly I heard him tell
(However he came to know)
How I'd smothered a bomb that fell
Into the trench, and so
None of my men were hit,
Though it busted me up a bit.

Well, I didn't quiver an eye,
And he chattered and there she sat;
And I fancied I heard her sigh—
But I wouldn't just swear to that.
And maybe she wasn't so bright,
Though she talked in a merry strain,
And I closed my eyes ever so tight,
Yet I saw her ever so plain:
Her dear little tilted nose,
Her delicate, dimpled chin,
Her mouth like a budding rose,
And the glistening pearls within;
Her eyes like the violet:
Such a rare little queen—Fleurette.

And at last when she rose to go,
The light was a little dim,
And I ventured to peep, and so
I saw her, graceful and slim,
And she kissed him and kissed him, and oh
How I envied and envied him!

So when she was gone I said
In rather a dreary voice
To him of the opposite bed:
"Ah, friend, how you must rejoice!
But me, I'm a thing of dread.
For me nevermore the bliss,
The thrill of a woman's kiss."

Then I stopped, for lo! she was there,
And a great light shone in her eyes.
And me! I could only stare,
I was taken so by surprise,
When gently she bent her head:
"*May I kiss you, Sergeant?*" she said.

Then she kissed my burning lips
With her mouth like a scented flower,
And I thrilled to the finger-tips,
And I hadn't even the power
To say: "God bless you, dear!"
And I felt such a precious tear
Fall on my withered cheek,
And darn it! I couldn't speak.

And so she went sadly away,
And I knew that my eyes were wet.
Ah, not to my dying day
Will I forget, forget!
Can you wonder now I am gay?
God bless her, that little Fleurette!

FUNK

When your marrer bone seems 'oller,
And you're glad you ain't no taller,
And you're all a-shakin' like you 'ad the chills;
When your skin creeps like a pullet's,
And you're duckin' all the bullets,
And you're green as gorgonzola round the gills;
When your legs seem made of jelly,
And you're squeamish in the belly,
And you want to turn about and do a bunk:
For Gawd's sake, kid, don't show it!
Don't let your mateys know it—
You're just sufferin' from funk, funk, funk.

Of course there's no denyin'
That it ain't so easy tryin'
To grin and grip your rifle by the butt,
When the 'ole world rips asunder,
And you sees yer pal go under,
As a bunch of shrapnel sprays 'im on the nut;
I admit it's 'ard contrivin'
When you 'ears the shells arrivin',
To discover you're a bloomin' bit o' spunk;
But, my lad, you've got to do it,
And your God will see you through it,
For wot 'E 'ates is funk, funk, funk.

So stand up, son; look gritty,
And just 'um a lively ditty,
And only be afraid to be afraid;

Just 'old yer rifle steady,
And 'ave yer bay'nit ready,
For that's the way good soldier-men is made.
And if you 'as to die,
As it sometimes 'appens, why,
Far better die a 'ero than a skunk;
A-doin' of yer bit,
And so—to 'ell with it,
There ain't no bloomin' funk, funk, funk.

OUR HERO

"FLOWERS, only flowers—bring me dainty posies,
Blossoms for forgetfulness," that was all he said;
So we sacked our gardens, violets and roses,
Lilies white and bluebells laid we on his bed.
Soft his pale hands touched them, tenderly caressing;
Soft into his tired eyes came a little light;
Such a wistful love-look, gentle as a blessing;
There amid the flowers waited he the night.

"I would have you raise me; I can see the West then:
I would see the sun set once before I go."
So he lay a-gazing, seemed to be at rest then,
Quiet as a spirit in the golden glow.
So he lay a-watching rosy castles crumbling,
Moats of blinding amber, bastions of flame,
Rugged rifts of opal, crimson turrets tumbling;
So he lay a-dreaming till the shadows came.

"Open wide the window; there's a lark a-singing;
There's a glad lark singing in the evening sky.
How it's wild with rapture, radiantly winging:
Oh, it's good to hear that when one has to die.
I am horror-haunted from the hell they found me;
I am battle-broken, all I want is rest.
Ah! It's good to die so, blossoms all around me,
And a kind lark singing in the golden West.

"Flowers, song and sunshine, just one thing is wanting,
Just the happy laughter of a little child."

326

So we brought our dearest, Doris all-enchanting;
Tenderly he kissed her; radiant he smiled.
"In the golden peace-time you will tell the story
How for you and yours, sweet, bitter deaths were ours. . . .
God bless little children!" So he passed to glory,
So we left him sleeping, still amid the flow'rs.

MY MATE

I'VE been sittin' starin', starin' at 'is muddy pair of boots,
And tryin' to convince meself it's 'im.
(Look out there, lad! That sniper—'e's a dysey when 'e shoots;
'E'll be layin' of you out the same as Jim.)
Jim as lies there in the dug-out wiv 'is blanket round 'is 'ead,
To keep 'is brains from mixin' wiv the mud;
And 'is face as white as putty, and 'is overcoat all red,
Like 'e's spilt a bloomin' paint-pot—but it's blood.

And I'm tryin' to remember of a time we wasn't pals.
'Ow often we've played 'ookey, 'im and me,
And sometimes it was music-'alls, and sometimes it was gals,
And even there we 'ad no disagree.
For when 'e copped Mariar Jones, the one I liked the best,
I shook 'is 'and and loaned 'im 'arf a quid;
I saw 'im through the parson's job, I 'elped 'im make 'is nest,
I even stood god-farther to the kid.

So when the war broke out, sez 'e: "Well, wot abaht it, Joe?"
"Well, wot abaht it, lad?" sez I to 'im.
'Is missis made a awful fuss, but 'e was mad to go,
('E always was 'igh-sperrited was Jim).
Well, none of it's been 'eaven, and the most of it's been 'ell,
But we've shared our baccy, and we've 'alved our bread.
We'd all the luck at Wipers, and we shaved through Noove
    Chapelle,
And . . . that snipin' barstard gits 'im on the 'ead.

Now wot I wants to know is, why it wasn't me was took?
I've only got meself, 'e stands for three.

I'm plainer than a louse, while 'e was 'andsome as a dook;
'E always *was* a better man than me.
'E was goin' 'ome next Toosday; 'e was 'appy as a lark,
And 'e'd just received a letter from 'is kid;
And 'e struck a match to show me, as we stood there in the dark,
When ∴ . . . that bleedin' bullet got 'im on the lid.

'E was killed so awful sudden that 'e 'adn't time to die.
'E sorto jumped, and came down wiv a thud.
Them corpsy-lookin' star-shells kept a-streamin' in the sky,
And there 'e lay like nothin' in the mud.
And there 'e lay so quiet wiv no mansard to 'is 'ead,
And I'm sick, and blamed if I can understand:
The pots of 'alf and 'alf we've 'ad, and *zip!* like that—'e's dead,
Wiv the letter of 'is nipper in 'is 'and.

There's some as fights for freedom and there's some as fights for
    fun,
But me, my lad, I fights for bleedin' 'ate.
You can blame the war and blast it, but I 'opes it won't be done
Till I gets the bloomin' blood-price for me mate.
It'll take a bit o' bayonet to level up for Jim;
Then if I'm spared I think I'll 'ave a bid,
Wiv 'er that was Mariar Jones to take the place of 'im,
To sorter be a farther to 'is kid.

MILKING TIME

THERE's a drip of honeysuckle in the deep green lane;
There's old Martin jogging homeward on his worn old wain;
There are cherry petals falling, and a cuckoo calling, calling,
And a score of larks (God bless 'em) . . . but it's all pain, pain.
For you see I am not really there at all, not at all;
For you see I'm in the trenches where the crump-crumps fall;
And the bits o' shells are screaming and it's only blessed dreaming
That in fancy I am seeming back in old Saint Pol.

Oh I've thought of it so often since I've come down here;
And I never dreamt that any place could be so dear;
The silvered whinstone houses, and the rosy men in blouses,
And the kindly, white-capped women with their eyes spring-
    clear.
And mother's sitting knitting where her roses climb,
And the angelus is calling with a soft, soft chime,
And the sea-wind comes caressing, and the light's a golden
    blessing.
And Yvonne, Yvonne is guessing that it's milking time.

Oh it's Sunday, for she's wearing of her broidered gown;
And she draws the pasture pickets and the cows come down;
And their feet are powdered yellow, and their voices honey-
    mellow,
And they bring a scent of clover, and their eyes are brown.
And Yvonne is dreaming after, but her eyes are blue;
And her lips are made for laughter, and her white teeth too;
And her mouth is like a cherry, and a dimple mocking merry
Is lurking in the very cheek she turns to you.

So I walk beside her kindly, and she laughs at me;
And I heap her arms with lilac from the lilac tree;
And a golden light is welling, and a golden peace is dwelling,
And a thousand birds are telling how it's good to be.
And what are pouting lips for if they can't be kissed?
And I've filled her arms with blossom so she can't resist;
And the cows are sadly straying, and her mother must be saying
That Yvonne is long delaying . . . *God! How close that missed!*

A nice polite reminder that the Boche are nigh;
That we're here to fight like devils, and if need-be die;
That from kissing pretty wenches to the frantic firing-benches
Of the battered, tattered trenches is a far, far cry.
Yet still I'm sitting dreaming in the glare and grime;
And once again I'm hearing of the church-bells chime;
And how I wonder whether in the golden summer weather
We will fetch the cows together when it's milking time. . . .
    (English voice, months later):—
"Ow Bill! A rottin' Frenchy. Whew! 'E ain't 'arf prime."

YOUNG FELLOW MY LAD

"WHERE are you going, Young Fellow My Lad,
On this glittering morn of May?"
"I'm going to join the Colours, Dad;
They're looking for men, they say."
"But you're only a boy, Young Fellow My Lad;
You aren't obliged to go."
"I'm seventeen and a quarter, Dad,
And ever so strong, you know."

. . . .

"So you're off to France, Young Fellow My Lad,
And you're looking so fit and bright."
"I'm terribly sorry to leave you, Dad,
But I feel that I'm doing right."
"God bless you and keep you, Young Fellow My Lad,
You're all of my life, you know."
"Don't worry. I'll soon be back, dear Dad,
And I'm awfully proud to go."

. . . .

"Why don't you write, Young Fellow My Lad?
I watch for the post each day;
And I miss you so, and I'm awfully sad,
And it's months since you went away.
And I've had the fire in the parlour lit,
And I'm keeping it burning bright
Till my boy comes home; and here I sit
Into the quiet night."

. . . .

"What is the matter, Young Fellow My Lad?
No letter again to-day.
Why did the postman look so sad,
And sigh as he turned away?
I hear them tell that we've gained new ground,
But a terrible price we've paid:
God grant, my boy, that you're safe and sound;
But oh I'm afraid, afraid."

.   .   .   .

"They've told me the truth, Young Fellow My Lad:
You'll never come back again:
(*Oh God! the dreams and the dreams I've had,
And the hopes I've nursed in vain!*)
For you passed in the night, Young Fellow My Lad,
And you proved in the cruel test
Of the screaming shell and the battle hell
That my boy was one of the best.

"So you'll live, you'll live, Young Fellow My Lad,
In the gleam of the evening star,
In the wood-note wild and the laugh of the child,
In all sweet things that are.
And you'll never die, my wonderful boy,
While life is noble and true;
For all our beauty and hope and joy
We will owe to our lads like you."

A SONG OF THE SANDBAGS

No, Bill, I'm not a-spooning out no patriotic tosh
(The cove be'ind the sandbags ain't a death-or-glory cuss).
And though I strafes 'em good and 'ard I doesn't 'ate the Boche,
I guess they're mostly decent, just the same as most of us.
I guess they loves their 'omes and kids as much as you or me;
And just the same as you or me they'd rather shake than fight;
And if we'd 'appened to be born at Berlin-on-the-Spree,
We'd be out there with 'Ans and Fritz, dead sure that we was
    right.

> A-standin' up to the sandbags
> It's funny the thoughts wot come;
> Starin' into the darkness,
> 'Earin' the bullets 'um;
> (*Zing! Zip! Ping! Rip!*
> *'Ark 'ow the bullets 'um!*)
> A-leanin' against the sandbags
> Wiv me rifle under me ear,
> Oh, I've 'ad more thoughts on a sentry-go
> Than I used to 'ave in a year.

I wonder, Bill, if 'Ans and Fritz is wonderin' like me
Wot's at the bottom of it all? Wot all the slaughter's for?
'E thinks 'e's right (of course 'e ain't) but this we both agree,
If them as made it 'ad to fight, there wouldn't be no war.
If them as lies in feather beds while we kips in the mud;
If them as makes their fortoons while we fights for 'em like 'ell;
If them as slings their pot of ink just 'ad to sling their blood:
By Crust! I'm thinkin' there 'ud be another tale to tell.

334

Shiverin' up to the sandbags,
With a hicicle 'stead of a spine,
Don't it seem funny the things you think
'Ere in the firin' line:
(*Whee! Whut! Ziz! Zut!*
Lord! 'Ow the bullets whine!)
Hunkerin' down when a star-shell
Cracks in a sputter of light,
You can jaw to yer soul by the sandbags
Most any old time o' night.

They talks o' England's glory and a-'oldin' of our trade,
Of Empire and 'igh destiny until we're fair flim-flammed;
But if it's for the likes o' that that bloody war is made,
Then wot I say is: Empire and 'igh destiny be damned!
There's only one good cause, Bill, for poor blokes like us to
    fight:
That's self-defence, for 'earth and 'ome, and them that bears our
    name;
And that's wot I'm a-doin' by the sandbags 'ere to-night. . . .
But Fritz out there will tell you 'e's a-doin' of the same.

Starin' over the sandbags,
Sick of the 'ole damn thing;
Firin' to keep meself awake,
'Earin' the bullets sing.
(*Hiss! Twang! Tsing! Pang!*
Saucy the bullets sing.)
Dreamin' 'ere by the sandbags
Of a day when war will cease,
When 'Ans and Fritz and Bill and me
Will clink our mugs in fraternity,
And the Brotherhood of Labour will be
The Brotherhood of Peace.

ON THE WIRE

O GOD, take the sun from the sky!
It's burning me, scorching me up.
God, can't You hear my cry?
Water! A poor, little cup!
It's laughing, the cursed sun!
See how it swells and swells
Fierce as a hundred hells!
God, will it never have done?
It's searing the flesh on my bones;
It's beating with hammers red
My eyeballs into my head;
It's parching my very moans.
See! It's the size of the sky,
And the sky is a torrent of fire,
Foaming on me as I lie
Here on the wire . . . the wire. . . .

Of the thousands that wheeze and hum
Heedlessly over my head,
Why can't a bullet come,
Pierce to my brain instead,
Blacken forever my brain,
Finish forever my pain?
Here in the hellish glare
Why must I suffer so?
Is it God doesn't care?
Is it God doesn't know?
Oh, to be killed outright,
Clean in the clash of the fight!
That is a golden death,

That is a boon; but this . . .
Drawing an anguished breath
Under a hot abyss,
Under a stooping sky
Of seething, sulphurous fire,
Scorching me up as I lie
Here on the wire . . . the wire. . . .

Hasten, O God, Thy night!
Hide from my eyes the sight
Of the body I stare and see
Shattered so hideously.
I can't believe that it's mine.
My body was white and sweet,
Flawless and fair and fine,
Shapely from head to feet;
Oh no, I can never be
The thing of horror I see
Under the rifle fire,
Trussed on the wire . . . the wire. . . .

Of night and of death I dream;
Night that will bring me peace,
Coolness and starry gleam,
Stillness and death's release:
Ages and ages have passed,—
Lo! it is night at last.
Night! but the guns roar out.
Night! but the hosts attack.
Red and yellow and black
Geysers of doom upspout.
Silver and green and red
Star-shells hover and spread.
Yonder off to the right

Fiercely kindles the fight;
Roaring near and more near,
Thundering now in my ear;
Close to me, close . . . Oh, hark!
Someone moans in the dark.
I hear, but I cannot see,
I hear as the rest retire,
Someone is caught like me,
Caught on the wire . . . the wire. . . .

Again the shuddering dawn,
Weird and wicked and wan;
Again, and I've not yet gone.
The man whom I heard is dead.
Now I can understand:
A bullet hole in his head,
A pistol gripped in his hand.
Well, he knew what to do,—
Yes, and now I know too. . . .

Hark the resentful guns!
Oh, how thankful am I
To think my beloved ones
Will never know how I die!
I've suffered more than my share;
I'm shattered beyond repair;
I've fought like a man the fight,
And now I demand the right
(God! how his fingers cling!)
To do without shame this thing.
Good! there's a bullet still;
Now I'm ready to fire;
Blame me, God, if You will,
Here on the wire . . . the wire. . . .

BILL'S GRAVE

I'м gatherin' flowers by the wayside to lay on the grave of Bill;
I've sneaked away from the billet, 'cause Jim wouldn't under-
    stand;
'E'd call me a silly fat'ead, and larf till it made 'im ill,
To see me 'ere in the cornfield, wiv a big bookay in me 'and.

For Jim and me are rough uns, but Bill was one o' the best;
We 'listed and learned together to larf at the wust wot comes;
Then Bill copped a packet proper, and took 'is departure West,
So sudden 'e 'adn't a minit to say good-bye to 'is chums.

And they took me to where 'e was planted, a sort of a measly
    mound,
And, thinks I, 'ow Bill would be tickled, bein' so soft and queer,
If I gathered a bunch o' them wild-flowers, and sort of arranged
    them round
Like a kind of a bloody headpiece . . . and that's the reason
    I'm 'ere.

But not for the love of glory I wouldn't 'ave Jim to know.
'E'd call me a slobberin' Cissy, and larf till 'is sides was sore;
I'd 'ave larfed at meself too, it isn't so long ago;
But some'ow it changes a feller, 'avin' a taste o' war.

It 'elps a man to be 'elpful, to know wot 'is pals is worth
(Them golden poppies is blazin' like lamps some fairy 'as lit);
I'm fond o' them big white dysies. . . . Now Jim's o' the salt
    o' the earth;
But 'e 'as got a tongue wot's a terror, and 'e ain't sentimental a
    bit.

I likes them blue chaps wot's 'idin' so shylike among the corn.
Won't Bill be glad! We was allus thicker 'n thieves, us three.
Why! 'Oo's that singin' so 'earty? *Jim!* And as sure as I'm born
'E's there in the giddy cornfields, a-gatherin' flowers like me.

Quick! Drop me posy be'ind me. I watches 'im for a while,
Then I says: "Wot 'o, there, Chummy! Wot price the little
    bookay?"
And 'e starts like a bloke wot's guilty, and 'e says with a sheep-
    ish smile:
"She's a bit of orl right, the widder wot keeps the estaminay."

So 'e goes away in a 'urry, and I wishes 'im best o' luck,
And I picks up me bunch o' wild-flowers, and the light's gettin'
    sorto dim,
When I makes me way to the boneyard, and . . . I stares like
    a man wot's stuck,
For wot do I see? *Bill's grave-mound strewn with the flowers
    of Jim.*

Of course I won't never tell 'im, bein' a tactical lad;
And Jim parley-voos to the widder: "Trez beans, lamoor; com-
    pree?"
Oh, 'e'd die of shame if 'e knew I knew; but say! won't Bill be
    glad
When 'e stares through the bleedin' clods and sees the blossoms
    of Jim and me?

JEAN DESPREZ

Oh, ye whose hearts are resonant, and ring to War's romance,
Hear ye the story of a boy, a peasant boy of France;
A lad uncouth and warped with toil, yet who, when trial came,
Could feel within his soul upleap and soar the sacred flame;
Could stand upright, and scorn and smite, as only heroes may:
Oh, hearken! Let me try to tell the tale of Jean Desprez.

With fire and sword the Teuton horde was ravaging the land,
And there was darkness and despair, grim death on every hand;
Red fields of slaughter sloping down to ruin's black abyss;
The wolves of war ran evil-fanged, and little did they miss.
And on they came with fear and flame, to burn and loot and slay,
Until they reached the red-roofed croft, the home of Jean Des-
    prez.

"Rout out the village, one and all!" the Uhlan Captain said.
"Behold! Some hand has fired a shot. My trumpeter is dead.
Now shall they Prussian vengeance know; now shall they rue
    the day,
For by this sacred German slain, ten of these dogs shall pay."
They drove the cowering peasants forth, women and babes and
    men,
And from the last, with many a jeer, the Captain chose he ten;
Ten simple peasants, bowed with toil; they stood, they knew not
    why,
Against the grey wall of the church, hearing their children cry;
Hearing their wives and mothers wail, with faces dazed they
    stood.
A moment only. . . . *Ready! Fire!* They weltered in their
    blood.

But there was one who gazed unseen, who heard the frenzied
    cries,
Who saw these men in sabots fall before their children's eyes;
A Zouave wounded in a ditch, and knowing death was nigh,
He laughed with joy: "Ah! here is where I settle ere I die."
He clutched his rifle once again, and long he aimed and well. . . .
A shot! Beside his victims ten the Uhlan Captain fell.

They dragged the wounded Zouave out; their rage was like a
    flame.
With bayonets they pinned him down, until their Major came.
A blond, full-blooded man he was, and arrogant of eye;
He stared to see with shattered skull his favourite Captain lie.
"Nay, do not finish him so quick, this foreign swine," he cried;
"Go nail him to the big church door: he shall be crucified."

With bayonets through hands and feet they nailed the Zouave
    there,
And there was anguish in his eyes, and horror in his stare;
"Water! A single drop!" he moaned; but how they jeered at
    him,
And mocked him with an empty cup, and saw his sight grow
    dim;
And as in agony of death with blood his lips were wet,
The Prussian Major gaily laughed, and lit a cigarette.

But mid the white-faced villagers who cowered in horror by,
Was one who saw the woeful sight, who heard the woeful cry:
"Water! One little drop, I beg! For love of Christ who
    died. . . ."
It was the little Jean Desprez who turned and stole aside;
It was the little bare-foot boy who came with cup abrim
And walked up to the dying man, and gave the drink to him.

A roar of rage! They seize the boy; they tear him fast away.
The Prussian Major swings around; no longer is he gay.
His teeth are wolfishly agleam; his face all dark with spite:
"Go, shoot the brat," he snarls, "that dare defy our Prussian
    might.
Yet stay! I have another thought. I'll kindly be, and spare;
Quick! give the lad a rifle charged, and set him squarely there,
And bid him shoot, and shoot to kill. Haste! Make him under-
    stand
The dying dog he fain would save shall perish by his hand.
And all his kindred they shall see, and all shall curse his name,
Who bought his life at such a cost, the price of death and shame."

They brought the boy, wild-eyed with fear; they made him
    understand;
They stood him by the dying man, a rifle in his hand.
"Make haste!" said they; "the time is short, and you must kill or
    die."
The Major puffed his cigarette, amusement in his eye.
And then the dying Zouave heard, and raised his weary head:
"Shoot, son, 'twill be the best for both; shoot swift and straight,"
    he said.
"Fire first and last, and do not flinch; for lost to hope am I;
And I will murmur: *Vive La France!* and bless you ere I die."

Half-blind with blows the boy stood there; he seemed to swoon
    and sway;
Then in that moment woke the soul of little Jean Desprez.
He saw the woods go sheening down; the larks were singing
    clear;
And oh! the scents and sounds of spring, how sweet they were!
    how dear!

He felt the scent of new-mown hay, a soft breeze fanned his
  brow;
O God! the paths of peace and toil! How precious were they
  now!
The summer days and summer ways, how bright with hope and
  bliss!
The autumn such a dream of gold . . . and all must end in this:
This shining rifle in his hand, that shambles all around;
The Zouave there with dying glare; the blood upon the ground;
The brutal faces round him ringed, the evil eyes aflame;
That Prussian bully standing by, as if he watched a game.
"Make haste and shoot," the Major sneered; "a minute more I
  give;
A minute more to kill your friend, if you yourself would live."

They only saw a bare-foot boy, with blanched and twitching
  face;
They did not see within his eyes the glory of his race;
The glory of a million men who for fair France have died,
The splendour of self-sacrifice that will not be denied.
Yet . . . he was but a peasant lad, and oh! but life was
  sweet. . . .
"Your minute's nearly gone, my lad," he heard a voice repeat.
"Shoot! Shoot!" the dying Zouave moaned; "Shoot! Shoot!" the
  soldiers said.
Then Jean Desprez reached out and shot . . . *the Prussian
  Major dead!*

GOING HOME

I'M goin' 'ome to Blighty—ain't I glad to 'ave the chance!
I'm loaded up wiv fightin', and I've 'ad my fill o' France;
I'm feelin' so excited-like, I want to sing and dance,
 For I'm goin' 'ome to Blighty in the mawnin'.

I'm goin' 'ome to Blighty: can you wonder as I'm gay?
I've got a wound I wouldn't sell for 'alf a year o' pay;
A harm that's mashed to jelly in the nicest sort o' way,
 For it takes me 'ome to Blighty in the mawnin'.

'Ow everlastin' keen I was on gettin' to the front!
I'd ginger for a dozen, and I 'elped to bear the brunt;
But Cheese and Crust! I'm crazy, now I've done me little stunt,
 To sniff the air of Blighty in the mawnin'.

I've looked upon the wine that's white, and on the wine that's
 red;
I've looked on cider flowin', till it fairly turned me 'ead;
But oh, the finest scoff will be, when all is done and said,
 A pint o' Bass in Blighty in the mawnin'.

I'm goin' back to Blighty, which I left to strafe the 'Un;
I've fought in bloody battles, and I've 'ad a 'eap of fun;
But now me flipper's busted, and I think me dooty's done,
 And I'll kiss me gel in Blighty in the mawnin'.

Oh, there be furrin lands to see, and some of 'em be fine;
And there be furrin gels to kiss, and scented furrin wine;
But there's no land like England, and no other gel like mine:
 Thank Gawd for dear old Blighty in the mawnin'.

COCOTTE

WHEN a girl's sixteen, and as poor as she's pretty,
And she hasn't a friend and she hasn't a home,
Heigh-ho! She's as safe in Paris city
As a lamb night-strayed where the wild wolves roam;
And that was I; oh, it's seven years now
(Some water's run down the Seine since then),
And I've almost forgotten the pangs and the tears now,
And I've almost taken the measure of men.

Oh, I found me a lover who loved me only,
Artist and poet, and almost a boy.
And my heart was bruised, and my life was lonely,
And him I adored with a wonderful joy.
If he'd come to me with his pockets empty,
How we'd have laughed in a garret gay!
But he was rich, and in radiant plenty
We lived in a villa at Viroflay.

Then came the War, and of bliss bereft me;
Then came the call, and he went away;
All that he had in the world he left me,
With the rose-wreathed villa at Viroflay.
Then came the news and the tragic story:
My hero, my splendid lover was dead,
Sword in hand on the field of glory,
And he died with my name on his lips, they said.

So here am I in my widow's mourning,
The weeds I've really no right to wear;

And women fix me with eyes of scorning,
Call me "cocotte," but I do not care.
And men look at me with eyes that borrow
The brightness of love, but I turn away;
Alone, say I, I will live with Sorrow,
In my little villa at Viroflay.

And lo! I'm living alone with *Pity*,
And they say that pity from love's not far;
Let me tell you all: last week in the city
I took the metro at Saint Lazare;
And the carriage was crowded to overflowing,
And when there entered at Chateaudun
Two wounded *poilus* with medals showing,
I eagerly gave my seat to one.

You should have seen them: they'd slipped death's clutches,
But sadder a sight you will rarely find;
One had a leg off and walked on crutches,
The other, a bit of a boy, was blind.
And they both sat down, and the lad was trying
To grope his way as a blind man tries;
And half of the women around were crying,
And some of the men had tears in their eyes.

How he stirred me, this blind boy, clinging
Just like a child to his crippled chum.
But I did not cry. Oh no; a singing
Came to my heart for a year so dumb,
Then I knew that at three-and-twenty
There is wonderful work to be done,
Comfort and kindness and joy in plenty,
Peace and light and love to be won.

Oh, thought I, could mine eyes be given
To one who will live in the dark alway!
To love and to serve—'twould make life Heaven
Here in my villa at Viroflay.
So I left my *poilus:* and now you wonder
Why to-day I am so elate. . . .
Look! In the glory of sunshine yonder
They're bringing my blind boy in at the gate.

MY BAY'NIT

WHEN first I left Blighty they gave me a bay'nit
And told me it 'ad to be smothered wiv gore;
But blimey! I 'aven't been able to stain it,
So far as I've gone wiv the vintage of war.
For ain't it a fraud! when a Boche and yours truly
Gits into a mix in the grit and the grime,
'E jerks up 'is 'ands wiv a yell and 'e's duly
                Part of me outfit every time.

    Left, right, Hans and Fritz!
    Goose step, keep up yer mits!
    Oh my, ain't it a shyme!
    Part of me outfit every time.

At toasting a biscuit me bay'nit's a dandy;
I've used it to open a bully beef can;
For pokin' the fire it comes in werry 'andy;
For any old thing but for stickin' a man.
'Ow often I've said: " 'Ere, I'm goin' to press you
Into a 'Un till you're seasoned for prime,"
And fiercely I rushes to do it, but bless you!
                Part of me outfit every time.

    Lor, yus; *don't* they look glad?
    Right O! 'Owl Kamerad!
    Oh my, always the syme!
    Part of me outfit every time.

I'm 'untin' for someone to christen me bay'nit,
Some nice juicy Chewton wot's fightin' in France;

349

I'm fairly down-'earted—'ow *can* yer explain it?
I keeps gettin' prisoners every chance.
As soon as they sees me they ups and surrenders,
Extended like monkeys wot's tryin' to climb;
And I uses me bay'nit—to slit their suspenders—
                    Part of me outfit every time.

        Four 'Uns; lor, wot a bag!
        'Ere, Fritz, sample a fag!
        Oh my, ain't it a gyme!
        Part of me outfit every time.

CARRY ON!

It's easy to fight when everything's right,
And you're mad with the thrill and the glory;
It's easy to cheer when victory's near,
And wallow in fields that are gory.
It's a different song when everything's wrong.
When you're feeling infernally mortal;
When it's ten against one, and hope there is none,
Buck up, little soldier, and chortle:

  Carry on! Carry on!
  There isn't much punch in your blow.
You're glaring and staring and hitting out blind;
You're muddy and bloody, but never you mind.
  Carry on! Carry on!
  You haven't the ghost of a show.
It's looking like death, but while you've a breath,
  Carry on, my son! Carry on!

And so in the strife of the battle of life
It's easy to fight when you're winning;
It's easy to slave, and starve and be brave,
When the dawn of success is beginning.
But the man who can meet despair and defeat
With a cheer, there's the man of God's choosing;
The man who can fight to Heaven's own height
Is the man who can fight when he's losing.

  Carry on! Carry on!
  Things never were looming so black.

But show that you haven't a cowardly streak,
And though you're unlucky you never are weak.
  Carry on! Carry on!
 Brace up for another attack.
It's looking like hell, but—you never can tell:
  Carry on, old man! Carry on!

There are some who drift out in the deserts of doubt,
And some who in brutishness wallow;
There are others, I know, who in piety go
Because of a Heaven to follow.
But to labour with zest, and to give of your best,
For the sweetness and joy of the giving;
To help folks along with a hand and a song;
Why, there's the real sunshine of living.

  Carry on! Carry on!
 Fight the good fight and true;
Believe in your mission, greet life with a cheer;
There's big work to do, and that's why you are here.
  Carry on! Carry on!
 Let the world be the better for you;
And at last when you die, let this be your cry:
  Carry on, my soul! Carry on!

OVER THE PARAPET

ALL day long when the shells sail over
I stand at the sandbags and take my chance;
But at night, at night I'm reckless rover,
And over the parapet gleams Romance.
Romance! Romance! How I've dreamed it, writing
Dreary old records of money and mart,
Me with my head chuckful of fighting
And the blood of vikings to thrill my heart.

But little I thought that my time was coming,
Sudden and splendid, supreme and soon;
And here I am with the bullets humming
As I crawl and I curse the light of the moon.
Out alone, for adventure thirsting,
Out in mysterious No Man's Land;
Prone with the dead when a star-shell, bursting,
Flares on the horrors on every hand.
There are ruby stars and they drip and wiggle;
And the grasses gleam in a light blood-red;
There are emerald stars, and their tails they wriggle,
And ghastly they glare on the face of the dead.
But the worst of all are the stars of whiteness,
That spill in a pool of pearly flame,
Pretty as gems in their silver brightness,
And etching a man for a bullet's aim.

Yet oh, it's great to be here with danger,
Here in the weird, death-pregnant dark,
In the devil's pasture a stealthy-ranger,

When the moon is decently hiding. Hark!
What was that? Was it just the shiver
Of an eerie wind or a clammy hand?
The rustle of grass, or the passing quiver
Of one of the ghosts of No Man's Land?

It's only at night when the ghosts awaken,
And gibber and whisper horrible things;
For to every foot of this God-forsaken
Zone of jeopard some horror clings.
Ugh! What was that? It felt like a jelly,
That flattish mound in the noisome grass;
You three big rats running free of its belly,
Out of my way and let me pass!

But if there's horror, there's beauty, wonder;
The trench lights gleam and the rockets play.
That flood of magnificent orange yonder
Is a battery blazing miles away.
With a rush and a singing a great shell passes;
The rifles resentfully bicker and brawl,
And here I crouch in the dew-drenched grasses,
And look and listen and love it all.

God! What a life! But I must make haste now,
Before the shadow of night be spent.
It's little the time there is to waste now,
If I'd do the job for which I was sent.
My bombs are right and my clippers ready,
And I wriggle out to the chosen place,
When I hear a rustle . . . Steady! . . . Steady!
Who am I staring slap in the face?

There in the dark I can hear him breathing,
A foot away, and as still as death;
And my heart beats hard, and my brain is seething,
And I know he's a Hun by the smell of his breath.
Then: "Will you surrender?" I whisper hoarsely,
For it's death, swift death to utter a cry.
"English schwein-hund!" he murmurs coarsely.
"Then we'll fight it out in the dark," say I.

So we grip and we slip and we trip and wrestle
There in the gutter of No Man's Land;
And I feel my nails in his wind-pipe nestle,
And he tries to gouge, but I bite his hand.
And he tries to squeal, but I squeeze him tighter:
"Now," I say, "I can kill you fine;
But tell me first, you Teutonic blighter!
Have you any children?" He answers: "Nein."

Nine! Well, I cannot kill such a father,
So I tie his hands and I leave him there.
Do I finish my little job? Well, rather;
And I get home safe with some light to spare.
Heigh-ho! by day it's just prosy duty,
Doing the same old song and dance;
But oh! with the night—joy, glory, beauty:
Over the parapet—Life, Romance!

THE BALLAD OF SOULFUL SAM

You want me to tell you a story, a yarn of the firin' line,
Of our thin red kharki 'eroes, out there where the bullets whine;
Out there where the bombs are bustin', and the cannons like
    'ell-doors slam—
Just order another drink, boys, and I'll tell you of Soulful Sam.

Oh, Sam, he was never 'ilarious, though I've 'ad some mates as
    was wus;
He 'adn't C. B. on his programme, he never was known to cuss.
For a card or a skirt or a beer-mug he 'adn't a friendly word;
But when it came down to Scriptures, say! Wasn't he just a bird!

He always 'ad tracts in his pocket, the which he would haste to
    present,
And though the fellers would use them in ways that they never
    was meant,
I used to read 'em religious, and frequent I've been impressed
By some of them bundles of 'oly dope he carried around in his
    vest.

For I—and oh, 'ow I shudder at the 'orror the word conveys!
'Ave been—let me whisper it 'oarsely—a gambler 'alf of me
    days;
A gambler, you 'ear—a gambler. It makes me wishful to weep,
And yet 'ow it's true, my brethren!—I'd rather gamble than
    sleep.

I've gambled the 'ole world over, from Monte Carlo to Maine;
From Dawson City to Dover, from San Francisco to Spain.

Cards! They 'ave been me ruin. They've taken me pride and me
    pelf,
And when I'd no one to play with—why, I'd go and I'd play
    by meself.

And Sam 'e would sit and watch me, as I shuffled a greasy deck,
And 'e'd say: "You're bound to Perdition," And I'd answer: "Git
    off me neck!"
And that's 'ow we came to get friendly, though built on a
    different plan,
Me wot's a desprite gambler, 'im sich a good young man.

But on to me tale. Just imagine . . . Darkness! The battle-front!
The furious 'Uns attackin'! Us ones a-bearin' the brunt!
Me crouchin' be'ind a sandbag, tryin' 'ard to keep calm,
When I 'ears someone singin' a 'ymn toon; be'old! it is Soulful
    Sam.

Yes; right in the crash of the combat, in the fury of flash and
    flame,
'E was shootin' and singin' serenely as if 'e enjoyed the same.
And there in the 'eat of the battle, as the 'ordes of demons
    attacked,
He dipped down into 'is tunic, and 'e 'anded me out a tract.

Then a star-shell flared, and I read it: Oh, Flee From the Wrath
    to Come!
Nice cheerful subject, I tell yer, when you're 'earin' the bullets
    'um.
And before I 'ad time to thank 'im, just one of them bits of lead
Comes slingin' along in a 'urry, and it 'its my partner. . . .
    Dead?

No, siree! not by a long sight! For it plugged 'im 'ard on the
    chest,
Just where 'e'd tracts for a army corps stowed away in 'is vest.
On its mission of death that bullet 'ustled along, and it caved
A 'ole in them tracts to 'is 'ide, boys—but the life o' me pal was
    saved.

And there as 'e showed me in triumph, and 'orror was chokin'
    me breath,
On came another bullet on its 'orrible mission of death;
On through the night it cavorted, seekin' its 'aven of rest,
And it zipped through a crack in the sandbags, and it walloped
    me bang on the breast.

Was I killed, do you ask? Oh no, boys. Why am I sittin' 'ere
Gazin' with mournful vision at a mug long empty of beer?
With a throat as dry as a—oh, thanky! I don't much mind if I do.
Beer with a dash of 'ollands, that's my particular brew.

Yes, that was a terrible moment. It 'ammered me 'ard o'er the
    'eart;
It bowled me down like a nine-pin, and I looked for the gore to
    start;
And I saw in the flash of a moment, in that thunder of hate and
    strife,
Me wretched past like a pitchur—the sins of a gambler's life.

For I 'ad no tracts to save me, to thwart that mad missile's doom;
I 'ad no pious pamphlets to 'elp me to cheat the tomb;
I 'ad no 'oly leaflets to baffle a bullet's aim;
I'd only—a deck of cards, boys, but . . . *it seemed to do just
    the same.*

ONLY A BOCHE

WE brought him in from between the lines: we'd better have let
    him lie;
For what's the use of risking one's skin for a *tyke* that's going
    to die?
What's the use of tearing him loose under a gruelling fire,
When he's shot in the head, and worse than dead, and all messed
    up on the wire?

However, I say, we brought him in. *Diable!* The mud was bad;
The trench was crooked and greasy and high, and oh, what a
    time we had!
And often we slipped, and often we tripped, but never he made
    a moan;
And how we were wet with blood and with sweat! but we
    carried him in like our own.

Now there he lies in the dug-out dim, awaiting the ambulance,
And the doctor shrugs his shoulders at him, and remarks, "He
    hasn't a chance."
And we squat and smoke at our game of bridge on the glistening,
    straw-packed floor,
And above our oaths we can hear his breath deep-drawn in a
    kind of snore.

For the dressing station is long and low, and the candles gutter
    dim,
And the mean light falls on the cold clay walls and our faces
    bristly and grim;
And we flap our cards on the lousy straw, and we laugh and
    jibe as we play,

And you'd never know that the cursed foe was less than a mile
away.
As we con our cards in the rancid gloom, oppressed by that
snoring breath,
You'd never dream that our broad roof-beam was swept by the
broom of death.

Heigh-ho! My turn for the dummy hand; I rise and I stretch a
bit;
The fetid air is making me yawn, and my cigarette's unlit,
So I go to the nearest candle flame, and the man we brought
is there,
And his face is white in the shabby light, and I stand at his feet
and stare.
Stand for a while, and quietly stare: for strange though it seems
to be,
The dying Boche on the stretcher there has a queer resemblance
to me.

It gives one a kind of a turn, you know, to come on a thing like
that.
It's just as if I were lying there, with a turban of blood for a hat,
Lying there in a coat grey-green instead of a coat grey-blue,
With one of my eyes all shot away, and my brain half tumbling
through;
Lying there with a chest that heaves like a bellows up and down,
And a cheek as white as snow on a grave, and lips that are coffee
brown.

And confound him, too! He wears, like me, on his finger a
wedding ring,
And around his neck, as around my own, by a greasy bit of
string,

A locket hangs with a woman's face, and I turn it about to see:
Just as I thought . . . on the other side the faces of children
    three;
Clustered together cherub-like, three little laughing girls,
With the usual tiny rosebud mouths and the usual silken curls.
"Zut!" I say. "He has beaten me; for me, I have only two,"
And I push the locket beneath his shirt, feeling a little blue.

Oh, it isn't cheerful to see a man, the marvellous work of God,
Crushed in the mutilation mill, crushed to a smeary clod;
Oh, it isn't cheerful to hear him moan; but it isn't that I mind,
It isn't the anguish that goes with him, it's the anguish he leaves
    behind.
For his going opens a tragic door that gives on a world of pain,
And the death he dies, those who live and love, will die again
    and again.

So here I am at my cards once more, but it's kind of spoiling
    my play,
Thinking of those three brats of his so many a mile away.
War is war, and he's only a Boche, and we all of us take our
    chance;
But all the same I'll be mighty glad when I'm hearing the
    ambulance.
One foe the less, but all the same I'm heartily glad I'm not
The man who gave him his broken head, the sniper who fired
    the shot.

No trumps you make it, I think you said? You'll pardon me if I
    err;
For a moment I thought of other things . . . *Mon Dieu! Quelle
vache de guerre.*

PILGRIMS

For oh, when the war will be over
We'll go and we'll look for our dead;
We'll go when the bee's on the clover,
And the plume of the poppy is red:
We'll go when the year's at its gayest,
When meadows are laughing with flow'rs;
And there where the crosses are greyest,
We'll seek for the cross that is ours.

For they cry to us: *Friends, we are lonely,*
A-weary the night and the day;
But come in the blossom-time only,
Come when our graves will be gay:
When daffodils all are a-blowing,
And larks are a-thrilling the skies,
Oh, come with the hearts of you glowing,
And the joy of the Spring in your eyes.

But never, oh, never come sighing,
For ours was the Splendid Release;
And oh, but 'twas joy in the dying
To know we were winning you Peace!
So come when the valleys are sheening,
And fledged with the promise of grain;
And here where our graves will be greening,
Just smile and be happy again.

And so, when the war will be over,
We'll seek for the Wonderful One;

And maiden will look for her lover,
And mother will look for her son;
And there will be end to our grieving,
And gladness will gleam over loss,
As—glory beyond all believing!
We point . . . to a name on a cross.

MY PRISONER

We was in a crump-'ole, 'im and me;
Fightin' wiv our bayonets was we;
Fightin' 'ard as 'ell we was,
Fightin' fierce as fire because
It was 'im or me as must be downed;
'E was twice as big as me;
I was 'arf the weight of 'e;
We was like a terryer and a 'ound.

'Struth! But 'e was sich a 'andsome bloke.
Me, I'm 'andsome as a chunk o' coke.
Did I give it 'im? Not 'arf!
Why, it fairly made me laugh,
'Cos 'is bloomin' bellows wasn't sound.
Couldn't fight for monkey nuts.
Soon I gets 'im in the guts,
There 'e lies a-floppin' on the ground.

In I goes to finish up the job.
Quick 'e throws 'is 'ands above 'is nob;
Speakin' English good as me:
" 'Tain't no use to kill," says 'e;
"Can't yer tyke me prisoner instead?"
"Why, I'd like to, sir," says I;
"But—yer knows the reason why.
If we pokes our noses out we're dead.

"Sorry, sir. Then on the other 'and
(As a gent like you must understand),
364

If I 'olds you longer 'ere,
Wiv yer pals so werry near,
It's me 'oo'll 'ave a free trip to Berlin;
If I lets yer go away,
Why, you'll fight another day:
See the sitooation I am in.

"Anyway I'll tell you wot I'll do,
Bein' kind and seein' as it's you,
Knowin' 'ow it's cold, the feel
Of a 'alf a yard o' steel,
I'll let yer 'ave a rifle ball instead;
Now, jist think yerself in luck. . . .
'Ere, ol' man! You keep 'em stuck,
Them saucy dooks o' yours, above yer 'ead."

'Ow 'is mits shot up it made me smile!
'Ow 'e seemed to ponder for a while!
Then 'e says: "It seems a shyme,
Me, a man wot's known ter Fyme:
Give me blocks of stone, I'll give yer gods.
Whereas, pardon me, I'm sure
You, my friend, are still obscure. . . ."
"In war," says I, "that makes no blurry odds."

Then says 'e: "I've painted picters too. . . .
Oh, dear God! The work I planned to do,
And to think this is the end!"
" 'Ere," says I, "my hartist friend,
Don't you give yerself no friskin' airs.
Picters, statoos, is that why
You should be let off to die?
That the best ye done? Just say yer prayers."

Once again 'e seems ter think awhile.
Then 'e smiles a werry 'aughty smile:
"Why, no, sir, it's not the best;
There's a locket next me breast,
Picter of a gel 'oo's eyes are blue.
That's the best I've done," says 'e.
"That's me darter, aged three. . . ."
"Blimy!" says I, "I've a nipper, too."

Straight I chucks my rifle to one side;
Shows 'im wiv a lovin' farther's pride
Me own little Mary Jane.
Proud 'e shows me 'is Elaine,
And we talks as friendly as can be;
Then I 'elps 'im on 'is way,
'Opes 'e's sife at 'ome to-day,
Wonders—*'ow would 'e 'ave treated me?*

TRI-COLOUR

Poppies, you try to tell me, glowing there in the wheat;
Poppies! Ah no! You mock me: It's blood, I tell you, it's blood.
It's gleaming wet in the grasses; it's glist'ning warm in the wheat;
It dabbles the ferns and the clover; it brims in an angry flood;
It leaps to the startled heavens; it smothers the sun; it cries
With scarlet voices of triumph from blossom and bough and
    blade.
See the bright horror of it! It's roaring out of the skies,
And the whole red world is a-welter. . . . O God! I'm afraid!
    I'm afraid!

Cornflowers, you say, just cornflowers, gemming the golden
    grain;
Ah no! You can't deceive me. Can't I believe my eyes?
Look! It's the dead, my comrades, stark on the dreadful plain,
All in their dark-blue blouses, staring up at the skies.
Comrades of canteen laughter, dumb in the yellow wheat.
See how they sprawl and huddle! See how their brows are
    white!
Goaded on to the shambles, there in death and defeat. . . .
Father of Pity, hide them! Hasten, O God, Thy night!

Lilies (the light is waning), only lilies you say,
Nestling and softly shining there where the spear-grass waves.
No, my friend, I know better; brighter I see than day:
It's the poor little wooden crosses over their quiet graves.
Oh, how they're gleaming, gleaming! See! Each cross has a
    crown.

Yes, it's true I am dying; little will be the loss. . . .

Darkness . . . but look! In Heaven a light, and it's shining
down. . . .

God's accolade! Lift me up, friends. I'm going to win—*my
Cross*.

A POT OF TEA

You make it in your mess-tin by the brazier's rosy gleam;
You watch it cloud, then settle amber clear;
You lift it with your bay'nit, and you sniff the fragrant steam;
The very breath of it is ripe with cheer.
You're awful cold and dirty, and a-cursin' of your lot;
You scoff the blushin' 'alf of it, so rich and rippin' 'ot;
It bucks you up like anythink, just seems to touch the spot:
    God bless the man that first discovered Tea!

Since I came out to fight in France, which ain't the other day,
I think I've drunk enough to float a barge;
All kinds of fancy foreign dope, from caffy and doo lay,
To rum they serves you out before a charge.
In back rooms of estaminays I've gurgled pints of cham;
I've swilled down mugs of cider till I've felt a bloomin' dam;
But 'struth! they all ain't in it with the vintage of Assam:
    God bless the man that first invented Tea!

I think them lazy lumps o' gods wot kips on asphodel
Swigs nectar that's a flavour of Oolong;
I only wish them sons o' guns a-grillin' down in 'ell
Could 'ave their daily ration of Suchong.
Hurrah! I'm off to battle, which is 'ell and 'eaven too;
And if I don't give some poor bloke a sexton's job to do,
To-night, by Fritz's camp-fire, won't I 'ave a gorgeous brew
    (For fightin' mustn't interfere with Tea).
To-night we'll all be tellin' of the Boches that we slew,
    As we drink the giddy victory in Tea.

THE REVELATION

*The same old sprint in the morning, boys, to the same old din
and smut;*
Chained all day to the same old desk, down in the same old rut;
Posting the same old greasy books, catching the same old train:
Oh, how will I manage to stick it all, if I ever get back again?

We've bidden good-bye to life in a cage, we're finished with
pushing a pen;
They're pumping us full of bellicose rage, they're showing us
how to be men.
We're only beginning to find ourselves; we're wonders of brawn
and thew;
But when we go back to our Sissy jobs,—oh, what are we going
to do?

For shoulders curved with the counter stoop will be carried
erect and square;
And faces white from the office light will be bronzed by the
open air;
And we'll walk with the stride of a new-born pride, with a
new-found joy in our eyes,
Scornful men who have diced with death under the naked skies.

And when we get back to the dreary grind, and the bald-headed
boss's call,
Don't you think that the dingy window-blind, and the dingier
office wall,
Will suddenly melt to a vision of space, of violent, flame-scarred
night?

Then . . . oh, the joy of the danger-thrill, and oh, the roar of
    the fight!

Don't you think as we peddle a card of pins the counter will fade
    away,
And again we'll be seeing the sand-bag rims, and the barb-wire's
    misty grey?
As a flat voice asks for a pound of tea, don't you fancy we'll
    hear instead
The night-wind moan and the soothing drone of the packet
    that's overhead?

Don't you guess that the things we're seeing now will haunt us
    through all the years;
Heaven and hell rolled into one, glory and blood and tears;
Life's pattern picked with a scarlet thread, where once we wove
    with a grey
To remind us all how we played our part in the shock of an epic
    day?

Oh, we're booked for the Great Adventure now, we're pledged
    to the Real Romance;
We'll find ourselves or we'll lose ourselves somewhere in giddy
    old France;
We'll know the zest of the fighter's life; the best that we have
    we'll give;
We'll hunger and thirst; we'll die . . . but first—we'll live; by
    the gods, we'll live!

We'll breathe free air and we'll bivouac under the starry sky;
We'll march with men and we'll fight with men, and we'll see
    men laugh and die;

We'll know such joy as we never dreamed; we'll fathom the
    deeps of pain:
But the hardest bit of it all will be—when we come back home
    again.

For some of us smirk in a chiffon shop, and some of us teach in
    a school;
Some of us help with the seat of our pants to polish an office
    stool;
The merits of somebody's soap or jam some of us seek to explain,
But all of us wonder what we'll do when we have to go back
    again.

GRAND-PÈRE

AND so when he reached my bed
The General made a stand:
"My brave young fellow," he said,
    "I would shake your hand."

So I lifted my arm, the right,
With never a hand at all;
Only a stump, a sight
    Fit to appal.

"Well, well. Now that's too bad!
That's sorrowful luck," he said;
"But there! You give me, my lad,
    The left instead."

So from under the blanket's rim
I raised and showed him the other,
A snag as ugly and grim
    As its ugly brother.

He looked at each jagged wrist;
He looked, but he did not speak;
And then he bent down and kissed
    Me on either cheek.

You wonder now I don't mind
I hadn't a hand to offer. . . .
They tell me (you know I'm blind)
    'Twas Grand-père Joffre.

SON

He hurried away, young heart of joy, under our Devon sky!
And I watched him go, my beautiful boy, and a weary woman
was I.
For my hair is grey, and his was gold; he'd the best of his life
to live;
And I'd loved him so, and I'm old, I'm old; and he's all I had
to give.

Ah yes, he was proud and swift and gay, but oh, how my eyes
were dim!
With the sun in his heart he went away, but he took the sun with
him.
For look! How the leaves are falling now, and the winter won't
be long. . . .
Oh, boy, my boy with the sunny brow, and the lips of love and
of song!

How we used to sit at the day's sweet end, we two by the fire-
light's gleam,
And we'd drift to the Valley of Let's Pretend, on the beautiful
river of Dream.
Oh, dear little heart! All wealth untold would I gladly, gladly
pay
Could I just for a moment closely hold that golden head to my
grey.

For I gaze in the fire, and I'm seeing there a child, and he waves
to me;
And I run and I hold him up in the air, and he laughs and shouts
with glee;

A little bundle of love and mirth, crying: "Come, Mumsie dear!"
Ah me! If he called from the ends of the earth I know that my
    heart would hear.

*   *   *   *   *   *   *   *

Yet the thought comes thrilling through all my pain: how
    worthier could he die?
Yea, a loss like that is a glorious gain, and pitiful proud am I.
For Peace must be bought with blood and tears, and the boys of
    our hearts must pay;
And so in our joy of the after-years, let us bless them every day.

And though I know there's a hasty grave with a poor little cross
    at its head,
And the gold of his youth he so gladly gave, yet to me he'll
    never be dead.
And the sun in my Devon lane will be gay, and my boy will be
    with me still,
So I'm finding the heart to smile and say: "Oh God, if it be Thy
    Will!"

3

THE BLACK DUDEEN

Humping it here in the dug-out,
Sucking me black dudeen,
I'd like to say in a general way,
There's nothing like Nickyteen;
There's nothing like Nickyteen, me boys,
Be it pipes or snipes or cigars;
So be sure that a bloke
Has plenty to smoke,
If you wants him to fight your wars.

When I've eat my fill and my belt is snug,
I begin to think of my baccy plug.
I whittle a fill in my horny palm,
And the bowl of me old clay pipe I cram.
I trim the edges, I tamp it down,
I nurse a light with an anxious frown;
I begin to draw, and my cheeks tuck in,
And all my face is a blissful grin;
And up in a cloud the good smoke goes,
And the good pipe glimmers and fades and glows;
In its throat it chuckles a cheery song,
For I likes it hot and I likes it strong.
Oh, it's good is grub when you're feeling hollow,
But the best of a meal's the smoke to follow.

There was Micky and me on a night patrol,
Having to hide in a fizz-bang hole;
And sure I thought I was worse than dead

Wi' them crump-crumps hustlin' over me head.
Sure I thought 'twas the dirty spot,
Hammer and tongs till the air was hot.
And mind you, water up to your knees.
And cold! A monkey of brass would freeze.
And if we ventured our noses out
A "typewriter" clattered its pills about.
The field of glory! Well, I don't think!
I'd sooner be safe and snug in clink.

Then Micky, he goes and he cops one bad,
He always was having ill-luck, poor lad.
Says he: "Old chummy, I'm booked right through;
Death and me 'as a wrongday voo.
But . . . 'aven't you got a pinch of shag?—
I'd sell me perishin' soul for a fag."
And there he shivered and cussed his luck,
So I gave him me old black pipe to suck.
And he heaves a sigh, and he takes to it
Like a babby takes to his mammy's tit;
Like an infant takes to his mother's breast,
Poor little Micky! he went to rest.

But the dawn was near, though the night was black,
So I left him there and I started back.
And I laughed as the silly old bullets came,
For the bullet ain't made wot's got me name.
Yet some of 'em buzzed onhealthily near,
And one little blighter just chipped me ear.
But there! I got to the trench all right,
When sudden I jumped wi' a start o' fright,
And a word that doesn't look well in type:
I'd clean forgotten me old clay pipe.

So I had to do it all over again,
Crawling out on that filthy plain.
Through shells and bombs and bullets and all—
Only this time—I do not crawl.
I run like a man wot's missing a train,
Or a tom-cat caught in a plump of rain.
I hear the spit of a quick-fire gun
Tickle my heels, but I run, I run.
Through crash and crackle, and flicker and flame,
(Oh, the packet ain't issued wot's got me name!)
I run like a man that's no ideer
Of hunting around for a sooveneer.
I run bang into a German chap,
And he stares like an owl, so I bash his map.
And just to show him that I'm his boss,
I gives him a kick on the parados.
And I marches him back with me all serene,
With, *tucked in me gub, me old dudeen.*

Sitting here in the trenches
Me heart's a-splittin' with spleen,
For a parcel o' lead comes missing me head,
But it smashes me old dudeen.
God blast that red-headed sniper!
I'll give him somethin' to snipe;
Before the war's through
Just see how I do
That blighter that smashed me pipe.

THE LITTLE PIOU-PIOU *

OH, some of us lolled in the château,
And some of us slinked in the slum;
But now we are here with a song and a cheer
To serve at the sign of the drum.
They put us in trousers of scarlet,
In big sloppy ulsters of blue;
In boots that are flat, a box of a hat,
And they call us the little piou-piou,
            Piou-piou,
The laughing and quaffing piou-piou,
The swinging and singing piou-piou;
And so with a rattle we march to the battle,
The weary but cheery piou-piou.

> *Encore un petit verre de vin,*
> *Pour nous mettre en route;*
> *Encore un petit verre de vin*
> *Pour nous mettre en train.*

They drive us head-on for the slaughter;
We haven't got much of a chance;
The issue looks bad, but we're awfully glad
To battle and die for La France.
For some must be killed, that is certain;
There's only one's duty to do;
So we leap to the fray in the glorious way
They expect of the little piou-piou.
            En avant!

* The French "Tommy."

379

The way of the gallant piou-piou,
The dashing and smashing piou-piou;
The way grim and gory that leads us to glory
Is the way of the little piou-piou.

  Allons, enfants de la Patrie,
  Le jour de gloire est arrivé.

To-day you would scarce recognise us,
Such veterans war-wise are we;
So grimy and hard, so calloused and scarred,
So "crummy," yet gay as can be.
We've finished with trousers of scarlet,
They're giving us breeches of blue,
With a helmet instead of a cap on our head,
Yet still we're the little piou-piou.
    Nous les aurons!
The jesting, unresting piou-piou;
The cheering, unfearing piou-piou;
The keep-your-head-level and fight-like-the-devil;
The dying, defying piou-piou.

  À la bayonette! Jusqu'à la mort!
  Sonnez la charge, clairons!

BILL THE BOMBER

The poppies gleamed like bloody pools through cotton-woolly
  mist;
The Captain kept a-lookin' at the watch upon his wrist;
And there we smoked and squatted, as we watched the shrapnel
  flame;
'Twas wonnerful, I'm tellin' you, how fast them bullets came.
'Twas weary work the waiting, though; I tried to sleep a wink,
For waitin' means a-thinkin', and it doesn't do to think.
So I closed my eyes a little, and I had a niceish dream
Of a-standin' by a dresser with a dish of Devon cream;
But I hadn't time to sample it, for suddenlike I woke:
"Come on, me lads!" the Captain says, 'n I climbed out through
  the smoke.

We spread out in the open: it was like a bath of lead;
But the boys they cheered and hollered fit to raise the bloody
  dead,
Till a beastly bullet copped 'em, then they lay without a sound,
And it's odd—we didn't seem to heed them corpses on the
  ground.
And I kept on thinkin', thinkin', as the bullets faster flew,
How they picks the werry best men, and they lets the rotters
  through;
So indiscriminatin' like, they spares a man of sin,
And a rare lad wot's a husband and a father gets done in.
And while havin' these reflections and advancin' on the run,
A bullet biffs me shoulder, and says I: "That's number one."

Well, it downed me for a jiffy, but I didn't lose me calm,
For I knew that I was needed: I'm a bomber, so I am.

I 'ad lost me cap and rifle, but I "carried on" because
I 'ad me bombs and knew that they was needed, so they was.
We didn't 'ave no singin' now, nor many men to cheer;
Maybe the shrapnel drowned 'em, crashin' out so werry near;
And the Maxims got us sideways, and the bullets faster flew,
And I copped one on me flipper, and says I: "That's number
  two."

I was pleased it was the left one, for I 'ad me bombs, ye see.
And 'twas 'ard if they'd be wasted like, and all along o' me.
And I'd lost me 'at and rifle—but I told you that before,
So I packed me mit inside me coat and "carried on" once more.
But the rumpus it was wicked, and the men were scarcer yet,
And I felt me ginger goin', but me jaws I kindo set,
And we passed the Boche first trenches, which was 'eapin' 'igh
  with dead,
And we started for their second, which was fifty feet ahead;
When something like a 'ammer smashed me savage on the knee,
And down I came all muck and blood: Says I: "That's number
  three."

So there I lay all 'elpless like, and bloody sick at that,
And worryin' like anythink, because I'd lost me 'at;
And thinkin' of me missis, and the partin' words she said:
"If you gets killed, write quick, ol' man, and tell me as you're
  dead."
And lookin' at me bunch o' bombs—that was the 'ardest blow,
To think I'd never 'ave the chance to 'url them at the foe.
And there was all our boys in front, a-fightin' there like mad,
And me as could 'ave 'elped 'em wiv the lovely bombs I 'ad.
And so I cussed and cussed, and then I struggled back again,
Into that bit of battered trench, packed solid with its slain.

Now as I lay a-lyin' there and blastin' of me lot,
And wishin' I could just dispose of all them bombs I'd got,
I sees within the doorway of a shy, retirin' dug-out
Six Boches all a-grinnin', and their Captain stuck 'is mug out;
And they 'ad a nice machine gun, and I twigged what they was
    at;
And they fixed it on a tripod, and I watched 'em like a cat;
And they got it in position, and they seemed so werry glad,
Like they'd got us in a death-trap, which, condemn their souls!
    they 'ad.
For there our boys was fightin' fifty yards in front, and 'ere
This lousy bunch of Boches they 'ad got us in the rear.

Oh, it set me blood a-boilin' and I quite forgot me pain,
So I started crawlin', crawlin' over all them mounds of slain;
And them barstards was so busy-like they 'ad no eyes for me,
And me bleedin' leg was draggin', but me right arm it was
    free. . . .
And now they 'ave it all in shape, and swingin' sweet and clear;
And now they're all excited like, but—I am drawin' near;
And now they 'ave it loaded up, and now they're takin'
    aim. . . .
Rat-tat-tat-tat! Oh, here, says I, is where I join the game.
And my right arm it goes swingin', and a bomb it goes a-slingin',
And that "typewriter" goes wingin' in a thunderbolt of flame.

Then these Boches, wot was left of 'em, they tumbled down
    their 'ole,
And up I climbed a mound of dead, and down on them I stole.
And, oh, that blessed moment when I heard their frightened yell,
And I laughed down in that dug-out, ere I bombed their souls
    to hell.

And now I'm in the hospital, surprised that I'm alive;
We started out a thousand men, we came back thirty-five.
And I'm minus of a trotter, but I'm most amazin' gay,
For me bombs they wasn't wasted, though, you might say,
    "thrown away."

THE WHISTLE OF SANDY McGRAW

You may talk o' your lutes and your dulcimers fine,
Your harps and your tabors and cymbals and a',
But here in the trenches jist gie me for mine
The wee penny whistle o' Sandy McGraw.
Oh, it's: "Sandy, ma lad, will you lilt us a tune?"
And Sandy is willin' and trillin' like mad;
Sae silvery sweet that we a' throng aroun',
And some o' it's gay, but the maist o' it's sad.
Jist the wee simple airs that sink intae your hert,
And grup ye wi' love and wi' longin' for hame;
And ye glour like an owl till you're feelin' the stert
O' a tear, and you blink wi' a feelin' o' shame.
For his song's o' the heather, and here in the dirt
You listen and dream o' a land that's sae braw,
And he mak's you forget a' the harm and the hurt,
For he pipes like a laverock, does Sandy McGraw.

.   .   .   .   .   .

At Eepers I mind me when rank upon rank
We rose from the trenches and swept like the gale,
Till the rapid-fire guns got us fell on the flank
And the murderin' bullets came swishin' like hail:
Till a' that were left o' us faltered and broke;
Till it seemed for a moment a panicky rout,
When shrill through the fume and the flash and the smoke
The wee valiant voice o' a whistle piped out.
The Campbells are Comin': Then into the fray

We bounded wi' bayonets reekin' and raw,
And, oh, we fair revelled in glory that day,
Jist thanks to the whistle o' Sandy McGraw.

.   .   .   .

At Loose, it wis after a sconnersome fecht,
On the field o' the slain I wis crawlin' aboot;
And the rockets were burnin' red holes in the nicht;
And the guns they were veciously thunderin' oot;
When sudden I heard a bit sound like a sigh,
And there in a crump-hole a kiltie I saw:
"Whit ails ye, ma lad? Are ye woundit?" says I.
"I've lost ma wee whustle," says Sandy McGraw.
" 'Twas oot by yon bing where we pressed the attack,
It drapped frae ma pooch, and between noo and dawn
There isna much time so I'm jist crawlin' back. . . ."
"Ye're daft, man!" I telt him, but Sandy wis gone.

Weel, I waited a wee, then I crawled oot masel.
And the big stuff wis gorin' and roarin' around,
And I seemed tae be under the oxter o' hell,
And Creation wis crackin' tae bits by the sound.
And I says in ma mind: "Gang ye back, ye auld fule!"
When I thrilled tae a note that wis saucy and sma';
And there in a crater, collected and cool,
Wi' his wee penny whistle wis Sandy McGraw.
Ay, there he wis playin' as gleg as could be,
And listenin' hard wis a spectacled Boche;
Then Sandy turned roon' and he noddit tae me,
And he says: "Dinna blab on me, Sergeant McTosh.
The auld chap is deein'. He likes me tae play.
It's makin' him happy. Jist see his een shine!"

And thrillin' and sweet in the hert o' the fray
Wee Sandy wis playin' *The Watch on the Rhine.*

.   .   .   .

The last scene o' a'—'twas the day that we took
That bit o' black ruin they ca' Labbiesell.
It seemed the hale hillside jist shivered and shook,
And the red skies were roarin' and spewin' oot shell.
And the Sergeants were cursin' tae keep us in hand,
And hard on the leash we were strainin' like dugs,
When upward we shot at the word o' command,
And the bullets were dingin' their songs in oor lugs.
And onward we swept wi' a yell and a cheer,
And a' wis destruction, confusion and din,
And we knew that the trench o' the Boches wis near,
And it seemed jist the safest bit hole tae be in.
So we a' tumbled doon, and the Boches were there,
And they held up their hands, and they yelled: "Kamarad!"
And I merched aff wi' ten, wi' their palms in the air,
And my! I wis prood-like, and my! I wis glad.
And I thocht: if ma lassie could see me jist then. . . .
When sudden I sobered at somethin' I saw,
And I stopped and I stared, and I halted ma men,
For there on a stretcher wis Sandy McGraw.

Weel, he looks in ma face, jist as game as ye please:
"Ye ken hoo I hate tae be workin'," says he;
"But noo I can play in the street for bawbees,
Wi' baith o' ma legs taken aff at the knee."
And though I could see he wis rackit wi' pain,
He reached for his whistle and stertit tae play;
And quaverin' sweet wis the pensive refrain:

The flowers o' the forest are a' wede awae.
Then sudden he stoppit: "Man, wis it no grand
Hoo we took a' them trenches?" . . . He shakit his heid:
"I'll—no—play—nae—mair——" feebly doon frae his hand
Slipped the wee penny whistle and—*Sandy wis deid.*

.   .   .   .

And so you may talk o' your Steinways and Strads,
Your wonderful organs and brasses sae braw;
But oot in the trenches jist gie me, ma lads,
Yon wee penny whistle o' Sandy McGraw.

THE STRETCHER-BEARER

My stretcher is one scarlet stain,
And as I tries to scrape it clean,
I tell you wot—I'm sick with pain
For all I've 'eard, for all I've seen;
Around me is the 'ellish night,
And as the war's red rim I trace,
I wonder if in 'Eaven's height,
Our God don't turn away 'Is face.

I don't care 'oose the Crime may be;
I 'olds no brief for kin or clan;
I 'ymns no 'ate: I only see
As man destroys his brother man;
I waves no flag: I only know,
As 'ere beside the dead I wait,
A million 'earts is weighed with woe,
A million 'omes is desolate.

In drippin' darkness, far and near,
All night I've sought them woeful ones.
Dawn shudders up and still I 'ear
The crimson chorus of the guns.
Look! like a ball of blood the sun
'Angs o'er the scene of wrath and wrong. . . .
"Quick! Stretcher-bearers on the run!"
O Prince of Peace! 'Ow long, 'ow long?

WOUNDED

Is it not strange? A year ago to-day,
With scarce a thought beyond the hum-drum round,
I did my decent job and earned my pay;
Was averagely happy, I'll be bound.
Ay, in my little groove I was content,
Seeing my life run smoothly to the end,
With prosy days in stolid labour spent,
And jolly nights, a pipe, a glass, a friend.
In God's good time a hearth fire's cosy gleam,
A wife and kids, and all a fellow needs;
When presto! like a bubble goes my dream:
I leap upon the Stage of Splendid Deeds.
I yell with rage; I wallow deep in gore:
I, that was clerk in a drysalter's store.

Stranger than any book I've ever read.
Here on the reeking battlefield I lie,
Under the stars, propped up with smeary dead,
Like too, if no one takes me in, to die.
Hit on the arms, legs, liver, lungs and gall;
Damn glad there's nothing more of me to hit;
But calm, and feeling never pain at all,
And full of wonder at the turn of it.
For of the dead around me three are mine,
Three foemen vanquished in the whirl of fight;
So if I die I have no right to whine,
I feel I've done my little bit all right.
I don't know how—but there the beggars are,
As dead as herrings pickled in a jar.

And here am I, worse wounded than I thought;
For in the fight a bullet bee-like stings;
You never heed; the air is metal-hot,
And all alive with little flicking wings.
But on you charge. You see the fellows fall;
Your pal was by your side, fair fighting-mad;
You turn to him, and lo! no pal at all;
You wonder vaguely if he's copped it bad.
But on you charge. The heavens vomit death;
And vicious death is besoming the ground.
You're blind with sweat; you're dazed, and out of breath,
And though you yell, you cannot hear a sound.
But on you charge. Oh, War's a rousing game!
Around you smoky clouds like ogres tower;
The earth is rowelled deep with spurs of flame,
And on your helmet stones and ashes shower.
But on you charge. It's odd! You have no fear.
Machine-gun bullets whip and lash your path;
Red, yellow, black the smoky giants rear;
The shrapnel rips, the heavens roar in wrath.
But on you charge. Barbed wire all trampled down.
The ground all gored and rent as by a blast;
Grim heaps of grey where once were heaps of brown;
A ragged ditch—the Hun first line at last.
All smashed to hell. Their second right ahead,
So on you charge. There's nothing else to do.
More reeking holes, blood, barbed wire, gruesome **dead**;
(Your puttee strap's undone—that worries you).
You glare around. You think you're all alone.
But no; your chums come surging left and right.
The nearest chap flops down without a groan,
His face still snarling with the rage of fight.
Ha! here's the second trench—just like the first,

Only a little more so, more "laid out";
More pounded, flame-corroded, death-accurst;
A pretty piece of work, beyond a doubt.
Now for the third, and there your job is done,
So on you charge. You never stop to think.
Your cursed puttee's trailing as you run;
You feel you'd sell your soul to have a drink.
The acrid air is full of cracking whips.
You wonder how it is you're going still.
You foam with rage. Oh, God! to be at grips
With someone you can rush and crush and kill.
Your sleeve is dripping blood; you're seeing red;
You're battle-mad; your turn is coming now.
See! there's the jagged barbed wire straight ahead,
And there's the trench—you'll get there anyhow.
Your puttee catches on a strand of wire,
And down you go; perhaps it saves your life,
For over sandbag rims you see 'em fire,
Crop-headed chaps, their eyes ablaze with strife.
You crawl, you cower; then once again you plunge
With all your comrades roaring at your heels.
Have at 'em, lads! You stab, you jab, you lunge;
A blaze of glory, then the red world reels.
A crash of triumph, then . . . you're faint a bit . . .
That cursed puttee! Now to fasten it. . . .

Well, that's the charge. And now I'm here alone.
I've built a little wall of Hun on Hun,
To shield me from the leaden bees that drone
(It saves me worry, and it hurts 'em none).
The only thing I'm wondering is when
Some stretcher-men will stroll along my way?
It isn't much that's left of me, but then

Where life is, hope is, so at least they say.
Well, if I'm spared I'll be the happy lad.
I tell you I won't envy any king.
I've stood the racket, and I'm proud and glad;
I've had my crowning hour. Oh, War's the thing!
It gives us common, working chaps our chance,
A taste of glory, chivalry, romance.

Ay, War, they say, is hell; it's heaven, too.
It lets a man discover what he's worth.
It takes his measure, shows what he can do,
Gives him a joy like nothing else on earth.
It fans in him a flame that otherwise
Would flicker out, these drab, discordant days;
It teaches him in pain and sacrifice
Faith, fortitude, grim courage past all praise.
Yes, War is good. So here beside my slain,
A happy wreck I wait amid the din;
For even if I perish mine's the gain. . . .
Hi, there, you fellows! *Won't* you take me in?
Give me a fag to smoke upon the way. . . .
We've taken La Boiselle! The hell, you say!
Well, that would make a corpse sit up and grin. . . .
Lead on! I'll live to fight another day.

FAITH

Since all that is was ever bound to be;
Since grim, eternal laws our Being bind;
And both the riddle and the answer find,
And both the carnage and the calm decree;
Since plain within the Book of Destiny
Is written all the journey of mankind
Inexorably to the end; since blind
And mortal puppets playing parts are we:

Then let's have faith; good cometh out of ill;
The power that shaped the strife shall end the strife;
Then let's bow down before the Unknown Will;
Fight on, believing all is well with life;
Seeing within the worst of War's red rage
The gleam, the glory of the Golden Age.

THE COWARD

'Ave you seen Bill's mug in the Noos to-day?
'E's gyned the Victoriar Cross, they say;
Little Bill wot would grizzle and run away,
   If you 'it 'im a swipe on the jawr.
'E's slaughtered the Kaiser's men in tons;
'E's captured one of their quick-fire guns,
And 'e 'adn't no practice in killin' 'Uns
   Afore 'e went off to the war.

   Little Bill wot I nussed in 'is by-by clothes;
   Little Bill wot told me 'is childish woes;
   'Ow often I've tidied 'is pore little nose
      Wiv the 'em of me pinnyfore.
   And now all the papers 'is praises ring,
   And 'e's been and 'e's shaken the 'and of the King
   And I sawr 'im to-day in the ward, pore thing,
      Where they're patchin' 'im up once more.

And 'e says: "Wot d'ye think of it, Lizer Ann?"
And I says: "Well, I can't make it out, old man;
You'd 'ook it as soon as a scrap began,
   When you was a bit of a kid."
And 'e whispers: " 'Ere, on the quiet, Liz,
They're makin' too much of the 'ole damn biz,
And the papers is printin' me ugly phiz,
   But . . . I'm 'anged if I know wot I did.

"Oh, the Captain comes and 'e says: 'Look 'ere!
They're far too quiet out there: it's queer.

They're up to somethin'—'oo'll volunteer
　To crawl in the dark and see?'
Then I felt me 'eart like a 'ammer go,
And up jumps a chap and 'e says: 'Right O!'
But I chips in straight, and I says 'Oh no!
　'E's a missis and kids—take me.'

　　"And the next I knew I was sneakin' out,
　　And the oozy corpses was all about,
　　And I felt so scared I wanted to shout,
　　　And me skin fair prickled wiv fear;
　　And I sez: 'You coward! You 'ad no right
　　To take on the job of a man this night,'
　　Yet still I kept creepin' till ('orrid sight!)
　　　The trench of the 'Uns was near.

"It was all so dark, it was all so still;
Yet somethin' pushed me against me will;
'Ow I wanted to turn! Yet I crawled until
　I was seein' a dim light shine.
Then thinks I: 'I'll just go a little bit,
And see wot the doose I can make of it,'
And it seemed to come from the mouth of a pit:
　'Christmas!' sez I, 'a *mine*.'

"Then 'ere's the part wot I can't explain:
I wanted to make for 'ome again,
But somethin' was blazin' inside me brain,
　So I crawled to the trench instead;
Then I saw the bullet 'ead of a 'Un,
And 'e stood by a rapid-firer gun,
And I lifted a rock and I 'it 'im one,
　And 'e dropped like a chunk o' lead.

"Then all the 'Uns that was underground,
Comes up with a rush and on with a bound,
And I swings that giddy old Maxim round
   And belts 'em solid and square.
You see I was off me chump wiv fear:
'If I'm sellin' me life,' sez I, 'it's dear.'
And the trench was narrow and they was near,
   So I peppered the brutes for fair.

"So I 'eld 'em back and I yelled wiv fright,
And the boys attacked and we 'ad a fight,
And we 'captured a section o' trench' that night
   Which we didn't expect to get;
And they found me there with me Maxim gun,
And I'd laid out a score if I'd laid out one,
And I fainted away when the thing was done,
   And I 'aven't got over it yet."

So that's the 'istory Bill told me.
Of course it's all on the strict Q. T.;
It wouldn't do to get out, you see,
   As 'e hacted against 'is will.
But 'e's convalescin' wiv all 'is might,
And 'e 'opes to be fit for another fight—
Say! Ain't 'e a bit of the real all right?
   Wot's the matter with Bill!

MISSIS MORIARTY'S BOY

Missis Moriarty called last week, and says she to me, says she:
"Sure the heart of me's broken entirely now—it's the fortunate
    woman you are;
You've still got your Dinnis to cheer up your home, but me
    Patsy boy where is he?
Lyin' alone, cold as a stone, kilt in the weariful wahr.
Oh, I'm seein' him now as I looked on him last, wid his hair all
    curly and bright,
And the wonderful, tenderful heart he had, and his eyes as he
    wint away,
Shinin' and lookin' down on me from the pride of his proper
    height:
Sure I'll remember me boy like that if I live to me dyin' day."

And just as she spoke them very same words me Dinnis came in
    at the door,
Came in from McGonigle's ould shebeen, came in from drinkin'
    his pay;
And Missis Moriarty looked at him, and she didn't say anny
    more,
But she wrapped her head in her ould black shawl, and she
    quietly wint away.
And what was I thinkin', I ask ye now, as I put me Dinnis to bed,
Wid him ravin' and cursin' one half of the night, as cold by his
    side I sat;
Was I thinkin' the poor ould woman she was wid her Patsy
    slaughtered and dead?
Was I weepin' for Missis Moriarty? I'm not so sure about that.

Missis Moriarty goes about wid a shinin' look on her face;

Wid her grey hair under her ould black shawl, and the eyes of
her mother-mild;

Some say she's a little bit off her head; but annyway it's the
case,

Her timper's so swate that you nivver would tell she'd be losin'
her only child.

And I think, as I wait up ivery night for me Dinnis to come home
blind,

And I'm hearin' his stumblin' foot on the stair along about half-
past three:

Sure there's many a way of breakin' a heart, and I haven't made
up me mind—

Would I be Missis Moriarty, or Missis Moriarty me?

MY FOE

A Belgian Priest-Soldier Speaks:—

Gurr! You *cochon!* Stand and fight!
Show your mettle! Snarl and bite!
Spawn of an accursed race,
Turn and meet me face to face!
Here amid the wreck and rout
Let us grip and have it out!
Here where ruins rock and reel
Let us settle, steel to steel!
Look! Our houses, how they spit
Sparks from brands your friends have lit.
See! Our gutters running red,
Bright with blood your friends have shed.
Hark! Amid your drunken brawl
How our maidens shriek and call.
Why have *you* come here alone,
To this hearth's blood-spattered stone?
Come to ravish, come to loot,
Come to play the ghoulish brute.
Ah, indeed! We well are met,
Bayonet to bayonet.
God! I never killed a man:
Now I'll do the best I can.
Rip you to the evil heart,
Laugh to see the life-blood start.
Bah! You swine! I hate you so.
Show you mercy? No! . . . and no! . . .

There! I've done it. See! He lies
Death a-staring from his eyes;
Glazing eyeballs, panting breath,
How it's horrible, is Death!
Plucking at his bloody lips
With his trembling finger-tips;
Choking in a dreadful way
As if he would something say
In that uncouth tongue of his. . . .
Oh, how horrible Death is!

How I wish that he would die!
So unnerved, unmanned am I.
See! His twitching face is white!
See! His bubbling blood is bright.
Why do I not shout with glee?
What strange spell is over me?
There he lies; the fight was fair;
Let me toss my cap in air.
Why am I so silent? Why
Do I pray for him to die?
Where is all my vengeful joy?
Ugh! *My foe is but a boy.*

I'd a brother of his age
Perished in the war's red rage;
Perished in the Ypres hell:
Oh, I loved my brother well.
And though I be hard and grim,
How it makes me think of him!
He had just such flaxen hair
As the lad that's lying there.
Just such frank blue eyes were his. . . .
God! How horrible war is!

I have reason to be gay:
There is one less foe to slay.
I have reason to be glad:
Yet—my foe is such a lad.
So I watch in dull amaze,
See his dying eyes a-glaze,
See his face grow glorified,
See his hands outstretched and wide
To that bit of ruined wall
Where the flames have ceased to crawl,
Where amid the crumbling bricks
Hangs *a blackened crucifix.*

Now, oh, now I understand.
Quick I press it in his hand,
Close his feeble finger-tips,
Hold it to his faltering lips.
As I watch his welling blood
I would stem it if I could.
God of Pity, let him live!
God of Love, forgive, forgive.

　　•　　•　　•　　•　　•　　•

His face looked strangely, as he died,
Like that of One they crucified.
And in the pocket of his coat
I found a letter; thus he wrote:
The things I've seen! Oh, mother dear,
I'm wondering can God be here?
To-night amid the drunken brawl
I saw a Cross hung on a wall;
I'll seek it now, and there alone
Perhaps I may atone, atone. . . .

Ah no! 'Tis I who must atone.
No other saw but God alone;
Yet how can I forget the sight
Of that face so woeful white!
Dead I kissed him as he lay,
Knelt by him and tried to pray;
Left him lying there at rest,
Crucifix upon his breast.

Not for him the pity be.
Ye who pity, pity me,
Crawling now the ways I trod,
Blood-guilty in sight of God.

MY JOB

I'VE got a little job on 'and, the time is drawin' nigh;
At seven by the Captain's watch I'm due to go and do it;
I wants to 'ave it nice and neat, and pleasin' to the eye,
And I 'opes the God of soldier men will see me safely through it.
Because, you see, it's somethin' I 'ave never done before;
And till you 'as experience noo stunts is always tryin';
The chances is I'll never 'ave to do it any more:
At seven by the Captain's watch my little job is . . . *dyin'*.

I've got a little note to write; I'd best begin it now.
I ain't much good at writin' notes, but here goes: "Dearest
    Mother,
I've been in many 'ot old 'do's'; I've scraped through safe
    some'ow,
But now I'm on the very point of tacklin' another.
A little job of hand-grenades; they called for volunteers.
They picked me out; I'm proud of it; it seems a trifle dicky.
If anythin' should 'appen, well, there ain't no call for tears,
And so . . . I 'opes this finds you well.—Your werry lovin'
    Micky."

I've got a little score to settle wiv them swine out there.
I've 'ad so many of me pals done in it's quite upset me.
I've seen so much of bloody death I don't seem for to care,
If I can only even up, how soon the blighters get me.
I'm sorry for them perishers that corpses in a bed;
I only 'opes mine's short and sweet, no linger-longer-lyin';
I've made a mess of life, but now I'll try to make instead . . .
It's seven sharp. Good-bye, old pals! . . . *a decent job in dyin'*.

THE SONG OF THE PACIFIST

WHAT do they matter, our headlong hates, when we take the toll
    of our Dead?
Think ye our glory and gain will pay for the torrent of blood we
    have shed?
By the cheers of our Victory will the heart of the mother be
    comforted?

If by the Victory all we mean is a broken and brooding foe;
Is the pomp and power of a glitt'ring hour, and a truce for an
    age or so:
By the clay-cold hand on the broken blade we have smitten a
    bootless blow!

If by the Triumph we only prove that the sword we sheathe is
    bright;
That justice and truth and love endure; that freedom's throned
    on the height;
That the feebler folks shall be unafraid; that Might shall never be
    Right;

If this be all: by the blood-drenched plains, by the havoc of fire
    and fear,
By the rending roar of the War of Wars, by the Dead so doubly
    dear. . . .
Then our Victory is a vast defeat, and it mocks us as we cheer.

Victory! there can be but one, hallowed in every land:
When by the graves of our common dead we who were foemen
    stand;
And in the hush of our common grief hand is tendered to hand.

Triumph! Yes, when out of the dust in the splendour of their
    release
The spirits of those who fell go forth and they hallow our hearts
    to peace,
And, brothers in pain, with world-wide voice, we clamour that
    War shall cease.

Glory! Ay, when from blackest loss shall be born most radiant
    gain;
When over the gory fields shall rise a star that never shall wane:
Then, and then only, our Dead shall know that they have not
    fall'n in vain.

When our children's children shall talk of War as a madness
    that may not be;
When we thank our God for our grief to-day, and blazon from
    sea to sea
In the name of the Dead the banner of Peace . . . *that will be
    Victory.*

THE TWINS

THERE were two brothers, John and James,
And when the town went up in flames,
To save the house of James dashed John,
Then turned, and lo! his own was gone.

And when the great World War began,
To volunteer John promptly ran;
And while he learned live bombs to lob,
James stayed at home and—sneaked his job.

John came home with a missing limb;
That didn't seem to worry him;
But oh, it set his brain awhirl
To find that James had—sneaked his girl!

Time passed. John tried his grief to drown;
To-day James owns one-half the town;
His army contracts riches yield;
And John? Well, *search the Potter's Field.*

THE SONG OF THE SOLDIER-BORN

Give me the scorn of the stars and a peak defiant;
Wail of the pines and a wind with the shout of a giant;
Night and a trail unknown and a heart reliant.

Give me to live and love in the old, bold fashion;
A soldier's billet at night and a soldier's ration;
A heart that leaps to the fight with a soldier's passion.

For I hold as a simple faith there's no denying;
The trade of a soldier's the only trade worth plying;
The death of a soldier's the only death worth dying.

So let me go and leave your safety behind me;
Go to the spaces of hazard where nothing shall bind me;
Go till the word is War—and then you will find me.

Then you will call me and claim me because you will need me;
Cheer me and gird me and into the battle-wrath speed me. . . .
And when it's over, spurn me and no longer heed me.

For guile and a purse gold-greased are the arms you carry;
With deeds of paper you fight and with pens you parry;
You call on the hounds of the law your foes to harry.

You with your "Art for its own sake," posing and prinking;
You with your "Live and be merry," eating and drinking;
You with your "Peace at all hazard," from bright blood shrink-
    ing.

Fools! I will tell you now: though the red rain patters,
And a million of men go down, it's little it matters. . . .
There's the Flag upflung to the stars, though it streams in tatters.

There's a glory gold never can buy to yearn and to cry for;
There's a hope that's as old as the sky to suffer and sigh for;
There's a faith that out-dazzles the sun to martyr and die for.

Ah no! it's my dream that War will never be ended;
That men will perish like men, and valour be splendid;
That the Flag by the sword will be served, and honour defended.

That the tale of my fights will never be ancient story;
That though my eye may be dim and my beard be hoary,
I'll die as a soldier dies on the Field of Glory.

So give me a strong right arm for a wrong's swift righting;
Stave of a song on my lips as my sword is smiting;
Death in my boots may-be, but fighting, fighting.

AFTERNOON TEA

As I was saying . . . (No, thank you; I never take cream with
    my tea;
Cows weren't allowed in the trenches—got out of the habit,
    y'see.)
As I was saying, our Colonel leaped up like a youngster of ten:
"Come on, lads!" he shouts, "and we'll show 'em." And he
    sprang to the head of the men.
Then some bally thing seemed to trip him, and he fell on his face
    with a slam. . . .
Oh, he died like a true British soldier, and the last word he ut-
    tered was "Damn!"
And hang it! I loved the old fellow, and something just burst in
    my brain,
And I cared no more for the bullets than I would for a shower
    of rain.
'Twas an awf'ly funny sensation (I say, this is jolly nice tea);
I felt as if something had broken; by gad! I was suddenly free.
Free for a glorified moment, beyond regulations and laws,
Free just to wallow in slaughter, as the chap of the Stone Age
    was.
So on I went joyously nursing a Berserker rage of my own,
And though all my chaps were behind me, feeling most frightf'ly
    alone;
With the bullets and shells ding-donging, and the "krock" and
    the swish of the shrap;
And I found myself humming "Ben Bolt" . . . (Will you pass
    me the sugar, old chap?
Two lumps, please). . . . What was I saying? Oh yes, the jolly
    old dash;

We simply ripped through the barrage, and on with a roar and
a crash.
My fellows—Old Nick couldn't stop 'em. On, on they went
with a yell,
Till they tripped on the Boches' sand-bags,—nothing much left
to tell:
A trench so tattered and battered that even a rat couldn't live;
Some corpses tangled and mangled, wire you could pass through
a sieve.
The jolly old guns had bilked us, cheated us out of our show,
And my fellows were simply yearning for a red mix-up with
the foe.
So I shouted to them to follow, and on we went roaring again,
Battle-tuned and exultant, on in the leaden rain.
Then all at once a machine gun barks from a bit of a bank,
And our Major roars in a fury: "We've got to take it on flank."
He was running like fire to lead us, when down like a stone he
comes,
As full of "typewriter" bullets as a pudding is full of plums.
So I took his job and we got 'em. . . . By gad! we got 'em like
rats;
Down in a deep shell-crater we fought like Kilkenny cats.
'Twas pleasant just for a moment to be sheltered and out of
range,
With someone you *saw* to go for—it made an agreeable change.
And the Boches that missed my bullets, my chaps gave a bayo-
net jolt,
And all the time, I remember, I whistled and hummed "Ben
Bolt."

Well, that little job was over, so hell for leather we ran,
On to the second line trenches,—that's where the fun began.

For though we had strafed 'em like fury, there still were some
    Boches about,
And my fellows, teeth set and eyes glaring, like terriers routed
    'em out.
Then I stumbled on one of their dug-outs, and I shouted: "Is
    anyone there?"
And a voice, "Yes, one; but I'm wounded," came faint up the
    narrow stair;
And my man was descending before me, when sudden a cry!
    a shot!
(I say, this cake is delicious. You make it yourself, do you not?)
My man? Oh, they killed the poor devil; for if there was one
    there was ten;
So after I'd bombed 'em sufficient I went down at the head of
    my men,
And four tried to sneak from a bunk-hole, but we cornered the
    rotters all right;
I'd rather not go into details, 'twas messy that bit of the fight.
But all of it's beastly messy; let's talk of pleasanter things:
The skirts that the girls are wearing, ridiculous fluffy things,
So short that they show. . . . Oh, hang it! Well, if I must, I
    must.
We cleaned out the second trench line, bomb and bayonet
    thrust;
And on we went to the third one, quite calloused to crumping
    by now;
And some of our fellows who'd passed us were making a deuce
    of a row;
And my chaps—well, I just couldn't hold 'em; (It's strange how
    it is with gore;
In some ways it's just like whiskey: if you taste it you must
    have more.)

Their eyes were like beacons of battle; by gad, sir! they *couldn't* be calmed,

So I headed 'em bang for the bomb-belt, racing like billy-be-damned.

Oh, it didn't take long to arrive there, those who arrived at all;

The machine guns were certainly chronic, the shindy enough to appal.

Oh yes, I omitted to tell you, I'd wounds on the chest and the head,

And my shirt was torn to a gun-rag, and my face blood-gummy and red.

I'm thinking I looked like a madman; I fancy I felt one too,

Half naked and swinging a rifle. . . . God! what a glorious "do."

As I sit here in old Piccadilly, sipping my afternoon tea,

I see a blind, bullet-chipped devil, and it's hard to believe that it's me;

I see a wild, war-damaged demon, smashing out left and right,

And humming "Ben Bolt" rather loudly, and hugely enjoying the fight.

And as for my men, may God bless 'em! I've loved 'em ever since then:

They fought like the shining angels; they're the pick o' the land, my men.

And the trench was a reeking shambles, not a Boche to be seen alive—

So I thought; but on rounding a traverse I came on a covey of five;

And four of 'em threw up their flippers, but the fifth chap, a sergeant, was game,

And though I'd a bomb and revolver he came at me just the same.

A sporty thing that, I tell you; I just couldn't blow him to hell,
So I swung to the point of his jaw-bone, and down like a nine-
pin he fell.
And then when I'd brought him to reason, he wasn't half bad,
that Hun;
He bandaged my head and my short-rib as well as the Doc could
have done.
So back I went with my Boches, as gay as a two-year-old colt,
And it suddenly struck me as rummy, I still was a-humming
"Ben Bolt."
And now, by Jove! how I've bored you. You've just let me
babble away;
Let's talk of the things that *matter*—your car or the newest
play. . . .

THE MOURNERS

I LOOK into the aching womb of night;
I look across the mist that masks the dead;
The moon is tired and gives but little light,
    The stars have gone to bed.

The earth is sick and seems to breathe with pain;
A lost wind whimpers in a mangled tree;
I do not see the foul, corpse-cluttered plain,
    The dead I do not see.

The slain I *would* not see . . . and so I lift
My eyes from out the shambles where they lie;
When lo! a million woman-faces drift
    Like pale leaves through the sky.

The cheeks of some are channelled deep with tears;
But some are tearless, with wild eyes that stare
Into the shadow of the coming years
    Of fathomless despair.

And some are young, and some are very old;
And some are rich, some poor beyond belief;
Yet all are strangely like, set in the mould
    Of everlasting grief.

They fill the vast of Heaven, face on face;
And then I see one weeping with the rest,
Whose eyes beseech me for a moment's space. . . .
    Oh eyes I love the best!

Nay, I but dream. The sky is all forlorn,
And there's the plain of battle writhing red:
God pity them, the women-folk who mourn!
How happy are the dead!

L'ENVOI

My job is done; my rhymes are ranked and ready,
My word-battalions marching verse by verse;
Here stanza-companies are none too steady;
There print-platoons are weak, but might be worse.
And as in marshalled order I review them,
My type-brigades, unfearful of the fray,
My eyes that seek their faults are seeing through them
Immortal visions of an epic day.

It seems I'm in a giant bowling-alley;
The hidden heavies round me crash and thud;
A spire snaps like a pipe-stem in the valley;
The rising sun is like a ball of blood.
Along the road the "fantassins" are pouring,
And some are gay as fire, and some steel-stern. . . .
Then back again I see the red tide pouring,
Along the reeking road from Hebuterne.

And once again I seek Hill Sixty-Seven,
The Hun lines grey and peaceful in my sight;
When suddenly the rosy air is riven—
A "coal-box" blots the "boyou" on my right.
Or else to evil Carnoy I am stealing,
Past sentinels who hail with bated breath;
Where not a cigarette spark's dim revealing
May hint our mission in that zone of death.

I see across the shrapnel-seeded meadows
The jagged rubble-heap of La Boiselle;

Blood-guilty Fricourt brooding in the shadows,
And Thiepval's château empty as a shell.
Down Albert's riven streets the moon is leering;
The Hanging Virgin takes its bitter ray;
And all the road from Hamel I am hearing
The silver rage of bugles over Bray.

Once more within the sky's deep sapphire hollow
I sight a swimming Taube, a fairy thing;
I watch the angry shell flame flash and follow
In feather puffs that flick a tilted wing;
And then it fades, with shrapnel mirror's flashing;
The flashes bloom to blossoms lily gold;
The batteries are rancorously crashing,
And life is just as full as it can hold.

Oh spacious days of glory and of grieving!
Oh sounding hours of lustre and of loss!
Let us be glad we lived you, still believing
The God who gave the cannon gave the Cross.
Let us be sure amid these seething passions,
The lusts of blood and hate our souls abhor:
The Power that Order out of Chaos fashions
Smites fiercest in the wrath-red forge of War. . . .
Have faith! Fight on! Amid the battle-hell
Love triumphs, Freedom beacons, all is well.

Book Five

BALLADS OF A BOHEMIAN

PRELUDE

Alas! upon some starry height,
The Gods of Excellence to please,
This hand of mine will never smite
The Harp of High Serenities.
Mere minstrel of the street am I,
To whom a careless coin you fling;
But who, beneath the bitter sky,
Blue-lipped, yet insolent of eye,
Can shrill a song of Spring;
A song of merry mansard days,
The cheery chimney-tops among;
Of rolics and of roundelays
When we were young . . . when we were young;
A song of love and lilac nights,
Of wit, of wisdom and of wine;
Of Folly whirling on the Heights,
Of hunger and of hope divine;
Of Blanche, Suzette and Celestine,
And all that gay and tender band
Who shared with us the fat, the lean,
The hazard of Illusion-land;
When scores of Philistines we slew
As mightily with brush and pen
We sought to make the world anew,
And scorned the gods of other men;
When we were fools divinely wise,
Who held it rapturous to strive;
When Art was sacred in our eyes,
And it was Heav'n to be alive. . . .

O days of glamour, glory, truth,
To you to-night I raise my glass;

O freehold of immortal youth,
Bohemia, the lost, alas!
O laughing lads who led the romp,
Respectable you've grown, I'm told;
Your heads you bow to power and pomp,
You've learned to know the worth of gold.
O merry maids who shared our cheer,
Your eyes are dim, your locks are grey;
And as you scrub I sadly fear
Your daughters speed the dance to-day.
O windmill land and crescent moon!
O Columbine and Pierrette!
To you my old guitar I tune
Ere I forget, ere I forget. . . .

So come, good men who toil and tire,
Who smoke and sip the kindly cup,
Ring round about the tavern fire
Ere yet you drink your liquor up;
And hear my simple songs of earth,
Of youth and truth and living things;
Of poverty and proper mirth,
Of rags and rich imaginings;
Of cock-a-hoop, blue-heavened days,
Of hearts elate and eager breath,
Of wonder, worship, pity, praise,
Of sorrow, sacrifice and death;
Of lusting, laughter, passion, pain,
Of lights that lure and dreams that thrall . . .
And if a golden word I gain,
Oh, kindly folks, God save you all!
And if you shake your heads in blame . . .
Good friends, God love you all the same.

BOOK ONE

SPRING

I

All day the sun has shone into my little attic, a bitter sunshine that brightened yet did not warm. And so as I toiled and toiled doggedly enough, many were the looks I cast at the three faggots I had saved to cook my evening meal. Now, however, my supper is over, my pipe alight, and as I stretch my legs before the embers I have at last a glow of comfort, a glimpse of peace.

MY GARRET

Here is my Garret up five flights of stairs;
Here's where I deal in dreams and ply in fancies,
Here is the wonder-shop of all my wares,
My sounding sonnets and my red romances.
Here's where I challenge Fate and ring my rhymes,
And grope at glory—aye, and starve at times.

Here is my Stronghold: stout of heart am I,
Greeting each dawn as songful as a linnet;
And when at night on yon poor bed I lie
(Blessing the world and every soul that's in it),
Here's where I thank the Lord no shadow bars
My skylight's vision of the valiant stars.

Here is my Palace tapestried with dreams.
Ah! though to-night ten *sous* are all my treasure,
While in my gaze immortal beauty gleams,
Am I not dowered with wealth beyond all measure?
Though in my ragged coat my songs I sing,
King of my soul, I envy not the king.

Here is my Haven: it's so quiet here;
Only the scratch of pen, the candle's flutter;
Shabby and bare and small, but O how dear!
Mark you—my table with my work a-clutter,
My shelf of tattered books along the wall,
My bed, my broken chair—that's nearly all.

Only four faded walls, yet mine, all mine.
Oh, you fine folks, a pauper scorns your pity.
Look, where above me stars of rapture shine;
See, where below me gleams the siren city . . .
Am I not rich?—a millionaire no less,
If wealth be told in terms of Happiness.

Ten *sous*. . . . I think one can sing best of poverty when one is
holding it at arm's length. I'm sure that when I wrote these lines,
fortune had for a moment tweaked me by the nose. To-night, how-
ever, I am truly down to ten *sous*. It is for that I have stayed in my
room all day, rolled in my blankets and clutching my pen with
clammy fingers. I must work, work, work. I must finish my book
before poverty crushes me. I am not only writing for my living but
for my life. Even to-day my Muse was mutinous. For hours and
hours anxiously I stared at a paper that was blank; nervously I paced
up and down my garret; bitterly I flung myself on my bed. Then
suddenly it all came. Line after line I wrote with hardly a halt. So I
made another of my Ballads of the Boulevards. Here it is:

JULOT THE *APACHE*

You've heard of Julot the *apache*, and Gigolette, his *môme*. . . .
Montmartre was their hunting-ground, but Belville was their
      home.
A little chap just like a boy, with smudgy black mustache,—
Yet there was nothing juvenile in Julot the *apache*.
From head to heel as tough as steel, as nimble as a cat,
With every trick of twist and kick, a master of *savate*.

And Gigolette was tall and fair, as stupid as a cow,
With three combs in the greasy hair she banged upon her brow.
You'd see her on the Place Pigalle on any afternoon,
A primitive and strapping wench as brazen as the moon.
And yet there is a tale that's told of Clichy after dark,
And two *gendarmes* who swung their arms with Julot for a
mark.
And oh, but they'd have got him too; they banged and blazed
away,
When like a flash a woman leapt between them and their prey.
She took the medicine meant for him; she came down with a
crash . . .
"Quick now, and make your get-away, O Julot the *apache!*"
But no! He turned, ran swiftly back, his arms around her met;
They nabbed him sobbing like a kid, and kissing Gigolette.

Now I'm a reckless painter chap who loves a jamboree,
And one night in Cyrano's bar I got upon a spree;
And there were trollops all about, and crooks of every kind,
But though the place was reeling round I didn't seem to mind.
Till down I sank, and all was blank when in the bleary dawn
I woke up in my studio to find—my money gone;
Three hundred francs I'd scraped and squeezed to pay my
quarter's rent.
"Someone has pinched my wad," I wailed; "it never has been
spent."
And as I racked my brains to seek how I could raise some more,
Before my cruel landlord kicked me cowering from the door:
A knock . . . "Come in," I gruffly groaned; I did not raise
my head,
Then lo! I heard a husky voice, a swift and silky tread:
"You got so blind, last night, *mon vieux*, I collared all your
cash—

Three hundred francs. . . . There! *Nom de Dieu*," said Julot
 the *apache*.

And that was how I came to know Julot and Gigolette,
And we would talk and drink a *bock*, and smoke a cigarette.
And I would meditate upon the artistry of crime,
And he would tell of cracking cribs and cops and doing time;
Or else when he was flush of funds he'd carelessly explain
He'd biffed some bloated *bourgeois* on the border of the Seine.
So gentle and polite he was, just like a man of peace,
And not a desperado and the terror of the police.

Now one day in a *bistro* that's behind the Place Vendôme
I came on Julot the *apache*, and Gigolette his *môme*.
And as they looked so very grave, says I to them, says I,
"Come on and have a little glass, it's good to rinse the eye.
You both look mighty serious; you've something on the heart."
"Ah, yes," said Julot the *apache*, "we've something to impart.
When such things come to folks like us, it isn't very gay . . .
It's Gigolette—she tells me that a *gosse* is on the way."
Then Gigolette, she looked at me with eyes like stones of gall:
"If we were honest folks," said she, "I wouldn't mind at all.
But then . . . you know the life we lead; well, anyway I mean
(That is, providing it's a girl) to call her Angeline."
"Cheer up," said I; "it's all in life. There's gold within the dross.
Come on, we'll drink another *verre* to Angeline the *gosse*."

And so the weary winter passed, and then one April morn
The worthy Julot came at last to say the babe was born.
"I'd like to chuck it in the Seine," he sourly snarled, "and yet
I guess I'll have to let it live, because of Gigolette."
I only laughed, for sure I saw his spite was all a bluff,
And he was prouder than a prince behind his manner gruff.

Yet every day he'd blast the brat with curses deep and grim,
And swear to me that Gigolette no longer thought of *him.*
And then one night he dropped the mask; his eyes were sick with
    dread,
And when I offered him a smoke he groaned and shook his head:
"I'm all upset; it's Angeline . . . she's covered with a rash . . .
She'll maybe die, my little *gosse,*" cried Julot the *apache.*

But Angeline, I joy to say, came through the test all right,
Though Julot, so they tell me, watched beside her day and night.
And when I saw him next, says he: "Come up and dine with me.
We'll buy a beefsteak on the way, a bottle and some *brie.*"
And so I had a merry night within his humble home,
And laughed with Angeline the *gosse* and Gigolette the *môme.*
And every time that Julot used a word the least obscene,
How Gigolette would frown at him and point to Angeline:
Oh, such a little innocent, with hair of silken floss,
I do not wonder they were proud of Angeline the *gosse.*
And when her arms were round his neck, then Julot says to me:
"I must work harder now, *mon vieux,* since I've to work for
    three."
He worked so very hard indeed, the police dropped in one day,
And for a year behind the bars they put him safe away.

So dark and silent now, their home; they'd gone—I wondered
    where,
Till in a laundry near I saw a child with shining hair;
And o'er the tub a strapping wench, her arms in soapy foam;
Lo! it was Angeline the *gosse,* and Gigolette the *môme.*
And so I kept an eye on them and saw that all went right,
Until at last came Julot home, half crazy with delight.
And when he'd kissed them both, says he: "I've had my fill this
    time.

I'm on the honest now, I am; I'm all fed up with crime.
You mark my words, the page I turn is going to be clean,
I swear it on the head of her, my little Angeline."

And so, to finish up my tale, this morning as I strolled
Along the boulevard I heard a voice I knew of old.
I saw a rosy little man with walrus-like mustache . . .
I stopped, I stared. . . . By all the gods! 'twas Julot the *apache*.
"I'm in the garden way," he said, "and doing mighty well;
I've half an acre under glass, and heaps of truck to sell.
Come out and see. Oh come, my friend, on Sunday, wet or
    shine . . .
Say!—*it's the First Communion of that little girl of mine*."

II

Chez Moi, Montparnasse,
The same evening.

To-day is an anniversary. A year ago to-day I kicked over an
office stool and came to Paris thinking to make a living by my pen.
I was twenty then, and in my pocket I had twenty pounds. Of that,
my ten *sous* are all that remain. And so to-night I am going to spend
them, not prudently on bread, but prodigally on beer.

As I stroll down the Boul' Mich' the lingering light has all the
exquisite tenderness of violet; the trees are in their first translucent
green; beneath them the lamps are lit with purest gold, and from the
Little Luxembourg comes a silver jangle of tiny voices. Taking the
gay side of the street, I enter a café. Although it isn't its true name,
I choose to call my café—

L'ESCARGOT D'OR

O Tavern of the Golden Snail!
Ten *sous* have I, so I'll regale;
Ten *sous* your amber brew to sip

(Eight for the *bock* and two the tip),
And so I'll sit the evening long,
And smoke my pipe and watch the throng,
The giddy crowd that drains and drinks,
I'll watch it quiet as a sphinx;
And who among them all shall buy
For ten poor *sous* such joy as I?
As I who, snugly tucked away,
Look on it all as on a play,
A frolic scene of love and fun,
To please an audience of One.

O Tavern of the Golden Snail!
You've stuff indeed for many a tale.
All eyes, all ears, I nothing miss:
Two lovers lean to clasp and kiss;
The merry students sing and shout,
The nimble *garçons* dart about;
Lo! here come Mimi and Musette
With: "*S'il vous plait, une cigarette?*"
Marcel and Rudolf, Schaunard too,
Behold the old rapscallion crew,
With flowing tie and shaggy head . . .
Who says Bohemia is dead?
Oh shades of Murger! prank and clown,
And I will watch and write it down.

O Tavern of the Golden Snail!
What crackling throats have gulped your ale!
What sons of Fame from far and near
Have glowed and mellowed in your cheer!
Within this corner where I sit
Banville and Coppée clashed their wit;

And hither too, to dream and drain,
And drown despair, came poor Verlaine.
Here Wilde would talk and Synge would muse,
Maybe like me with just ten *sous*.
Ah! one is lucky, is one not?
With ghosts so rare to drain a pot!
So may your custom never fail,
O Tavern of the Golden Snail!

There! my pipe is out. Let me light it again and consider. I have
no illusions about myself. I am not fool enough to think I am a poet,
but I have a knack of rhyme and I love to make verses. Mine is a
tootling, tin-whistle music. Humbly and afar I follow in the foot-
steps of Praed and Lampson, of Field and Riley, hoping that in time
my Muse may bring me bread and butter. So far, however, it has
been all kicks and no coppers. And to-night I am at the end of my
tether. I wish I knew where to-morrow's breakfast was coming
from. Well, since rhyming's been my ruin, let me rhyme to the
bitter end.

IT IS LATER THAN YOU THINK

Lone amid the café's cheer,
Sad of heart am I to-night;
Dolefully I drink my beer,
But no single line I write.
There's the wretched rent to pay,
Yet I glower at pen and ink:
Oh, inspire me, Muse, I pray,
It is later than you think!

Hello! there's a pregnant phrase.
Bravo! let me write it down;
Hold it with a hopeful gaze,
Gauge it with a fretful frown;

Tune it to my lyric lyre . . .
Ah! upon starvation's brink,
How the words are dark and dire:
It is later than you think.

Weigh them well. . . . Behold yon band,
Students drinking by the door,
Madly merry, *bock* in hand,
Saucers stacked to mark their score.
Get you gone, you jolly scamps;
Let your parting glasses clink;
Seek your long neglected lamps:
It is later than you think.

Look again: yon dainty blonde,
All allure and golden grace,
Oh so willing to respond
Should you turn a smiling face.
Play your part, poor pretty doll;
Feast and frolic, pose and prink;
There's the Morgue to end it all,
And it's later than you think.

Yon's a playwright—mark his face,
Puffed and purple, tense and tired;
Pasha-like he holds his place,
Hated, envied and admired.
How you gobble life, my friend;
Wine, and woman soft and pink!
Well, each tether has its end:
Sir, it's later than you think.

See yon living scarecrow pass
With a wild and wolfish stare

At each empty absinthe glass,
As if he saw Heaven there.
Poor damned wretch, to end your pain
There is still the Greater Drink.
Yonder waits the sanguine Seine . . .
It is later than you think.

Lastly, you who read; aye, you
Who this very line may scan:
Think of all you planned to do . . .
Have you done the best you can?
See! the tavern lights are low;
Black's the night, and how you shrink!
God! and is it time to go?
Ah! the clock is always slow;
It is later than you think;
Sadly later than you think;
Far, far later than you think.

Scarcely do I scribble that last line on the back of an old envelope when a voice hails me. It is a fellow free-lance, a short-story man called MacBean. He is having a feast of *Marennes* and he asks me to join him.

MacBean is a Scotsman with the soul of an Irishman. He has a keen, lean, spectacled face, and if it were not for his grey hair he might be taken for a student of theology. However, there is nothing of the Puritan in MacBean. He loves wine and women, and money melts in his fingers.

He has lived so long in the Quarter he looks at life from the Parisian angle. His knowledge of literature is such that he might be a Professor, but he would rather be a vagabond of letters. We talk shop. We discuss the American short story, but MacBean vows they do these things better in France. He says that some of the *contes* printed every day in the *Journal* are worthy of Maupassant. After that he buys more beer, and we roam airily over the fields of litera-

ture, plucking here and there a blossom of quotation. A fine talk,
vivid and eager. It puts me into a kind of glow.

MacBean pays the bill from a handful of big notes, and the thought
of my own empty pockets for a moment damps me. However, when
we rise to go, it is well after midnight, and I am in a pleasant daze.
The rest of the evening may be summed up in the following jingle:

NOCTAMBULE

ZUT! it's two o'clock.
See! the lights are jumping.
Finish up your *bock*,
Time we all were humping.
Waiters stack the chairs,
Pile them on the tables;
Let us to our lairs
Underneath the gables.

Up the old Boul' Mich'
Climb with steps erratic.
Steady . . . how I wish
I was in my attic!
Full am I with cheer;
In my heart the joy stirs;
Couldn't be the beer,
Must have been the oysters.

In obscene array
Garbage cans spill over;
How I wish that they
Smelled as sweet as clover!
Charing women wait;
Cafés drop their shutters;
Rats perambulate
Up and down the gutters.

Down the darkened street
Market carts are creeping;
Horse with wary feet,
Red-faced driver sleeping.
Loads of vivid greens,
Carrots, leeks, potatoes,
Cabbages and beans,
Turnips and tomatoes.

Pair of dapper chaps,
Cigarettes and sashes,
Stare at me, perhaps
Desperate *Apachès*.
"Needn't bother me,
Jolly well you know it;
Parceque je suis
Quartier Latin poète.

"Give you villanelles,
Madrigals and lyrics;
Ballades and rondels,
Odes and panegyrics.
Poet pinched and poor,
Pricked by cold and hunger;
Trouble's troubadour,
Misery's balladmonger."

Think how queer it is!
Every move I'm making,
Cosmic gravity's
Center I am shaking;
Oh, how droll to feel
(As I now am feeling),

Even as I reel,
All the world is reeling.

Reeling too the stars,
Neptune and Uranus,
Jupiter and Mars,
Mercury and Venus;
Suns and moons with me,
As I'm homeward straying,
All in sympathy
Swaying, swaying, swaying.

Lord! I've got a head.
Well, it's not surprising.
I must gain my bed
Ere the sun be rising;
When the merry lark
In the sky is soaring,
I'll refuse to hark,
I'll be snoring, snoring.

Strike a sulphur match . . .
Ha! at last my garret.
Fumble at the latch,
Close the door and bar it.
Bed, you graciously
Wait, despite my scorning . . .
So, bibaciously
Mad old world, good morning.

III

MY GARRET, MONTPARNASSE,
April.

INSOMNIA

HEIGH ho! to sleep I vainly try;
Since twelve I haven't closed an eye,
And now it's three, and as I lie,
From Notre Dame to St. Denis
The bells of Paris chime to me;
"You're young," they say, "and strong and free."

I do not turn with sighs and groans
To ease my limbs, to rest my bones,
As if my bed were stuffed with stones,
No peevish murmur tips my tongue—
Ah no! for every sound upflung
Says: "Lad, you're free and strong and young."

And so beneath the sheet's caress
My body purrs with happiness;
Joy bubbles in my veins. . . . Ah yes,
My very blood that leaps along
Is chiming in a joyous song,
Because I'm young and free and strong.

Maybe it is the springtide. I am so happy I am afraid. The sense of
living fills me with exultation. I want to sing, to dance; I am dithy-
rambic with delight.

I think the moon must be to blame:
It fills the room with fairy flame;

It paints the wall, it seems to pour
A dappled flood upon the floor.
I rise and through the window stare . . .
Ye gods! how marvellously fair!
From Montrouge to the Martyr's Hill,
A silver city rapt and still;
Dim, drowsy deeps of opal haze,
And spire and dome in diamond blaze;
The little lisping leaves of spring
Like sequins softly glimmering;
Each roof a plaque of argent sheen,
A gauzy gulf the space between;
Each chimney-top a thing of grace,
Where merry moonbeams prank and chase;
And all that sordid was and mean,
Just Beauty, deathless and serene.

O magic city of a dream!
From glory unto glory gleam;
And I will gaze and pity those
Who on their pillows drowse and doze . . .
And as I've nothing else to do,
Of tea I'll make a rousing brew,
And coax my pipes until they croon,
And chant a ditty to the moon.

There! my tea is black and strong. Inspiration comes with every
sip. Now for the moon.

The moon peeped out behind the hill
As yellow as an apricot;
Then up and up it climbed until
Into the sky it fairly got;

The sky was vast and violet;
The poor moon seemed to faint in fright,
And pale it grew and paler yet,
Like fine old silver, rinsed and bright.
And yet it climbed so bravely on
Until it mounted heaven-high;
Then earthward it serenely shone,
A silver sovereign of the sky,
A bland sultana of the night,
Surveying realms of lily light.

MOON SONG

A CHILD saw in the morning skies
The dissipated-looking moon,
And opened wide her big blue eyes,
And cried: "Look, look, my lost balloon!"
And clapped her rosy hands with glee:
"Quick, mother! Bring it back to me."

A poet in a lilied pond
Espied the moon's reflected charms,
And ravished by that beauty blonde,
Leapt out to clasp her in his arms.
And as he'd never learnt to swim,
Poor fool! that was the end of him.

A rustic glimpsed amid the trees
The bluff moon caught as in a snare.
"They say it do be made of cheese,"
Said Giles, "and that a chap bides there. . . .
That Blue Boar ale be strong, I vow—
The lad's a-winkin' at me now."

Two lovers watched the new moon hold
The old moon in her bright embrace.
Said she: "There's mother, pale and old,
And drawing near her resting place."
Said he: "Be mine, and with me wed,"
Moon-high she stared . . . she shook her head.

A soldier saw with dying eyes
The bleared moon like a ball of blood,
And thought of how in other skies,
So pearly bright on leaf and bud
Like peace its soft white beams had lain;
Like Peace! . . . He closed his eyes again.

Child, lover, poet, soldier, clown,
Ah yes, old Moon, what things you've seen!
I marvel now, as you look down,
How can your face be so serene?
And tranquil still you'll make your round,
Old Moon, when we are underground.

"And now, blow out your candle, lad, and get to bed. See, the
dawn is in the sky. Open your window and let its freshness rouge
your cheek. You've earned your rest. Sleep."

Aye, but before I do so, let me read again the last of my *Ballads*.

THE SEWING-GIRL

THE humble garret where I dwell
Is in that Quarter called the Latin;
It isn't spacious—truth to tell,
There's hardly room to swing a cat in.
But what of that! It's there I fight
For food and fame, my Muse inviting,

And all the day and half the night
You'll find me writing, writing, writing.

Now, it was in the month of May
As, wrestling with a rhyme rheumatic,
I chanced to look across the way,
And lo! within a neighbor attic,
A hand drew back the window shade,
And there, a picture glad and glowing,
I saw a sweet and slender maid,
And she was sewing, sewing, sewing.

So poor the room, so small, so scant,
Yet somehow oh, so bright and airy.
There was a pink geranium plant,
Likewise a very pert canary.
And in the maiden's heart it seemed
Some fount of gladness must be springing,
For as alone I sadly dreamed
I heard her singing, singing, singing.

God love her! how it cheered me then
To see her there so brave and pretty;
So she with needle, I with pen,
We slaved and sang above the city.
And as across my streams of ink
I watched her from a poet's distance,
She stitched and sang . . . I scarcely think
She was aware of my existence.

And then one day she sang no more.
That put me out, there's no denying.
I looked—she labored as before,
But, bless me! she was crying, crying.

Her poor canary chirped in vain;
Her pink geranium drooped in sorrow;
"Of course," said I, "she'll sing again.
Maybe," I sighed, "she will to-morrow."

Poor child; 'twas finished with her song:
Day after day her tears were flowing;
And as I wondered what was wrong
She pined and peaked above her sewing.
And then one day the blind she drew,
Ah! though I sought with vain endeavor
To pierce the darkness, well I knew
My sewing-girl had gone forever.

And as I sit alone to-night
My eyes unto her room are turning . . .
I'd give the sum of all I write
Once more to see her candle burning,
Once more to glimpse her happy face,
And while my rhymes of cheer I'm ringing,
Across the sunny sweep of space
To hear her singing, singing, singing.

Heigh ho! I realize I am very weary. It's nice to be so tired, and to
know one can sleep as long as one wants. The morning sunlight
floods in at my window, so I draw the blind, and throw myself on
my bed. . . .

IV

MY GARRET, MONTPARNASSE,
April.

Hurrah! As I opened my eyes this morning to a hard, unfeeling
world, little did I think what a surprise awaited me. A big blue
envelope had been pushed under my door. Another rejection, I

thought, and I took it up distastefully. The next moment I was staring at my first cheque.

It was an express order for two hundred francs, in payment of a bit of verse. . . . So to-day I will celebrate. I will lunch at the D'Harcourt, I will dine on the Grand Boulevard, I will go to the theater.

Well, here's the thing that has turned the tide for me. It is somewhat in the vein of "Sourdough" Service, the Yukon bard. I don't think much of his stuff, but they say he makes heaps of money. I can well believe it, for he drives a Hispano-Suiza in the Bois every afternoon. The other night he was with a crowd at the Dome Café, a chubby chap who sits in a corner and seldom speaks. I was disappointed. I thought he was a big, hairy man who swore like a trooper and mixed brandy with his beer. He only drank Vichy, poor fellow!

LUCILLE

Of course you've heard of the *Nancy Lee,* and how she sailed
  away
On her famous quest of the Arctic flea, to the wilds of Hudson's
  Bay?
For it was a foreign Prince's whim to collect this tiny cuss,
And a golden quid was no more to him than a copper to coves
  like us.
So we sailed away and our hearts were gay as we gazed on the
  gorgeous scene;
And we laughed with glee as we caught the flea of the wolf and
  the wolverine;
Yea, our hearts were light as the parasite of the ermine rat we
  slew,
And the great musk ox, and the silver fox, and the moose and
  the caribou.
And we laughed with zest as the insect pest of the marmot
  crowned our zeal,

And the wary mink and the wily "link," and the walrus and the
seal.

And with eyes aglow on the scornful snow we danced a riga-
doon,

Round the lonesome lair of the Arctic hare, by the light of the
silver moon.

But the time was nigh to homeward hie, when, imagine our
despair!

For the best of the lot we hadn't got—the flea of the polar bear.

Oh, his face was long and his breath was strong, as the Skipper he
says to me:

"I wants you to linger 'ere, my lad, by the shores of the Hartic
Sea;

I wants you to 'unt the polar bear the perishin' winter through,

And if flea ye find of its breed and kind, there's a 'undred quid
for you."

But I shook my head: "No, Cap," I said; "it's yourself I'd like to
please,

But I tells ye flat I wouldn't do that if ye went on yer bended
knees."

Then the Captain spat in the seething brine, and he says: "Good
luck to you,

If it can't be did for a 'undred quid, supposin' we call it two?"

So that was why they said good-by, and they sailed and left me
there—

Alone, alone in the Arctic Zone to hunt for the polar bear.

Oh, the days were slow and packed with woe, till I thought they
would never end;

And I used to sit when the fire was lit, with my pipe for my only
friend.

And I tried to sing some rollicky thing, but my song broke off
in a prayer,
And I'd drowse and dream by the driftwood gleam; I'd dream of
a polar bear;
I'd dream of a cloudlike polar bear that blotted the stars on high,
With ravenous jaws and flenzing claws, and the flames of hell
in his eye.
And I'd trap around on the frozen ground, as a proper hunter
ought,
And beasts I'd find of every kind, but never the one I sought.
Never a track in the white ice-pack that humped and heaved
and flawed,
Till I came to think: "Why, strike me pink! if the creature ain't
a fraud."
And then one night in the waning light, as I hurried home to sup,
I hears a roar by the cabin door, and a great white hulk heaves
up.
So my rifle flashed, and a bullet crashed; dead, dead as a stone
fell he,
And I gave a cheer, for there in his ear—Gosh ding me!—a
tiny flea.

At last, at last! Oh, I clutched it fast, and I gazed on it with
pride;
And I thrust it into a biscuit-tin, and I shut it safe inside;
With a lid of glass for the light to pass, and space to leap and
play;
Oh, it kept alive; yea, seemed to thrive, as I watched it night
and day.
And I used to sit and sing to it, and I shielded it from harm,
And many a hearty feed it had on the heft of my hairy arm.
For you'll never know in that land of snow how lonesome a man
can feel;

So I made a fuss of the little cuss, and I christened it "Lucille."
But the longest winter has its end, and the ice went out to sea,
And I saw one day a ship in the bay, and there was the *Nancy
    Lee*.
So a boat was lowered and I went aboard, and they opened wide
    their eyes—
Yes, they gave a cheer when the truth was clear, and they saw
    my precious prize.
And then it was all like a giddy dream; but to cut my story short,
We sailed away on the fifth of May to the foreign Prince's court;
To a palmy land and a palace grand, and the little Prince was
    there,
And a fat Princess in a satin dress with a crown of gold on her
    hair.
And they showed me into a shiny room, just him and her and me,
And the Prince he was pleased and friendly-like, and he calls
    for drinks for three.
And I shows them my battered biscuit-tin, and I makes my
    modest spiel,
And they laughed, they did, when I opened the lid, and out there
    popped Lucille.

Oh, the Prince was glad, I could soon see that, and the Princess
    she was too;
And Lucille waltzed round on the tablecloth as she often used
    to do.
And the Prince pulled out a purse of gold, and he put it in my
    hand;
And he says: "It was worth all that, I'm told, to stay in that nasty
    land."
And then he turned with a sudden cry, and he clutched at his
    royal beard;

And the Princess screamed, and well she might—for Lucille had
 disappeared.

"She must be here," said his Noble Nibs, so we hunted all
 around;
Oh, we searched that place, but never a trace of the little beast
 we found.
So I shook my head, and I glumly said: "Gol darn the saucy cuss!
It's mighty queer, but she isn't here; so . . . she must be on
 one of us.
You'll pardon me if I make so free, but—there's just one thing
 to do:
If you'll kindly go for a half a mo' I'll search me garments
 through."
Then all alone on the shiny throne I stripped from head to heel;
In vain, in vain; it was very plain that I hadn't got Lucille.
So I garbed again, and I told the Prince, and he scratched his
 august head;
"I suppose if she hasn't selected you, it must be me," he said.
So *he* retired; but he soon came back, and his features showed
 distress:
"Oh, it isn't you and it isn't me." . . . Then we looked at the
 Princess.
So *she* retired; and we heard a scream, and she opened wide the
 door;
And her fingers twain were pinched to pain, but a radiant smile
 she wore:
"It's here," she cries, "our precious prize. Oh, I found it right
 away. . . ."
Then I ran to her with a shout of joy, but I choked with a wild
 dismay.

I clutched the back of the golden throne, and the room began to
    reel . . .
What she held to me was, ah yes! a flea, but . . . *it wasn't my*
    Lucille.

After all, I did not celebrate. I sat on the terrace of the Café
Napolitain on the Grand Boulevard, half hypnotized by the passing
crowd. And as I sat I fell into conversation with a god-like stranger
who sipped some golden ambrosia. He told me he was an actor and
introduced me to his beverage, which he called a "Suze-Anni." He
soon left me, but the effect of the golden liquid remained, and there
came over me a desire to write. *C'était plus fort que moi.* So instead
of going to the Folies Bergère I spent all evening in the Omnium Bar
near the Bourse, and wrote the following:

ON THE BOULEVARD

> Oh, it's pleasant sitting here,
> Seeing all the people pass;
> You beside your *bock* of beer,
> I behind my *demi-tasse.*
> Chatting of no matter what.
> You the Mummer, I the Bard;
> Oh, it's jolly, is it not?—
> Sitting on the Boulevard.
>
> More amusing than a book,
> If a chap has eyes to see;
> For, no matter where I look,
> Stories, stories jump at me.
> Moving tales my pen might write;
> Poems plain on every face;
> Monologues you could recite
> With inimitable grace.

(Ah! Imagination's power)
See yon *demi-mondaine* there,
Idly toying with a flower,
Smiling with a pensive air . . .
Well, her smile is but a mask,
For I saw within her muff
Such a wicked little flask:
Vitriol—ugh! the beastly stuff.

Now look back beside the bar.
See yon curled and scented *beau*,
Puffing at a fine cigar—
Sale espèce de maquereau.
Well (of course, it's all surmise),
It's for him she holds her place;
When he passes she will rise,
Dash the vitriol in his face.

Quick they'll carry him away,
Pack him in a Red Cross car;
Her they'll hurry, so they say,
To the cells of St. Lazare.
What will happen then, you ask?
What will all the sequel be?
Ah! Imagination's task
Isn't easy . . . let me see . . .

She will go to jail, no doubt,
For a year, or maybe two;
Then as soon as she gets out
Start her bawdy life anew.
He will lie within a ward,
Harmless as a man can be.

With his face grotesquely scarred,
And his eyes that cannot see.

Then amid the city's din
He will stand against a wall,
With around his neck a tin
Into which the pennies fall.
She will pass (I see it plain,
Like a cinematograph),
She will halt and turn again,
Look and look, and maybe laugh.

Well, I'm not so sure of that—
Whether she will laugh or cry.
He will hold a battered hat
To the lady passing by.
He will smile a cringing smile,
And into his grimy hold,
With a laugh (or sob) the while,
She will drop a piece of gold.

"Bless you, lady," he will say,
And get grandly drunk that night.
She will come and come each day,
Fascinated by the sight.
Then somehow he'll get to know
(Maybe by some kindly friend)
Who she is, and so . . . and so
Bring my story to an end.

How his heart will burst with hate!
He will curse and he will cry.
He will wait and wait and wait,

Till again she passes by.
Then like tiger from its lair
He will leap from out his place,
Down her, clutch her by the hair,
Smear the vitriol on her face.

(Ah! Imagination rare)
See . . . he takes his hat to go;
Now he's level with her chair;
Now she rises up to throw. . . .
God! and she has done it too . . .
Oh, those screams; those hideous screams!
I imagined and . . . it's true:
How his face will haunt my dreams!

What a sight! It makes me sick.
Seems I am to blame somehow.
Garçon, fetch a brandy quick . . .
There! I'm feeling better now.
Let's collaborate, we two,
You the Mummer, I the Bard;
Oh, what ripping stuff we'll do,
Sitting on the Boulevard!

It is strange how one works easily at times. I wrote this so quickly
that I might almost say I had reached the end before I had come to
the beginning. In such a mood I wonder why everybody does not
write poetry. Get a Roget's *Thesaurus*, a rhyming dictionary: sit
before your typewriter with a strong glass of coffee at your elbow,
and just click the stuff off.

FACILITY

So easy 'tis to make a rhyme,
That did the world but know it,

Your coachman might Parnassus climb,
Your butler be a poet.

Then, oh, how charming it would be
If, when in haste hysteric
You called the page, you learned that he
Was grappling with a lyric.

Or else what rapture it would yield,
When cook sent up the salad,
To find within its depths concealed
A touching little ballad.

Or if for tea and toast you yearned,
What joy to find upon it
The chambermaid had coyly laid
A palpitating sonnet.

Your baker could the fashion set;
Your butcher might respond well;
With every tart a triolet,
With every chop a rondel.

Your tailor's bill . . . well, I'll be blowed!
Dear chap! I never knowed him . . .
He's gone and written me an ode,
Instead of what I *owed* him.

So easy 'tis to rhyme . . . yet stay!
Oh, terrible misgiving!
Please do not give the game away . . .
I've got to make my living.

V

My Garret
May 1914.

GOLDEN DAYS

Another day of toil and strife,
Another page so white,
Within that fateful Log of Life
That I and all must write;
Another page without a stain
To make of as I may,
That done, I shall not see again
Until the Judgment Day.

Ah, could I, could I backward turn
The pages of that Book,
How often would I blench and burn!
How often loathe to look!
What pages would be meanly scrolled;
What smeared as if with mud;
A few, maybe, might gleam like gold,
Some scarlet seem as blood.

O Record grave, God guide my hand
And make me worthy be,
Since what I write to-day shall stand
To all eternity;
Aye, teach me, Lord of Life, I pray,
As I salute the sun,
To bear myself that every day
May be a Golden One.

I awoke this morning to see the bright sunshine flooding my garret. No chamber in the palace of a king could have been more fair. How I sang as I dressed! How I lingered over my coffee, savoring every drop! How carefully I packed my pipe, gazing serenely over the roofs of Paris.

Never is the city so lovely as in this month of May, when all the trees are in the fullness of their foliage. As I look, I feel a freshness of vision in my eyes. Wonder wakes in me. The simplest things move me to delight.

THE JOY OF LITTLE THINGS

It's good the great green earth to roam,
Where sights of awe the soul inspire;
But oh, it's best, the coming home,
The crackle of one's own hearth-fire!
You've hob-nobbed with the solemn Past;
You've seen the pageantry of kings;
Yet oh, how sweet to gain at last
The peace and rest of Little Things!

Perhaps you're counted with the Great;
You strain and strive with mighty men;
Your hand is on the helm of State;
Colossus-like you stride . . . and then
There comes a pause, a shining hour,
A dog that leaps, a hand that clings:
O Titan, turn from pomp and power;
Give all your heart to Little Things.

Go couch you childwise in the grass,
Believing it's some jungle strange,
Where mighty monsters peer and pass,
Where beetles roam and spiders range.

'Mid gloom and gleam of leaf and blade,
What dragons rasp their painted wings!
O magic world of shine and shade!
O beauty land of Little Things!

I sometimes wonder, after all,
Amid this tangled web of fate,
If what is great may not be small,
And what is small may not be great.
So wondering I go my way,
Yet in my heart contentment sings . . .
O may I ever see, I pray,
God's grace and love in Little Things.

So give to me, I only beg,
A little roof to call my own,
A little cider in the keg,
A little meat upon the bone;
A little garden by the sea,
A little boat that dips and swings . . .
Take wealth, take fame, but leave to me,
O Lord of Life, just Little Things.

Yesterday I finished my tenth ballad. When I have done about a score I will seek a publisher. If I cannot find one, I will earn, beg or steal the money to get them printed. Then if they do not sell I will hawk them from door to door. Oh, I'll succeed, I know I'll succeed. And yet I don't want an easy success; give me the joy of the fight, the thrill of the adventure. Here's my last ballad:

THE ABSINTHE DRINKERS

HE's yonder, on the terrace of the Café de la Paix,
The little wizened Spanish man, I see him every day.

He's sitting with his Pernod on his customary chair;
He's staring at the passers with his customary stare.
He never takes his piercing eyes from off that moving throng,
That current cosmopolitan meandering along:
Dark diplomats from Martinique, pale Rastas from Peru,
An Englishman from Bloomsbury, a Yank from Kalamazoo;
A poet from Montmartre's heights, a dapper little Jap,
Exotic citizens of all the countries on the map;

A tourist horde from every land that's underneath the sun—
That little wizened Spanish man, he misses never one.
Oh, foul or fair he's always there, and many a drink he buys,
And there's a fire of red desire within his hollow eyes.
And sipping of my Pernod, and a-knowing what I know,
Sometimes I want to shriek aloud and give away the show.
I've lost my nerve; he's haunting me; he's like a beast of prey,
That Spanish man that's watching at the Café de la Paix.

Say! Listen and I'll tell you all . . . the day was growing dim,
And I was with my Pernod at the table next to him;
And he was sitting soberly as if he were asleep,
When suddenly he seemed to tense, like tiger for a leap.
And then he swung around to me, his hand went to his hip,
My heart was beating like a gong—my arm was in his grip;
His eyes were glaring into mine; aye, though I shrank with fear,
His fetid breath was on my face, his voice was in my ear:
"Excuse my *brusquerie*," he hissed; "but, sir, do you suppose—
That portly man who passed us had a *wen upon his nose?*"

And then a last it dawned on me, the fellow must be mad;
And when I soothingly replied: "I do not think he had,"
The little wizened Spanish man subsided in his chair,
And shrouded in his raven cloak resumed his owlish stare.

But when I tried to slip away he turned and glared at me,
And oh, that fishlike face of his was sinister to see:
"Forgive me if I startled you; of course you think I'm queer;
No doubt you wonder who I am, so solitary here;
You question why the passers-by I piercingly review . . .
Well, listen, my bibacious friend, I'll tell my tale to you.

"It happened twenty years ago, and in another land:
A maiden young and beautiful, two suitors for her hand.
My rival was the lucky one; I vowed I would repay;
Revenge has mellowed in my heart, it's rotten ripe to-day.
My happy rival skipped away, vamoosed, he left no trace;
And so I'm waiting, waiting here to meet him face to face;
For has it not been ever said that all the world one day
Will pass in pilgrimage before the Café de la Paix?"

"But, sir," I made remonstrance, "if it's twenty years ago,
You'd scarcely recognize him now, he must have altered so."
The little wizened Spanish man he laughed a hideous laugh,
And from his cloak he quickly drew a faded photograph.
"You're right," said he, "but there are traits (oh, this you must
        allow)
That never change; Lopez was fat, he must be fatter now.
His paunch is senatorial, he cannot see his toes,
I'm sure of it; and then, behold! that wen upon his nose.
I'm looking for a man like that. I'll wait and wait until . . ."
"What will you do?" I sharply cried; he answered me: "Why,
        kill!
He robbed me of my happiness—nay, stranger, do not start;
I'll firmly and politely put—a bullet in his heart."

And then that little Spanish man, with big cigar alight,
Uprose and shook my trembling hand and vanished in the night.

And I went home and thought of him and had a dreadful dream
Of portly men with each a wen, and woke up with a scream.
And sure enough, next morning, as I prowled the Boulevard,
A portly man with wenny nose roamed into my regard;
Then like a flash I ran to him and clutched him by the arm:
"Oh, sir," said I, "I do not wish to see you come to harm;
But if your life you value aught, I beg, entreat and pray—
Don't pass before the terrace of the Café de la Paix."
That portly man he looked at me with such a startled air,
Then bolted like a rabbit down the rue Michaudière.
"Ha! ha! I've saved a life," I thought; and laughed in my relief,
And straightway joined the Spanish man o'er his *apéritif*.
And thus each day I dodged about and kept the strictest guard
For portly men with each a wen upon the Boulevard.
And then I hailed my Spanish pal, and sitting in the sun,
We ordered many Pernods and we drank them every one.
And sternly he would stare and stare until my hand would shake,
And grimly he would glare and glare until my heart would
    quake.
And I would say: "Alphonso, lad, I must expostulate;
Why keep alive for twenty years the furnace of your hate?
Perhaps his wedded life was hell; and you, at least, are free . . ."
"That's where you've got it wrong," he snarled; "the fool she
    took was *me*.
My rival sneaked, threw up the sponge, betrayed himself a churl:
'Twas he who got the happiness, I only got—the girl."
With that he looked so devil-like he made me creep and shrink,
And there was nothing else to do but buy another drink.

Now yonder like a blot of ink he sits across the way,
Upon the smiling terrace of the Café de la Paix;
That little wizened Spanish man, his face is ghastly white,
His eyes are staring, staring like a tiger's in the night.

I know within his evil heart the fires of hate are fanned,
I know his automatic's ready waiting to his hand.
I know a tragedy is near. I dread, I have no peace . . .
Oh, don't you think I ought to go and call upon the police?
Look there . . . he's rising up . . . my God! He leaps from out
    his place . . .
Yon millionaire from Argentine . . . the two are face to
    face . . .
A shot! A shriek! A heavy fall! A huddled heap! Oh, see
The little wizened Spanish man is dancing in his glee. . . .
I'm sick . . . I'm faint . . . I'm going mad. . . . Oh, please
    take me away . . .
There's BLOOD upon the terrace of the Café de la Paix. . . .

    And now I'll leave my work and sally forth. The city is *en fête*.
I'll join the crowd and laugh and sing with the best.

        The sunshine seeks my little room
        To tell me Paris streets are gay;
        That children cry the lily bloom
        All up and down the leafy way;
        That half the town is mad with May,
        With flame of flag and boom of bell:
        For Carnival is King to-day;
        So pen and page, awhile farewell.

BOOK TWO

EARLY SUMMER

I

Parc Montsouris
June 1914.

THE RELEASE

To-day within a grog-shop near
I saw a newly captured linnet,
Who beat against his cage in fear,
And fell exhausted every minute;
And when I asked the fellow there
If he to sell the bird were willing,
He told me with a careless air
That I could have it for a shilling.

And so I bought it, cage and all
(Although I went without my dinner),
And where some trees were fairly tall
And houses shrank and smoke was thinner,
The tiny door I open threw,
As down upon the grass I sank me:
Poor little chap! How quick he flew . . .
He didn't even wait to thank me.

Life's like a cage; we beat the bars,
We bruise our breasts, we struggle vainly;
Up to the glory of the stars
We strain with flutterings ungainly.
And then—God opens wide the door;
Our wondrous wings are arched for flying;
We poise, we part, we sing, we soar . . .
Light, freedom, love. . . . Fools call it—Dying.

463

Yes, that wretched little bird haunted me. I had to let it go. Since I have seized my own liberty I am a fanatic for freedom. It is now a year ago I launched on my great adventure. I have had hard times, been hungry, cold, weary. I have worked harder than ever I did and discouragement has slapped me on the face. Yet the year has been the happiest of my life.

And all because I am free. By reason of filthy money no one can say to me: Do this, or do that. "Master" doesn't exist in my vocabulary. I can look any man in the face and tell him to go to the devil. I belong to myself. I am not for sale. It's glorious to feel like that. It sweetens the dry crust and warms the heart in the icy wind. For that I will hunger and go threadbare; for that I will live austerely and deny myself all pleasure. After health, the best thing in life is freedom.

Here is the last of my ballads. It is by way of being an experiment. Its theme is commonplace, its language that of everyday. It is a bit of realism in rhyme.

THE WEE SHOP

She risked her all, they told me, bravely sinking
The pinched economies of thirty years;
And there the little shop was, meek and shrinking,
The sum of all her dreams and hopes and fears.
Ere it was opened I would see them in it,
The grey-haired dame, the daughter with her crutch;
So fond, so happy, hoarding every minute,
Like artists, for the final tender touch.

The opening day! I'm sure that to their seeming
Was never shop so wonderful as theirs;
With pyramids of jam-jars rubbed to gleaming;
Such vivid cans of peaches, prunes and pears;
And chocolate, and biscuits in glass cases,
And bon-bon bottles, many-hued and bright;

Yet nothing half so radiant as their faces,
Their eyes of hope, excitement and delight.

I entered: how they waited all a-flutter!
How awkwardly they weighed my acid-drops!
And then with all the thanks a tongue could utter
They bowed me from the kindliest of shops.
I'm sure that night their customers they numbered;
Discussed them all in happy, breathless speech;
And though quite worn and weary, ere they slumbered,
Sent heavenward a little prayer for each.

And so I watched with interest redoubled
That little shop, spent in it all I had;
And when I saw it empty I was troubled,
And when I saw them busy I was glad.
And when I dared to ask how things were going,
They told me, with a fine and gallant smile:
"Not badly . . . slow at first . . . There's never knowing . . .
'Twill surely pick up in a little while."

I'd often see them through the winter weather,
Behind the shutters by a light's faint speck,
Poring o'er books, their faces close together,
The lame girl's arm around her mother's neck.
They dressed their windows not one time but twenty,
Each change more pinched, more desperately neat;
Alas! I wondered if behind that plenty
The two who owned it had enough to eat.

Ah, who would dare to sing of tea and coffee?
The sadness of a stock unsold and dead;
The petty tragedy of melting toffee,

The sordid pathos of stale gingerbread.
Ignoble themes! And yet—those haggard faces!
Within that little shop. . . . Oh, here I say
One does not need to look in lofty places
For tragic themes, they're round us every day.

And so I saw their agony, their fighting,
Their eyes of fear, their heartbreak, their despair;
And there the little shop is, black and blighting,
And all the world goes by and does not care.
They say she sought her old employer's pity,
Content to take the pittance he would give.
The lame girl? yes, she's working in the city;
She coughs a lot—she hasn't long to live.

Last night MacBean introduced me to Saxon Dane the Poet. Truly, he is more like a blacksmith than a Bard—a big bearded man whose black eyes brood somberly or flash with sudden fire. We talked of Walt Whitman, and then of others.

"The trouble with poetry," he said, "is that it is too exalted. It has a phraseology of its own; it selects themes that are quite outside of ordinary experience. As a medium of expression it fails to reach the great mass of the people."

Then he added: "To hell with the great mass of the people! What have they got to do with it? Write to please yourself, as if not a single reader existed. The moment a man begins to be conscious of an audience he is artistically damned. You're not a Poet, I hope?"

I meekly assured him I was a mere maker of verse.

"Well," said he, "better good verse than middling poetry. And maybe even the humblest of rhymes has its uses. Happiness is happiness, whether it be inspired by a Rossetti sonnet or a ballad by G. R. Sims. Let each one who has something to say, say it in the best way he can, and abide the result. . . . After all," he went on, "what does it matter? We are living in a pygmy day. With Tennyson and Browning the line of great poets passed away, perhaps forever. The world to-day is full of little minstrels, who echo one another and who pipe away tunefully enough. But with one exception they do not matter."

I dared to ask who was his one exception. He answered, "Myself, of course."

Here's a bit of light verse which it amused me to write to-day, as I sat in the sun on the terrace of the Closerie de Lilas:

THE PHILISTINE AND THE BOHEMIAN

SHE was a Philistine spick and span,
He was a bold Bohemian.
She had the *mode*, and the last at that;
He had a cape and a brigand hat.
She was so *riante* and *chic* and trim;
He was so shaggy, unkempt and grim.
On the rue de la Paix she was wont to shine;
The rue de la Gaîté was more his line.
She doted on Barclay and Dell and Caine;
He quoted Mallarmé and Paul Verlaine.
She was a triumph at Tango teas;
At Vorticist's suppers he sought to please.
She thought that Franz Lehar was utterly great;
Of Strauss and Stravinski he'd piously prate.
She loved elegance, he loved art;
They were as wide as the poles apart:
Yet—Cupid and Caprice are hand and glove—
They met at a dinner, they fell in love.

Home he went to his garret bare,
Thrilling with rapture, hope, despair.
Swift he gazed in his looking-glass,
Made a grimace and murmured: "Ass!"
Seized his scissors and fiercely sheared,

Severed his buccaneering beard;
Grabbed his hair, and clip! clip! clip!
Off came a bunch with every snip.
Ran to a tailor's in startled state,
Suits a dozen commanded straight;
Coats and overcoats, pants in pairs,
Everything that a dandy wears;
Socks and collars, and shoes and ties,
Everything that a dandy buys.
Chums looked at him with wondering stare,
Fancied they'd seen him before somewhere;
A Brummell, a D'Orsay, a *beau* so fine,
A shining, immaculate Philistine.

Home she went in a raptured daze,
Looked in a mirror with startled gaze,
Didn't seem to be pleased at all;
Savagely muttered: "Insipid Doll!"
Clutched her hair and a pair of shears,
Cropped and bobbed it behind the ears;
Aimed at a wan and willowy-necked
Sort of a Holman Hunt effect;
Robed in subtile and sage-green tones,
Like the dames of Rossetti and E. Burne-Jones;
Girdled her garments billowing wide,
Moved with an undulating glide;
All her frivolous friends forsook,
Cultivated a soulful look;
Gushed in a voice with a creamy throb
Over some weirdly Futurist daub—
Did all, in short, that a woman can
To be a consummate Bohemian.

A year went past with its hopes and fears,
A year that seemed like a dozen years.
They met once more. . . . Oh, at last! At last!
They rushed together, they stopped aghast.
They looked at each other with blank dismay,
They simply hadn't a word to say.
He thought with a shiver: "Can this be she?"
She thought with a shudder: "This can't be he?"
This simpering dandy, so sleek and spruce;
This languorous lily in garments loose;
They sought to brace from the awful shock:
Taking a seat, they tried to talk.
She spoke of Bergson and Pater's prose,
He prattled of dances and ragtime shows;
She purred of pictures, Matisse, Cezanne,
His tastes to the girls of Kirchner ran;
She raved of Tschaikowsky and Cæsar Franck,
He owned that he was a jazz-band crank!
They made no headway. Alas! alas!
He thought her a bore, she thought him an ass.
And so they arose and hurriedly fled;
Perish Illusion, Romance, you're dead.
He loved elegance, she loved art,
Better at once to part, to part.

And what is the moral of all this rot?
Don't try to be what you know you're not.
And if you're made on a muttonish plan,
Don't seek to seem a Bohemian;
And if to the goats your feet incline,
Don't try to pass for a Philistine.

II

A Small Café in a Side Street,
June 1914.

THE BOHEMIAN DREAMS

Because my overcoat's in pawn,
I choose to take my glass
Within a little *bistro* on
The rue du Montparnasse;
The dusty bins with bottles shine,
The counter's lined with zinc,
And there I sit and drink my wine,
And think and think and think.

I think of hoary old Stamboul,
Of Moslem and of Greek,
Of Persian in coat of wool,
Of Kurd and Arab sheikh;
Of all the types of weal and woe,
And as I raise my glass,
Across Galata bridge I know
They pass and pass and pass.

I think of citron-trees aglow,
Of fan-palms shading down,
Of sailors dancing heel and toe
With wenches black and brown;
And though it's all an ocean far
From Yucatan to France,
I'll bet beside the old bazaar
They dance and dance and dance.

I think of Monte Carlo, where
The pallid croupiers call,
And in the gorgeous, guilty air
The gamblers watch the ball;
And as I flick away the foam
With which my beer is crowned,
The wheels beneath the gilded dome
Go round and round and round.

I think of vast Niagara,
Those gulfs of foam a-shine,
Whose mighty roar would stagger a
More prosy bean than mine;
And as the hours I idly spend
Against a greasy wall,
I know that green the waters bend
And fall and fall and fall.

I think of Nijni Novgorod
And Jews who never rest;
And womenfolk with spade and hod
Who slave in Buda-Pest;
Of squat and sturdy Japanese
Who pound the paddy soil,
And as I loaf and smoke at ease
They toil and toil and toil.

I think of shrines in Hindustan,
Of cloistral glooms in Spain,
Of minarets in Ispahan,
Of St. Sophia's fane,
Of convent towers in Palestine,
Of temples in Cathay,

And as I stretch and sip my wine
They pray and pray and pray.

And so my dreams I dwell within,
And visions come and go,
And life is passing like a Cin-
Ematographic Show;
Till just as surely as my pipe
Is underneath my nose,
Amid my visions rich and ripe
I doze and doze and doze.

Alas! it is too true. Once more I am counting the coppers, living on the ragged edge. My manuscripts come back to me like boomerangs, and I have not the postage, far less the heart, to send them out again.

MacBean seems to take an interest in my struggles. I often sit in his room in the rue Saint-Julien-le-Pauvre, smoking and sipping whisky into the small hours. He is an old hand, who knows the market and frankly manufactures for it.

"Give me short pieces," he says; "things of three verses that will fill a blank half-page of a magazine. Let them be sprightly, and, if possible, have a snapper at the end. Give me that sort of article. I think I can place it for you."

Then he looked through a lot of my verse: "This is the kind of stuff I might be able to sell," he said:

A DOMESTIC TRAGEDY

CLORINDA met me on the way
As I came from the train;
Her face was anything but gay,
In fact, suggested pain.
"Oh hubby, hubby dear!" she cried,

"I've awful news to tell. . . ."
"What is it, darling?" I replied;
"Your mother—is she well?"

"Oh no! oh no! it is not that,
It's something else," she wailed,
My heart was beating pit-a-pat,
My ruddy visage paled.
Like lightning flash in heaven's dome
The fear within me woke:
"Don't say," I cried, "our little home
Has all gone up in smoke!"

She shook her head. Oh, swift I clasped
And held her to my breast;
"The children! Tell me quick," I gasped,
"Believe me, it is best."
Then, then she spoke; 'mid sobs I caught
These words of woe divine:
"It's coo-coo-cook has gone and bought
A new hat just like mine."

At present I am living on bread and milk. By doing this I can rub along for another ten days. The thought pleases me. As long as I have a crust I am master of my destiny. Some day, when I am rich and famous, I shall look back on all this with regret. Yet I think I shall always remain a Bohemian. I hate regularity. The clock was never made for me. I want to eat when I am hungry, sleep when I am weary, drink—well, any old time.

I prefer to be alone. Company is a constraint on my spirit. I never make an engagement if I can avoid it. To do so is to put a mortgage on my future. I like to be able to rise in the morning with the thought that the hours before me are all mine, to spend in my own way—to work, to dream, to watch the unfolding drama of life.

Here is another of my ballads. It is longer than most, and gave me
more trouble, though none the better for that.

THE PENCIL SELLER

A PENCIL, sir; a penny—won't you buy?
I'm cold and wet and tired, a sorry plight;
Don't turn your back, sir; take one just to try;
I haven't made a single sale to-night.
Oh, thank you, sir; but take the pencil too;
I'm not a beggar, I'm a business man.
Pencils I deal in, red and black and blue;
It's hard, but still I do the best I can.
Most days I make enough to pay for bread,
A cup o' coffee, stretching room at night.
One needs so little—to be warm and fed,
A hole to kennel in—oh, one's all right . . .

Excuse me, you're a painter, are you not?
I saw you looking at that dealer's show,
The *croûtes* he has for sale, a shabby lot—
What do I know of Art? What do I know . . .
Well, look! That David Strong so well displayed,
"White Sorcery" it's called, all gossamer,
And pale moon-magic and a dancing maid
(You like the little elfin face of her?)—
That's good; but still, the picture as a whole,
The values,— Pah! He never painted worse;
Perhaps because his fire was lacking coal,
His cupboard bare, no money in his purse.
Perhaps . . . they say he labored hard and long,
And see now, in the harvest of his fame,

When round his pictures people gape and throng,
A scurvy dealer sells this on his name.
A wretched rag, wrung out of want and woe;
A soulless daub, not David Strong a bit,
Unworthy of his art. . . . How should I know?
How should I know? I'm *Strong*—I painted it.

There now, I didn't mean to let that out.
It came in spite of me—aye, stare and stare.
You think I'm lying, crazy, drunk, no doubt—
Think what you like, it's neither here nor there.
It's hard to tell so terrible a truth,
To gain to glory, yet be such as I.
It's true; that picture's mine, done in my youth,
Up in a garret near the Paris sky.
The child's my daughter; aye, she posed for me.
That's why I come and sit here every night.
The painting's bad, but still—oh, still I see
Her little face all laughing in the light.
So now you understand.—I live in fear
Lest one like you should carry it away;
A poor, pot-boiling thing, but oh, how dear!
"Don't let them buy it, pitying God!" I pray!
And hark ye, sir—sometimes my brain's awhirl.
Some night I'll crash into that window pane
And snatch my picture back, my little girl,
And run and run. . . .
                        I'm talking wild again;
A crab can't run. I'm crippled, withered, lame,
Palsied, as good as dead all down one side.
No warning had I when the evil came:
It struck me down in all my strength and pride.
Triumph was mine, I thrilled with perfect power;

Honor was mine, Fame's laurel touched my brow;
Glory was mine—within a little hour
I was a god and . . . what you find me now.

My child, that little, laughing girl you see,
She was my nurse for all ten weary years;
Her joy, her hope, her youth she gave for me;
Her very smiles were masks to hide her tears.
And I, my precious art, so rich, so rare,
Lost, lost to me—what could my heart but break!
Oh, as I lay and wrestled with despair,
I would have killed myself but for her sake. . . .

By luck I had some pictures I could sell,
And so we fought the wolf back from the door;
She painted too, aye, wonderfully well.
We often dreamed of brighter days in store.
And then quite suddenly she seemed to fail;
I saw the shadows darken round her eyes.
So tired she was, so sorrowful, so pale,
And oh, there came a day she could not rise.
The doctor looked at her; he shook his head,
And spoke of wine and grapes and Southern air:
"If you can get her out of this," he said,
"She'll have a fighting chance with proper care."

"With proper care!" When he had gone away,
I sat there, trembling, twitching, dazed with grief.
Under my old and ragged coat she lay,
Our room was bare and cold beyond belief.
"Maybe," I thought, "I still can paint a bit,
Some lilies, landscape, anything at all."
Alas! My brush, I could not steady it.

Down from my fumbling hand I let it fall.
"With proper care"—how could I give her that,
Half of me dead? . . . I crawled down to the street.
Cowering beside the wall, I held my hat
And begged of every one I chanced to meet.
I got some pennies, bought her milk and bread,
And so I fought to keep the Doom away;
And yet I saw with agony of dread
My dear one sinking, sinking day by day.
And then I was awakened in the night:
"Please take my hands, I'm cold," I heard her sigh;
And soft she whispered, as she held me tight:
"Oh daddy, we've been happy you and I!"
I do not think she suffered any pain,
She breathed so quietly . . . but though I tried,
I could not warm her little hands again:
And so there in the icy dark she died. . . .
The dawn came groping in with fingers grey
And touched me, sitting silent as a stone;
I kissed those piteous lips, as cold as clay—
I did not cry, I did not even moan.
At last I rose, groped down the narrow stair;
An evil fog was oozing from the sky;
Half-crazed I stumbled on, I knew not where,
Like phantoms were the folks that passed me by.
How long I wandered thus I do not know,
But suddenly I halted, stood stock-still—
Beside a door that spilled a golden glow
I saw a name, *my name*, upon a bill.
"A Sale of Famous Pictures," so it read,
"A Notable Collection, each a gem,
Distinguished Works of Art by painters dead."
The folks were going in, I followed them.

I stood upon the outskirts of the crowd,
I only hoped that none might notice me.
Soon, soon I heard them call my name aloud:
"A 'David Strong,' his *Fête in Brittany*."
(A brave big picture that, the best I've done,
It glowed and kindled half the hall away,
With all its memories of sea and sun,
Of pipe and bowl, of joyous work and play.
I saw the sardine nets blue as the sky,
I saw the nut-brown fisher-boats put out.)
"Five hundred pounds!" rapped out a voice near by;
"Six hundred!" "Seven!" "Eight!" And then a shout:
"A thousand pounds!" Oh, how I thrilled to hear!
Oh, how the bids went up by leaps, by bounds!
And then a silence; then the auctioneer:
"It's going! Going! Gone! *Three thousand pounds!*"
Three thousand pounds! A frenzy leapt in me.
"That picture's mine," I cried; "I'm David Strong.
I painted it, this famished wretch you see;
I did it, I, and sold it for a song.
And in a garret three small hours ago
My daughter died for want of Christian care.
Look, look at me! . . . Is it to mock my woe
You pay three thousand for my picture there?" . . .

O God! I stumbled blindly from the hall;
The city crashed on me, the fiendish sounds
Of cruelty and strife, but over all
"Three thousand pounds!" I heard; "Three thousand pounds!"

There, that's my story, sir; it isn't gay.
Tales of the Poor are never very bright . . .

You'll look for me next time you pass this way . . .
I hope you'll find me, sir; good-night, good-night.

III

THE LUXEMBOURG,
June 1914.

On a late afternoon, when the sunlight is mellow on the leaves, I
often sit near the Fontaine de Medicis, and watch the children at
their play. Sometimes I make bits of verse about them, such as:

FI-FI IN BED

UP into the sky I stare;
All the little stars I see;
And I know that God is there
O, how lonely He must be!

Me, I laugh and leap all day,
Till my head begins to nod;
He's so great, He cannot play:
I am glad I am not God.

Poor kind God upon His throne,
Up there in the sky so blue,
Always, always all alone . . .
"Please, dear God, I pity You."

Or else, sitting on the terrace of a café on the Boul' Mich', I sip
slowly a Dubonnet or a Byrrh, and the charm of the Quarter pos-
sesses me. I think of men who have lived and loved there, who have
grovelled and gloried, who have drunk deep and died. And then I
scribble things like this:

GODS IN THE GUTTER

I DREAMED I saw three demi-gods who in a café sat,
And one was small and crapulous, and one was large and fat;
And one was eaten up with vice and verminous at that.

The first he spoke of secret sins, and gems and perfumes rare;
And velvet cats and courtesans voluptuously fair:
"Who is the Sybarite?" I asked. They answered: "Baudelaire."

The second talked in tapestries, by fantasy beguiled;
As frail as bubbles, hard as gems, his pageantries he piled;
"This Lord of Language, who is he?" They whispered "Oscar
    Wilde."

The third was staring at his glass from out abysmal pain;
With tears his eyes were bitten in beneath his bulbous brain.
"Who is the sodden wretch?" I said. They told me: "Paul
    Verlaine."

Oh, Wilde, Verlaine and Baudelaire, their lips were wet with
    wine;
Oh poseur, pimp and libertine! Oh cynic, sot and swine!
Oh votaries of velvet vice! . . . Oh gods of light divine!

Oh Baudelaire, Verlaine and Wilde, they knew the sinks of
    shame;
Their sun-aspiring wings they scorched at passion's altar flame;
Yet lo! enthroned, enskied they stand, Immortal Sons of Fame.

I dreamed I saw three demi-gods who walked with feet of clay,
With cruel crosses on their backs, along a miry way;
Who climbed and climbed the bitter steep to which men turn
    and pray.

And while I am on the subject of the Quarter, let me repeat this, which is included in my Ballads of the Boulevards:

THE DEATH OF MARIE TORO

WE'RE taking Marie Toro to her home in Père-La-Chaise;
We're taking Marie Toro to her last resting-place.
Behold! her hearse is hung with wreaths till everything is hid
Except the blossoms heaping high upon her coffin lid.
A week ago she roamed the street, a draggle and a slut,
A by-word of the Boulevard and everybody's butt;
A week ago she haunted us, we heard her whining cry,
We brushed aside the broken blooms she pestered us to buy;
A week ago she had not where to rest her weary head . . .
But now, oh, follow, follow on, for Marie Toro's dead.

Oh Marie, she was once a queen—ah yes, a queen of queens.
High-throned above the Carnival she held her splendid sway.
For four-and-twenty crashing hours she knew what glory
    means,
The cheers of half a million throats, the *délire* of a day.
Yet she was only one of us, a little sewing-girl,
Though far the loveliest and best of all our laughing band;
Then Fortune beckoned; off she danced, amid the dizzy whirl,
And we who once might kiss her cheek were proud to kiss her
    hand.
For swiftly as a star she soared; she had her every wish;
We saw her roped with pearls of price, with princes at her call;
And yet, and yet I think her dreams were of the old Boul' Mich',
And yet I'm sure within her heart she loved us best of all.
For one night in the Purple Pig, upon the rue Saint-Jacques,
We laughed and quaffed . . . a limousine came swishing to the
    door;

Then Raymond Jolicœur cried out: "It's Queen Marie come
　　back,
In satin clad to make us glad, and witch our hearts once more."
But no, her face was strangely sad, and at the evening's end:
"Dear lads," she said; "I love you all, and when I'm far away,
Remember, oh, remember, little Marie is your friend,
And though the world may lie between, I'm coming back some
　　day."
And so she went, and many a boy who's fought his way to Fame,
Can look back on the struggle of his garret days and bless
The loyal heart, the tender hand, the Providence that came
To him and all in hour of need, in sickness and distress.
Time passed away. She won their hearts in London, Moscow,
　　Rome;
They worshipped her in Argentine, adored her in Brazil;
We smoked our pipes and wondered when she might be coming
　　home,
And then we learned the luck had turned, the things were going
　　ill.
Her health had failed, her beauty paled, her lovers fled away;
And someone saw her in Peru, a common drab at last.
So years went by, and faces changed; our beards were sadly
　　grey,
And Marie Toro's name became an echo of the past.

You know that old and withered man, that derelict of art,
Who for a paltry franc will make a crayon sketch of you?
In slouching hat and shabby cloak he looks and is the part,
A sodden old Bohemian, without a single *sou*.
A boon companion of the days of Rimbaud and Verlaine,
He broods and broods, and chews the cud of bitter souvenirs;
Beneath his mop of grizzled hair his cheeks are gouged with pain,
The saffron sockets of his eyes are hollowed out with tears.

Well, one night in the D'Harcourt's din I saw him in his place,
When suddenly the door was swung, a woman halted there;
A woman cowering like a dog, with white and haggard face,
A broken creature, bent of spine, a daughter of Despair.
She looked and looked, as to her breast she held some withered
    bloom;
"Too late! Too late! . . . they all are dead and gone," I heard
    her say.
And once again her weary eyes went round and round the room;
"Not one of all I used to know . . ." she turned to go away . . .
But quick I saw the old man start: "Ah no!" he cried, "not all.
Oh Marie Toro, queen of queens, don't you remember Paul?"

"Oh Marie, Marie Toro, in my garret next the sky,
Where many a day and night I've crouched with not a crust to
    eat,
A picture hangs upon the wall a fortune couldn't buy,
A portrait of a girl whose face is pure and angel-sweet."
Sadly the woman looked at him: "Alas! it's true," she said;
"That little maid, I knew her once. It's long ago—she's dead."
He went to her; he laid his hand upon her wasted arm:
"Oh, Marie Toro, come with me, though poor and sick am I.
For old times' sake I cannot bear to see you come to harm;
Ah! there are memories, God knows, that never, never die. . . ."
"Too late!" she sighed; "I've lived my life of splendor and of
    shame;
I've been adored by men of power, I've touched the highest
    height;
I've squandered gold like heaps of dirt—oh, I have played the
    game;
I've had my place within the sun . . . and now I face the night.
Look! look! you see I'm lost to hope; I live no matter how . . .
To drink and drink and so forget . . . that's all I care for now."

And so she went her heedless way, and all our help was vain.
She trailed along with tattered shawl and mud-corroded skirt;
She gnawed a crust and slept beneath the bridges of the Seine,
A garbage thing, a composite of alcohol and dirt.
The students learned her story and the cafés knew her well,
The Pascal and the Panthéon, the Sufflot and Vachette;
She shuffled round the tables with the flowers she tried to sell
A living mask of misery that no one will forget.
And then last week I missed her, and they found her in the street
One morning early, huddled down, for it was freezing cold;
But when they raised her ragged shawl her face was still and
    sweet;
Some bits of broken bloom were clutched within her icy hold.
That's all. . . . Ah yes, they say that saw: her blue, wide-open
    eyes
Were beautiful with joy again, with radiant surprise. . . .

A week ago she begged for bread; we've bought for her a stone,
And a peaceful place in Père-La-Chaise where she'll be well
    alone.
She cost a king his crown, they say; oh, wouldn't she be proud
If she could see the wreaths to-day, the coaches and the crowd!
So follow, follow, follow on with slow and sober tread,
For Marie Toro, gutter waif and queen of queens, is dead.

IV

THE CAFÉ DE DEUX MAGOTS,
June 1914.

THE BOHEMIAN

Up in my garret bleak and bare
I tilted back on my broken chair,

And my three old pals were with me there,
　　Hunger and Thirst and Cold;
Hunger scowled at his scurvy mate:
Cold cowered down by the hollow grate,
And I hated them with a deadly hate
　　As old as life is old.

So up in my garret that's near the sky
I smiled a smile that was thin and dry:
"You've roomed with me twenty year," said I,
　　"Hunger and Thirst and Cold;
But now, begone down the broken stair!
I've suffered enough of your spite . . . so there!"
Bang! Bang! I slapped on the table bare
　　A glittering heap of gold.

"Red flames will jewel my wine to-night;
I'll loose my belt that you've lugged so tight;
Ha! Ha! Dame Fortune is smiling bright;
　　The stuff of my brain I've sold;
Canaille of the gutter, up! Away!
You've battened on me for a bitter-long day;
But I'm driving you forth, and forever and aye,
　　Hunger and Thirst and Cold."

So I kicked them out with a scornful roar;
Yet, oh, they turned at the garret door;
Quietly there they spoke once more:
　　"The tale is not all told.
It's *au revoir*, but it's not good-by;
We're yours, old chap, till the day you die;
Laugh on, you fool! Oh, you'll never defy
　　Hunger and Thirst and Cold."

Hurrah! The crisis in my financial career is over. Once more I have weathered the storm, and never did money jingle so sweetly in my pocket. It was MacBean who delivered me. He arrived at the door of my garret this morning, with a broad grin of pleasure on his face.

"Here," said he; "I've sold some of your rubbish. They'll take more too, of the same sort."

With that he handed me three crisp notes. For a moment I thought that he was paying the money out of his own pocket, as he knew I was desperately hard up; but he showed me the letter enclosing the cheque he had cashed for me.

So we sought the Grand Boulevard, and I had a Pernod, which rose to my head in delicious waves of joy. I talked ecstatic nonsense, and seemed to walk like a god in clouds of gold. We dined on frogs' legs and Vouvray, and then went to see the Revue at the Marigny. A very merry evening.

Such is the life of Bohemia, up and down, fast and feast; its very uncertainty its charm.

Here is my latest ballad, another attempt to express the sentiment of actuality:

THE AUCTION SALE

HER little head just topped the window-sill;
She even mounted on a stool, maybe;
She pressed against the pane, as children will,
And watched us playing, oh so wistfully!
And then I missed her for a month or more,
And idly thought: "She's gone away, no doubt,"
Until a hearse drew up beside the door . . .
I saw a tiny coffin carried out.

And after that, towards dusk I'd often see
Behind the blind another face that looked:
Eyes of a young wife watching anxiously,
Then rushing back to where her dinner cooked.

She often gulped it down alone, I fear,
Within her heart the sadness of despair,
For near to midnight I would vaguely hear
A lurching step, a stumbling on the stair.

These little dramas of the common day!
A man weak-willed and fore-ordained to fail . . .
The window's empty now, they've gone away,
And yonder, see, their furniture's for sale.
To all the world their door is open wide,
And round and round the bargain-hunters roam,
And peer and gloat, like vultures avid-eyed,
Above the corpse of what was once a home.

So reverent I go from room to room,
And see the patient care, the tender touch,
The love that sought to brighten up the gloom,
The woman-courage tested overmuch.
Amid those things so intimate and dear,
Where now the mob invades with brutal tread,
I think: "What happiness is buried here,
What dreams are withered and what hopes are dead!"

Oh, woman dear, and were you sweet and glad
Over the lining of your little nest!
What ponderings and proud ideas you had!
What visions of a shrine of peace and rest!
For there's his easy-chair upon the rug,
His reading-lamp, his pipe-rack on the wall,
All that you could devise to make him snug—
And yet you could not hold him with it all.

Ah, patient heart, what homelike joys you planned
To stay him by the dull domestic flame!

Those silken cushions that you worked by hand
When you had time, before the baby came.
Oh, how you wove around him cozy spells,
And schemed so hard to keep him home of nights!
Aye, every touch and turn some story tells
Of sweet conspiracies and dead delights.

And here upon the scratched piano stool,
Tied in a bundle, are the songs you sung;
That cozy that you worked in colored wool,
The Spanish lace you made when you were young,
And lots of modern novels, cheap reprints,
And little dainty knick-knacks everywhere;
And silken bows and curtains of gay chintz . . .
And oh, her tiny crib, her folding chair!

Sweet woman dear, and did your heart not break,
To leave this precious home you made in vain?
Poor shabby things! so prized for old times' sake,
With all their memories of love and pain.
Alas! while shouts the raucous auctioneer,
And rat-faced dames are prying everywhere,
The echo of old joy is all I hear,
All, all I see just heartbreak and despair.

Imagination is the great gift of the gods. Given it, one does not
need to look afar for subjects. There is romance in every face.
Those who have Imagination live in a land of enchantment which
the eyes of others cannot see. Yet if it brings marvellous joy it also
brings exquisite pain. Who lives a hundred lives must die a hundred
deaths.
I do not know any of the people who live around me. Sometimes
I pass them on the stairs. However, I am going to give my imagina-
tion rein, and string some rhymes about them.

Before doing so, having money in my pocket and seeing the prospect of making more, let me blithely chant about

THE JOY OF BEING POOR

I

Let others sing of gold and gear, the joy of being rich;
But oh, the days when I was poor, a vagrant in a ditch!
When every dawn was like a gem, so radiant and rare,
And I had but a single coat, and not a single care;
When I would feast right royally on bacon, bread and beer,
And dig into a stack of hay and doze like any peer;
When I would wash beside a brook my solitary shirt,
And though it dried upon my back I never took a hurt;
When I went romping down the road contemptuous of care,
And slapped Adventure on the back—by Gad! we were a pair;
When, though my pockets lacked a coin, and though my coat
    was old,
The largess of the stars was mine, and all the sunset gold;
When time was only made for fools, and free as air was I,
And hard I hit and hard I lived beneath the open sky;
When all the roads were one to me, and each had its allure . . .
Ye Gods! these were the happy days, the days when I was poor.

II

Or else, again, old pal of mine, do you recall the times
You struggled with your storyettes, I wrestled with my rhymes;
Oh, we were happy, were we not?—we used to live so "high"
(A little bit of broken roof between us and the sky);
Upon the forge of art we toiled with hammer and with tongs;
You told me all your ripping yarns, I sang to you my songs.

Our hats were frayed, our jackets patched, our boots were down
 at heel,
But oh, the happy men were we, although we lacked a meal.
And if I sold a bit of rhyme, or if you placed a tale,
What feasts we had of tenderloins and apple-tarts and ale!
And yet how often we would dine as cheerful as you please,
Beside our little friendly fire on coffee, bread and cheese.
We lived upon the ragged edge, and grub was never sure,
But oh, these were the happy days, the days when we were poor.

III

Alas! old man, we're wealthy now, it's sad beyond a doubt;
We cannot dodge prosperity, success has found us out.
Your eye is very dull and drear, my brow is creased with care,
We realize how hard it is to be a millionaire.
The burden's heavy on our backs—you're thinking of your
 rents,
I'm worrying if I'll invest in five or six per cents.
We've limousines, and marble halls, and flunkeys by the score,
We play the part . . . but say, old chap, oh, isn't it a bore?
We work like slaves, we eat too much, we put on evening dress;
We've everything a man can want, I think . . . but happiness.

Come, let us sneak away, old chum; forget that we are rich,
And earn an honest appetite, and scratch an honest itch.
Let's be two jolly garreteers, up seven flights of stairs,
And wear old clothes and just pretend we aren't millionaires;
And wonder how we'll pay the rent, and scribble ream on ream,
And sup on sausages and tea, and laugh and loaf and dream.

And when we're tired of that, my friend, oh, you will come with
 me;

And we will seek the sunlit roads that lie beside the sea.
We'll know the joy the gipsy knows, the freedom nothing mars,
The golden treasure-gates of dawn, the mintage of the stars.
We'll smoke our pipes and watch the pot, and feed the crackling
    fire,
And sing like two old jolly boys, and dance to heart's desire;
We'll climb the hill and ford the brook and camp upon the
    moor . . .
Old chap, let's haste, I'm mad to taste the Joy of Being Poor.

V

My Garret, Montparnasse,
June 1914.

MY NEIGHBORS

To rest my fagged brain now and then,
When wearied of my proper labors,
I lay aside my lagging pen
And get to thinking on my neighbors;
For, oh, around my garret den
There's woe and poverty a-plenty,
And life's so interesting when
A lad is only two-and-twenty.

Now, there's that artist gaunt and wan,
A little card his door adorning;
It reads: "Je ne suis pour personne,"
A very frank and fitting warning.
I fear he's in a sorry plight;
He starves, I think, too proud to borrow,

I hear him moaning every night:
Maybe they'll find him dead to-morrow.

ROOM 4

THE PAINTER CHAP

HE gives me such a bold and curious look,
That young American across the way,
As if he'd like to put me in a book
(Fancies himself a poet, so they say.)
Ah well! He'll make no "document" of me.
I lock my door. Ha!ha! Now none shall see. . . .

Pictures, just pictures piled from roof to floor,
Each one a bit of me, a dream fulfilled,
A vision of the beauty I adore,
My own poor glimpse of glory, passion-thrilled . . .
But now my money's gone, I paint no more.

For three days past I have not tasted food;
The jewelled colors run . . . I reel, I faint;
They tell me that my pictures are no good,
Just crude and childish daubs, a waste of paint.
I burned to throw on canvas all I saw—
Twilight on water, tenderness of trees,
Wet sands at sunset and the smoking seas,
The peace of valleys and the mountain's awe:
Emotion swayed me at the thought of these.
I sought to paint ere I had learned to draw,
And that's the trouble. . . .

Ah well! here am I,

Facing my failure after struggle long;
And there they are, my *croutes* that none will buy
(And doubtless they are right and I am wrong);
Well, when one's lost one's faith it's time to die. . . .

This knife will do . . . and now to slash and slash;
Rip them to ribands, rend them every one,
My dreams and visions—tear and stab and gash,
So that their crudeness may be known to none;
Poor, miserable daubs! Ah! there, it's done. . . .

And now to close my little window tight.
Lo! in the dusking sky, serenely set,
The evening star is like a beacon bright.
And see! to keep her tender tryst with night
How Paris veils herself in violet. . . .

Oh, why does God create such men as I?—
All pride and passion and divine desire,
Raw, quivering nerve-stuff and devouring fire,
Foredoomed to failure though they try and try;
Abortive, blindly to destruction hurled;
Unfound, unfit to grapple with the world. . . .

And now to light my wheezy jet of gas;
Chink up the window-crannies and the door,
So that no single breath of air may pass;
So that I'm sealed air-tight from roof to floor.
There, there, that's done; and now there's nothing more. . . .

Look at the city's myriad lamps a-shine;
See, the calm moon is launching into space . . .
There will be darkness in these eyes of mine

Ere it can climb to shine upon my face.
Oh, it will find such peace upon my face! . . .

City of Beauty, I have loved you well,
A laugh or two I've had, but many a sigh;
I've run with you the scale from Heav'n to Hell.
Paris, I love you still . . . good-bye, good-bye.
Thus it all ends—unhappily, alas!
It's time to sleep, and now . . . *blow out the gas*. . . .

> *Now there's that little* midinette
> *Who goes to work each morning daily;*
> *I choose to call her Blithe Babette,*
> *Because she's always humming gaily;*
> *And though the Goddess "Comme-il-faut"*
> *May look on her with prim expression,*
> *It's Pagan Paris where, you know,*
> *The queen of virtues is Discretion.*

Room 6

THE LITTLE WORKGIRL

THREE gentlemen live close beside me—
A painter of pictures bizarre,
A poet whose virtues might guide me,
A singer who plays the guitar;
And there on my lintel is Cupid;
I leave my door open, and yet
These gentlemen, aren't they stupid!
They never make love to Babette.

I go to the shop every morning;
I work with my needle and thread;

Silk, satin and velvet adorning,
Then luncheon on coffee and bread.
Then sewing and sewing till seven;
Or else, if the order I get,
I toil and I toil till eleven—
And such is the day of Babette.

It doesn't seem cheerful, I fancy;
The wage is unthinkably small;
And yet there is one thing I can say:
I keep a bright face through it all.
I chaff though my head may be aching;
I sing a gay song to forget;
I laugh though my heart may be breaking—
It's all in the life of Babette.

That gown, O my lady of leisure,
You begged to be "finished in haste."
It gives you an exquisite pleasure,
Your lovers remark on its taste.
Yet . . . oh, the poor little white faces,
The tense midnight toil and the fret . . .
I fear that the foam of its laces
Is salt with the tears of Babette.

It takes a brave heart to be cheery
With no gleam of hope in the sky;
The future's so utterly dreary,
I'm laughing—in case I should cry.
And if, where the gay lights are glowing,
I dine with a man I have met,
And snatch a bright moment—who's going
To blame a poor little Babette?

And you, Friend beyond all the telling,
.Although you're an ocean away,
Your pictures, they tell me, are selling,
You're married and settled, they say.
Such happiness one wouldn't barter;
Yet, oh, do you never regret
The Springtide, the roses, Montmartre,
Youth, poverty, love and—Babette?

That blond-haired chap across the way
With sunny smile and voice so mellow,
He sings in some cheap cabaret,
Yet what a gay and charming fellow!
His breath with garlic may be strong,
What matters it? his laugh is jolly;
His day he gives to sleep and song:
His night's made up of song and folly.

Room 5

THE CONCERT SINGER

I'm one of these haphazard chaps
Who sit in cafés drinking;
A most improper taste, perhaps,
Yet pleasant, to my thinking.
For, oh, I hate discord and strife;
I'm sadly, weakly human;
And I do think the best of life
Is wine and song and woman.

Now, there's that youngster on my right
Who thinks himself a poet,

And so he toils from morn to night
And vainly hopes to show it;
And there's that dauber on my left,
Within his chamber shrinking—
He looks like one of hope bereft;
He lives on air, I'm thinking.

But me, I love the things that are,
My heart is always merry;
I laugh and tune my old guitar:
Sing ho! and hey-down-derry.
Oh, let them toil their lives away
To gild a tawdry era,
But I'll be gay while yet I may:
Sing tira-lira-lira.

I'm sure you know that picture well,
A monk, all else unheeding,
Within a bare and gloomy cell
A musty volume reading;
While through the window you can see
In sunny glade entrancing,
With cap and bells beneath a tree
A jester dancing, dancing.

Which is the fool and which the sage?
I cannot quite discover;
But you may look in learning's page
And I'll be laughter's lover.
For this our life is none too long,
And hearts were made for gladness;
Let virtue lie in joy and song,
The only sin be sadness.

So let me troll a jolly air,
Come what come will to-morrow;
I'll be no *cabotin* of care,
No *souteneur* of sorrow.
Let those who will indulge in strife,
To my most merry thinking,
The true philosophy of life
Is laughing, loving, drinking.

And there's that weird and ghastly hag
Who walks head bent, with lips a-mutter;
With twitching hands and feet that drag,
And tattered skirts that sweep the gutter.
An outworn harlot, lost to hope,
With staring eyes and hair that's hoary
I hear her gibber, dazed with dope:
I often wonder what's her story.

ROOM 7

THE COCO-FIEND

I LOOK at no one, me;
I pass them on the stair;
Shadows! I don't see;
Shadows! everywhere.
Haunting, taunting, staring, glaring,
Shadows! I don't care.
Once my room I gain
Then my life begins.
Shut the door on pain;
How the Devil grins!
Grin with might and main;

Grin and grin in vain;
Here's where Heav'n begins:
Cocaine! Cocaine!

A whiff! Ah, that's the thing.
How it makes me gay!
Now I want to sing,
Leap, laugh, play.
Ha! I've had my fling!
Mistress of a king
In my day.
Just another snuff . . .
Oh, the blessed stuff!
How the wretched room
Rushes from my sight;
Misery and gloom
Melt into delight;
Fear and death and doom
Vanish in the night.
No more cold and pain,
I am young again,
Beautiful again,
Cocaine! Cocaine!

Oh, I was made to be good, to be good,
For a true man's love and a life that's sweet;
Fireside blessings and motherhood.
Little ones playing around my feet.
How it all unfolds like a magic screen,
Tender and glowing and clear and glad,
The wonderful mother I might have been,
The beautiful children I might have had;
Romping and laughing and shrill with glee,

Oh, I see them now and I see them plain.
Darlings! Come nestle up close to me,
You comfort me so, and you're just . . . Cocaine.

It's Life that's all to blame:
We can't do what we will;
She robes us with her shame,
She crowns us with her ill.
I do not care, because
I see with bitter calm,
Life made me what I was,
Life makes me what I am.
Could I throw back the years,
It all would be the same;
Hunger and cold and tears,
Misery, fear and shame,
And then the old refrain,
Cocaine! Cocaine!

A love-child I, so here my mother came,
Where she might live in peace with none to blame.
And how she toiled! Harder than any slave,
What courage! patient, hopeful, tender, brave.
We had a little room at Lavilette,
So small, so neat, so clean, I see it yet.
Poor mother! sewing, sewing late at night,
Her wasted face beside the candlelight,
This Paris crushed her. How she used to sigh!
And as I watched her from my bed I knew
She saw red roofs against a primrose sky
And glistening fields and apples dimmed with dew.
Hard times we had. We counted every *sou*,

We sewed sacks for a living. I was quick . . .
Four busy hands to work instead of two.
Oh, we were happy there, till she fell sick. . . .

My mother lay, her face turned to the wall,
And I, a girl of sixteen, fair and tall,
Sat by her side, all stricken with despair,
Knelt by her bed and faltered out a prayer.
A doctor's order on the table lay,
Medicine for which, alas! I could not pay;
Medicine to save her life, to soothe her pain.
I sought for something I could sell, in vain . . .
All, all was gone! The room was cold and bare;
Gone blankets and the cloak I used to wear;
Bare floor and wall and cupboard, every shelf—
Nothing that I could sell . . . except myself.

I sought the street, I could not bear
To hear my mother moaning there.
I clutched the paper in my hand.
'Twas hard. You cannot understand . . .
I walked as martyr to the flame,
Almost exalted in my shame.
They turned, who heard my voiceless cry,
"For Sale, a virgin, who will buy?"
And so myself I fiercely sold,
And clutched the price, a piece of gold.
Into a pharmacy I pressed;
I took the paper from my breast.
I gave my money . . . how it gleamed!
How precious to my eyes it seemed!
And then I saw the chemist frown,

Quick on the counter throw it down,
Shake with an angry look his head:
"Your *louis d'or* is bad," he said.

Dazed, crushed, I went into the night,
I clutched my gleaming coin so tight.
No, no, I could not well believe
That any one could so deceive.
I tried again and yet again—
Contempt, suspicion and disdain;
Always the same reply I had:
"Get out of this. Your money's bad."

Heart broken to the room I crept,
To mother's side. All still . . . she slept . . .
I bent, I sought to raise her head . . .
"Oh, God, have pity!" she was dead.

That's how it all began.
Said I: Revenge is sweet.
So in my guilty span
I've ruined many a man.
They've grovelled at my feet,
I've pity had for none;
I've bled them every one.
Oh, I've had interest for
That worthless *louis d'or*.

But now it's over; see,
I care for no one, me;
Only at night sometimes
In dreams I hear the chimes
Of wedding-bells and see

A woman without stain
With children at her knee.
Ah, how you comfort me,
Cocaine! . . .

BOOK THREE

LATE SUMMER

I

MacBean, before he settled down to the manufacture of mercantile fiction, had ideas of a nobler sort, which bore their fruit in a slender book of poems. In subject they are either erotic, mythologic, or descriptive of nature. So polished are they that the mind seems to slide over them: so faultless in form that the critics hailed them with highest praise, and as many as a hundred copies were sold.

Saxon Dane, too, has published a book of poems, but he, on the other hand, defies tradition to an eccentric degree. Originality is his sin. He strains after it in every line. I must confess I think much of the free verse he writes is really prose, and a good deal of it blank verse chopped up into odd lengths. He talks of assonance and colour, of stress and pause and accent, and bewilders me with his theories.

He and MacBean represent two extremes, and at night, as we sit in the Café du Dôme, they have the hottest of arguments. As for me, I listen with awe, content that my medium is verse, and that the fashions of Hood, Thackeray and Bret Harte are the fashions of to-day.

Of late I have been doing light stuff, "fillers" for MacBean. Here are three of my specimens:

THE PHILANDERER

Oh, have you forgotten those afternoons
With riot of roses and amber skies,
When we thrilled to the joy of a million Junes,
And I sought for your soul in the deeps of your eyes?
I would love you, I promised, forever and aye,
And I meant it too; yet, oh, isn't it odd?
When we met in the Underground to-day
I addressed you as Mary instead of as Maude.

Oh, don't you remember that moonlit sea,
With us on a silver trail afloat,
When I gracefully sank on my bended knee
At the risk of upsetting our little boat?
Oh, I vowed that my life was blighted then,
As friendship you proffered with mournful mien;
But now as I think of your children ten,
I'm glad you refused me, Evangeline.

Oh, is that moment eternal still
When I breathed my love in your shell-like ear,
And you plucked at your fan as a maiden will,
And you blushed so charmingly, Guinivere?
Like a worshipper at your feet I sat;
For a year and a day you made me mad;
But now, alas! you are forty, fat,
And I think: What a lucky escape I had!

Oh, maidens I've set in a sacred shrine,
Oh, Rosamond, Molly and Mignonette,
I've deemed you in turn the most divine,
In turn you've broken my heart . . . and yet
It's easily mended. What's past is past.
To-day on Lucy I'm going to call;
For I'm sure that I know true love at last,
And *She* is the fairest girl of all.

THE *PETIT VIEUX*

"Sow your wild oats in your youth," so we're always told;
But I say with deeper sooth: "Sow them when you're old."
I'll be wise till I'm about seventy or so:
Then, by Gad! I'll blossom out as an ancient *beau*.

I'll assume a dashing air, laugh with loud Ha! ha! . . .
How my grandchildren will stare at their grandpapa!
Their perfection aureoled I will scandalize:
Won't I be a hoary old sinner in their eyes!

Watch me, how I'll learn to chaff barmaids in a bar;
Scotches daily, gayly quaff, puff a fierce cigar.
I will haunt the Tango teas, at the stage-door stand;
Wait for Dolly Dimpleknees, bouquet in my hand.

Then at seventy I'll take flutters at roulette;
While at eighty hope I'll make good at poker yet;
And in fashionable togs to the races go,
Gayest of the gay old dogs, ninety years or so.

"Sow your wild oats while you're young," that's what you are
        told;
Don't believe the foolish tongue—sow 'em when you're old.
Till you're threescore years and ten, take my humble tip,
Sow your nice tame oats and then . . . Hi, boys! Let 'er rip.

MY MASTERPIECE

It's slim and trim and bound in blue;
Its leaves are crisp and edged with gold;
Its words are simple, stalwart too;
Its thoughts are tender, wise and bold.
Its pages scintillate with wit;
Its pathos clutches at my throat:
Oh, how I love each line of it!
That Little Book I Never Wrote.

In dreams I see it praised and prized
By all, from plowman unto peer;

It's pencil-marked and memorized,
It's loaned (and not returned, I fear);
It's worn and torn and travel-tossed,
And even dusky natives quote
That classic that the world has lost,
The Little Book I Never Wrote.

Poor ghost! For homes you've failed to cheer,
For grieving hearts uncomforted,
Don't haunt me now. . . . Alas! I fear
The fire of Inspiration's dead.
A humdrum way I go to-night,
From all I hoped and dreamed remote:
Too late . . . a better man must write
That Little Book I Never Wrote.

Talking about writing books, there is a queer character who shuffles up and down the little streets that neighbor the Place Maubert, and who, they say, has been engaged on one for years. Sometimes I see him cowering in some cheap *bouge*, and his wild eyes gleam at me through the tangle of his hair. But I do not think he ever sees me. He mumbles to himself, and moves like a man in a dream. His pockets are full of filthy paper on which he writes from time to time. The students laugh at him and make him tipsy; the street boys pelt him with ordure; the better cafés turn him from their doors. But who knows? At least, this is how I see him:

MY BOOK

BEFORE I drink myself to death,
God, let me finish up my Book!
At night, I fear, I fight for breath,
And wake up whiter than a spook;
And crawl off to a *bistro* near,
And drink until my brain is clear.

Rare Absinthe! Oh, it gives me strength
To write and write; and so I spend
Day after day, until at length
With joy and pain I'll write The End:
Then let this carcase rot; I give
The world my Book—my Book will live.

For every line is tense with truth,
There's hope and joy on every page;
A cheer, a clarion call to Youth,
A hymn, a comforter to Age:
All's there that I was meant to be,
My part divine, the God in me.

It's of my life the golden sum;
Ah! who that reads this Book of mine,
In stormy centuries to come,
Will dream I rooted with the swine?
Behold! I give mankind my best:
What does it matter, all the rest?

It's this that makes sublime my day;
It's this that makes me struggle on.
Oh, let them mock my mortal clay,
My spirit's deathless as the dawn;
Oh, let them shudder as they look . . .
I'll be immortal in my Book.

And so beside the sullen Seine
I fight with dogs for filthy food,
Yet know that from my sin and pain
Will soar serene a Something Good;
Exultantly from shame and wrong
A Right, a Glory and a Song.

How charming it is, this Paris of the summer skies! Each morning I leap up with joy in my heart, all eager to begin the day of work. As I eat my breakfast and smoke my pipe, I ponder over my task. Then in the golden sunshine that floods my little attic I pace up and down, absorbed and forgetful of the world. As I compose I speak the words aloud. There are difficulties to overcome; thoughts that will not fit their mould; rebellious rhymes. Ah! those moments of despair and defeat.

Then suddenly the mind grows lucid, imagination glows, the snarl unravels. In the end is always triumph and success. O delectable *métier!* Who would not be a rhymesmith in Paris, in Bohemia, in the heart of youth!

I have now finished my twentieth ballad. Five more and they will be done. In quiet corners of cafés, on benches of the Luxembourg, on the sunny Quays I read them over one by one. Here is my latest:

MY HOUR

DAY after day behold me plying
My pen within an office drear;
The dullest dog, till homeward hieing,
Then lo! I reign a king of cheer.
A throne have I of padded leather,
A little court of kiddies three,
A wife who smiles whate'er the weather,
A feast of muffins, jam and tea.

The table cleared, a romping battle,
A fairy tale, a "Children, bed,"
A kiss, a hug, a hush of prattle
(God save each little drowsy head!)
A cozy chat with wife a-sewing,
A silver lining clouds that low'r,
Then she too goes, and with her going,
I come again into my Hour.

I poke the fire, I snugly settle,
My pipe I prime with proper care;
The water's purring in the kettle,
Rum, lemon, sugar, all are there.
And now the honest grog is steaming,
And now the trusty briar's aglow:
Alas! in smoking, drinking, dreaming,
How sadly swift the moments go!

Oh, golden hour! 'twixt love and duty,
All others I to others give;
But you are mine to yield to Beauty,
To glean Romance, to greatly live.
For in my easy-chair reclining . . .
I feel the sting of ocean spray;
And yonder wondrously are shining
The Magic Isles of Far Away.

Beyond the comber's crashing thunder
Strange beaches flash into my ken;
On jetties heaped head-high with plunder
I dance and dice with sailor-men.
Strange stars swarm down to burn above me,
Strange shadows haunt, strange voices greet;
Strange women lure and laugh and love me,
And fling their bastards at my feet.

Oh, I would wish the wide world over,
In ports of passion and unrest,
To drink and drain, a tarry rover
With dragons tattooed on my chest,
With haunted eyes that hold red glories
Of foaming seas and crashing shores,

With lips that tell the strangest stories
Of sunken ships and gold moidores;

Till sick of storm and strife and slaughter,
Some ghostly night when hides the moon,
I slip into the milk-warm water
And softly swim the stale lagoon.
Then through some jungle python-haunted,
Or plumed morass, or woodland wild,
I win my way with heart undaunted,
And all the wonder of a child.

The pathless plains shall swoon around me,
The forests frown, the floods appall;
The mountains tiptoe to confound me,
The rivers roar to speed my fall.
Wild dooms shall daunt, and dawns be gory,
And Death shall sit beside my knee;
Till after terror, torment, glory,
I win again the sea, the sea. . . .

Oh, anguish sweet! Oh, triumph splendid!
Oh, dreams adieu! my pipe is dead.
My glass is dry, my Hour is ended,
It's time indeed I stole to bed.
How peacefully the house is sleeping!
Ah! why should I strange fortunes plan?
To guard the dear ones in my keeping—
That's task enough for any man.

So through dim seas I'll ne'er go spoiling;
The red Tortugas never roam;
Please God! I'll keep the pot a-boiling,

And make at least a happy home.
My children's path shall gleam with roses,
Their grace abound, their joy increase.
And so my Hour divinely closes
With tender thoughts of praise and peace.

II

THE GARDEN OF THE LUXEMBOURG,
Late July 1914.

When on some scintillating summer morning I leap lightly up to
the seclusion of my garret, I often think of those lines: "In the brave
days when I was twenty-one."

True, I have no loving, kind Lisette to pin her petticoat across
the pane, yet I do live in hope. Am I not in Bohemia the Magical,
Bohemia of Murger, of de Musset, of Verlaine? Shades of Mimi
Pinson, of Trilby, of all that immortal line of laughterful grisettes,
do not tell me that the days of love and fun are forever at an end!

Yes, youth is golden, but what of age? Shall it too not testify to
the rhapsody of existence? Let the years between be those of strug-
gle, of sufferance—of disillusion if you will; but let youth and age
affirm the ecstasy of being. Let us look forward all to a serene sun-
set, and in the still skies "a late lark singing."

This thought comes to me as, sitting on a bench near the band-
stand, I see an old savant who talks to all the children. His clean-
shaven face is alive with kindliness; under his tall silk hat his white
hair falls to his shoulders. He wears a long black cape over a black
frock-coat, very neat linen, and a flowing tie of black silk. I call him
"Silvester Bonnard." As I look at him I truly think the best of life
are the years between sixty and seventy.

A SONG OF SIXTY-FIVE

BRAVE Thackeray has trolled of days when he was twenty-one,
And bounded up five flights of stairs, a gallant garreteer;

And yet again in mellow vein when youth was gaily run,
Has dipped his nose in Gascon wine, and told of Forty Year
But if I worthy were to sing a richer, rarer time,
I'd tune my pipes before the fire and merrily I'd strive
To praise that age when prose again has given way to rhyme,
The Indian Summer days of life when I'll be Sixty-five;

For then my work will all be done, my voyaging be past,
And I'll have earned the right to rest where folding hills are
　　green;
So in some glassy anchorage I'll make my cable fast,—
Oh, let the seas show all their teeth, I'll sit and smile serene.
The storm may bellow round the roof, I'll bide beside the fire,
And many a scene of sail and trail within the flame I'll see;
For I'll have worn away the spur of passion and desire. . . .
Oh yes, when I am Sixty-five, what peace will come to me.

I'll take my breakfast in my bed, I'll rise at half-past ten,
When all the world is nicely groomed and full of golden song;
I'll smoke a bit and joke a bit, and read the news, and then
I'll potter round my peach-trees till I hear the luncheon gong.
And after that I think I'll doze an hour, well, maybe two,
And then I'll show some kindred soul how well my roses thrive;
I'll do the things I never yet have found the time to do. . . .
Oh, won't I be the busy man when I am Sixty-five.

I'll revel in my library; I'll read De Morgan's books;
I'll grow so garrulous I fear you'll write me down a bore;
I'll watch the ways of ants and bees in quiet sunny nooks,
I'll understand Creation as I never did before.
When gossips round the tea-cups talk I'll listen to it all;
On smiling days some kindly friend will take me for a drive:
I'll own a shaggy collie dog that dashes to my call:
I'll celebrate my second youth when I am Sixty-five.

Ah, though I've twenty years to go, I see myself quite plain,
A wrinkling, twinkling, rosy-cheeked, benevolent old chap;
I think I'll wear a tartan shawl and lean upon a cane.
I hope that I'll have silver hair beneath a velvet cap.
I see my little grandchildren a-romping round my knee;
So gay the scene, I almost wish 'twould hasten to arrive.
Let others sing of Youth and Spring, still will it seem to me
The golden time's the olden time, some time round Sixty-five.

From old men to children is but a step, and there too, in the shadow of the Fontaine de Medicis, I spend much of my time watching the little ones. Childhood, so innocent, so helpless, so trusting, is somehow pathetic to me.

There was one jolly little chap who used to play with a large white Teddy Bear. He was always with his mother, a sweet-faced woman, who followed his every movement with delight. I used to watch them both, and often spoke a few words.

Then one day I missed them, and it struck me I had not seen them for a week, even a month, maybe. After that I looked for them a time or two and soon forgot.

Then this morning I saw the mother in the rue D'Assas. She was alone and in deep black. I wanted to ask after the boy, but there was a look in her face that stopped me.

I do not think she will ever enter the garden of the Luxembourg again.

TEDDY BEAR

O Teddy Bear! with your head awry
And your comical twisted smile,
You rub your eyes—do you wonder why
You've slept such a long, long while?
As you lay so still in the cupboard dim,
And you heard on the roof the rain,
Were you thinking . . . what has become of *him?*
And when will he play again?

Do you sometimes long for a chubby hand,
And a voice so sweetly shrill?
O Teddy Bear! don't you understand
Why the house is awf'ly still?
You sit with your muzzle propped on your paws,
And your whimsical face askew.
Don't wait, don't wait for your friend . . . because
He's sleeping and dreaming too.

Aye, sleeping long. . . . You remember how
He stabbed our hearts with his cries?
And oh, the dew of pain on his brow,
And the deeps of pain in his eyes!
And, Teddy Bear! you remember, too,
As he sighed and sank to his rest,
How all of a sudden he smiled to you,
And he clutched you close to his breast.

I'll put you away, little Teddy Bear,
In the cupboard far from my sight;
Maybe he'll come and he'll kiss you there,
A wee white ghost in the night.
But me, I'll live with my love and pain
A weariful lifetime through;
And my Hope: will I see him again, again?
Ah, God! If I only knew!

After old men and children I am greatly interested in dogs. I will
go out of my way to caress one who shows any desire to be friendly.
There is a very filthy fellow who collects cigarette stubs on the Boul'
Mich', and who is always followed by a starved yellow cur. The
other day I came across them in a little side street. The man was
stretched on the pavement brutishly drunk and dead to the world.
The dog, lying by his side, seemed to look at me with sad, imploring

eyes. Though all the world despise that man, I thought, this poor
brute loves him and will be faithful unto death.

From this incident I wrote the verses that follow:

THE OUTLAW

A WILD and woeful race he ran
Of lust and sin by land and sea;
Until, abhorred of God and man,
They swung him from the gallows-tree.
And then he climbed the Starry Stair,
And dumb and naked and alone,
With head unbowed and brazen glare,
He stood before the Judgment Throne.

The Keeper of the Records spoke:
"This man, O Lord, has mocked Thy Name.
The weak have wept beneath his yoke,
The strong have fled before his flame.
The blood of babes is on his sword;
His life is evil to the brim:
Look down, decree his doom, O Lord!
Lo! there is none will speak for him."

The golden trumpets blew a blast
That echoed in the crypts of Hell,
For there was Judgment to be passed,
And lips were hushed and silence fell.
The man was mute; he made no stir,
Erect before the Judgment Seat . . .
When all at once a mongrel cur
Crept out and cowered and licked his feet.

It licked his feet with whining cry.
Come Heav'n, come Hell, what did it care?
It leapt, it tried to catch his eye;
Its master, yea, its God was there.
Then, as a thrill of wonder sped
Through throngs of shining seraphim,
The Judge of All looked down and said:
"Lo! here is ONE who pleads for him.

"And who shall love of these the least,
And who by word or look or deed
Shall pity show to bird or beast,
By Me shall have a friend in need.
Aye, though his sin be black as night,
And though he stand 'mid men alone,
He shall be softened in My sight,
And find a pleader by My Throne.

"So let this man to glory win;
From life to life salvation glean;
By pain and sacrifice and sin,
Until he stand before Me—*clean*.
For he who loves the least of these
(And here I say and here repeat)
Shall win himself an angel's pleas
For Mercy at My Judgment Seat."

I take my exercise in the form of walking. It keeps me fit and leaves me free to think. In this way I have come to know Paris like my pocket. I have explored its large and little streets, its stateliness and its slums.

But most of all I love the Quays, between the leafage and the sunlit Seine. Like shuttles the little steamers dart up and down, weaving the water into patterns of foam. Cigar-shaped barges stream under the lacework of the many bridges and make me think of tranquil days and willow-fringed horizons.

But what I love most is the stealing in of night, when the sky takes on that strange elusive purple; when eyes turn to the evening star and marvel at its brightness; when the Eiffel Tower becomes a strange, shadowy stairway yearning in impotent effort to the care-less moon.

Here is my latest ballad, short if not very sweet:

THE WALKERS

(He speaks.)

WALKING, walking, oh, the joy of walking!
Swinging down the tawny lanes with head held high;
Striding up the green hills, through the heather stalking,
Swishing through the woodlands where the brown leaves lie;
Marvelling at all things—windmills gaily turning,
Apples for the cider-press, ruby-hued and gold;
Tails of rabbits twinkling, scarlet berries burning,
Wedge of geese high-flying in the sky's clear cold,
Light in little windows, field and furrow darkling;
Home again returning, hungry as a hawk;
Whistling up the garden, ruddy-cheeked and sparkling,
Oh, but I am happy as I walk, walk, walk!

(She speaks.)

Walking, walking, oh, the curse of walking!
Slouching round the grim square, shuffling up the street,
Slinking down the by-way, all my graces hawking,
Offering my body to each man I meet.
Peering in the gin-shop where the lads are drinking,
Trying to look gay-like, crazy with the blues;
Halting in a doorway, shuddering and shrinking

(Oh, my draggled feather and my thin, wet shoes).
Here's a drunken drover: "Hullo, there, old dearie!"
No, he only curses, can't be got to talk. . . .
On and on till daylight, famished, wet and weary,
God in Heaven help me as I walk, walk, walk!

III

THE CAFÉ DE LA SOURCE,
Late in July 1914.

The other evening MacBean was in a pessimistic mood.

"Why do you write?" he asked me gloomily.

"Obviously," I said, "to avoid starving. To produce something that will buy me food, shelter, raiment."

"If you were a millionaire, would you still write?"

"Yes," I said, after a moment's thought. "You get an idea. It haunts you. It seems to clamour for expression. It begins to obsess you. At last in desperation you embody it in a poem, an essay, a story. There! it is disposed of. You are at rest. It troubles you no more. Yes; if I were a millionaire I should write, if it were only to escape from my ideas."

"You have given two reasons why men write," said MacBean: "for gain, for self-expression. Then, again, some men write to amuse themselves, some because they conceive they have a mission in the world; some because they have real genius, and are conscious they can enrich the literature of all time. I must say I don't know of any belonging to the latter class. We are living in an age of mediocrity. There is no writer of to-day who will read twenty years after he is dead. That's a truth that must come home to the best of them."

"I guess they're not losing much sleep over it," I said.

"Take novelists," continued MacBean. "The line of first-class novelists ended with Dickens and Thackeray. Then followed some of the second class, Stevenson, Meredith, Hardy. And to-day we have three novelists of the third class, good, capable craftsmen. We can trust ourselves comfortably in their hands. We read and enjoy them, but do you think our children will?"

"Yours won't, anyway," I said.

"Don't be too sure. I may surprise you yet. I may get married and turn *bourgeois*."

The best thing that could happen to MacBean would be that. It might change his point of view. He is so painfully discouraging. I have never mentioned my ballads to him. He would be sure to throw cold water on them. And as it draws near to its end the thought of my book grows more and more dear to me. How I will get it published I know not; but I will. Then even if it doesn't sell, even if nobody reads it, I will be content. Out of this brief, perishable Me I will have made something concrete, something that will preserve my thought within its dusty covers long after I am dead and dust.

Here is one of my latest:

POOR PETER

BLIND PETER PIPER used to play
All up and down the city;
I'd often meet him on my way,
And throw a coin for pity.
But all amid his sparkling tones
His ear was quick as any
To catch upon the cobble-stones
The jingle of my penny.

And as upon a day that shone
He piped a merry measure:
"How well you play!" I chanced to say;
Poor Peter glowed with pleasure.
You'd think the words of praise I spoke
Were all the pay he needed;
The artist in the player woke,
The penny lay unheeded.

Now Winter's here; the wind is shrill,
His coat is thin and tattered;

Yet hark! he's playing trill on trill
As if his music mattered.
And somehow though the city looks
Soaked through and through with shadows,
He makes you think of singing brooks
And larks and sunny meadows.

Poor chap! he often starves, they say;
Well, well, I can believe it;
For when you chuck a coin his way
He'll let some street-boy thieve it.
I fear he freezes in the night;
My praise I've long repented,
Yet look! his face is all alight . . .
Blind Peter seems contented.

A day later.

On the terrace of the Closerie de Lilas I came on Saxon Dane. He was smoking his big briar and drinking a huge glass of brown beer. The tree gave a pleasant shade, and he had thrown his sombrero on a chair. I noted how his high brow was bronzed by the sun and there were golden lights in his broad beard. There was something massive and imposing in the man as he sat there in brooding thought.

MacBean, he told me, was sick and unable to leave his room. Rheumatism. So I bought a cooked chicken and a bottle of Barsac, and mounting to the apartment of the invalid, I made him eat and drink. MacBean was very despondent, but cheered up greatly.

I think he rather dreads the future. He cannot save money, and all he makes he spends. He has always been a rover, often tried to settle down but could not. Now I think he wishes for security. I fear, however, it is too late.

THE WISTFUL ONE

I sought the trails of South and North,
I wandered East and West;

But pride and passion drove me forth
And would not let me rest.

And still I seek, as still I roam,
A snug roof overhead;
Four walls, my own; a quiet home. . . .
"You'll have it—*when you're dead.*"

MacBean is one of Bohemia's victims. It is a country of the young.
The old have no place in it. He will gradually lose his grip, go down
and down. I am sorry. He is my nearest approach to a friend. I do
not make them easily. I have deep reserves. I like solitude. I am never
so surrounded by boon companions as when I am all alone.

But though I am a solitary I realize the beauty of friendship, and
on looking through my note-book I find the following:

IF YOU HAD A FRIEND

IF you had a friend strong, simple, true,
Who knew your faults and who understood;
Who believed in the very best of you,
And who cared for you as a father would;
Who would stick by you to the very end,
Who would smile however the world might frown:
I'm sure you would try to please your friend,
You never would think to throw him down.

And supposing your friend was high and great,
And he lived in a palace rich and tall,
And sat like a King in shining state,
And his praise was loud on the lips of all;
Well then, when he turned to you alone,
And he singled you out from all the crowd,
And he called you up to his golden throne,
Oh, wouldn't you just be jolly proud?

If you had a friend like this, I say,
So sweet and tender, so strong and true,
You'd try to please him in every way,
You'd live at your bravest—now, wouldn't you?
His worth would shine in the words you penned;
You'd shout his praises . . . yet now it's odd!
You tell me you haven't got such a friend;
You haven't? I wonder . . . *What of God?*

To how few is granted the privilege of doing the work which lies closest to the heart, the work for which one is best fitted. The happy man is he who knows his limitations, yet bows to no false gods.

MacBean is not happy. He is overridden by his appetites, and to satisfy them he writes stuff that in his heart he despises.

Saxon Dane is not happy. His dream exceeds his grasp. His twisted, tortured phrases mock the vague grandiosity of his visions.

I am happy. My talent is proportioned to my ambition. The things I like to write are the things I like to read. I prefer the lesser poets to the greater, the cackle of the barnyard fowl to the scream of the eagle. I lack the divinity of discontent.

True Contentment comes from within. It dominates circumstance. It is resignation wedded to philosophy, a Christian quality seldom attained except by the old.

There is such an one I sometimes see being wheeled about in the Luxembourg. His face is beautiful in its thankfulness.

THE CONTENTED MAN

"How good God is to me," he said;
"For have I not a mansion tall,
With trees and lawns of velvet tread,
And happy helpers at my call?
With beauty is my life abrim,
With tranquil hours and dreams apart;
You wonder that I yield to Him
That best of prayers, a grateful heart?"

"How good God is to me," he said;
"For look! though gone is all my wealth,
How sweet it is to earn one's bread
With brawny arms and brimming health.
Oh, now I know the joy of strife!
To sleep so sound, to wake so fit.
Ah yes, how glorious is life!
I thank Him for each day of it."

"How good God is to me," he said;
"Though health and wealth are gone, it's true;
Things might be worse, I might be dead,
And here I'm living, laughing too.
Serene beneath the evening sky
I wait, and every man's my friend;
God's most contented man am I . . .
He keeps me smiling to the End."

To-day the basin of the Luxembourg is bright with little boats.
Hundreds of happy children romp around it. Little ones every-
where; yet there is no other city with so many childless homes.

THE SPIRIT OF THE UNBORN BABE

THE Spirit of the Unborn Babe peered through the window-
    pane,
Peered through the window-pane that glowed like beacon in the
    night;
For, oh, the sky was desolate and wild with wind and rain;
And how the little room was crammed with coziness and light!
Except the flirting of the fire there was no sound at all;
The Woman sat beside the hearth, her knitting on her knee,
The shadow of her husband's head was dancing on the wall;

She looked with staring eyes at it, she looked yet did not see.
She only saw a childish face that topped the table rim,
A little wistful ghost that smiled and vanished quick away;
And then because her tender eyes were flooding to the brim,
She lowered her head. . . . "Don't sorrow, dear," she heard
    him softly say;
"It's over now. We'll try to be as happy as before
(Ah! they who little children have, grant hostages to pain).
We gave Life chance to wound us once, but never, never
    more. . . ."
The Spirit of the Unborn Babe fled through the night again.

The Spirit of the Unborn Babe went wildered in the dark;
Like termagants the winds tore down and whirled it with the
    snow.
And then amid the writhing storm it saw a tiny spark,
A window broad, a spacious room all goldenly aglow,
A woman slim and Paris-gowned and exquisitely fair,
Who smiled with rapture as she watched her jewels catch the
    blaze;
A man in faultless evening dress, young, handsome, debonnaire,
Who smoked his cigarette and looked with frank admiring gaze.
"Oh, we are happy, sweet," said he; "youth, health, and wealth
    are ours.
What if a thousand toil and sweat that we may live at ease!
What if the hands are worn and torn that strew our path with
    flowers!
Ah, well! we did not make the world; let us not think of these.
Let's seek the beauty-spots of earth, Dear Heart, just you and I;
Let other women bring forth life with sorrow and with pain.
Above our door we'll hang the sign: 'No children need
    apply. . . .' "
The Spirit of the Unborn Babe sped through the night again

The Spirit of the Unborn Babe went whirling on and on;
It soared above a city vast, it swept down to a slum;
It saw within a grimy house a light that dimly shone;
It peered in through a window-pane and lo! a voice said:
    "Come!"
And so a little girl was born amid the dirt and din,
And lived in spite of everything, for life is ordered so;
A child whose eyes first opened wide to swinishness and sin,
A child whose love and innocence met only curse and blow.
And so in due and proper course she took the path of shame,
And gladly died in hospital, quite old at twenty years;
And when God comes to weigh it all, ah! whose shall be the
    blame
For all her maimed and poisoned life, her torture and her tears?
For oh, it is not what we do, but what we have not done!
And on that day of reckoning, when all is plain and clear,
What if we stand before the Throne, blood-guilty every
    one? . . .
Maybe the blackest sins of all are Selfishness and Fear.

IV

THE CAFÉ DE LA PAIX,
August 1, 1914.

Paris and I are out of tune. As I sit at this famous corner the faint
breeze is stale and weary; stale and weary too the faces that swirl
around me; while overhead the electric sign of Somebody's Choco-
late appears and vanishes with irritating insistency. The very trees
seem artificial, gleaming under the arc-lights with a raw virility that
rasps my nerves.

"Poor little trees," I mutter, "growing in all this grime and glare,
your only dryads the loitering ladies with the complexions of such
brilliant certainty, your only Pipes of Pan orchestral echoes from
the clamorous cafés. Exiles of the forest! what know you of full-
blossomed winds, of red-embered sunsets, of the gentle admonition

of spring rain! Life, that would fain be a melody, seems here almost
a malady. I crave for the balm of Nature, the anodyne of solitude,
the breath of Mother Earth. Tell me, O wistful trees, what shall
I do?"

Then that stale and weary wind rustles the leaves of the nearest
sycamore, and I am sure it whispers: "Brittany."

So to-morrow I am off, off to the Land of Little Fields.

FINISTÈRE

HURRAH! I'm off to Finistère, to Finistère, to Finistère;
My satchel's swinging on my back, my staff is in my hand;
I've twenty *louis* in my purse, I know the sun and sea are there,
And so I'm starting out to-day to tramp the golden land.
I'll go alone and glorying, with on my lips a song of joy;
I'll leave behind the city with its canker and its care;
I'll swing along so sturdily—oh, won't I be the happy boy!
A-singing on the rocky roads, the roads of Finistère.

Oh, have you been to Finistère, and do you know a whin-grey
    town
That echoes to the clatter of a thousand wooden shoes?
And have you seen the fisher-girls go gallivantin' up and down,
And watched the tawny boats go out, and heard the roaring
    crews?
Oh, would you sit with pipe and bowl, and dream upon some
    sunny quay,
Or would you walk the windy heath and drink the cooler air;
Oh, would you seek a cradled cove and tussle with the topaz
    sea!—
Pack up your kit to-morrow, lad, and haste to Finistère.

Oh, I will go to Finistère, there's nothing that can hold me back.
I'll laugh with Yves and Léon, and I'll chaff with Rose and
    Jeanne;

I'll seek the little, quaint *buvette* that's kept by Mother Mer-
   drinac,
Who wears a cap of many frills, and swears just like a man.
I'll yarn with hearty, hairy chaps who dance and leap and crack
   their heels;
Who swallow cupfuls of cognac and never turn a hair;
I'll watch the nut-brown boats come in with mullet, plaice and
   conger eels,
The jewelled harvest of the sea they reap in Finistère.

Yes, I'll come back from Finistère with memories of shining
   days,
Of scaly nets and salty men in overalls of brown;
Of ancient women knitting as they watch the tethered cattle
   graze
By little nestling beaches where the gorse goes blazing down;
Of headlands silvering the sea, of Calvarys against the sky,
Of scorn of angry sunsets, and of Carnac grim and bare;
Oh, won't I have the leaping veins, and tawny cheek and spar-
   kling eye,
When I come back to Montparnasse and dream of Finistère.

Two days later.

Behold me with staff and scrip, footing it merrily in the Land of
Pardons. I have no goal. When I am weary I stop at some *auberge;*
when I am rested I go on again. Neither do I put any constraint on
my spirit. No subduing of the mind to the task of the moment. I
dream to heart's content.

My dreams stretch into the future. I see myself a singer of simple
songs, a laureate of the under-dog. I will write books, a score of
them. I will voyage far and wide. I will . . .

But there! Dreams are dangerous. They waste the time one
should spend in making them come true. Yet when we do make them
come true, we find the vision sweeter than the reality. How much

of our happiness do we owe to dreams? I have in mind one old chap
who used to herd the sheep on my uncle's farm.

OLD DAVID SMAIL

HE dreamed away his hours in school;
He sat with such an absent air,
The master reckoned him a fool,
And gave him up in dull despair.

When other lads were making hay
You'd find him loafing by the stream;
He's take a book and slip away,
And just pretend to fish . . . and dream.

His brothers passed him in the race;
They climbed the hill and clutched the prize.
He did not seem to heed, his face
Was tranquil as the evening skies.

He lived apart, he spoke with few;
Abstractedly through life he went;
Oh, what he dreamed of no one knew,
And yet he seemed to be content.

I see him now, so old and grey,
His eyes with inward vision dim;
And though he faltered on the way,
Somehow I almost envied him.

At last beside his bed I stood:
"And is Life done so soon?" he sighed;
"It's been so rich, so full, so good,
I've loved it all . . ."—and so he died.

Another day.

Framed in hedgerows of emerald, the wheat glows with a caloric fervor, as if gorged with summer heat. In the vivid green of pastures old women are herding cows. Calm and patient are their faces as with gentle industry they bend over their knitting. One feels that they are necessary to the landscape.

To gaze at me the field-workers suspend the magnificent lethargy of their labours. The men with the reaping hooks improve the occasion by another pull at the cider bottle under the stook; the women raise apathetic brown faces from the sheaf they are tying; every one is a study in deliberation, though the crop is russet ripe and crying to be cut.

Then on I go again amid high banks overgrown with fern and honeysuckle. Sometimes I come on an old mill that seems to have been constructed by Constable, so charmingly does Nature imitate Art. By the deserted house, half drowned in greenery, the velvety wheel, dipping in the crystal water, seems to protest against this prolongation of its toil.

Then again I come on its brother, the Mill of the Wind, whirling its arms so cheerily, as it turns its great white stones for its master, the floury miller by the door.

These things delight me. I am in a land where Time has lagged, where simple people timorously hug the Past. How far away now seems the welter and swelter of the city, the hectic sophistication of the streets. The sense of wonder is strong in me again, the joy of looking at familiar things as if one were seeing them for the first time.

THE WONDERER

I wish that I could understand
The moving marvel of my Hand;
I watch my fingers turn and twist,
The supple bending of my wrist,
The dainty touch of finger-tip,
The steel intensity of grip;
A tool of exquisite design,
With pride I think: "It's mine! It's mine!"

Then there's the wonder of my Eyes,
Where hills and houses, seas and skies,
In waves of light converge and pass,
And print themselves as on a glass.
Line, form and color live in me;
I am the Beauty that I see;
Ah! I could write a book of size
About the wonder of my Eyes.

What of the wonder of my Heart,
That plays so faithfully its part?
I hear it running sound and sweet;
It does not seem to miss a beat;
Between the cradle and the grave
It never falters, stanch and brave.
Alas! I wish I had the art
To tell the wonder of my Heart.

Then oh! but how can I explain
The wondrous wonder of my **Brain**?
That marvellous machine that brings
All consciousness of wonderings;
That lets me from myself leap out
And watch my body walk about;
It's hopeless—all my words are vain
To tell the wonder of my Brain.

But do not think, O patient friend,
Who reads these stanzas to the end,
That I myself would glorify. . . .
You're just as wonderful as I,
And all Creation in our view
Is quite as marvellous as you.
Come, let us on the sea-shore stand

And wonder at a grain of sand;
And then into the meadow pass
And marvel at a blade of grass;
Or cast our vision high and far
And thrill with wonder at a star;
A host of stars—night's holy tent
Huge-glittering with wonderment.

If wonder is in great and small,
Then what of Him who made it all?
In eyes and brain and heart and limb
Let's see the wondrous work of Him.
In house and hill and sward and sea,
In bird and beast and flower and tree,
In everything from sun to sod,
The wonder and the awe of God.

August 9, 1914.

For some time the way has been growing wilder. Thickset hedges
have yielded to dykes of stone, and there is every sign that I am ap-
proaching the rugged region of the coast. At each point of vantage
I can see a Cross, often a relic of the early Christians, stumpy and
corroded. Then I come on a slab of grey stone upstanding about
fifteen feet. Like a sentinel on that solitary plain it overwhelms me
with a sense of mystery.

But as I go on through this desolate land these stones become more
and more familiar. Like soldiers they stand in rank, extending over
the moor. The sky is cowled with cloud, save where a sullen sunset
shoots blood-red rays across the plain. Bathed in that sinister light
stands my army of stone, and a wind swooping down seems to wail
amid its ranks. As in a glass darkly I can see the skin-clad men, the
women with the tangled hair, the beast-like feast, the cowering
terror of the night. Then the sunset is cut off suddenly, and a
clammy mist shrouds that silent army. So it is almost with a shudder
I take my last look at the Stones of Carnac.

But now my pilgrimage is drawing to an end. A painter friend who lives by the sea has asked me to stay with him awhile. Well, I have walked a hundred miles, singing on the way. I have dreamed and dawdled, planned, exulted. I have drunk buckets of cider, and eaten many an omelette that seemed like a golden glorification of its egg. It has all been very sweet, but it will also be sweet to loaf awhile.

OH, IT IS GOOD

OH, it is good to drink and sup,
And then beside the kindly fire
To smoke and heap the faggots up,
And rest and dream to heart's desire.

Oh, it is good to ride and run,
To roam the greenwood wild and free;
To hunt, to idle in the sun,
To leap into the laughing sea.

Oh, it is good with hand and brain
To gladly till the chosen soil,
And after honest sweat and strain
To see the harvest of one's toil.

Oh, it is good afar to roam,
And seek adventure in strange lands;
Yet oh, so good the coming home,
The velvet love of little hands.

So much is good. . . . We thank Thee, God,
For all the tokens Thou hast given,
That here on earth our feet have trod
Thy little shining trails of Heaven.

V

August 10, 1914.

I am living in a little house so near the sea that at high tide I can see on my bedroom wall the reflected ripple of the water. At night I waken to the melodious welter of waves; or maybe there is a great stillness, and then I know that the sand and sea-grass are lying naked to the moon. But soon the tide returns, and once more I hear the roistering of the waves.

Calvert, my friend, is a lover as well as a painter of nature. He rises with the dawn to see the morning mist kindle to coral and the sun's edge clear the hill-crest. As he munches his coarse bread and sips his white wine, what dreams are his beneath the magic changes of the sky! He will paint the same scene under a dozen conditions of light. He has looked so long for Beauty that he has come to see it everywhere.

I love this friendly home of his. A peace steals over my spirit, and I feel as if I could stay here always. Some day I hope that I too may have such an one, and that I may write like this:

I HAVE SOME FRIENDS

I HAVE some friends, some worthy friends,
And worthy friends are rare:
These carpet slippers on my feet,
That padded leather chair;
This old and shabby dressing-gown,
So well the worse of wear.

I have some friends, some honest friends,
And honest friends are few;
My pipe of briar, my open fire,
A book that's not too new;
My bed so warm, the nights of storm
I love to listen to.

I have some friends, some good, good friends
Who faithful are to me:
My wrestling partner when I rise,
The big and burly sea;
My little boat that's riding there
So saucy and so free.

I have some friends, some golden friends,
Whose worth will not decline:
A tawny Irish terrier, a purple shading pine,
A little red-roofed cottage that
So proudly I call mine.

All other friends may come and go,
All other friendships fail;
But these, the friends I've worked to win,
Oh, they will never stale;
And comfort me till Time shall write
The finish to my tale.

Calvert tries to paint more than the thing he sees; he tries to paint behind it, to express its spirit. He believes that Beauty is God made manifest, and that when we discover Him in Nature we discover Him in ourselves.

But Calvert did not always see thus. At one time he was a Pagan, content to paint the outward aspect of things. It was after his little child died he gained in vision. Maybe the thought that the dead are lost to us was too unbearable. He had to believe in a coming together again.

THE QUEST

I sought Him on the purple seas,
I sought Him on the peaks aflame;
Amid the gloom of giant trees

And canyons lone I called His name;
The wasted ways of earth I trod:
In vain! In vain! I found not God.

I sought Him in the hives of men,
The cities grand, the hamlets grey,
The temples old beyond my ken,
The tabernacles of to-day;
All life that is, from cloud to clod
I sought. . . . Alas! I found not God.

Then after roamings far and wide,
In streets and seas and deserts wild,
I came to stand at last beside
The death-bed of my little child.
Lo! as I bent beneath the rod
I raised my eyes . . . and there was God.

A golden mile of sand swings hammock-like between two tusks
of rock. The sea is sleeping sapphire that wakes to cream and crash
upon the beach. There is a majesty in the detachment of its lazy
waves, and it is good in the night to hear its friendly roar. Good, too,
to leap forth with the first sunshine and fall into its arms, to let it
pummel the body to living ecstasy and send one to breakfast glad-
eyed, and glowing.

Behind the house the greensward slopes to a wheat-field that is
like a wall of gold. Here I lie and laze away the time, or dip into a
favorite book, Stevenson's *Letters* or Belloc's *Path to Rome*. Bees
drone in the wild thyme; a cuckoo keeps calling, a lark spills jewelled
melody. Then there is a seeming silence, but it is the silence of a
deeper sound.

After all, Silence is only man's confession of his deafness. Like
Death, like Eternity, it is a word that means nothing. So lying there
I hear the breathing of the trees, the crepitation of the growing
grass, the seething of the sap and the movements of innumerable
insects. Strange how I think with distaste of the spurious glitter of
Paris, of my garret, even of my poor little book.

I watch the wife of my friend gathering poppies in the wheat. There is a sadness in her face, for it is only a year ago they lost their little one. Often I see her steal away to the village graveyard, sitting silent for long and long.

THE COMFORTER

As I sat by my baby's bed
That's open to the sky,
There fluttered round and round my head
A radiant butterfly.

And as I wept—of hearts that ache
The saddest in the land—
It left a lily for my sake,
And lighted on my hand.

I watched it, oh, so quietly,
And though it rose and flew,
As if it fain would comfort me
It came and came anew.

Now, where my darling lies at rest,
I do not dare to sigh,
For look! there gleams upon my breast
A snow-white butterfly.

My friends will have other children, and if some day they should read this piece of verse, perhaps they will think of the city lad who used to sit under the old fig-tree in the garden and watch the lizards sun themselves on the time-worn wall.

THE OTHER ONE

"GATHER around me, children dear;
The wind is high and the night is cold;

Closer, little ones, snuggle near;
Let's seek a story of ages old;
A magic tale of a bygone day,
Of lovely ladies and dragons dread;
Come, for you're all so tired of play,
We'll read till it's time to go to bed."

So they all are glad, and they nestle in,
And squat on the rough old nursery rug,
And they nudge and hush as I begin,
And the fire leaps up and all's so snug;
And there I sit in the big arm-chair,
And how they are eager and sweet and wise,
And they cup their chins in their hands and stare
At the heart of the flame with thoughtful eyes.

And then, as I read by the ruddy glow
And the little ones sit entranced and still . . .
He's drawing near, ah! I know, I know
He's listening too, as he always will.
He's there—he's standing beside my knee;
I see him so well, my wee, wee son. . . .
Oh, children dear, don't look at me—
I'm reading now for—the Other One.

For the firelight glints in his golden hair,
And his wondering eyes are fixed on my face,
And he rests on the arm of my easy-chair,
And the book's a blur and I lose my place:
And I touch my lips to his shining head,
And my voice breaks down and—the story's done. . . .
Oh, children, kiss me and go to bed:
Leave me to think of the Other One.

Of the One who will never grow up at all,
Who will always be just a child at play,
Tender and trusting and sweet and small,
Who will never leave me and go away;
Who will never hurt me and give me pain;
Who will comfort me when I'm all alone;
A heart of love that's without a stain,
Always and always my own, my own.

Yet a thought shines out from the dark of pain,
And it gives me hope to be reconciled:
That each of us must be born again,
And live and die as a little child;
So that with souls all shining white,
White as snow and without one sin,
We may come to the Gates of Eternal Light,
Where only children may enter in.

So, gentle mothers, don't ever grieve
Because you have lost, but kiss the rod;
From the depths of your woe be glad, believe
You've given an angel unto God.
Rejoice! You've a child whose youth endures,
Who comes to you when the day is done,
Wistful for love, oh, yours, just yours,
Dearest of all, the Other One.

CATASTROPHE

BRITTANY,
August 14, 1914.

And now I fear I must write in another strain. Up to this time
I have been too happy. I have existed in a magic Bohemia, largely

of my own making. Hope, faith, enthusiasm have been mine. Each day has had its struggle, its failure, its triumph. However, that is all ended. During the past week we have lived breathlessly. For in spite of the exultant sunshine our spirits have been under a cloud, a deepening shadow of horror and calamity. . . . . WAR.

Even as I write, in our little village steeple the bells are ringing madly, and in every little village steeple all over the land. As he hears it the harvester checks his scythe on the swing; the clerk throws down his pen; the shopkeeper puts up his shutters. Only in the cafés there is a clamour of voices and a drowning of care.

For here every man must fight, every home give tribute. There is no question, no appeal. By heredity and discipline all minds are shaped to this great hour. So to-morrow each man will seek his barracks and become a soldier as completely as if he had never been anything else. With the same docility as he dons his baggy red trousers will he let some muddle-headed General hurl him to destruction for some dubious gain. To-day a father, a home-maker; to-morrow fodder for cannon. So they all go without hesitation, without bitterness; and the great military machine that knows not humanity swings them to their fate. I marvel at the sense of duty, the resignation, the sacrifice. It is magnificent, it is FRANCE.

And the Women. Those who wait and weep. Ah! to-day I have not seen one who did not weep. Yes, one. She was very old, and she stood by her garden gate with her hand on the uplifted latch. As I passed she looked at me with eyes that did not see. She had no doubt sons and grandsons who must fight, and she had good reason, perhaps, to remember the war of *soixante-dix*. When I passed an hour later she was still there, her hand on the uplifted latch.

August 30th.

The men have gone. Only remain greybeards, women and children. Calvert and I have been helping our neighbours to get in the harvest. No doubt we aid; but there with the old men and children a sense of uneasiness and even shame comes over me. I would like to return to Paris, but the railway is mobilized. Each day I grow more discontented. Up there in the red North great things are doing and I am out of it. I am thoroughly unhappy.

Then Calvert comes to me with a plan. He has a Ford car. We will all three go to Paris. He intends to offer himself and his car to the Red Cross. His wife will nurse. So we are very happy at the solution, and to-morrow we are off.

PARIS.

Back again. Closed shutters, deserted streets. How glum everything is! Those who are not mobilized seem uncertain how to turn. Every one buys the papers and reads grimly of disaster. No news is bad news.

I go to my garret as to a beloved friend. Everything is just as I left it, so that it seems I have never been away. I sigh with relief and joy. I will take up my work again. Serene above the storm I will watch and wait. Although I have been brought up in England I am American born. My country is not concerned.

So, going to the Dôme Café, I seek some of my comrades. Strange! They have gone. MacBean, I am told, is in England. By dyeing his hair and lying about his age he has managed to enlist in the Seaforth Highlanders. Saxon Dane too. He has joined the Foreign Legion, and even now may be fighting.

Well, let them go. I will keep out of the mess. But why did they go? I wish I knew. War is murder. Criminal folly. Against Humanity. Imperialism is at the root of it. We are fools and dupes. Yes, I will think and write of other things. . . .

MacBean has enlisted.

I hate violence. I would not willingly cause pain to anything breathing. I would rather be killed than kill. I will stand above the Battle and watch it from afar.

Dane is in the Foreign Legion.

How disturbing it all is! One cannot settle down to anything. Every day I meet men who tell the most wonderful stories in the most casual way. I envy them. I too want to have experiences, to live where-life's beat is most intense. But that's a poor reason for going to war.

And yet, though I shrink from the idea of fighting, I might in some way help those who are. MacBean and Dane, for example. Sitting lonely in the Dôme, I seem to see their ghosts in the corner. MacBean listening with his keen, sarcastic smile, Saxon Dane banging his great hairy fist on the table till the glasses jump. Where are they now? Living a life that I will never know. When they come back, if they ever do, shall I not feel ashamed in their presence?

Oh, this filthy war! Things were going on so beautifully. We were all so happy, so full of ambition, of hope; laughing and talking over pipe and bowl, and in our garrets seeking to realize our dreams. Ah, these days will never come again!

Then, as I sit there, Calvert seeks me out. He has joined an ambulance corps that is going to the Front. Will I come in?

"Yes," I say; "I'll do anything."

So it is all settled. To-morrow I give up my freedom.

I

There is an avenue of noble beeches leading to the Château, and
in the shadow of each glimmers the pale oblong of an ambulance.
We have to keep them thus concealed, for only yesterday morning
a Taube flew over. The beggars are rather partial to Red Cross
cars. One of our chaps, taking in a load of wounded, was chased
and pelted the other day.

The Château seems all spires and towers, the glorified dream of
a Parisian pastrycook. On its terrace figures in khaki are lounging.
They are the volunteers, the owner-drivers of the Corps, many of
them men of wealth and title. Curious to see one who owns all the
coal in two counties proudly signing for his *sou* a day; or another,
who lives in a Fifth Avenue palace, contentedly sleeping on the
straw-strewn floor of a hovel.

Here is a rhyme I have made of such an one:

PRISCILLA

Jerry MacMullen, the millionaire,
Driving a red-meat bus out there—
How did he win his *Croix de Guerre?*
Bless you, that's all old stuff:
Beast of a night on the Verdun road,
Jerry stuck with a woeful load,
Stalled in the mud where the red lights glowed,
Prospect devilish tough.

"Little Priscilla" he called his car,
Best of our battered bunch by far,

549

Branded with many a bullet scar,
Yet running so sweet and true.
Jerry he loved her, knew her tricks;
Swore: "She's the beat of the best big six,
And if ever I get in a deuce of a fix
Priscilla will pull me through."

"Looks pretty rotten right now," says he;
"Hanged if the devil himself could see.
Priscilla, it's up to you and me
To show 'em what we can do."
Seemed that Priscilla just took the word;
Up with a leap like a horse that's spurred,
On with the joy of a homing bird,
Swift as the wind she flew.

Shell-holes shoot at them out of the night;
A lurch to the left, a wrench to the right,
Hands grim-gripping and teeth clenched tight,
Eyes that glare through the dark.
"Priscilla, you're doing me proud this day;
Hospital's only a league away,
And, honey, I'm longing to hit the hay,
So hurry, old girl. . . . But hark!"

Howl of a shell, harsh, sudden, dread;
Another . . . another. . . . "Strike me dead
If the Huns ain't strafing the road ahead
So the convoy can't get through!
A barrage of shrap, and us alone;
Four rush-cases—you hear 'em moan?
Fierce old messes of blood and bone. . . .
Priscilla, what shall we do?"

Again it seems that Priscilla hears.
With a rush and a roar her way she clears,
Straight at the hell of flame she steers,
Full at its heart of wrath.
Fury of death and dust and din!
Havoc and horror! She's in, she's in;
She's almost over, she'll win, she'll win!
Woof! Crump! right in the path.

Little Priscilla skids and stops,
Jerry MacMullen sways and flops;
Bang in his map the crash he cops;
Shriek from the car: "Mon Dieu!"
One of the *blessés* hears him say,
Just at the moment he faints away:
"Reckon this isn't my lucky day,
Priscilla, it's up to you."

Sergeant raps on the doctor's door;
"Car in the court with *couchés* four;
Driver dead on the dashboard floor;
Strange how the bunch got here."
"No," says the Doc, "this chap's alive;
But tell me, how could a man contrive
With both arms broken, a car to drive?
Thunder of God! it's queer."

Same little *blessé* makes a spiel;
Says he: "When I saw our driver reel,
A Strange Shape leapt to the driving wheel
And sped us safe through the night."
But Jerry, he says in his drawling tone:
"Rats! Why, Priscilla came in on her own.

Bless her, she did it alone, alone. . . ."
Hanged if I know who's right.

As I am sitting down to my midday meal an orderly gives me
a telegram:

Hill 71. Two couchés. Send car at once.

The uptilted country-side is a checker-board of green and grey,
and, except where groves of trees rise like islands, cultivated to
the last acre. But as we near the firing-line all efforts to till the land
cease, and the ungathered beets of last year have grown to seed.
Amid rank unkempt fields I race over a road that is pitted with
obus-holes; I pass a line of guns painted like snakes, and drawn by
horses dyed khaki-color; then soldiers coming from the trenches,
mud-caked and ineffably weary; then a race over a bit of road that
is exposed; then, buried in the hill-side, the dressing station.

The two wounded are put into my car. From hip to heel one is
swathed in bandages; the other has a great white turban on his head,
with a red patch on it that spreads and spreads. They stare dully,
but make no sound. As I crank the car there is a shrill screaming
noise. . . . About thirty yards away I hear an explosion like a mine-
blast, followed by a sudden belch of coal-black smoke. I stare at it
in a dazed way. Then the doctor says: "Don't trouble to analyze
your sensations. Better get off. You're only drawing their fire."

Here is one of my experiences:

A CASUALTY

That boy I took in the car last night,
With the body that awfully sagged away,
And the lips blood-crisped, and the eyes flame-bright,
And the poor hands folded and cold as clay—
Oh, I've thought and I've thought of him all the day.

For the weary old doctor says to me:
"He'll only last for an hour or so."

Both of his legs below the knee
Blown off by a bomb. . . . So, lad, go slow,
And please remember, he doesn't know."

So I tried to drive with never a jar;
And there was I cursing the road like mad,
When I hears a ghost of a voice from the car:
"Tell me, old chap, have I 'copped it' bad?"
So I answers "No," and he says, "I'm glad."

"Glad," says he, "for at twenty-two
Life's so splendid, I hate to go.
There's so much good that a chap might do,
And I've fought from the start and I've suffered so.
'Twould be hard to get knocked out now, you know."

"Forget it," says I; then I drove awhile,
And I passed him a cheery word or two;
But he didn't answer for many a mile,
So just as the hospital hove in view,
Says I: "Is there nothing that I can do?"

Then he opens his eyes and he smiles at me;
And he takes my hand in his trembling hold;
"Thank you—you're far too kind," says he:
"I'm awfully comfy—stay . . . let's see:
I fancy my blanket's come unrolled—
My *feet*, please wrap 'em—they're cold . . . they're cold."

There is a city that glitters on the plain. Afar off we can see its
tall cathedral spire, and there we often take our wounded from the
little village hospitals to the rail-head. Tragic little buildings, these
emergency hospitals—town-halls, churches, schools; their cots are
never empty, their surgeons never still.

So every day we get our list of cases and off we go, a long line of cars swishing through the mud. Then one by one we branch off to our village hospital, puzzling out the road on our maps. Arrived there, we load up quickly.

The wounded make no moan. They lie, limp, heavily bandaged, with bare legs and arms protruding from their blankets. They do not know where they are going; they do not care. Like live stock, they are labelled and numbered. An orderly brings along their battle-scarred equipment, throwing open their rifles to see that no charge remains. Sometimes they shake our hands and thank us for the drive.

In the streets of the city I see French soldiers wearing the *fourragère*. It is a cord of green, yellow or red, and corresponds to the *Croix de Guerre*, the *Médaille militaire* and the Legion of Honor. The red is the highest of all, and has been granted only to one or two regiments. This incident was told to me by a man who saw it:

THE BLOOD-RED *FOURRAGÈRE*

WHAT was the blackest sight to me
Of all that campaign?
A naked woman tied to a tree
With jagged holes where her breasts should be,
Rotting there in the rain.

On we pressed to the battle fray,
Dogged and dour and spent.
Sudden I heard my Captain say:
"*Voilà!* Kultur has passed this way,
And left us a monument."

So I looked and I saw our Colonel there,
And his grand head, snowed with the years,
Unto the beat of the rain was bare;
And, oh, there was grief in his frozen stare,
And his cheeks were stung with tears!

Then at last he turned from the woeful tree,
And his face like stone was set;
"Go, march the Regiment past," said he,
"That every father and son may see,
And none may ever forget."

Oh, the crimson strands of her hair downpoured
Over her breasts of woe;
And our grim old Colonel leaned on his sword,
And the men filed past with their rifles lowered,
Solemn and sad and slow.

But I'll never forget till the day I die,
As I stood in the driving rain,
And the jaded columns of men slouched by,
How amazement leapt into every eye,
Then fury and grief and pain.

And some would like madmen stand aghast,
With their hands upclenched to the sky;
And some would cross themselves as they passed,
And some would curse in a scalding blast,
And some like children cry.

Yea, some would be sobbing, and some would pray,
And some hurl hateful names;
But the best had never a word to say;
They turned their twitching faces away,
And their eyes were like hot flames.

They passed; then down on his bended knee
The Colonel dropped to the Dead:
"Poor martyred daughter of France!" said he,

"O dearly, dearly avenged you'll be
Or ever a day be sped!"

Now they hold that we are the best of the best,
And each of our men may wear,
Like a gash of crimson across his chest,
As one fierce-proved in the battle-test,
The blood-red *Fourragère*.

For each as he leaps to the top can see,
Like an etching of blood on his brain,
A wife or a mother lashed to a tree,
With two black holes where her breasts should be,
Left to rot in the rain.

So we fight like fiends, and of us they say
That we neither yield nor spare.
Oh, we have the bitterest debt to pay. . . .
Have we paid it?—Look—how we wear to-day
Like a trophy, gallant and proud and gay,
Our blood-red *Fourragère*.

It is often weary waiting at the little *poste de secours*. Some of
us play solitaire, some read a "sixpenny," some doze or try to talk
in bad French to the *poilus*. Around us is discomfort, dirt and
drama.

For my part, I pass the time only too quickly, trying to put into
verse the incidents and ideas that come my way. In this way I hope
to collect quite a lot of stuff which may some day see itself in print.

Here is one of my efforts:

JIM

Never knew Jim, did you? Our boy Jim?
Bless you, there was the likely lad;

Supple and straight and long of limb,
Clean as a whistle, and just as glad.
Always laughing, wasn't he, dad?
Joy, pure joy to the heart of him,
And, oh, but the soothering ways he had,
                              Jim, our Jim!

But I see him best as a tiny tot,
A bonny babe, though it's me that speaks;
Laughing there in his little cot,
With his sunny hair and his apple cheeks.
And my! but the blue, blue eyes he'd got,
And just where his wee mouth dimpled dim
Such a fairy mark like a beauty spot—
                              That was Jim.

Oh, the war, the war! How my eyes were wet!
But he says: "Don't be sorrowing, mother dear;
You never knew me to fail you yet,
And I'll be back in a year, a year."
'Twas at Mons he fell, in the first attack;
For so they said, and their eyes were dim;
But I laughed in their faces: "He'll come back,
                              Will my Jim."

Now, we'd been wedded for twenty year,
And Jim was the only one we'd had;
So when I whispered in father's ear,
He wouldn't believe me—would you, dad?
There! I must hurry . . . hear him cry?
My new little baby. . . . See! that's him.
What are we going to call him? Why,
                              Jim, just Jim.

Jim! For look at him laughing there
In the same old way in his tiny cot,
With his rosy cheeks and his sunny hair,
And look, just look . . . his beauty spot
In the selfsame place. . . . Oh, I can't explain,
And of course you think it's a mother's whim,
But I know, I know it's my boy again,
                              Same wee Jim.

Just come back as he said he would;
Come with his love and his heart of glee.
Oh, I cried and I cried, but the Lord was good;
From the shadow of Death he set Jim free.
So I'll have him all over again, you see.
Can you wonder my mother-heart's a-brim?
Oh, how happy we're going to be!
                              Aren't we, Jim?

II

IN PICARDY,
January 1915.

The road lies amid a malevolent heath. It seems to lead us right
into the clutch of the enemy; for the star-shells, that at first were
bursting overhead, gradually encircle us. The fields are strangely
sinister; the splintered trees are like giant toothpicks. There is a
lisping and a twanging overhead.

As we wait at the door of the dugout that serves as a first-aid
dressing station, I gaze up into that mysterious dark, so alive with
musical vibrations. Then a small shadow detaches itself from the
greater shadow, and a grey-bearded sentry says to me: "You'd better
come in out of the bullets."

So I keep under cover, and presently they bring my load. Two
men drip with sweat as they carry their comrade. I can see that
they all three belong to the Foreign Legion. I think for a moment

of Saxon Dane. How strange if some day I should carry him! Half fearfully I look at my passenger, but he is a black man. Such things only happen in fiction.

This is what I have written of the finest troops in the Army of France:

KELLY OF THE LEGION

Now Kelly was no fighter;
He loved his pipe and glass;
An easygoing blighter,
Who lived in Montparnasse.
But 'mid the tavern tattle
He heard some guinney say:
"When France goes forth to battle,
The Legion leads the way.

"The scourings of creation,
Of every sin and station,
The men who've known damnation,
Are picked to lead the way."

Well, Kelly joined the Legion;
They marched him day and night;
They rushed him to the region
Where largest loomed the fight.
"Behold your mighty mission,
Your destiny," said they;
"By glorious tradition
The Legion leads the way.

"With tattered banners flying
With trail of dead and dying,

On! On! All hell defying,
The Legion sweeps the way."

With grim, hard-bitten faces,
With jests of savage mirth,
They swept into their places,
The men of iron worth;
Their blooded steel was flashing;
They swung to face the fray;
Then rushing, roaring, crashing,
The Legion cleared the way.

 The trail they blazed was gory;
 Few lived to tell the story;
 Through death they plunged to glory;
 But, oh, they cleared the way!

Now Kelly lay a-dying,
And dimly saw advance,
With split new banners flying,
The *fantassins* of France.
Then up amid the *mêlée*
He rose from where he lay;
"Come on, me boys," says Kelly,
"The Layjun lades the way!"

 Aye, while they faltered, doubting
 (Such flames of doom were spouting),
 He caught them, thrilled them, shouting:
 "The Layjun lades the way!"

They saw him slip and stumble,
Then stagger on once more;

They marked him trip and tumble,
A mass of grime and gore;
They watched him blindly crawling
Amid hell's own affray,
And calling, calling, calling:
"The Layjun lades the way!"

> *And even while they wondered,*
> *The battle-wrack was sundered;*
> *To Victory they thundered,*
> *But . . . Kelly led the way.*

Still Kelly kept agoing;
Berserker-like he ran;
His eyes with fury glowing,
A lion of a man;
His rifle madly swinging,
His soul athirst to slay,
His slogan ringing, ringing,
"The Layjun lades the way!"

> *Till in a pit death-baited,*
> *Where Huns with Maxims waited,*
> *He plunged . . . and there, blood-sated,*
> *To death he stabbed his way.*

Now Kelly was a fellow
Who simply loathed a fight:
He loved a tavern mellow,
Grog hot and pipe alight;
I'm sure the Show appalled him,
And yet without dismay,
When Death and Duty called him,
He up and led the way.

So in Valhalla drinking
(If heroes meek and shrinking
Are suffered there), I'm thinking
'Tis Kelly leads the way.

We have just had one of our men killed, a young sculptor of immense promise.

When one thinks of all the fine work he might have accomplished, it seems a shame. But, after all, to-morrow it may be the turn of any of us. If it should be mine, my chief regret will be for work undone.

Ah! I often think of how I will go back to the Quarter and take up the old life again. How sweet it will all seem. But first I must earn the right. And if ever I do go back, how I will find Bohemia changed! Missing how many a face!

It was in thinking of our lost comrade I wrote the following:

THE THREE TOMMIES

THAT Barret, the painter of pictures, what feeling for colour he
    had!
And Fanning, the maker of music, such melodies mirthful and
    mad!
And Harley, the writer of stories, so whimsical, tender and
    glad!

To hark to their talk in the trenches, high heart unfolding to
    heart,
Of the day when the war would be over, and each would be true
    to his part,
Upbuilding a Palace of Beauty to the wonder and glory of
    Art . . .

Yon's Barret, the painter of pictures, yon carcass that rots on
    the wire;

His hand with its sensitive cunning is crisped to a cinder with
fire;
His eyes with their magical vision are bubbles of glutinous mire.

Poor Fanning! He sought to discover the symphonic note of a
shell;
There are bits of him broken and bloody, to show you the place
where he fell;
I've reason to fear on his exquisite ear the rats have been banquet-
ing well.

And speaking of Harley, the writer, I fancy I looked on him
last,
Sprawling and staring and writhing in the roar of the battle
blast;
Then a mad gun-team crashed over, and scattered his brains as
it passed.

Oh, Harley and Fanning and Barret, they were bloody good
mates o' mine;
Their bodies are empty bottles; Death has guzzled the wine;
What's left of them's filth and corruption. . . . Where is the
Fire Divine?

I'll tell you. . . . At night in the trenches, as I watch and I do
my part,
Three radiant spirits I'm seeing, high heart revealing to heart,
And they're building a peerless palace to the splendour and tri-
umph of Art.

Yet, alas! for the fame of Barret, the glory he might have trailed!
And alas! for the name of Fanning, a star that beaconed and
paled,

Poor Harley, obscure and forgotten. . . . Well, who shall say
  that they failed!

No, each did a Something Grander than ever he dreamed to do;
And as for the work unfinished, all will be paid their due;
The broken ends will be fitted, the balance struck will be true.

So painters, and players, and penmen, I tell you: Do as you
  please;
Let your fame outleap on the trumpets, you'll never rise up to
  these—
To three grim and gory Tommies, down, down on your bended
  knees!

Daventry, the sculptor, is buried in a little graveyard near one
of our posts. Just now our section of the line is quiet, so I often go
and sit there. Stretching myself on a flat stone, I dream for hours.
   Silence and solitude! How good the peace of it all seems! Around
me the grasses weave a pattern, and half hide the hundreds of little
wooden crosses. Here is one with a single name:

AUBREY.

Who was Aubrey I wonder? Then another:

To Our Beloved Comrade.

   Then one which has attached to it, in the cheapest of little frames,
the crude water-colour daub of a child, three purple flowers stand-
ing in a yellow vase. Below it, painfully printed, I read:

To My Darling Papa—Thy Little Odette.

   And beyond the crosses many fresh graves have been dug. With
hungry open mouths they wait. Even now I can hear the guns that
are going to feed them. Soon there will be more crosses, and more
and more. Then they will cease, and wives and mothers will come
here to weep.

Ah! Peace so precious must be bought with blood and tears. Let us honour and bless the men who pay, and envy them the manner of their dying; for not all the jewelled orders on the breasts of the living can vie in glory with the little wooden cross the humblest of these has won. . . .

THE TWA JOCKS

Says Bauldy MacGreegor frae Gleska tae Hecky MacCrimmon frae Skye:
"That's whit I hate maist aboot fechtin'—it makes ye sae deevilish dry;
Noo jist hae a keek at yon ferm-hoose them Gairmans are poundin' sae fine,
Weel, think o' it, doon in the dunnie there's bottles and bottles o' wine.
A' hell's fairly belchin' oot yonner, but oh, lad, I'm ettlin' tae try. . . ."
"If it's poose she'll be with ye whateffer," says Hecky MacCrimmon frae Skye.

Says Bauldy MacGreegor frae Gleska: "Whit price fur a funeral wreath?
We're dodgin' a' kinds o' destruction, an' jist by the skin o' oor teeth.
Here, spread yersel oot on yer belly, and slither along in the glaur;
Confoond ye, ye big Hielan' deevil! Ye don't realize there's a war.
Ye think that ye're back in Dunvegan, and herdin' the wee bits o' kye."
"She'll neffer trink wine in Dunfegan," says Hecky MacCrimmon frae Skye.

Says Bauldy MacGreegor frae Gleska: "Thank goodness! the
    ferm-hoose at last;
There's no muckle left but the cellar, an' even that's vanishin'
    fast.
Look oot, there's the corpse o' a wumman, sair mangelt and deid
    by her lane.
Quick! Strike a match. . . . Whit did I tell ye! A hale bonny
    box o' shampane;
Jist knock the heid aff o' a bottle. . . . Haud on, mon, I'm
    hearing a cry. . . ."
"She'll think it's a wean that wass greetin'," says Hecky Mac-
Crimmon frae Skye.

Says Bauldy MacGreegor frae Gleska: "Ma conscience! I'm
    hanged but yer richt.
It's yin o' thae waifs of the war-field, a' sobbin' and shakin' wi'
    fricht.
Wheesht noo, dear, we're no gaun tae hurt ye. We're takin' ye
    hame, my wee doo!
We've got tae get back wi' her, Hecky. Whit mercy we didna
    get fou!
We'll no touch a drap o' that likker—that's hard, man, ye canna
    deny. . . ."
"It's the last thing she'll think o' denyin'," says Hecky Mac-
Crimmon frae Skye.

Says Bauldy MacGreegor frae Gleska: "If I should get struck
    frae the rear,
Ye'll tak' and ye'll shield the wee lassie, and rin for the lines like
    a deer.
God! Wis that the breenge o' a bullet? I'm thinkin' it's cracket
    ma spine.

I'm doon on ma knees in the glabber; I'm fearin', auld man, I've
  got mine.
Here, quick! Pit yer erms roon the lassie. Noo, rin, lad! good
  luck and good-by. . . .
*"Hoots, mon! it's ye baith she'll be takin'," says Hecky Mac-
Crimmon frae Skye.*

Says Corporal Muckle frae Rannoch: "Is that no' a picture tae
  frame?
Twa sair woundit Jocks wi' a lassie jist like ma wee Jeannie at
  hame.
We're prood o' ye baith, ma brave heroes. We'll gie ye a medal,
  I think."
Says Bauldy MacGreegor frae Gleska: "I'd raither ye gied me a
  drink.
I'll no speak for Private MacCrimmon, but oh, mon, I'm perishin'
  dry. . . ."
*"She'll wush that Loch Lefen wass whuskey," says Hecky Mac-
Crimmon frae Skye.*

III

Near Albert,
February 1915.

Over the spine of the ridge a horned moon of reddish hue peers
through the splintered, hag-like trees. Where the trenches are,
rockets are rising, green and red. I hear the coughing of the Maxims,
the peevish nagging of the rifles, the boom of a "heavy" and the
hollow sound of its exploding shell.

Running the car into the shadow of a ruined house, I try to sleep.
But a battery starts to blaze away close by, and the flame lights
up my shelter. Near me some soldiers are in deep slumber; one stirs
in his sleep as a big rat runs over him, and I know by experience
that when one is sleeping a rat feels as heavy as a sheep.

But how *can* one possibly sleep? Out there in the dark there is the wild tattoo of a thousand rifles; and hark! that dull roar is the explosion of a mine. There! the purring of the rapid firers. Desperate things are doing. There will be lots of work for me before this night is over. What a cursed place!

As I cannot sleep, I think of a story I heard to-day. It is of a Canadian Colonel, and in my mind I shape it like this:

HIS BOYS

"I'm going, Billy, old fellow. Hist, lad! Don't make any noise.
There's Boches to beat all creation, the pitch of a bomb away.
I've fixed the note to your collar, you've got to get back to my
    Boys,
You've got to get back to warn 'em before it's the break of day."

The order came to go forward to a trench-line traced on the
    map;
I knew the brass-hats had blundered, I knew and I told 'em so;
I knew if I did as they ordered I would tumble into a trap,
And I tried to explain, but the answer came like a pistol: "Go."

Then I thought of the Boys I commanded—I always called them
    "my Boys"—
The men of my own recruiting, the lads of my countryside;
Tested in many a battle, I knew their sorrows and joys,
And I loved them all like a father, with more than a father's
    pride.

To march my Boys to a shambles as soon as the dawn of day;
To see them helplessly slaughtered, if all that I guessed was true;
My Boys that trusted me blindly, I thought and I tried to pray,
And then I arose and I muttered: "It's either them or it's you."

I rose and I donned my rain-coat; I buckled my helmet tight.
I remember you watched me, Billy, as I took my cane in my
  hand;
I vaulted over the sandbags into the pitchy night,
Into the pitted valley that served us as No Man's Land.

I strode out over the hollow of hate and havoc and death,
From the heights the guns were angry, with a vengeful snarling
  of steel;
And once in a moment of stillness I heard hard panting breath,
And I turned . . . it was you, old rascal, following hard on my
  heel.

I fancy I cursed you, Billy; but not so much as I ought!
And so we went forward together, till we came to the valley
  rim,
And then a star-shell sputtered . . . it was even worse than I
  thought,
For the trench they told me to move in was packed with Boche
  to the brim.

They saw me too, and they got me; they peppered me till I fell;
And there I scribbled my message with my life-blood ebbing
  away;
"Now, Billy, you fat old duffer, you've got to get back like
  hell;
And get them to cancel that order before it's the dawn of day.

"Billy, old boy, I love you, I kiss your shiny black nose;
Now, home there. . . . Hurry, you devil, or I'll cut you to rib-
  ands. . . . See . . ."
Poor brute! he's off! and I'm dying. . . . I go as a soldier goes.

I'm happy. My Boys, God bless 'em! . . . It had to be them
or me.

Ah! I never was intended for a job like this. I realize it more
and more every day, but I will stick it out till I break down. To
be nervous, over-imaginative, terribly sensitive to suffering, is a
poor equipment for the man who starts out to drive wounded on
the battlefield. I am haunted by the thought that my car may break
down when I have a load of wounded. Once indeed it did, and a
man died while I waited for help. Now I never look at what is given
me. It might unnerve me.

I have been at it for over six months without a rest. When an
attack has been going on I have worked day and night, until as I
drove I wanted to fall asleep at the wheel.

The winter has been trying; there is rain one day, frost the next.
Mud up to the axles. One sleeps in lousy barns or dripping dugouts.
Cold, hunger, dirt, I know them all singly and together. My only
consolation is that the war must soon be over, and that I will have
helped. When I have time and am not too tired, I comfort myself
with scribbling.

THE BOOBY-TRAP

I'm crawlin' out in the mangolds to bury wot's left o' Joe—
Joe, my pal, and a good un (God! 'ow it rains and rains).
I'm sick o' seein' him lyin' like a 'eap o' offal, and so
I'm crawlin' out in the beet-field to bury 'is last remains.

'E might 'a bin makin' munitions—'e 'adn't no need to go;
An' I tells 'im strite, but 'e arnsers, " 'Tain't no use chewin' the
    fat;
I've got to be doin' me dooty wiv the rest o' the boys" . . .
    an' so
Yon's 'im, yon blob on the beet-field wot I'm tryin' so 'ard to
    git at.

There was five of us lads from the brickyard; 'Enry was gassed
    at Bapome,
Sydney was drowned in a crater, 'Erbert was 'alved by a shell;
Joe was the pick o' the posy, might 'a bin sifely at 'ome,
Only son of 'is mother, 'er a widder as well.

She used to sell bobbins and buttons—'ad a plice near the Water-
    loo Road;
A little, old, bent-over lydy, wiv glasses an' silvery 'air;
Must tell 'er I planted 'im nicely, cheer 'er up like. . . . (Well,
    I'm blowed,
That bullet near catched me a biffer)—I'll see the old gel if I'm
    spared.

She'll tike it to 'eart, pore ol' lydy, fer 'e was 'er 'ope and 'er joy;
'Is dad used to drink like a knot-'ole, she kept the 'ome goin',
    she did:
She pinched and she scriped fer 'is scoolin', 'e was sich a fine
    'andsome boy
('Alf Flanders seems packed on me panties)—'e's 'andsome no
    longer, pore kid!

This bit o' a board that I'm packin' and draggin' around in the
    mire,
I was tickled to death when I found it. Says I, " 'Ere's a nice
    little glow."
I was chilled and wet through to the marrer, so I started to make
    me a fire;
And then I says: "No; 'ere, Goblimy, it'll do for a cross for Joe."

Well, 'ere 'e is. Gawd! 'Ow one chinges a-lyin' six weeks in the
    rain.
Joe, me old pal, 'ow I'm sorry; so 'elp me, I wish I could pray.

An' now I 'ad best get a-diggin' 'is grave (it seems more like a
    drain)—

And I 'opes that the Boches won't git me till I gits 'im safe
    planted away.

     (*As he touches the body there is a tremendous explosion.
     He falls back shattered.*)

A booby-trap! Ought to 'a known it! If that's not a bastardly
    trick!

Well, one thing, I won't be long goin'. Gawd! I'm a 'ell of a
    sight.

Wish I'd died fightin' and killin'; that's wot it is makes me
    sick. . . .

Ah, Joe! we'll be pushin' up dysies . . . together, old Chummie
    . . . good-night!

    To-day I heard that MacBean had been killed in Belgium. I be-
lieve he turned out a wonderful soldier. Saxon Dane, too, has been
missing for two months. We know what that means.

    It is odd how one gets callous to death, a mediæval callousness.
When we hear that the best of our friends have gone West, we
have a moment of the keenest regret; but how soon again we find
the heart to laugh! The saddest part of loss, I think, is that one
so soon gets over it.

    Is it that we fail to realize it all? Is it that it seems a strange and
hideous dream, from which we will awake and rub our eyes?

    Oh, how bitter I feel as the days go by! It is creeping more and
more into my verse. Read this:

BONEHEAD BILL

      I WONDER 'oo and wot 'e was,
      That 'Un I got so slick.
      I couldn't see 'is face because
      The night was 'ideous thick.

I just made out among the black
A blinkin' wedge o' white;
Then *biff!* I guess I got 'im *crack*—
The man I killed last night.

I wonder if account o' me
Some wench will go unwed,
And 'eaps o' lives will never be,
Because 'e's stark and dead?
Or if 'is missis damns the war,
And by some candle light,
Tow-headed kids are prayin' for
The Fritz I copped last night.

I wonder, 'struth, I wonder why
I 'ad that 'orful dream?
I saw up in the giddy sky
The gates o' God agleam;
I saw the gates o' 'eaven shine
Wiv everlastin' light:
And then . . . I knew that I'd got mine,
As 'e got 'is last night.

Aye, bang beyond the broodin' mists
Where spawn the mother stars,
I 'ammered wiv me bloody fists
Upon them golden bars;
I 'ammered till a devil's doubt
Fair froze me wiv affright:
To fink wot God would say about
The bloke I corpsed last night.

I 'ushed; I wilted wiv despair,
When, like a rosy flame,

I sees a angel standin' there
'Oo calls me by me name.
'E 'ad such soft, such shiny eyes;
'E 'eld 'is 'and and smiled;
And through the gates o' Paradise
'E led me like a child.

'E led me by them golden palms
Wot 'ems that jewelled street;
And seraphs was a-singin' psalms,
You've no ideer 'ow sweet;
Wiv cheroobs crowdin' closer round
Than peas is in a pod,
'E led me to a shiny mound
Where beams the throne o' God.

And then I 'ears God's werry voice:
"Bill 'agan, 'ave no fear.
Stand up and glory and rejoice
For 'im 'oo led you 'ere."
And in a nip I seemed to see:
Aye, like a flash o' light,
My angel pal I knew to be
The chap I plugged last night.

Now, I don't claim to understand—
They calls me Bonehead Bill;
They shoves a rifle in me 'and,
And show me 'ow to kill.
Me job's to risk me life and limb,
But . . . be it wrong or right,
This cross I'm makin', it's for 'im,
The cove I croaked last night.

IV

A LAPSE OF TIME AND A WORD OF EXPLANATION

THE AMERICAN HOSPITAL, NEUILLY,
January 1919.

Four years have passed and it is winter again. Much has happened. When I last wrote, on the Somme in 1915, I was sickening with typhoid fever. All that spring I was in hospital.

Nevertheless, I was sufficiently recovered to take part in the Champagne battle in the fall of that year, and to "carry on" during the following winter. It was at Verdun I got my first wound.

In the spring of 1917 I again served with my Corps; but on the entry of the United States into the War I joined the army of my country. In the Argonne I had my left arm shot away.

As far as time and health permitted, I kept a record of these years, and also wrote much verse. All this, however, has disappeared under circumstances into which there is no need to enter here. The loss was a cruel one, almost more so than that of my arm; for I have neither the heart nor the power to rewrite this material.

And now, in default of something better, I have bundled together this manuscript, and have added to it a few more verses, written in hospitals. Let it represent me. If I can find a publisher for it, *tant mieux*. If not, I will print it at my own cost, and anyone who cares for a copy can write to me—

STEPHEN POORE,
12 *bis*, RUE DES PETITS MOINEAUX,
PARIS.

MICHAEL

"THERE's something in your face, Michael, I've seen it all the
day;
There's something quare that wasn't there when first ye wint
away. . . ."

"It's just the Army life, mother, the drill, the left and right,
That puts the stiffinin' in yer spine and locks yer jaw up
    tight. . . ."

"There's something in your eyes, Michael, an' how they stare
    and stare—
You're lookin' at me now, me boy, as if I wasn't there. . . ."

"It's just the things I've seen, mother, the sights that come and
    come,
A bit o' broken, bloody pulp that used to be a chum. . . ."

"There's something on your heart, Michael, that makes ye wake
    at night,
And often when I hear ye moan, I trimble in me fright. . . ."

"It's just a man I killed, mother, a mother's son like me;
It seems he's always hauntin' me, he'll never let me be. . . ."

"But maybe he was bad, Michael, maybe it was right
To kill the inimy you hate in fair and honest fight. . . ."

"I did not hate at all, mother; he never did me harm;
I think he was a lad like me, who worked upon a farm. . . ."

"And what's it all about, Michael; why did you have to go,
A quiet, peaceful lad like you, and we were happy so? . . ."

"It's thim that's up above, mother, it's thim that sits an' rules;
We've got to fight the wars they make, it's us as are the
    fools. . . ."

"And what will be the end, Michael, and what's the use, I say,
Of fightin' if whoever wins it's us that's got to pay? . . ."

"Oh, it will be the end, mother, when lads like him and me,
That sweat to feed the ones above, decide that we'll be
    free. . . ."

"And when will that day come, Michael, and when will fightin'
    cease,
And simple folks may till their soil and live and love in
    peace? . . ."

"It's coming soon and soon, mother, it's nearer every day,
When only men who work and sweat will have a word to say;
When all who earn their honest bread in every land and soil
Will claim the Brotherhood of Man, the Comradeship of Toil;
When we, the Workers, all demand: 'What are we fighting
    for?' . . .
Then, then we'll end that stupid crime, that devil's madness—
    War."

THE WIFE

"TELL Annie I'll be home in time
To help her with her Christmas-tree."
That's what he wrote, and hark! the chime
Of Christmas bells, and where is he?
And how the house is dark and sad,
And Annie's sobbing on my knee!

The page beside the candle-flame
With cruel type was overfilled;
I read and read until a name
Leapt at me and my heart was stilled:
My eye crept up the column—up
Unto its hateful heading: *Killed*.

And there was Annie on the stair:
"And will he not be long?" she said.
Her eyes were bright and in her hair
She'd twined a bit of riband red;
And every step was daddy's sure,
Till tired out she went to bed.

And there alone I sat so still,
With staring eyes that did not see;
The room was desolate and chill,
And desolate the heart of me;
Outside I heard the news-boys shrill:
"Another Glorious Victory!"

A victory. . . . Ah! what care I?
A thousand victories are vain.
Here in my ruined home I cry
From out my black despair and pain,
I'd rather, rather damned defeat,
And have my man with me again.

They talk to us of pride and power,
Of Empire vast beyond the sea;
As here beside my hearth I cower,
What mean such words as these to me?
Oh, will they lift the clouds that low'r,
Or light my load in years to be?

What matters it to us poor folk?
Who win or lose, it's we who pay.
Oh, I would laugh beneath the yoke
If I had *him* at home to-day;
One's home before one's country comes:
Aye, so a million women say.

"Hush, Annie dear, don't sorrow so."
(How can I tell her?) "See, we'll light
With tiny star of purest glow
Each little candle pink and white."
(They make mistakes. I'll tell myself
I did not read that name aright.)
Come, dearest one; come, let us pray
Beside our gleaming Christmas-tree;
Just fold your little hands and say
These words so softly after me:
"God pity mothers in distress,
And little children fatherless."

"God pity mothers in distress,
And little children fatherless."

.   .   .   .   .

What's that?—a step upon the stair;
A shout!—the door thrown open wide!
My hero and my man is there,
And Annie's leaping by his side. . . .
The room reels round, I faint, I fall. . . .
"O God! Thy world is glorified."

VICTORY STUFF

What d'ye think, lad; what d'ye think,
As the roaring crowds go by?
As the banners flare and the brasses blare
And the great guns rend the sky?
As the women laugh like they'd all gone mad,
And the champagne glasses clink:

Oh, you're grippin' me hand so tightly, lad,
I'm a-wonderin': what d'ye think?

D'ye think o' the boys we used to know,
And how they'd have topped the fun?
Tom and Charlie, and Jack and Joe—
Gone now, every one.
How they'd have cheered as the joy-bells chime
And they grabbed each girl for a kiss!
And now—they're rottin' in Flanders slime,
And they gave their lives—for *this*.

Or else d'ye think of the many a time
We wished we too was dead,
Up to our knees in the freezin' grime,
With the fires of hell overhead;
When the youth and the strength of us sapped away,
And we cursed in our rage and pain?
And yet—we haven't a word to say. . . .
We're glad. We'd do it again.

I'm scared that they pity us. Come, old boy,
Let's leave them their flags and their fuss.
We'd surely be hatin' to spoil their joy
With the sight of such wrecks as us.
Let's slip away quietly, you and me,
And we'll talk of our chums out there:
You with your eyes that'll never see,
Me that's wheeled in a chair.

WAS IT YOU?

"HULLO, young Jones! with your tie so gay
And your pen behind your ear;

Will you mark my cheque in the usual way?
For I'm overdrawn, I fear."
Then you look at me in a manner bland,
As you turn your ledger's leaves,
And you hand it back with a soft white hand,
And the air of a man who grieves. . . .

"Was it you, young Jones, was it you I saw
(And I think I see you yet)
With a live bomb gripped in your grimy paw
And your face to the parapet?
With your lips asnarl and your eyes gone mad
With a fury that thrilled you through. . . .
Oh, I look at you now and I think, my lad,
Was it you, young Jones, was it you?

"Hullo, young Smith, with your well-fed look
And your coat of dapper fit,
Will you recommend me a decent book
With nothing of War in it?"
Then you smile as you polish a finger-nail,
And your eyes serenely roam,
And you suavely hand me a thrilling tale
By a man who stayed at home.

"Was it you, young Smith, was it you I saw
In the battle's storm and stench,
With a roar of rage and a wound red-raw
Leap into the reeking trench?
As you stood like a fiend on the firing-shelf
And you stabbed and hacked and slew. . . .
Oh, I look at you and I ask myself,
Was it you, young Smith, was it you?

"Hullo, old Brown, with your ruddy cheek
And your tummy's rounded swell,
Your garden's looking jolly *chic*
And your kiddies awf'ly well.
Then you beam at me in your cheery way
As you swing your water-can;
And you mop your brow and you blithely say:
'What about golf, old man?'

"Was it you, old Brown, was it you I saw
Like a bull-dog stick to your gun,
A cursing devil of fang and claw
When the rest were on the run?
Your eyes aflame with the battle-hate. . . .
As you sit in the family pew,
And I see you rising to pass the plate,
I ask: Old Brown, was it you?

"Was it me and you? Was it you and me?
(Is that grammar, or is it not?)
Who grovelled in filth and misery,
Who gloried and groused and fought?
Which is the wrong and which is the right?
Which is the false and the true?
The man of peace or the man of fight?
Which is the ME and the YOU?"

V

LES GRANDS MUTILES

I saw three wounded of the war:
And the first had lost his eyes;

And the second went on wheels and had
No legs below the thighs;
And the face of the third was featureless,
And his mouth ran cornerwise,
So I made a rhyme about each one,
And this is how my fancies run.

THE SIGHTLESS MAN

OUT of the night a crash,
A roar, a rampart of light;
A flame that leaped like a lash,
Searing forever my sight;
Out of the night a flash,
Then, oh, forever the Night!

Here in the dark I sit,
I who so loved the sun;
Supple and strong and fit,
In the dark till my days be done;
Aye, that's the hell of it,
Stalwart and twenty-one.

Marie is stanch and true,
Willing to be my wife;
Swears she has eyes for two . . .
Aye, but it's long, is Life.
What is a lad to do
With his heart and his brain at strife?

There now, my pipe is out;
No one to give me a light;
I grope and I grope about.
Well, it is nearly night;

Sleep may resolve my doubt,
Help me to reason right. . . .

(*He sleeps and dreams.*)

I heard them whispering there by the bed . . .
Oh, but the ears of the blind are quick!
Every treacherous word they said
Was a stab of pain and my heart turned sick.
Then lip met lip and they looked at me,
Sitting bent by the fallen fire,
And they laughed to think that I couldn't see;
But I felt the flame of their hot desire.
He's helping Marie to work the farm,
A dashing, upstanding chap, they say;
And look at me with my flabby arm,
And the fat of sloth, and my face of clay—
Look at me as I sit and sit,
By the side of a fire that's seldom lit,
Sagging and weary the livelong day,
When everyone else is out on the field,
Sowing the seed for a golden yield,
Or tossing around the new-mown hay. . . .

Oh, the shimmering wheat that frets the sky,
Gold of plenty and blue of hope,
I'm seeing it all with an inner eye
As out of the door I grope and grope.
And I hear my wife and her lover there,
Whispering, whispering, round the rick,
Mocking me and my sightless stare,
As I fumble and stumble everywhere,
Slapping and tapping with my stick;
Old and weary at thirty-one.

Heartsick, wishing it all was done.
Oh, I'll tap my way around to the byre,
And I'll hear the cows as they chew their hay;
There at least there is none to tire,
There at least I am not in the way.
And they'll look at me with their velvet eyes
And I'll stroke their flanks with my woman's hand,
And they'll answer to me with soft replies,
And somehow I fancy they'll understand.
And the horses too, they know me well;
I'm sure that they pity my wretched lot,
And the big fat ram with the jingling bell . . .
Oh, the beasts are the only friends I've got.
And my old dog, too, he loves me more,
I think, than ever he did before.
Thank God for the beasts that are all so kind,
That know and pity the helpless blind!

Ha! they're coming, the loving pair.
My hand's a-shake as my pipe I fill.
What if I steal on them unaware
With a reaping-hook, to kill, to kill? . . .
I'll do it . . . they're there in the mow of hay,
I hear them saying: "He's out of the way!"
Hark! how they're kissing and whispering. . . .
Closer I creep . . . I crouch . . . I spring. . . .

(*He wakes.*)

Ugh! What a horrible dream I've had!
And it isn't real . . . I'm glad, I'm glad!
Marie is good and Marie is true . . .
But now I know what it's best to do.
I'll sell the farm and I'll seek my kind,

I'll live apart with my fellow-blind,
And we'll eat and drink, and we'll laugh and joke,
And we'll talk of our battles, and smoke and smoke;
And brushes of bristle we'll make for sale,
While one of us reads a book of Braille.
And there will be music and dancing too,
And we'll seek to fashion our life anew;
And we'll walk the highways hand in hand,
The Brotherhood of the Sightless Band;
Till the years at last shall bring respite
And our night is lost in the Greater Night.

THE LEGLESS MAN

(*The Dark Side.*)

My mind goes back to Fumin Wood, and how we stuck it out,
Eight days of hunger, thirst and cold, mowed down by steel and
*   flame;*
Waist-deep in mud and mad with woe, with dead men all about,
We fought like fiends and waited for relief that never came.
Eight days and nights they rolled on us in battle-frenzied mass!
"Debout les morts!" We hurled them back. By God! they did
*   not pass.*

They pinned two medals on my chest, a yellow and a brown,
And lovely ladies made me blush, such pretty words they said.
I felt a cheerful man, almost, until my eyes went down,
And there I saw the blankets—how they sagged upon my bed.
And then again I drank the cup of sorrow to the dregs:
Oh, they can keep their medals if they give me back my legs.

I think of how I used to run and leap and kick the ball,
And ride and dance and climb the hills and frolic in the sea;

And all the thousand things that now I'll never do at all. . . .
Mon Dieu! there's nothing left in life, it often seems to me.
And as the nurses lift me up and strap me in my chair,
If they would chloroform me off I feel I wouldn't care.

Ah yes! we're "heroes all" to-day—they point to us with pride;
To-day their hearts go out to us, the tears are in their eyes!
But wait a bit; to-morrow they will blindly look aside;
No more they'll talk of what they owe, the dues of sacrifice
(One hates to be reminded of an everlasting debt).
It's all in human nature. Ah! the world will soon forget.

My mind goes back to where I lay wound-rotted on the plain,.
And ate the muddy mangold roots, and drank the drops of dew,
And dragged myself for miles and miles when every move was
   pain,
And over me the carrion-crows were retching as they flew.
Oh, ere I closed my eyes and stuck my rifle in the air
I wish that those who picked me up had passed and left me there.

(*The Bright Side.*)

Oh, one gets used to everything!
I hum a merry song,
And up the street and round the square
I wheel my chair along;
For look you, how my chest is sound
And how my arms are strong!

Oh, one gets used to anything!
It's awkward at the first,
And jolting o'er the cobbles gives
A man a grievous thirst;
But of all ills that one must bear
That's surely not the worst.

For there's the café open wide,
And there they set me up;
And there I smoke my *caporal*
Above my cider cup;
And play *manille* a while before
I hurry home to sup.

At home the wife is waiting me
With smiles and pigeon-pie;
And little Zi-Zi claps her hands
With laughter loud and high;
And if there's cause to growl, I fail
To see the reason why.

And all the evening by the lamp
I read some tale of crime,
Or play my old accordion
With Marie keeping time,
Until we near the hour of ten
From out the steeple chime.

Then in the morning bright and soon,
No moment do I lose;
Within my little cobbler's shop
To gain the silver *sous*
(Good luck one has no need of legs
To make a pair of shoes).

And every Sunday—oh, it's then
I am the happy man;
They wheel me to the river-side,
And there with rod and can
I sit and fish and catch a dish
Of *goujons* for the pan.

Aye, one gets used to everything,
And doesn't seem to mind;
Maybe I'm happier than most
Of my two-legged kind;
For look you at the darkest cloud,
Lo! how it's silver-lined.

THE FACELESS MAN

I'm dead.
Officially I'm dead. Their hope is past.
How long I stood as missing! Now, at last
                         I'm dead.
Look in my face—no likeness can you see,
No tiny trace of him they knew as "me."
How terrible the change!
Even my eyes are strange.
So keyed are they to pain,
That if I chanced to meet
My mother in the street
She'd look at me in vain.

When she got home I think she'd say:
"I saw the saddest sight to-day—
A *poilu* with no face at all.
Far better in the fight to fall
Than go through life like that, I think.
Poor fellow! how he made me shrink.
No face. Just eyes that seemed to stare
At me with anguish and despair.
This ghastly war! I'm almost cheered
To think my son who disappeared,

My boy so handsome and so gay,
Might have come home like him to-day."

I'm dead. I think it's better to be dead
When little children look at you with dread;
And when you know your coming home again
Will only give the ones who love you pain.
Ah! who can help but shrink? One cannot blame.
They see the hideous husk, not, not the flame
Of sacrifice and love that burns within;
While souls of satyrs, riddled through with sin,
Have bodies fair and excellent to see.
Mon Dieu! how different we all would be
If this our flesh was ordained to express
Our spirit's beauty or its ugliness.

(Oh, you who look at me with fear to-day,
And shrink despite yourselves, and turn away—
It was for you I suffered woe accurst;
For you I braved red battle at its worst;
For you I fought and bled and maimed and slew;
                              For you, for you!
For you I faced hell-fury and despair;
The reeking horror of it all I knew:
I flung myself into the furnace there;
I faced the flame that scorched me with its glare;
I drank unto the dregs the devil's brew—
Look at me now—for *you* and *you* and *you*. . . .)

    .   .   .   .

I'm thinking of the time we said good-by:
We took our dinner in Duval's that night,
Just little Jacqueline, Lucette and I;

We tried our very utmost to be bright.
We laughed. And yet our eyes, they weren't gay.
I sought all kinds of cheering things to say.
"Don't grieve," I told them. "Soon the time will pass;
My next permission will come quickly round;
We'll all meet at the Gare du Montparnasse;
Three times I've come already, safe and sound."
(But oh, I thought, it's harder every time,
After a home that seems like Paradise,
To go back to the vermin and the slime,
The weariness, the want, the sacrifice.
"Pray God," I said, "the war may soon be done,
But no, oh never, never till we've won!")

Then to the station quietly we walked;
I had my rifle and my haversack,
My heavy boots, my blankets on my back;
And though it hurt us, cheerfully we talked.
We chatted bravely at the platform gate.
I watched the clock. My train must go at eight.
One minute to the hour . . . we kissed good-by,
Then, oh, they both broke down, with piteous cry.
I went. . . . Their way was barred; they could not pass.
I looked back as the train began to start;
Once more I ran with anguish at my heart
And through the bars I kissed my little lass. . . .

Three years have gone; they've waited day by day.
I never came. I did not even write.
For when I saw my face was such a sight
I thought that I had better . . . stay away.
And so I took the name of one who died,
A friendless friend who perished by my side.

In Prussian prison camps three years of hell
I kept my secret; oh, I kept it well!
And now I'm free, but none shall ever know;
They think I died out there . . . it's better so.

To-day I passed my wife in widow's weeds.
I brushed her arm. She did not even look.
So white, so pinched her face, my heart still bleeds,
And at the touch of her, oh, how I shook!
And then last night I passed the window where
They sat together; I could see them clear,
The lamplight softly gleaming on their hair,
And all the room so full of cozy cheer.
My wife was sewing, while my daughter read;
I even saw my portrait on the wall.
I wanted to rush in, to tell them all;
And then I cursed myself: "You're dead, you're dead!"
God! how I watched them from the darkness there,
Clutching the dripping branches of a tree,
Peering as close as ever I might dare,
And sobbing, sobbing, oh, so bitterly!

But no, it's folly; and I mustn't stay.
To-morrow I am going far away.
I'll find a ship and sail before the mast;
In some wild land I'll bury all the past.
I'll live on lonely shores and there forget,
Or tell myself that there has never been
The gay and tender courage of Lucette,
The little loving arms of Jacqueline.

A man lonely upon a lonely isle,
Sometimes I'll look towards the North and smile

To think they're happy, and they both believe
I died for France, and that I lie at rest;
And for my glory's sake they've ceased to grieve,
And hold my memory sacred. Ah! that's best.
And in that thought I'll find my joy and peace
As there alone I wait the Last Release.

L'ENVOI

We've finished up the filthy war;
We've won what we were fighting for . . .
(Or have we? I don't know).
But anyway I have my wish:
I'm back upon the old Boul' Mich',
And how my heart's aglow!
Though in my coat's an empty sleeve,
Ah! do not think I ever grieve
(The pension for it, I believe,
Will keep me on the go).

So I'll be free to write and write,
And give my soul to sheer delight,
Till joy is almost pain;
To stand aloof and watch the throng,
And worship youth and sing my song
Of faith and hope again;
To seek for beauty everywhere,
To make each day a living prayer
That life may not be vain.

To sing of things that comfort me,
The joy in mother-eyes, the glee
Of little ones at play;
The blessed gentleness of trees,
Of old men dreaming at their ease
Soft afternoons away;
Of violets and swallows' wings,

Of wondrous, ordinary things
In words of every day.

To rhyme of rich and rainy nights,
When like a legion leap the lights
And take the town with gold;
Of taverns quaint where poets dream,
Of cafés gaudily agleam,
And vice that's overbold;
Of crystal shimmer, silver sheen,
Of soft and soothing nicotine,
Of wine that's rich and old,

Of gutters, chimney-tops and stars,
Of apple-carts and motor-cars,
The sordid and sublime;
Of wealth and misery that meet
In every great and little street,
Of glory and of grime;
Of all the living tide that flows—
From princes down to puppet shows—
I'll make my humble rhyme.

So if you like the sort of thing
Of which I also like to sing,
Just give my stuff a look;
And if you don't, no harm is done—

In writing it I've had my fun;
Good luck to you and every one—
And so
         Here ends my book.

Book Six

BAR-ROOM BALLADS

FORE-WARNING

I'd rather be the Jester than the Minstrel of the King;
I'd rather jangle cap and bells than twang the stately harp;
I'd rather make His royal ribs with belly-laughter ring,
Than see him sitting in the suds and sulky as a carp.
I'd rather be the Court buffoon than its most high-browed sage:
      So you who read, take heed, take heed,—
      Ere yet you turn my page.

PRELUDE

To smite Apollo's lyre I am unable;
Of loveliness, alas! I cannot sing.
My lot it is, across the tavern table,
To start a chorus to the strumming string.
I have no gift to touch your heart to pity;
I have no power to ring the note of pain:
All I can do is pipe a pot-house ditty,
Or roar a Rabelaisian refrain.

Behold yon minstrel of the empty belly,
Who seeks to please the bored and waiting throng,
Outside the Opera with ukulele,
And raucous strains of syncopated song.
His rag-time mocks their eager hearts a-hunger
For golden voices, melody divine:
Yet . . . throw a penny to the ballad-monger;
Yet . . . listen idly to this song of mine.

For with a humble heart I clank rhyme's fetters,
And bare my buttocks to the critic knout;
A graceless hobo in the Land of Letters,
Piping my ditties of the down-and-out.
A bar-room bard . . . so if a coin you're flinging,
Pay me a pot, and let me dream and booze;
To stars of scorn my dour defiance ringing,
With battered banjo and a strumpet Muse.

THE BALLAD OF SALVATION BILL

'Twas in the bleary middle of the hard-boiled Arctic night,
I was lonesome as a loon, so if you can,
Imagine my emotions of amazement and delight
When I bumped into that Missionary Man.
He was lying lost and dying in the moon's unholy leer,
And frozen from his toes to finger-tips;
The famished wolf-pack ringed him; but he didn't seem to fear,
As he pressed his ice-bound Bible to his lips.

'Twas the limit of my trap-line, with the cabin miles away,
And every step was like a stab of pain;
But I packed him like a baby, and I nursed him night and day,
Till I got him back to health and strength again.
So there we were, benighted in the shadow of the Pole,
And he might have proved a priceless little pard,
If he hadn't got to worrying about my blessed soul,
And a-quotin' me his Bible by the yard.

Now there was I, a husky guy, whose god was Nicotine.
With a "coffin-nail" a fixture in my mug;
I rolled them in the pages of a pulpwood magazine,
And hacked them with my jack-knife from the plug.
For, oh to know the bliss and glow that good tobacco means,
Just live among the everlasting ice. . . .
So judge my horror when I found my stock of magazines
Was chewed into a chowder by the mice.

A woeful week went by and not a single pill I had,
Me that would smoke my forty in a day;

I sighed, I swore, I strode the floor; I felt I would go mad:
The gospel-plugger watched me in dismay.
My brow was wet, my teeth were set, my nerves were rasping
    raw;
And yet that preacher couldn't understand:
So with despair I wrestled there—when suddenly I saw
The volume he was holding in his hand.

Then something snapped inside my brain, and with an evil start
The wolf-man in me woke to rabid rage.
"I saved your lousy life," says I; "so show you have a heart,
And tear me out a solitary page."
He shrank and shrivelled at my words; his face went pewter
    white;
'Twas just as if I'd handed him a blow;
And then . . . and then he seemed to swell, and grow to
    Heaven's height,
And in a voice that rang he answered: "No!"

I grabbed my loaded rifle and I jabbed it to his chest:
"Come on, you shrimp, give up that Book," says I.
Well sir, he was a parson, but he stacked up with the best,
And for grit I got to hand it to the guy.
"If I should let you desecrate this Holy Word," he said,
"My soul would be eternally accurst;
So go on, Bill, I'm ready. You can pump me full of lead
And take it, but—you've got to kill me first."

Now I'm no foul assassin, though I'm full of sinful ways,
And I knew right there the fellow had me beat;
For I felt a yellow mongrel in the glory of his gaze,
And I flung my foolish firearm at his feet.
Then wearily I turned away, and dropped upon my bunk,

And there I lay and blubbered like a kid.
"Forgive me, pard," says I at last, "for acting like a skunk,
But hide the blasted rifle. . . ." Which he did.

And he also hid his Bible, which was maybe just as well,
For the sight of all that paper gave me pain;
And there were crimson moments when I felt I'd go to hell
To have a single cigarette again.
And so I lay day after day, and brooded dark and deep,
Until one night I thought I'd end it all;
Then rough I roused the preacher, where he stretched pretend-
    ing sleep,
With his map of horror turned towards the wall.

"See here, my pious pal," says I, "I've stood it long enough. . . .
Behold! I've mixed some strychnine in a cup;
Enough to kill a dozen men—believe me it's no bluff;
Now watch me, for I'm gonna drink it up.
You've seen me bludgeoned by despair through bitter days and
    nights,
And now you'll see me squirming as I die.
You're not to blame, you've played the game according to your
    lights. . . .
But how would Christ have played it?—Well, good-bye. . . ."

With that I raised the deadly drink and laid it to my lips,
But he was on me with a tiger-bound;
And as we locked and reeled and rocked with wild and wicked
    grips,
The poison cup went crashing to the ground.
"Don't do it, Bill," he madly shrieked. "Maybe I acted wrong.
See, here's my Bible—use it as you will;

But promise me—you'll read a little as you go along. . . .
You do! Then take it, Brother; smoke your fill."

And so I did. I smoked and smoked from Genesis to Job,
And as I smoked I read each blessed word;
While in the shadow of his bunk I heard him sigh and sob,
And then . . . a most peculiar thing occurred.
I got to reading more and more, and smoking less and less,
Till just about the day his heart was broke,
Says I: "Here, take it back, me lad. I've had enough, I guess.
Your paper makes a mighty rotten smoke."

So then and there with plea and prayer he wrestled for my soul,
And I was racked and ravaged by regrets.
But God was good, for lo! next day there came the police patrol,
With paper for a thousand cigarettes. . . .
So now I'm called Salvation Bill; I teach the Living Law,
And Bally-hoo the Bible with the best;
And if a guy won't listen—why, I sock him on the jaw,
And preach the Gospel sitting on his chest.

EACH DAY A LIFE

I COUNT each day a little life,
    With birth and death complete;
I cloister it from care and strife
    And keep it sane and sweet.

With eager eyes I greet the morn,
    Exultant as a boy,
Knowing that I am newly born
    To wonder and to joy.

And when the sunset splendours wane,
    And ripe for rest am I,
Knowing that I will live again,
    Exultantly I die.

O that all Life were but a Day,
    Sunny and sweet and sane!
And that at Even I might say:
    "I sleep to wake again."

DOLLS

SHE said: "I am too old to play
With dolls," and put them all away,
Into a box, one rainy day.

I think she must have felt some pain,
She looked so long into the rain,
Then sighed: "I'll bring you out again;

"For I'll have little children too,
With sunny hair and eyes of blue,
And they will play and play with you.

"And now good-bye, my pretty dears;
There in the dark for years and years,
Dream of your little mother's tears."

Eglantine, Pierrot and Marie Claire,
Topsy and Tiny and Teddy Bear,
Side by side in the coffer there.

Time went by; one day she kneeled
By a wooden Cross in Flanders Field,
And wept for the One the earth concealed;

And made a vow she would never wed,
But always be true to the deathless dead,
Until the span of her life be sped.

.   .   .   .   .   .

More years went on and they made her wise
By sickness and pain and sacrifice,
With greying tresses and tired eyes.

And then one evening of weary rain,
She opened the old oak box again,
And her heart was clutched with an ancient pain.

For there in the quiet dark they lay,
Just as they were when she put them away . . .
O but it seemed like yesterday!

Topsy and Tiny and Teddy Bear,
Eglantine, Pierrot and Marie Claire,
Ever so hopefully waiting there.

But she looked at them through her blinding tears,
And she said: "You've been patient, my pretty dears;
You've waited and waited all these years.

"I've broken a promise I made so true;
But my heart, my darlings, is broken too:
No little Mothers have I for you.

"My hands are withered, my hair is grey;
Yet just for a moment I'll try to play
With you as I did that long dead day. . . .

"Ah no, I cannot. I try in vain. . . .
I stare and I stare into the rain. . . .
I'll put you back in your box again.

"Bless you, darlings, perhaps one day,
Some little Mother will find you and play,
And once again you'll be glad and gay.

"But when in the friendly dark I lie,
No one will ever love you as I. . . .
My little children . . . good-bye . . . good-bye."

THE BALLAD OF HOW MACPHERSON HELD
THE FLOOR

Said President MacConnachie to Treasurer MacCall:
"We ought to have a piper for our next Saint Andrew's Ball.
Yon squakin' saxophone gives me the syncopated gripes.
I'm sick of jazz, I want to hear the skirling of the pipes."
"Alas! it's true," said Tam MacCall. "The young folk of to-day
Are fox-trot mad and dinna ken a reel from a Strathspey.
Now, what we want's a kiltie lad, primed up wi' mountain dew,
To strut the floor at supper time, and play a lilt or two.
In all the North there's only one; of him I've heard them speak:
His name is Jock MacPherson, and he lives on Boulder Creek;
An old-time hard-rock miner, and a wild and wastrel loon,
Who spends his nights in glory, playing pibrochs to the moon.
I'll seek him out; beyond a doubt on next Saint Andrew's Night
We'll proudly hear the pipes to cheer and charm our appetite."

Oh lads were neat and lassies sweet who graced Saint Andrew's
    Ball;
But there was none so full of fun as Treasurer MacCall.
And as Maloney's rag-time band struck up the newest hit,
He smiled a smile behind his hand, and chuckled: "Wait a bit."
And so with many a Celtic snort, with malice in his eye,
He watched the merry crowd cavort, till supper time drew nigh.
Then gleefully he seemed to steal, and sought the Nugget Bar,
Wherein there sat a tartaned chiel, as lonely as a star;
A huge and hairy Highlandman as hearty as a breeze,
A glass of whisky in his hand, his bag-pipes on his knees.

"Drink down your *doch and doris*, Jock," cried Treasurer Mac-
  Call;
"The time is ripe to up and pipe; they wait you in the hall.
Gird up your loins and grit your teeth, and here's a pint of
  hooch
To mind you of your native heath—jist pit it in your pooch.
Play on and on for all you're worth; you'll shame us if you stop.
Remember you're of Scottish birth—keep piping till you drop.
Aye, though a bunch of Willie boys should bluster and implore,
For the glory of the Highlands, lad, you've *got* to hold the
  floor."
The dancers were at supper, and the tables groaned with cheer,
When President MacConnachie exclaimed: "What do I hear?
Methinks it's like a chanter, and it's coming from the hall."
"It's Jock MacPherson tuning up," cried Treasurer MacCall
So up they jumped with shouts of glee, and gaily hurried forth.
Said they: "We never thought to see a piper in the North."
Aye, all the lads and lassies braw went buzzing out like bees,
And Jock MacPherson there they saw, with red and rugged
  knees.
Full six feet four he strode the floor, a grizzled son of Skye,
With glory in his whiskers and with whisky in his eye.
With skelping stride and Scottish pride he towered above them
  all:
"And is he no' a bonny sight?" said Treasurer MacCall.
While President MacConnachie was fairly daft with glee,
And there was jubilation in the Scottish Commy-tee.
But the dancers seemed uncertain, and they signified their doubt,
By dashing back to eat as fast as they had darted out.
And someone raised the question 'twixt the coffee and the cakes:
"Does the Piper walk to get away from all the noise he makes?"
Then reinforced with fancy food they slowly trickled forth,
And watched in patronizing mood the Piper of the North.

Proud, proud was Jock MacPherson, as he made his bag-pipes
 skirl,
And he set his sporran swinging, and he gave his kilts a whirl.
And President MacConnachie was jumping like a flea,
And there was joy and rapture in the Scottish Commy-tee.
"Jist let them have their saxophones, wi' constipated squall;
We're having heaven's music now," said Treasurer MacCall
But the dancers waxed impatient, and they rather seemed to fret
For Maloney and the jazz of his Hibernian Quartette.
Yet little recked the Piper, as he swung with head on high,
Lamenting with MacCrimmon on the heather hills of Skye.
With Highland passion in his heart he held the centre floor;
Aye, Jock MacPherson played as he had never played before.

Maloney's Irish melodists were sitting in their place,
And as Maloney waited, there was wonder in his face.
'Twas sure the gorgeous music— Golly! wouldn't it be grand
If he could get MacPherson as a member of his band?
But the dancers moped and mumbled, as around the room they
 sat:
"We paid to dance," they grumbled; "but we cannot dance to
 that.
Of course we're not denying that it's really splendid stuff;
But it's mighty satisfying—don't you think we've had enough?"
"You've raised a pretty problem," answered Treasurer Mac-
 Call;
"For on Saint Andrew's Night, ye ken, the Piper rules the Ball."
Said President MacConnachie: "You've said a solemn thing.
Tradition holds him sacred, and he's got to have his fling.
But soon, no doubt, he'll weary out. Have patience; bide a wee."
"That's right. Respect the Piper," said the Scottish Commy-tee.

And so MacPherson stalked the floor, and fast the moments
 flew,

Till half an hour went past, as irritation grew and grew.
Then the dancers held a council, and with faces fiercely set,
They hailed Maloney, heading his Hibernian Quartette:
"It's long enough we've waited. Come on, Mike, play up the
    Blues."
And Maloney hesitated, but he didn't dare refuse.
So banjo and piano, and guitar and saxophone
Contended with the shrilling of the chanter and the drone;
And the women's ears were muffled, so infernal was the din,
But MacPherson was unruffled, for he knew that he would win.
Then two bright boys jazzed round him, and they sought to play
    the clown,
But MacPherson jolted sideways, and the Sassenachs went down.
And as if it was a signal, with a wild and angry roar,
The gates of wrath were riven—yet MacPherson held the floor.

Aye, amid the rising tumult, still he strode with head on high,
With ribbands gaily streaming, yet with battle in his eye.
Amid the storm that gathered, still he stalked with Highland
    pride,
While President and Treasurer sprang bravely to his side.
And with ire and indignation that was glorious to see,
Around him in a body ringed the Scottish Commy-tee.
Their teeth were clenched with fury; their eyes with anger
    blazed:
"Ye manna touch the Piper," was the slogan that they raised.
Then blows were struck, and men went down; yet 'mid the ris-
    ing fray
MacPherson towered in triumph—and he never ceased to play.

Alas! his faithful followers were but a gallant few,
And faced defeat, although they fought with all the skill they
    knew.

For President MacConnachie was seen to slip and fall,
And o'er his prostrate body stumbled Treasurer MacCall.
And as their foes with triumph roared, and leaguered them about,
It looked as if their little band would soon be counted out.
For eyes were black and noses red, yet on that field of gore,
As resolute as Highland rock—MacPherson held the floor.

Maloney watched the battle, and his brows were bleakly set,
While with him paused and panted his Hibernian Quartette.
For sure it is an evil spite, and breaking to the heart,
For Irishmen to watch a fight and not be taking part.
Then suddenly on high he soared, and tightened up his belt:
"And shall we see them crush," he roared, "a brother and a
    Celt?
A fellow *artiste* needs our aid. Come on, boys, take a hand."
Then down into the *mêlée* dashed Maloney and his band.

Now though it was Saint Andrew's Ball, yet men of every race,
That bow before the Great God Jazz were gathered in that
    place.
Yea, there were those who grunt: "Ya! Ya!" and those who
    squeak: "We! We!"
Likewise Dutch, Dago, Swede and Finn, Polack and Portugee.
Yet like ripe grain before the gale that national hotch-potch
Went down before the fury of the Irish and the Scotch.
Aye, though they closed their gaping ranks and rallied to the
    fray,
To the Shamrock and the Thistle went the glory of the day.

You should have seen the carnage in the drooling light of dawn,
Yet 'mid the scene of slaughter Jock MacPherson playing on.
Though all lay low about him, yet he held his head on high,
And piped as if he stood upon the caller crags of Skye.

His face was grim as granite, and no favour did he ask,
Though weary were his mighty lungs and empty was his flask.
And when a fallen foe wailed out: "Say! when will you have
  .done?"
MacPherson grinned and answered: "Hoots! She's only ha'f
  begun."
Aye, though his hands were bloody, and his knees were gay
  with gore,
A Grampian of Highland pride—MacPherson held the floor.

And still in Yukon valleys where the silent peaks look down,
They tell of how the Piper was invited up to town,
And he went in kilted glory, and he piped before them all,
But he wouldn't stop his piping till he busted up the Ball.
Of that Homeric scrap they speak, and how the fight went on,
With sally and with rally till the breaking of the dawn.
And how the Piper towered like a rock amid the fray,
And the battle surged about him, but he never ceased to play.
Aye, by the lonely camp-fires, still they tell the story o'er—
How the Sassenach was vanquished and—MacPherson held the
  floor.

GIPSY

The poppies that in Spring I sow,
In rings of radiance gleam and glow,
Like lords and ladies gay.
A joy are they to dream beside,
As in the air of eventide
They flutter, dip and sway.

For some are scarlet, some are gold,
While some in fairy flame unfold,
And some are rose and white.
There's pride of breeding in their glance,
And pride of beauty as they dance
Cotillions of delight.

Yet as I lift my eyes I see
Their swarthy kindred, wild and free,
Who flaunt it in the field.
"Begone, you Romanies!" I say,
"Lest you defile this bright array
Whose loveliness I shield."

My poppies are a sheen of light;
They take with ecstasy the sight,
And hold the heart elate. . . .
Yet why do I so often turn
To where their outcast brothers burn
With passion at my gate?

My poppies are my joy and pride;
Yet wistfully I gaze outside
To where their sisters yearn;
Their blowzy crimson cups afire,
Their lips aflutter with desire
To give without return.

My poppies dance a minuet;
Like courtiers in silk they set
My garden all aglow. . . .
Yet O the vagrants at my gate!
The gipsy trulls who peer and wait! . . .
Calling the heart they know.

THE BALLAD OF HANK THE FINN

Now Fireman Flynn met Hank the Finn where lights of Lust-
    land glow;
"Let's leave," says he, "the lousy sea, and give the land a show.
I'm fed up to the molar mark with wallopin' the brine;
I feel the bloody barnacles a-carkin' on me spine.
Let's hit the hard-boiled North a crack, where creeks are paved
    with gold."
"You count me in," says Hank the Finn. "Ay do as Ay ban
    told."

And so they sought the Lonely Land and drifted down its
    stream,
Where sunny silence round them spanned, as dopey as a dream.
But to the spell of flood and fell their gold-grimed eyes were
    blind;
By pine and peak they paused to seek, but nothing did they find;
No yellow glint of dust to mint, just mud and mocking sand,
And a hateful hush that seemed to crush them down on every
    hand.
Till Fireman Flynn grew mean as sin, and cursed his comrade
    cold,
But Hank the Finn would only grin, and . . . do as he was told.

Now Fireman Flynn had pieces ten of yellow Yankee gold,
Which every night he would invite his partner to behold.
"Look hard," says he; "it's all you'll see in this god-blasted land;
But don't you fret, I'm gonna let you hold them in your hand.

Yeah! Watch 'em gleam, then go and *dream* they're yours to
    have and hold."
Then Hank the Finn would scratch his chin and . . . do as he
    was told.

But every night by camp-fire light, he'd incubate his woes,
And fan the hate of mate for mate, the evil Arctic knows.
In dreams the Lapland witches gloomed like gargoyles overhead,
While the devils three of Helsinkee came cowering by his bed.
"Go, take," said they, "the yellow loot he's clinking in his belt,
And leave the sneaking wolverines to snout around his pelt.
Last night he called you *Swedish* scum, from out the glory-hole;
To-day he said you were a bum, and damned your mother's
    soul.
Go, plug with lead his scurvy head, and grab his greasy
    gold. . . ."
Then Hank the Finn saw red within, and . . . did as he was told.

So in due course the famous Force of Men Who Get Their
    Man,
Swooped down on sleeping Hank the Finn, and popped him in
    the can.
And in due time his grievous crime was judged without a plea,
And he was dated up to swing upon the gallows tree.
Then Sheriff gave a party in the Law's almighty name,
He gave a neck-tie party, and he asked me to the same.
There was no hooch a-flowin' and his party wasn't gay,
For O our hearts were heavy at the dawning of the day.
There was no band a-playin' and the only dancin' there
Was Hank the Finn interpretin' his solo on the air.
We climbed the scaffold steps and stood beside the knotted rope.
We watched the hooded hangman and his eyes were dazed with
    dope.

The Sheriff was in evening dress; a bell began to toll,
A beastly bell that struck a knell of horror to the soul.
As if the doomed one was myself, I shuddered, waiting there.
I spoke no word, then . . . then I heard *his* step upon the stair;
His halting foot, moccasin clad . . . and then I saw him stand
Between a weeping warder and a priest with Cross in hand.
And at the sight a murmur rose of terror and of awe,
And all them hardened gallows fans were sick at what they saw:
For as he towered above the mob, his limbs with leather triced,
By all that's wonderful, I swear, *his face was that of Christ.*

Now I ain't no blaspheming cuss, so don't you start to shout.
You see, his beard had grown so long it framed his face about.
His rippling hair was long and fair, his cheeks were spirit-pale,
His face was bright with holy light that made us wince and
   quail.
He looked at us with eyes a-shine, and sore were we confused,
As if he were the Judge divine, and we were the accused.
Aye, as serene he stood between the hangman and the cord,
You would have sworn, with anguish torn, he was the Blessed
   Lord.

The priest was wet with icy sweat, the Sheriff's lips were dry,
And we were staring starkly at the man who had to die.
"Lo! I am raised above you all," his pale lips seemed to say,
"For in a moment I shall leap to God's Eternal Day.
Am I not happy! I forgive you each for what you do;
Redeemed and penitent I go, with heart of love for you."
So there he stood in mystic mood, with scorn sublime of death.
I saw him gently kiss the Cross, and then I held my breath.
That blessed smile was blotted out; they dropped the hood of
   black;
They fixed the noose around his neck, the rope was hanging
   slack.

I heard him pray, I saw him sway, then . . . then he was not
 there;
A rope, a ghastly yellow rope was jerking in the air;
A jigging rope that soon was still; a hush as of the tomb,
And Hank the Finn, that man of sin, had met his rightful doom.

His rightful doom! Now that's the point. I'm wondering, be-
 cause
I hold *a man is what he is*, and never what he was.
You see, the priest had filled that guy so full of holy dope,
That at the last he came to die as pious as the Pope.
A gentle ray of sunshine made a halo round his head.
I thought to see a sinner—lo! I saw a Saint instead.
Aye, as he stood as martyrs stand, clean-cleansed of mortal dross,
I think he might have gloried had . . . WE NAILED HIM TO A
 CROSS.

SHEILA

WHEN I played my penny whistle on the braes above Lochgyle
The heather bloomed about us, and we heard the peewit call;
As you bent above your knitting something *fey* was in your
    smile,
And fine and soft and slow the rain made silver on your shawl.
Your cheeks were pink like painted cheeks, your eyes a pansy
    blue . . .
My heart was in my playing, but my music was for you.

And now I play the organ in this lordly London town;
I play the lovely organ with a thousand folk in view.
They're wearing silk and satin, but I see a woollen gown,
And my heart's not in my music, for I'm thinking, lass, of you;
When you listened to a barefoot boy, who piped of ancient
    pain,
And your ragged shawl was pearly in the sweet, shy rain.

I'll play them mighty music— O I'll make them stamp and
    cheer;
I'll give the best that's in me, but I'll give it all for you.
I'll put my whole heart in it, for I feel that you are near,
Not yonder, sleeping always, where the peat is white with dew.
But I'll never live the rapture of that shepherd boy the while
I trilled for you my whistle on the braes above Lochgyle.

THE BALLAD OF TOUCH-THE-BUTTON NELL

Beyond the Rocking Bridge it lies, the burg of evil fame,
The huts where hive and swarm and thrive the sisterhood of
*   shame.*
Through all the night each cabin light goes out and then goes in,
A blood-red heliograph of lust, a semaphore of sin.
From Dawson Town, soft skulking down, each lewdster seeks
*   his mate;*
And glad and bad, kimono clad, the wanton women wait.
The Klondike gossips to the moon, and simmers o'er its bars;
Each silent hill is dark and chill, and chill the patient stars.
Yet hark! upon the Rocking Bridge a bacchanalian step;
A whispered: "Come," the skirl of some hell-raking demi-
*   rep. . . .*

.   .   .   .

They gave a dance in Lousetown, and the Tenderloin was there,
The girls were fresh and frolicsome, and nearly all were fair.
They flaunted on their backs the spoil of half-a-dozen towns;
And some they blazed in gems of price, and some wore Paris
    gowns.
The voting was divided as to who might be the belle;
But all opined, the winsomest was Touch-the-Button Nell.

Among the merry mob of men was one who did not dance,
But watched the "light fantastic" with a sour and sullen glance.
They saw his white teeth grit and gleam, they saw his thick lips
    twitch;
They knew him for the giant Slav, one Riley Dooleyvitch.

623

"Oh Riley Dooleyvitch, come forth," quoth Touch-the-Button
   Nell,
"And dance a step or two with me—the music's simply swell."
He crushed her in his mighty arms, a meek, beguiling witch:
"With you, oh Nell, I'd dance to Hell," said Riley Dooleyvitch.

He waltzed her up, he waltzed her down, he waltzed her round
   the hall;
His heart was putty in her hands, his very soul was thrall.
As Antony of old succumbed to Cleopatra's spell,
So Riley Dooleyvitch bowed down to Touch-the-Button Nell.

"And do you love me true?" she cried. "I love you as my life."
"How can you prove your love?" she sighed. "I beg you, be my
   wife.
I stake big pay up Hunker way; some day I be so rich;
I make you shine in satins fine," said Riley Dooleyvitch.

"Some day you'll be so rich," she mocked; "that old pipe-dream
   don't go.
Who gets an option on this kid must have the coin to show.
You work your ground. When Spring comes round, our wed-
   ding bells will ring.
I'm on the square, and *I'll* take care of all the gold you bring."

So Riley Dooleyvitch went back and worked upon his claim;
He ditched and drifted, sunk and stoped, with one unswerving
   aim;
And when his poke of raw moose-hide with dust began to swell,
He brought and laid it at the feet of Touch-the-Button Nell.

     .   .   .   .

Now like all others of her ilk, the lady had a friend,
And what she made by way of trade, she gave to him to spend;

To stake him in a poker game, or pay his bar-room score:
He was a pimp from Paris, and his name was Lew Lamore.

And so as Dooleyvitch went forth and worked as he was bid,
And wrested from the frozen muck the yellow stuff it hid,
And brought it to his Lady Nell, she gave him love galore—
But handed over all her gains to festive Lew Lamore.

.   .   .   .

A year had gone, a weary year of strain and bloody sweat;
Of pain and hurt in dark and dirt, of fear that she forget.
He sought once more her cabin door: "I've laboured like a
    beast;
But now, dear one, the time has come to go before the priest.

"I've brought you gold—a hundred-fold I'll bring you by-and-
    by;
But oh I want you, want you bad; I want you till I die.
Come, quit this life with evil rife—we'll joy while yet we
    can. . . ."
"I may not wed with you," she said; "I love another man.

"I love him and I hate him so. He holds me in a spell.
He beats me—see my bruisèd breast; he makes my life a hell.
He bleeds me, as by sin and shame I earn my daily bread:
Oh cruel Fate, I cannot mate till Lew Lamore be dead!"

.   .   .   .

The long, lean flume streaked down the hill, five hundred feet
    of fall;
The waters in the dam above chafed at their prison wall;
They surged and swept, they churned and leapt, with savage
    glee and strife;

With spray and spume the dizzy flume thrilled like a thing of
    life.

"We must be free," the waters cried, and scurried down the
    slope;
"No power can hold us back," they roared, and hurried in their
    hope.
Into a mighty pipe they plunged; like maddened steers they ran,
And crashed out through a shard of steel—to serve the will of
    Man.

And there, hydraulicking his ground beside a bedrock ditch,
With eye aflame and savage aim was Riley Dooleyvitch.
In long hip-boots and overalls, and dingy denim shirt,
Behind a giant monitor he pounded at the dirt.

A steely shaft of water shot, and smote the face of clay;
It burrowed in the frozen muck, and scooped the dirt away;
It gored the gravel from its bed, it bellowed like a bull;
It hurled the heavy rocks aloft like heaps of fleecy wool.

Strength of a hundred men was there, resistless might and skill,
And only Riley Dooleyvitch to swing it at his will.
He played it up, he played it down, nigh deafened by its roar,
'Til suddenly he raised his eyes, and there stood Lew Lamore.

Pig-eyed and heavy jowled he stood, and puffed a big cigar;
As cool as though he ruled the roost in some Montmartre bar.
He seemed to say: "I've got a cinch, a double diamond hitch:
I'll skin this Muscovitish oaf, this Riley Dooleyvitch."

He shouted: "Stop ze water gun; it stun me . . . *Sacré damn!*
I like to make one beezness deal; you know ze man I am.

Zat leetle girl, she love me so—I tell you what I do:
You geeve to me zees claim. . . . *Jeezcrize!* I geeve zat girl to
   you."

"I'll see you damned," says Dooleyvitch; but e'er he checked his
   tongue,
(It *may* have been an accident) the "Little Giant" swung;
Swift as a lightning flash it swung, until it plumply bore
And met with an obstruction in the shape of Lew Lamore.

It caught him up, and spun him round, and tossed him like a
   ball;
It played and pawed him in the air, before it let him fall.
Then just to show what it could do, with savage rend and thud,
It ripped the entrails from his spine, and dropped him in the
   mud.

They gathered up the broken bones, and sadly in a sack,
They bore to town the last remains of Lew Lamore, the *macque*.
And would you hear the full details of how it all befell,
Ask Missis Riley Dooleyvitch (late Touch-the-Button Nell).

ATOLL

THE woes of men beyond my ken
Mean nothing more to me.
Behold my world, an Eden hurled
From Heaven to the Sea;
A jewelled home, in fending foam
Tempestuously tossed;
A virgin isle none dare defile,
Far-flung, forgotten, lost.

And here I dwell, where none may tell
Me tales of mortal strife;
Let millions die, immune am I,
And radiant with life.
No echo comes of evil drums,
To vex my dawns divine;
Aloof, alone I hold my throne,
And Majesty is mine.

Ghost ships pass by, and glad am I
They make no sign to me.
The green corn springs, the gilt vine clings,
The net is in the sea.
My paradise around me lies,
Remote from wrath and wrong;
My isle is clean, unsought, unseen,
And innocent with song.

Here let me dwell in beauty's spell,
As tranquil as a tree;

Here let me bide, where wind and tide
Bourdon that I am free;
Here let me know from human woe
The rapture of release:
The rich caress of Loveliness,
The plenitude of Peace.

THE BALLAD OF THE ICE-WORM COCKTAIL

To Dawson Town came Percy Brown from London on the
     Thames.
A pane of glass was in his eye, and stockings on his stems.
Upon the shoulder of his coat a leather pad he wore,
To rest his deadly rifle when it wasn't seeking gore;
The which it must have often been, for Major Percy Brown,
According to his story was a hunter of renown,
Who in the Murrumbidgee wilds had stalked the kangaroo
And killed the cassowary on the plains of Timbuctoo.
And now the Arctic fox he meant to follow to its lair,
And it was also his intent to beard the Arctic hare. . . .
Which facts concerning Major Brown I merely tell because
I fain would have you know him for the Nimrod that he was.

Now Skipper Grey and Deacon White were sitting in the shack,
And sampling of the whisky that pertained to Sheriff Black.
Said Skipper Grey: "I want to say a word about this Brown:
The piker's sticking out his chest as if he owned the town."
Said Sheriff Black: "He has no lack of frigorated cheek;
He called himself a Sourdough when he'd just been here a
     week."
Said Deacon White: "Methinks you're right, and so I have a
     plan
By which I hope to prove to-night the mettle of the man.
Just meet me where the hooch-bird sings, and though our ways
     be rude
We'll make a *proper* Sourdough of this Piccadilly dude."

Within the Malamute Saloon were gathered all the gang;
The fun was fast and furious, and loud the hooch-bird sang.
In fact the night's hilarity had almost reached its crown,
When into its storm-centre breezed the gallant Major Brown
And at the apparition, with its glass eye and plus-fours,
From fifty alcoholic throats resounded fifty roars.
With shouts of stark amazement and with whoops of sheer de-
      light,
They surged around the stranger, but the first was Deacon
      White.
"We welcome you," he cried aloud, "to this the Great White
      Land.
The Arctic Brotherhood is proud to grip you by the hand.
Yea, sportsman of the bull-dog breed, from trails of far away,
To Yukoners this is indeed a memorable day.
Our jubilation to express, vocabularies fail. . . .
Boys, hail the Great Cheechako!" And the boys responded:
      "Hail!"

"And now," continued Deacon White to blushing Major Brown,
"Behold assembled the *eelight* and cream of Dawson Town.
And one ambition fills their hearts and makes their bosoms
      glow—
They want to make you, honoured sir, a *bony feed* Sourdough.
The same, some say, is one who's seen the Yukon ice go out,
But most profound authorities the definition doubt.
And to the genial notion of this meeting, Major Brown,
A Sourdough is a guy who drinks . . . an ice-worm cocktail
      down."

"By Gad!" responded Major Brown, "that's ripping, don't you
      know.
I've always felt I'd like to be a *certified* Sourdough.

And though I haven't any doubt your Winter's awf'ly nice,
Mayfair, I fear, may miss me ere the break-up of your ice.
Yet (pray excuse my ignorance of matters such as these)
A cocktail I can understand—but what's an ice-worm, please?"
Said Deacon White: "It is not strange that you should fail to
    know,
Since ice-worms are peculiar to the Mountain of Blue Snow.
Within the Polar rim it rears, a solitary peak,
And in the smoke of early Spring (a spectacle unique)
Like flame it leaps upon the sight and thrills you through and
    through,
For though its cone is piercing white, its base is blazing blue.
Yet all is clear as you draw near—for coyly peering out
Are hosts and hosts of tiny worms, each indigo of snout.
And as no nourishment they find, to keep themselves alive
They masticate each other's tails, till just the Tough survive.
Yet on this stern and Spartan fare so rapidly they grow,
That some attain six inches by the melting of the snow.
Then when the tundra glows to green and nigger heads ap-
    pear,
They burrow down and are not seen until another year."

"A toughish yarn," laughed Major Brown, "as well you may
    admit.
I'd like to see this little beast before I swallow it."
" 'Tis easy done," said Deacon White. "Ho! Barman, haste and
    bring
Us forth some pickled ice-worms of the vintage of last Spring."
But sadly still was Barman Bill, then sighed as one bereft:
"There's been a run on cocktails, Boss; there ain't an ice-worm
    left.
Yet wait. . . . By gosh! it seems to me that some of extra size
Were picked and put away to show the scientific guys."

Then deeply in a drawer he sought, and there he found a jar,
The which with due and proper pride he put upon the bar;
And in it, wreathed in queasy rings, or rolled into a ball,
A score of grey and greasy things were drowned in alcohol.
Their bellies were a bilious blue, their eyes a bulbous red;
Their backs were grey, and gross were they, and hideous of
   head.
And when with gusto and a fork the barman speared one out,
It must have gone four inches from its tail-tip to its snout.
Cried Deacon White with deep delight: "Say, isn't that a beaut?"
"I think it is," sniffed Major Brown, "a most disgustin' brute.
It's very sight gives me the pip. I'll bet my bally hat,
You're only spoofin' me, old chap. You'll never swallow that."
"The hell I won't!" said Deacon White. "Hey! Bill, that fel-
   low's fine.
Fix up four ice-worm cocktails, and just put that wop in mine."

So Barman Bill got busy, and with sacerdotal air
His art's supreme achievement he proceeded to prepare.
His silver cups, like sickle moon, went waving to and fro,
And four celestial cocktails soon were shining in a row.
And in the starry depths of each, artistically piled,
A fat and juicy ice-worm raised its mottled mug and smiled.
Then closer pressed the peering crowd, suspended was the fun,
As Skipper Grey in courteous way said: "Stranger, please take
   one."
But with a gesture of disgust the Major shook his head.
"You can't bluff me. You'll never drink that ghastly thing," he
   said.
"You'll see all right," said Deacon White, and held his cocktail
   high,
Till its ice-worm seemed to wiggle, and to wink a wicked eye.
Then Skipper Grey and Sheriff Black each lifted up a glass,

While through the tense and quiet crowd a tremor seemed to
    pass.
"Drink, Stranger, drink," boomed Deacon White. "Proclaim
    you're of the best,
A doughty Sourdough who has passed the Ice-worm Cocktail
    Test."
And at these words, with all eyes fixed on gaping Major Brown,
Like a libation to the gods, each dashed his cocktail down.
The Major gasped with horror as the trio smacked their lips.
He twiddled at his eye-glass with unsteady finger-tips.
Into his starry cocktail with a look of woe he peered,
And its ice-worm, to his thinking, most incontinently leered.
Yet on him were a hundred eyes, though no one spoke aloud,
For hushed with expectation was the waiting, watching crowd.
The Major's fumbling hand went forth—the gang prepared to
    cheer;
The Major's falt'ring hand went back, the mob prepared to jeer.
The Major gripped his gleaming glass and laid it to his lips,
And as despairfully he took some nauseated sips,
From out its coil of crapulence the ice-worm raised its head;
Its muzzle was a murky blue, its eyes a ruby red.
And then a roughneck bellowed forth: "This stiff comes here
    and struts,
As if he'd bought the blasted North—jest let him show his guts."
And with a roar the mob proclaimed: "Cheechako, Major
    Brown,
Reveal that you're of Sourdough stuff, and drink your cocktail
    down."

The Major took another look, then quickly closed his eyes,
For even as he raised his glass he felt his gorge arise.
Aye, even though his sight was sealed, in fancy he could see
That grey and greasy thing that reared and sneered in mockery.

Yet round him ringed the callous crowd—and how they seemed
    to gloat!
It must be done. . . . He swallowed hard. . . . The brute was
    at his throat.
He choked . . . he gulped. . . . Thank God! at last he'd got
    the horror down.
Then from the crowd went up a roar: "Hooray for Sourdough
    Brown!"
With shouts they raised him shoulder high, and gave a rousing
    cheer,
But though they praised him to the sky the Major did not hear.
Amid their demonstrative glee delight he seemed to lack;
Indeed it almost seemed that he—was "keeping something back."
A clammy sweat was on his brow, and pallid as a sheet:
"I feel I must be going now," he'd plaintively repeat.
Aye, though with drinks and smokes galore, they tempted him
    to stay,
With sudden bolt he gained the door, and made his get-away.

And ere next night his story was the talk of Dawson Town,
But gone and reft of glory was the wrathful Major Brown;
For that ice-worm (so they told him) of such formidable size
Was—*a stick of stained spaghetti with two red ink spots for
    eyes.*

GRANDAD

Heaven's mighty sweet, I guess;
Ain't no rush to git there;
Been a sinner, more or less;
Maybe wouldn't fit there.
Wicked still, bound to confess;
Might jest pine a bit there.

Heaven's swell, the preachers say:
Got so used to earth here;
Had such good times all the way,
Frolic, fun and mirth here;
Eighty Springs ago to-day,
Since I had my birth here.

Quite a spell of happy years.
Wish I could begin it;
Cloud and sunshine, laughter, tears,
Livin' every minute.
Women, too, the pretty dears;
Plenty of 'em in it.

Heaven! that's another tale.
Mightn't let me chew there.
Gotta have me pot of ale;
Would I like the brew there?
Maybe I'd get slack and stale—
No more chores to do there.

Here I weed the garden plot,
Scare the crows from pillage;

Simmer in the sun a lot,
Talk about the tillage.
Yarn of battles I have fought,
Greybeard of the village.

Heaven's mighty fine, I know. . . .
Still, it ain't so bad here.
See them maples all aglow;
Starlings seem so glad here:
I'll be mighty peeved to go,
Scrumptious times I've had here.

Lord, I know You'll understand.
With Your Light You'll lead me.
Though I'm not the pious brand,
I'm here when You need me.
Gosh! I know that Heaven's GRAND,
But dang it! God, *don't speed me.*

THE BALLAD OF THE LEATHER MEDAL

ONLY a Leather Medal, hanging there on the wall,
Dingy and frayed and faded, dusty and worn and old;
Yet of my humble treasures I value it most of all,
And I wouldn't part with that medal if you gave me its weight
    in gold.

Read the inscription: *For Valour—presented to Millie MacGee.*
Ah! how in mem'ry it takes me back to the "auld lang syne,"
When Millie and I were sweethearts, and fair as a flower was
    she—
Yet little I dreamt that her bosom held the heart of a heroine.

Listen! I'll tell you about it. . . . An orphan was Millie Mac-
    Gee,
Living with Billie her brother, under the Yukon sky.
Sam, her pa, was cremated in the winter of nineteen-three,
As duly and truly related by the pen of an author guy.

A cute little kid was Billie, solemn and silken of hair,
The image of Jackie Coogan in the days before movies could
    speak.
Devoted to him was Millie, with more than a mother's care,
And happy were they together in their cabin on Bunker Creek.

'Twas only a mining village, where hearts are simple and true,
And Millie MacGee was schoolma'am, loved and admired by
    all;

Yet no one dreamed for a moment she'd do what she dared to
  do—
But wait and I'll try to tell you, as clear as I can recall. . . .

.   .   .   .

Christmas Eve in the school-house! A scene of glitter and glee;
The children eager and joyful; parents and neighbours too;
Right in the forefront, Millie, close to the Christmas Tree,
While Billie, her brother, recited "The Shooting of Dan Mc-
  Grew."

I reckon you've heard the opus, a ballad of guts and gore;
Of a Yukon frail and a frozen trail and a fight in a drinking dive.
It's on a par, I figger, with "The Face on the Bar-Room Floor,"
And the boys who wrote them pieces ought to be skinned alive.

Picture that scene of gladness: the honest faces aglow;
The kiddies gaping and spellbound, as Billie strutted his stuff.
The stage with its starry candles, and there in the foremost row,
Millie, bright as a fairy, in radiant flounce and fluff.

More like an angel I thought her; all she needed was wings,
And I sought for a smile seraphic, but her eyes were only for
  Bill;
So there was I longing and loving, and dreaming the craziest
  things,
And Billie shouting and spouting, and everyone rapt and still.

Proud as a prince was Billie, bang in the footlights' glare,
And quaking for him was Millie, as she followed every word;
Then just as he reached the climax, ranting and sawing the air—
Ugh! How it makes me shudder! The horrible thing oc-
  curred. . . .

'Twas the day when frocks were frilly, and skirts were scraping
    the ground,
And the snowy flounces of Millie like sea foam round her swept;
Humbly adoring I watched her—when oh, my heart gave a
    bound!
Hoary and scarred and hideous, out from the tree . . . IT . . .
    crept.

A whiskered, beady-eyed monster, grisly and grim of hue;
Savage and slinking and silent, born of the dark and the dirt;
Dazed by the glare and the glitter, it wavered a moment or two—
Then like a sinister shadow, it vanished . . . 'neath Millie's skirt.

I stared. Had my eyes deceived me? I shivered. I held my breath.
Surely I must have dreamed it. I quivered. I made to rise. . . .
Then—my God! it was real. Millie grew pale as death;
And oh, such a look of terror woke in her lovely eyes.

Did her scream ring out? Ah no, sir. It froze at her very lips.
Clenching her teeth she checked it, and I saw her slim hands lock,
Grasping and gripping tensely, with desperate finger tips,
Something that writhed and wriggled under her dainty frock.

Quick I'd have dashed to her rescue, but fiercely she signalled:
    "No!"
Her eyes were dark with anguish, but her lips were set and grim;
Then I knew she was thinking of Billie—the kiddy must have
    his show,
Reap to the full his glory, nothing mattered but him.

So spiked to my chair with horror, there I shuddered and saw
Her fingers frenziedly clutching and squeezing with all their
    might

Something that squirmed and struggled, a demon of tooth and
    claw,
Fighting with fear and fury, under her garment white.

Oh could I only aid her! But the wide room lay between,
And again her eyes besought me: "Steady!" they seemed to say.
"Stay where you are, Bob Simmons; don't let us have a scene.
Billie will soon be finished. Only a moment . . . stay!"

A moment! Ah yes, I got her. I knew how night after night
She'd learned him each line of that ballad with patience and
    pride and glee;
With gesture and tone dramatic, she'd taught him how to re-
    cite. . . .
And now at the last to fail him—no, it must never be.

A moment! It seemed like ages. Why was Billie so slow?
He stammered. Twice he repeated: "The Lady that's known as
    Lou——"
The kiddy was stuck and she knew it. Her face was frantic with
    woe.
Could she but come to his rescue? Could she remember the cue?

I saw her whispering wildly as she leaned to the frightened boy;
But Billie stared like a dummy, and I stifled an anxious curse.
Louder, louder she prompted; then his face illumined with joy,
And panting, flushed and exultant, he finished the final verse.

So the youngster wound up like a whirlwind, while cheer re-
    sounded on cheer;
His piece was the hit of the evening. "Bravo!" I heard them say.
But there in the heart of the racket was one who could not
    hear—

The loving sister who'd coached him; for Millie had fainted
away.

I rushed to her side and grabbed her; then others saw her dis-
tress,
And all were eager to aid me, as I pillowed that golden head.
But her arms were tense and rigid, and clutched in the folds of
her dress,
Unlocking her hands they found it . . . A RAT . . . *and the
brute was dead.*

In silence she'd crushed its life out, rather than scare the crowd,
And queer little Billie's triumph. . . . Hey! Mother, what about
tea?
I've just been telling a story that makes me so mighty proud. . . .
Stranger, let me present you—*my wife, that was Millie MacGee.*

COURAGE

To-DAY I opened wide my eyes,
And stared with wonder and surprise,
To see beneath November skies
An apple blossom peer;
Upon a branch as bleak as night
It gleamed exultant on my sight,
A fairy beacon burning bright
Of hope and cheer.

"Alas!" said I, "poor foolish thing,
Have you mistaken this for Spring?
Behold, the thrush has taken wing,
And Winter's near."
Serene it seemed to lift its head:
"The Winter's wrath I do not dread,
Because I am," it proudly said,
"A Pioneer.

"Some apple blossom must be first,
With beauty's urgency to burst
Into a world for joy athirst,
And so I dare;
And I shall see what none shall see—
December skies gloom over me,
And mock them with my April glee,
And fearless fare.

"And I shall hear what none shall hear—
The hardy robin piping clear,

The Storm King gallop dark and drear
Across the sky;
And I shall know what none shall know—
The silent kisses of the snow,
The Christmas candles' silver glow,
Before I die.

"Then from your frost-gemmed window pane
One morning you will look in vain,
My smile of delicate disdain
No more to see;
But though I pass before my time,
And perish in the grale and grime,
Maybe you'll have a little rhyme
To spare for me."

A SOURDOUGH STORY

Hark to a Sourdough story, told at sixty below,
When the pipes are lit and we smoke and spit
Into the campfire glow.
Rugged are we and hoary, and statin' a general rule,
A genooine Sourdough story
Ain't no yarn for the Sunday School.

A Sourdough came to stake his claim in Heav'n one morning
    early.
Saint Peter cried: "Who waits outside them gates so bright and
    pearly?"
"I'm recent dead," the Sourdough said, "and crave to visit
    Hades,
Where haply pine some pals o' mine, includin' certain ladies."
Said Peter: "Go, you old Sourdough, from life so croolly riven;
And if ye fail to find their trail, we'll have a snoop round
    Heaven."

He waved, and lo! that old Sourdough dropped down to Hell's
    red spaces;
But though 'twas hot he couldn't spot them old familiar faces.
The bedrock burned, and so he turned, and climbed with foot-
    steps fleeter,
The stairway straight to Heaven's gate, and there, of course, was
    Peter.
"I cannot see my mates," sez he, "among those damned forever.
I have a hunch some of the bunch in Heaven I'll discover."
Said Peter: "True; and this I'll do (since Sourdoughs are my
    failing)

You see them guys in Paradise, lined up against the railing—
As bald as coots, in *birthday* suits, with beards below the mid-
dle . . .
Well, I'll allow you in right now, if you can solve a riddle:
Among that gang of stiffs who hang and dodder round the
portals,
Is one whose name is known to Fame—it's Adam, first of mortals.
For quiet's sake he makes a break from Eve, which is his Mad-
ame. . . .
Well, there's the gate.—To crash it straight, just spy the guy
that's Adam."

The old Sourdough went down the row of greybeards rumi-
natin'.
With optics dim they peered at him, and pressed agin the
gratin'.
In every face he sought some trace of our ancestral father;
But though he stared, he soon despaired the faintest clue to
gather.
Then suddenly he whooped with glee: "Ha! Ha! an inspira-
tion."
And to and fro along the row he ran with animation.
To Peter, bold he cried: "Behold, all told there are eleven.
Suppose I fix on Number Six—say Boy! How's that for
Heaven?"

"By gosh! you win," said Pete. "Step in. But tell me how you
chose him.
They're like as pins; all might be twins. There's nothing to dis-
close him."
The Sourdough said: " 'Twas hard; my head was seething with
commotion.
I felt a dunce; then all at once I had a gorgeous notion.

I stooped and peered beneath each beard that drooped like fleece
of mutton.

My search was crowned. . . . That bird I found—*ain't got no
belly button*."

ALLOUETTE

Singing larks I saw for sale—
(Ah! the pain of it)
Plucked and ready to impale
On the roasting spit;
Happy larks that summer-long
Stormed the radiant sky,
Adoration in their song . . .
Packed to make a pie.

Hark! from springs of joy unseen
Spray their jewelled notes.
Tangle them in nets of green,
Twist their lyric throats;
Clip their wings and string them tight,
Stab them with a skewer,
All to tempt the appetite
Of the epicure.

Shade of Shelley! Come not nigh
This accursèd spot,
Where for sixpence one can buy
Skylarks for the pot;
Dante, paint a blacker hell,
Plunge in deeper darks
Wretches who can slay and sell
Sunny-hearted larks.

You who eat, you are the worst:
By internal pains,

May you ever be accurst
Who pluck these poor remains.
But for you wingèd joy would soar
To heaven from the sod:
In ecstasy a lark would pour
Its gratitude to God.

THE BALLAD OF LENIN'S TOMB

This is the yarn he told to me
As we sat in Casey's Bar,
That Rooshun mug who scrammed from the jug
In the Land of the Crimson Star;
That Soveet guy with the single eye,
And the face like a flaming scar.

Where Lenin lies the red flag flies, and rat-grey workers wait
To tread the gloom of Lenin's Tomb, where the Comrade lies
    in state.
With lagging pace they scan his face, so weary yet so firm;
For years a score they've laboured sore to save him from the
    worm.
The Kremlin walls are grimly grey, but Lenin's Tomb is red,
And pilgrims from the Sour Lands say: "He sleeps and is not
    dead."
Before their eyes in peace he lies, a symbol and a sign,
And as they pass that dome of glass they see—a God Divine.
So Doctors plug him full of dope, for if he drops to dust,
So will collapse their faith and hope, the whole combine will
    bust.
But stay, Tovarich; hark to me . . . a secret I'll disclose,
For I did see what none did see; I know what no one knows.

I was a Cheka terrorist— Oh I served the Soviets well,
Till they put me down on the bone-yard list, for the fear that I
    might tell;
That I might tell the thing I saw, and that only I did see,

They held me in quod with a firing squad to make a corpse of
    me.
But I got away, and here to-day I'm telling my tale to you;
Though it may sound weird, by Lenin's beard, so help me God
    it's true.
I slouched across the great Red Square, and watched the waiting
    line.
The mongrel sons of Marx were there, convened to Lenin's
    shrine;
Ten thousand men of Muscovy, Mongol and Turkoman,
Black-bonnets of the Aral Sea and Tatars of Kazan.
Kalmuck and Bashkir, Lett and Finn, Georgian, Jew and Lapp,
Kirghiz and Kazakh, crowding in to gaze at Lenin's map.
Aye, though a score of years had run I saw them pause and pray,
As mourners at the Tomb of one who died but yesterday.
I watched them in a bleary daze of bitterness and pain,
For oh, I missed the cheery blaze of vodka in my brain.
I stared, my eyes were hypnotized by that saturnine host,
When with a start that shook my heart I saw—I saw a ghost.
As in foggèd glass I saw him pass, and peer at me and grin—
A man I knew, a man I *slew*, Prince Boris Mazarin.

Now do not think because I drink I love the flowing bowl;
But liquor kills remorse and stills the anguish of the soul.
And there's so much I would forget, stark horrors I have seen,
Faces and forms that haunt me yet, like shadows on a screen.
And of these sights that mar my nights the ghastliest by far
Is the death of Boris Mazarin, that soldier of the Czar.

A mighty nobleman was he; we took him by surprise;
His mother, son and daughters three we slew before his eyes.
We tortured him, with jibes and threats; then mad for glut of
    gore,

Upon our reeking bayonets we nailed him to the door.
But he defied us to the last, crying: "O carrion crew!
I'd die with joy could I destroy a hundred dogs like you."
I thrust my sword into his throat; the blade was gay with blood;
We flung him to his castle moat, and stamped him in its mud.
That mighty Cossack of the Don was dead with all his race. . . .
And now I saw him coming on, dire vengeance in his face.
(Or was it some fantastic dream of my besotted brain?)
He looked at me with eyes a-gleam, the man whom I had slain.
He looked and bade me follow him; I could not help but go;
I joined the throng that passed along, so sorrowful and slow.
I followed with a sense of doom that shadow gaunt and grim;
Into the bowels of the Tomb I followed, followed him.

The light within was weird and dim, and icy cold the air;
My brow was wet with bitter sweat, I stumbled on the stair.
I tried to cry; my throat was dry; I sought to grip his arm;
For well I knew this man I slew was there to do us harm.
Lo! he was walking by my side, his fingers clutched my own,
This man I knew so well had died, his hand was naked bone.
His face was like a skull, his eyes were caverns of decay . . .
And so we came to the crystal frame where lonely Lenin lay.

Without a sound we shuffled round. I sought to make a sign,
But like a vice his hand of ice was biting into mine.
With leaden pace around the place where Lenin lies at rest,
We slouched, I saw his bony claw go fumbling to his breast.
With ghastly grin he groped within, and tore his robe apart,
And from the hollow of his ribs he drew his blackened
    heart. . . .
Ah no! Oh God! A *bomb*, a BOMB! And as I shrieked with dread,
With fiendish cry he raised it high, and . . . swung at Lenin's
    head.

Oh I was blinded by the flash and deafened by the roar,
And in a mess of bloody mash I wallowed on the floor.
Then Alps of darkness on me fell, and when I saw again
The leprous light 'twas in a cell, and I was racked with pain;
And ringèd round by shapes of gloom, who hoped that I would
     die;
For of the crowd that crammed the Tomb the sole to live was I.
They told me I had dreamed a dream that must not be revealed,
But by their eyes of evil gleam I knew my doom was sealed.

I need not tell how from my cell in Lubianka gaol,
I broke away, but listen, here's the point of all my tale. . . .
Outside the "Gay Pay Oo" none knew of that grim scene of
     gore;
They closed the Tomb, and then they threw it open as before.
And there was Lenin, stiff and still, a symbol and a sign,
And rancid races come to thrill and wonder at his Shrine;
And hold the thought: if Lenin rot the Soviets will decay;
So there he sleeps and calm he keeps his watch and ward for aye.
Yet if you pass that frame of glass, peer closely at his phiz,
So stern and firm it mocks the worm, it looks like wax . . .
     and is.
They tell you he's a mummy—don't you make that bright mis-
     take:
I tell you—he's a dummy; aye, a fiction and a fake.
This eye beheld the bloody bomb that bashed him on the bean.
I heard the crash, I saw the flash, yet . . . there he lies serene.
And by the roar that rocked the Tomb I ask: how could that be?
But if you doubt that deed of doom, just go yourself and see.
You think I'm mad, or drunk, or both. . . . Well, I don't care
     a damn:
I tell you this: their Lenin is a waxen, show-case SHAM.

Such was the yarn he handed me,
Down there in Casey's Bar,
That Rooshun bug with the scrambled mug
From the Land of the Commissar.
It may be true, I leave it you
To figger out how far.

MAIDS IN MAY

THREE maids there were in meadow bright,
The eldest less than seven;
Their eyes were dancing with delight,
And innocent as Heaven.

Wild flowers they wound with tender glee,
Their cheeks with rapture rosy;
All radiant they smiled at me,
When I besought a posy.

So one gave me a columbine,
And one a poppy brought me;
The tiniest, with eyes ashine,
A simple daisy sought me.

And as I went my sober way,
I heard their careless laughter;
Their hearts too happy with to-day
To care for what comes after.

. . . . . .

That's long ago; they're gone, all three,
To walk amid the shadows;
Forgotten is their lyric glee
In still and sunny meadows.

For Columbine loved life too well,
And went adventure faring;

And sank into the pit of hell,
And passed but little caring.

While Poppy was a poor man's wife,
And children had a-plenty;
And went, worn out with toil and strife
When she was five-and-twenty.

And Daisy died while yet a child,
As fragile blossoms perish,
When Winter winds are harsh and wild,
With none to shield and cherish.

Ah me! How Fate is dark and dour
To little Children of the Poor.

THE BALLAD OF CASEY'S BILLY-GOAT

You've heard of "Casey at The Bat,"
And "Casey's Tabble Dote";
But now it's time
To write the rhyme
Of "Casey's Billy-goat."

Pat Casey had a billy-goat he gave the name of Shamus,
Because it was (the neighbours said) a national disgrace.
And sure enough that animal was eminently famous
For masticating every rag of laundry round the place.
From shirts to skirts prodigiously it proved its powers of chew-
    ing;
The question of digestion seemed to matter not at all;
But you'll agree, I think with me, its limit of misdoing
Was reached the day it swallowed Missis Rooney's ould red
    shawl.

Now Missis Annie Rooney was a winsome widow woman,
And many a bouncing boy had sought to make her change her
    name;
And living just across the way 'twas surely only human
A lonesome man like Casey should be wishfully the same.
So every Sunday, shaved and shined, he'd make the fine occa-
    sion
To call upon the lady, and she'd take his hat and coat;
And supping tea it seemed that she might yield to his persuasion,
But alas! he hadn't counted on that devastating goat.

For Shamus loved his master with a deep and dumb devotion,
And everywhere that Casey went that goat would want to go;

And though I cannot analyse a quadruped's emotion,
They said the baste was jealous, and I reckon it was so.
For every time that Casey went to call on Missis Rooney,
Beside the gate the goat would wait with woefulness intense;
Until one day it chanced that they were fast becoming spooney,
When Shamus spied that ould red shawl a-flutter on the fence.

Now Missis Rooney loved that shawl beyond all rhyme or
    reason,
And maybe 'twas an heirloom or a cherished souvenir;
For judging by the way she wore it season after season,
It might have been as precious as a product of Cashmere.
So Shamus strolled towards it, and no doubt the colour pleased
    him,
For he biffed it and he sniffed it, as most any goat might do;
Then his melancholy vanished as a sense of hunger seized him,
And he wagged his tail with rapture as he started in to chew.

"Begorrah! you're a daisy," said the doting Mister Casey
To the blushing Widow Rooney as they parted at the door.
"Wid yer tinderness an' tazin' sure ye've set me heart a-blazin',
And I dread the day I'll nivver see me Annie anny more."
"Go on now wid yer blarney," said the widow softly sighing;
And she went to pull his whiskers, when dismay her bosom
    smote. . . .
Her ould red shawl! 'Twas missin' where she'd left it bravely
    drying—
Then she saw it disappearing—down the neck of Casey's goat.

Fiercely flamed her Irish temper. "Look!" says she, "the thavin'
    divvle!
Sure he's made me shawl his supper. Well, I hope it's to his taste;
But excuse me, Mister Casey, if I seem to be oncivil,

For I'll nivver wed a man wid such a misbegotten baste."
So she slammed the door and left him in a state of consternation,
And he couldn't understand it, till he saw that grinning goat;
Then with eloquence he cussed it, and his final fulmination
Was a poem of profanity impossible to quote.

So blasting goats and petticoats, and feeling downright sinful,
Despairfully he wandered in to Shinnigan's shebeen;
And straightway he proceeded to absorb a mighty skinful
Of the deadliest variety of Shinnigan's potheen.
And when he started homeward it was in the early morning,
But Shamus followed faithfully, a yard behind his back;
Then Casey slipped and stumbled, and without the slightest
      warning
Like a lump of lead he tumbled—right across the railway track.

And there he lay, serenely, and defied the powers to budge him,
Reposing like a baby, with his head upon a rail;
But Shamus seemed unhappy, and from time to time would
      nudge him,
Though his prods of protestation were without the least avail.
Then to that goatish mind, maybe, a sense of fell disaster
Came stealing like a spectre in the dim and dreary dawn;
For his bleat of warning blended with the snoring of his master
In a chorus of calamity—but Casey slumbered on.

Yet oh, that goat was troubled, for his efforts were redoubled;
Now he tugged at Casey's whisker, now he nibbled at his ear;
Now he shook him by the shoulder, and with fear becoming
      bolder,
He bellowed like a fog-horn, but the sleeper did not hear.
Then up and down the railway line he scampered for assistance;
But anxiously he hurried back and sought with tug and strain

To pull his master off the track . . . when sudden! in the distance
He heard the roar and rumble of the fast approaching train.

Did Shamus faint and falter? No, he stood there stark and splendid.
True, his tummy was distended, but he gave his horns a toss.
By them his goathood's honour would be gallantly defended,
And if their valour failed him—he would perish with his boss.
So dauntlessly he lowered his head, and ever clearer, clearer,
He heard the throb and thunder of the Continental Mail.
He would face that mighty monster. It was coming nearer, nearer;
He would fight it, he would smite it, but he'd never show his tail.

Can you see that hirsute hero, standing there in tragic glory?
Can you hear the Pullman porters shrieking horror to the sky?
No, you can't; because my story has no end so grim and gory,
For Shamus did not perish and his master did not die.
At this very present moment Casey swaggers hale and hearty,
And Shamus strolls beside him with a bright bell at his throat;
While the recent Missis Rooney is the gayest of the party,
For now she's Missis Casey and she's crazy for that goat.

You're wondering what happened? Well, you know that truth is stranger
Than the wildest brand of fiction, so I'll tell you without shame. . . .
There was Shamus and his master in the face of awful danger,
And the giant locomotive dashing down in smoke and flame. . . .
What power on earth could save them? Yet a golden inspiration
To gods and goats alike may come, so in that brutish brain

A thought was born—*the ould red shawl.* . . . Then rearing
  with elation,
Like lightning Shamus *threw it up*—AND FLAGGED AND STOPPED
  THE TRAIN.

THE SMOKING FROG

THREE men I saw beside a bar,
Regarding o'er their bottle,
A frog who smoked a rank cigar
They'd jammed within its throttle.

A Pasha frog it must have been,
So big it was and bloated;
And from its lips the nicotine
In graceful festoon floated.

And while the trio jeered and joked,
As if it quite enjoyed it,
Impassively it smoked and smoked,
(It could not well avoid it).

A ring of fire its lips were nigh,
Yet it seemed all unwitting;
It could not spit, like you and I,
Who've learned the art of spitting.

It did not wink, it did not shrink,
As there serene it squatted;
Its eyes were clear, it did not fear
The fate the Gods allotted.

It squatted there with calm sublime,
Amid their cruel guying;
Grave as a god, and all the time
It knew that it was dying.

And somehow then it seemed to me
These men expectorating,
Were infinitely less than he,
The dumb thing they were baiting.

It seemed to say, despite their jokes:
"This is my hour of glory.
It isn't every frog that smokes:
My name will live in story."

Before its nose the smoke arose;
The flame grew nigher, nigher;
And then I saw its bright eyes close
Beside that ring of fire.

They turned it on its warty back,
From off its bloated belly;
Its legs jerked out, then dangled slack;
It quivered like a jelly.

And then the fellows went away,
Contented with their joking;
But even as in death it lay,
The frog continued smoking.

Life's like a lighted fag, thought I;
We smoke it stale; then after
Death turns our belly to the sky:
The Gods must have their laughter.

MADAME LA MARQUISE

SAID Hongray de la Glaciere unto his proud Papa:
"I want to take a wife, *mon Père*." The Marquis laughed: "Ha!
Ha!
And whose, my son?" he slyly said; but Hongray with a frown
Cried: "Fi! Papa, I mean—to wed. I want to settle down."
The Marquis de la Glaciere responded with a smile:
"You're young, my boy; I much prefer that you should wait
awhile."
But Hongray sighed: "I cannot wait, for I am twenty-four;
And I have met my blessed fate: I worship, I adore.
Such beauty, grace and charm has she, I'm sure you will ap-
prove,
For if I live a century none other can I love."
"I have no doubt," the Marquis shrugged, "that she's a proper
pet;
But has she got a decent *dot*, and is she of our set?"
"Her *dot*," said Hongray, "will suffice; her family you know.
The girl with whom I fain would splice is Mirabelle du Veau."

What made the Marquis start and stare, and clutch his perfumed
beard?
Why did he stagger to a chair, and murmur: "As I feared"?
Dilated were his eyes with dread, and in a voice of woe
He wailed: "My son, you cannot wed with Mirabelle du Veau."
"Why not? my Parent," Hongray cried. "Her name's without a
slur.
Why should you look so horrified that I should wed with her?"
The Marquis groaned: "Unhappy lad! Forget her if you can,
And see in your respected Dad a miserable man."

664

"What is the matter? I repeat," said Hongray growing hot.
"She's witty, pretty, rich and sweet. . . . Then—*mille diables!*
—what?"
The Marquis moaned: "Alas! that I your dreams of bliss should
banish;
It happened in the days gone-by, when I was Don Juanish.
Her mother was your mother's friend, and we were much to-
gether.
Ah well! You know how such things end. (I blame it on the
weather.)
We had a very sultry spell. One day, *mon Dieu!* I kissed her.
My son, you can't wed Mirabelle. She is . . . *she is your sister.*"

So broken-hearted Hongray went and roamed the world around,
Till hunting in the Occident forgetfulness he found.
Then quite recovered, he returned to the paternal nest,
Until one day, with brow that burned, the Marquis he ad-
dressed:
"Felicitate me, Father mine; my brain is in a whirl;
For I have found the mate divine, the one, the perfect girl.
She's healthy, wealthy, witching, wise, with loveliness serene.
Ah! Proud am I to win a prize, half angel and half queen."
" 'Tis time to wed," the Marquis said. "You must be twenty-
seven.
But who is she whose lot may be to make your life a heaven?"
"A friend of childhood," Hongray cried. "For whom regard
you feel.
The maid I fain would make my bride is Raymonde de la Veal."

The Marquis de la Glaciere collapsed upon the floor,
And all the words he uttered were: "Forgive me, I implore.
My sins are heavy on my head. Profound remorse I feel.
My son, you simply cannot wed with Raymonde de la Veal."

Then Hongray spoke with voice that broke, and corrugated
   brow:
"Inform me, Sir, why you demur. What is the matter now?"
The Marquis wailed: "My wicked youth! Ah! how it gives me
   pain.
But let me tell the awful truth, my agony explain. . . .
A cursed Casanova I; a finished flirt her mother;
And so alas! it came to pass we fell for one another.
Our lives were blent in bliss and joy. The sequel you may
   gather:
You cannot wed Raymonde, my boy, because I am . . . *her
   father.*"

Again sore-stricken Hongray fled, and sought his grief to
   smother,
And as he writhed upon his bed to him there came his Mother.
The Marquise de la Glaciere was snowy-haired and frigid.
Her wintry features chiselled were, her manner stiff and rigid.
The pride of race was in her face, her bearing high and stately,
And sinking down by Hongray's side she spoke to him sedately:
"What ails you so, my precious child? What thongs of sorrow
   smite you?
Why are your eyes so wet and wild? Come, tell me, I invite
   you."
"Ah! if I told you, Mother dear," said Hongray with a shiver,
"Another's honour would, I fear, be in the soup forever."
"Nay, trust," she begged, "my only boy, the fond Mama who
   bore you.
Perhaps I may your grief alloy. Please tell me, I implore you."

And so his story Hongray told, in accents choked and muffled.
The Marquise listened, calm and cold, her visage quite unruffled.
He told of Mirabelle du Veau, his agony revealing.

For Raymonde de la Veal his woe was quite beyond concealing.
And still she sat without a word, her look so high and haughty,
You'd ne'er have thought it was her lord who had behaved so naughty.
Then Hongray finished up: "For life my hopes are doomed to slaughter;
For if I choose another wife, she's *sure* to be his daughter."
The Marquise rose. "Cheer up," said she, "the last word is not spoken.
A Mother cannot sit and see her boy's heart rudely broken.
So dry your tears and calm your fears; no longer need you tarry;
To-day your bride you may decide, to-morrow you may marry.
Yes, you may wed with Mirabelle, or Raymonde if you'd rather. . . .
For I as well the truth may tell . . . *Papa is not your father*."

BEACHCOMBER

WHEN I have come with happy heart to sixty years and ten,
I'll buy a boat and sail away upon a summer sea;
And in a little lonely isle that's far and far from men,
In peace and praise I'll spend the days the Gods allow to me.
For I am weary of a strife so pitiless and vain;
And in a far and fairy isle, bewilderingly bright,
I'll learn to know the leap and glow of rapture once again,
And welcome every living dawn with wonder and delight.

And there I'll build a swan-white house above the singing foam,
With brooding eaves, where joyously rich roses climb and cling;
With crotons in a double row, like wine and honeycomb,
And flame trees dripping golden rain, and palms pavilioning
And there I'll let the wind and wave do what they will with me;
And I will dwell unto the end with loveliness and joy;
And drink from out the crystal spring, and eat from off the tree,
As simple as a savage is, as careless as a boy.

For I have come to think that Life's a lamentable tale,
And all we break our hearts to win is little worth our while;
For fame and fortune in the end are comfortless and stale,
And it is best to dream and rest upon a radiant isle.
So I'll blot out the bitter years of sufferance and scorn,
And I'll forget the fear and fret, the poverty and pain;
And in a shy and secret isle I'll be a man newborn,
And fashion life to heart's desire, and seek my soul again.

For when I come with happy heart to sixty years and ten,
I fondly hope the best of life will yet remain to me;

And so I'll burn my foolish books and break my futile pen,
And seek a tranced and tranquil isle, that dreams eternally.
I'll turn my back on all the world, I'll bid my friends adieu;
Unto the blind I'll leave behind what gold I have to give;
And in a jewelled solitude I'll mould my life anew,
And nestling close to Nature's heart, I'll learn at last . . . to
    live.

JOBSON OF THE *STAR*

WITHIN a pub that's off the Strand and handy to the bar,
With pipe in mouth and mug in hand sat Jobson of the *Star*.
"Come, sit ye down, ye wond'ring wight, and have a yarn," says
  he.
"I can't," says I, "because to-night I'm off to Tripoli;
To Tripoli and Trebizond and Timbuctoo mayhap,
Or any magic name beyond I find upon the map.
I go the errant trail to try, to clutch the skirts of Chance,
To make once more before I die the gesture of Romance."
Then Jobson yawned above his jug, and rumbled: "Is that so?
Well, anyway, sit down, you mug, and drink before you go."

Now Jobson is a chum of mine, and in a dusty den,
Within the street that's known as Fleet, he wields a wicked pen.
And every night it's his delight, above the fleeting show,
To castigate the living Great, and keep the lowly low.
And all there is to know he knows, for unto him is spurred
The knowledge of the knowledge of the Thing That Has Oc-
  curred.
And all that is to hear he hears, for to his ear is whirled
The echo of the echo of the Sound That Shocks The World.
Let Revolutions rage and rend, and Kingdoms rise and fall,
There Jobson sits and smokes and spits, and writes about it all.

And so we jawed a little while on matters small and great;
He told me with his cynic smile of grave affairs of state.
Of princes, peers and presidents, and folk beyond my ken,
He spoke as you and I might speak of ordinary men.
For Jobson is a scribe of worth, and has respect for none,

And all the mighty ones of earth are targets for his fun.
So when I said good-bye, says he, with his satyric leer:
"Too bad to go, when life is so damned interesting here.
The Government rides for a fall, and things are getting hot.
You'd better stick around, old pal; you'll miss an awful lot."

Yet still I went and wandered far, by secret ways and wide.
Adventure was the shining star I took to be my guide.
For fifty moons I followed on, and every moon was sweet,
And lit as if for me alone the trail before my feet.
From cities desolate with doom my moons swam up and set,
On tower and temple, tent and tomb, on mosque and minaret.
To heights that hailed the dawn I scaled, by cliff and chasm
    sheer;
To far Cathay I found my way, and fabulous Kashmir.
From camel-back I traced the track that bars the barren *bled*,
And leads to hell-and-blazes, and I followed where it led.
Like emeralds in sapphire set, and ripe for human rape,
I passed with passionate regret the Islands of Escape.
With death I clinched a time or two, and gave the brute a fall.
Hunger and cold and thirst I knew, yet . . . how I loved it all!
Then suddenly I seemed to tire of trekking up and down,
And longed for some domestic fire, and sailed for London Town.

And in a pub that's off the Strand, and handy to the bar,
With pipe in mouth and mug in hand sat Jobson of the *Star*
"Hullo!" says he. "Come, take a pew, and tell me where you've
    been.
It seems to me that lately you have vanished from the scene."
"I've been," says I, "to Kordovan and Kong and Calabar,
To Sarawak and Samarkand, to Ghat and Bolivar;
To Caracas and Guayaquil, to Lhasa and Pekin,
To Brahmaputra and Brazil, to Bagdad and Benin.

I've sailed the Black Sea and the White, the Yellow and the Red,
The Sula and the Celebes, the Bering and the Dead.
I've climbed on Chimborazo, and I've wandered in Peru;
I've camped on Kinchinjunga, and I've crossed the Great Kar-
roo.
I've drifted on the Hoang-ho, the Nile and Amazon;
I've swam the Tiber and the Po . . ." thus I was going on,
When Jobson yawned above his beer, and rumbled: "Is that
so? . . .
It's been so damned exciting here, too bad you had to go.
We've had the devil of a slump; the market's gone to pot;
You should have stuck around, you chump, you've missed an
awful lot."

.   .   .   .

In haggard lands where ages brood, on plains burnt out and dim,
I broke the bread of brotherhood with ruthless men and grim.
By ways untrod I walked with God, by parched and bitter path;
In deserts dim I talked with Him, and learned to know His
Wrath.
But in a pub that's off the Strand, sits Jobson every night,
And tells me what a fool I am, and maybe he is right.
For Jobson is a man of stamp, and proud of him am I;
And I am just a bloody tramp, and will be till I die.

BASTARD

The very skies were black with shame,
As near my moment drew;
The very hour before you came
I felt I hated you.

But now I see how fair you are,
How divine your eyes,
It seems I step upon a star
And leap to Paradise.

What care I who your father was:
('Twere better not to know);
You're mine and mine alone because
I love and love you so.

What though you only bear my name,
I hold my head on high;
For none shall have a right to claim
A right to you but I.

Because I've borne a human life,
I'm worthier, I know,
Than those who flaunt the name of wife,
And have no seed to show.

I have fulfilled, I think with joy,
My woman's destiny;
And glad am I you are a boy,
For you will fight for me.

And maybe there will come a day
You'll bear a famous name,
And men will be ashamed to say:
"He was a child of shame."

A day will dawn, divinely free,
With love in every breast,
When every child will welcome be,
And every mother blest.

When every woman, wed or no,
Will deem her highest good
On grateful mankind to bestow
The Gift of Motherhood.

BESSIE'S BOIL

A LANCASHIRE BALLAD

SAYS I to my Missis: "Ba goom, lass! you've something, I see, on
    your mind."
Says she: "You are right, Sam, I've something. It 'appens it's on
    me be'ind.
A Boil as 'ud make Job be jealous. It 'urts me no end when I sit."
Says I: "Go to 'ospittel, Missis. They might 'ave to coot it a bit."
Says she: "I just 'ate to be showin' the part of me person it's at."
Says I: "Don't be fussy; them doctors sees sights far more 'orrid
    than that."

So Missis goes off togged up tasty, and there at the 'ospittel door
They tells 'er to see the 'ouse Doctor, 'oose office is Room
    Thirty-four.
So she 'unts up and down till she finds it, and knocks and a voice
    says: "Come in,"
And there is a 'andsome young feller, in white from 'is 'eels to
    'is chin.
"I've got a big boil," says my Missis. "It 'urts me for fair when I
    sit,
And Sam (that's me 'usband) 'as asked me to ask you to coot it
    a bit."
Then blushin' she plucks up her courage, and bravely she shows
    'im the place,
And 'e gives it a proper inspection, wi' a 'eap o' surprise on 'is
    face.
Then 'e says wi' an accent o' Scotland: "Whit ye hae is a bile,
    Ah can feel,

But ye'd better consult the heid Dockter; they caw him Pro-
fessor O'Neil.

He's special for biles and carbuncles. Ye'll find him in Room
Sixty-three.

No charge, Ma'am. It's been a rale pleasure. Jist tell him ye're
comin' from me."

So Missis she thanks 'im politely, and 'unts up and down as
before,

Till she comes to a big 'andsome room with "Professor O'Neil"
on the door.

Then once more she plucks up her courage, and knocks, and a
voice says: "All right."

So she enters, and sees a fat feller wi' whiskers, all togged up in
white.

"I've got a big boil," says my Missis, "and if ye will kindly
permit,

I'd like for to 'ave you inspect it; it 'urts me like all when I sit."

So blushin' as red as a beet-root she 'astens to show 'im the spot,

And 'e says wi' a look o' amazement: "Sure, Ma'am, it must hurrt
ye a lot."

Then 'e puts on 'is specs to regard it, and finally says wi' a frown:

"I'll bet it's as sore as the divvle, espacially whin ye sit down.

I think it's a case for the Surgeon; ye'd better consult Doctor
Hoyle.

I've no hisitation in sayin' yer boil is a hill of a boil."

So Missis she thanks 'im for sayin' her boil is a hill of a boil,

And 'unts all around till she comes on a door that is marked:
"Doctor Hoyle."

But by now she 'as fair got the wind up, and trembles in every
limb;

But she thinks: "After all, 'e's a Doctor. Ah moosn't be bashful
    wi' 'im."

She's made o' good stoof is the Missis, so she knocks and a voice
    says: " 'Oos there?"

"It's me," says ma Bessie, an' enters a room which is spacious and
    bare.

And a wise-lookin' old feller greets 'er, and 'e too is togged up
    in white.

"It's the room where they coot ye," thinks Bessie; and shakes like
    a jelly wi' fright.

"Ah got a big boil," begins Missis, "and if ye are sure you don't
    mind,

I'd like ye to see it a moment. It 'urts me, because it's be'ind."

So thinkin' she'd best get it over, she 'astens to show 'im the
    place,

And 'e stares at 'er kindo surprised like, an' gets very red in the
    face.

But 'e looks at it most conscientious, from every angle of view,

Then 'e says wi' a shrug o' 'is shoulders: "Pore Lydy, I'm sorry
    for you.

It wants to be cut, but you should 'ave a medical bloke to do that.

Sye, why don't yer go to the *'orsespittel*, where all the *Doctors*
    is at?

Ye see, Ma'am, this part o' the buildin' is closed on account o'
    repairs;

Us fellers is only the pynters, a-pyntin' the 'alls and the stairs."

FIVE-PER-CENT

Because I have ten thousand pounds I sit upon my stern,
And leave my living tranquilly for other folks to earn.
For in some procreative way that isn't very clear,
Ten thousand pounds will breed, they say, five hundred every
 year.
So as I have a healthy hate of economic strife,
I mean to stand aloof from it the balance of my life.
And yet with sympathy I see the grimy son of toil,
And heartily congratulate the tiller of the soil.
I like the miner in the mine, the sailor on the sea,
Because up to five hundred pounds they sail and mine for me.
For me their toil is taxed unto that annual extent,
According to the holy shibboleth of Five-per-Cent.

So get ten thousand pounds, my friend, in any way you can,
And leave your future welfare to the noble Working Man.
He'll buy you suits of Harris tweed, an Airedale and a car;
Your golf clubs and your morning *Times*, your whisky and
 cigar.
He'll cosily install you in a cottage by a stream,
With every modern comfort, and a garden that's a dream.
Or if your tastes be urban, he'll provide you with a flat,
Secluded from the clamour of the proletariat.
With pictures, music, easy chairs, a table of good cheer,
A chap can manage nicely on five hundred pounds a year.
And though around you painful signs of industry you view,
Why should you work when you can make your money work
 for you?

So I'll get down upon my knees and bless the Working Man,
Who offers me a life of ease through all my mortal span;
Whose loins are lean to make me fat, who slaves to keep me free,
Who dies before his prime to let me round the century;
Whose wife and children toil in turn until their strength is
      spent,
That I may live in idleness upon my five-per-cent.
And if at times they curse me, why should I feel any blame?
For in my place I know that they would do the very same.
Aye, though they hoist a flag that's red on Sunday afternoon,
Just offer them ten thousand pounds and see them change their
      tune.
So I'll enjoy my dividends and live my life with zest,
And bless the mighty men who first—*invented Interest.*

SECURITY

THERE once was a limpet puffed with pride
Who said to the ribald sea:
"It isn't I who cling to the rock,
It's the rock who clings to me;
It's the silly old rock who hugs me tight,
Because he loves me so;
And though I struggle with all my might,
He will not let me go."

Then said the sea, who hates the rock
That defies him night and day:
"You want to be free—well, leave it to me,
I'll help you to get away.
I know such a beautiful silver beach,
Where blissfully you may bide;
Shove off to-night when the moon is bright,
And I'll swing you there on my tide."

"I'd like to go," said the limpet low,
"But what's a silver beach?"
"It's sand," said the sea, "bright baby rocks,
And you shall be lord of each."
"Righto!" said the limpet; "life allures,
And a rover I would be."
So greatly bold she slacked her hold
And launched on the laughing sea.

But when she got to the gelid deep
Where the waters swish and swing,

She began to know with a sense of woe
That a limpet's lot is to cling.
But she couldn't cling to a jelly fish,
Or clutch at a wastrel weed,
So she raised a cry as the waves went by,
But the waves refused to heed.

Then when she came to the glaucous deep
Where the congers coil and leer,
The flesh in her shell began to creep,
And she shrank in utter fear.
It was good to reach that silver beach,
That gleamed in the morning light,
Where a shining band of the silver sand
Looked up with a welcome bright.

Looked up with a smile that was full of guile,
Called up through the crystal blue:
"Each one of us is a baby rock,
And we want to cling to you."
Then the heart of the limpet leaped with joy,
For she hated the waters wide;
So down she sank to the sandy bank
That clung to her under-side.

That clung so close she couldn't breathe,
So fierce she fought to be free;
But the silver sand couldn't understand,
While above her laughed the sea.
Then to each wave that wimpled past
She cried in her woe and pain:
"Oh take me back, let me rivet fast
To my steadfast rock again."

She cried till she roused a taxi-crab
Who gladly gave her a ride;
But I grieve to say in his crabby way
He insisted she sit inside. . . .
So if of the limpet breed ye be,
Beware life's brutal shock;
Don't take the chance of the changing sea,
But—*cling like hell to your rock.*

LONGEVITY

I watched one day a parrot grey—'twas in a barber shop.
"Cuckold!" he cried, until I sighed: "You feathered devil, stop!"
Then balefully he looked at me, and slid along his perch,
With sneering eye that seemed to pry my very soul to search.
So fierce, so bold, so grim, so cold, so *agate* was his stare:
And then that bird I thought I heard this sentiment declare:—

"As it appears, a hundred years a parrot may survive,
When you are gone I'll sit upon this perch and be alive.
In this same spot I'll drop my crot, and crack my sunflower
    seeds,
And cackle loud when in a shroud you rot beneath the weeds.
I'll carry on when carrion you lie beneath the yew;
With claw and beak my grub I'll seek when grubs are seeking
    you."

"Foul fowl!" said I, "don't prophesy. I'll jolly well contrive
That when I rot in bone-yard lot *you* cease to be alive."
So I bespoke that barber bloke: "Joe, here's a five-pound note.
It's crisp and new, and yours if you will slice that parrot's
    throat."
"In part," says he, "I must agree, for poor I be in pelf.
With right good will I'll take your bill, but—cut his throat
    yourself."

So it occurred I took that bird to my ancestral hall,
And there he sat and sniggered at the portraits on the wall.
I sought to cut his wind-pipe but he gave me such a peck,
So cross was I, I swore I'd try to wring his blasted neck;

When shrill he cried: "It's *parrotcide* what you propose to do;
For every time you make a rhyme you're just a parrot too."

Said I: "It's true. I bow to you. Poor parrots are we all."
And now I sense with reverence the wisdom in his poll.
For every time I want a rhyme he seems to find the word;
In any doubt he helps me out—a most amazing bird.
This line that lies before your eyes he helped me to indite;
I sling the ink but often think it's he who ought to write.
It's he who should in mystic mood concoct poetic screeds,
And I who ought to drop my crot and crackle sunflower seeds.

A parrot nears a hundred years (or so the legend goes),
So were I he this century I might see to its close.
Then I might swing within my ring while revolutions roar,
And watch a world to ruin hurled—and find it all a bore.
As upside-down I cling and clown, I might with parrot eyes
Blink blandly when exalted men are moulding Paradise.
New Christs might die, while grimly I would croak and carry
    on,
Till gnarled and old I should behold the year TWO THOUSAND
    dawn.

But what a fate! How I should hate upon my perch to sit,
And nothing do to make anew a world for angels fit.
No, better far, though feeble are my lyric notes and flat,
Be dead and done than anyone who lives a life like that.
Though critic-scarred a humble bard I feel I'd rather be,
Than flap and flit and shriek and spit through all a century.

So feathered friend, until the end you may divide my den,
And make a mess, which (more or less) I clean up now and then.
But I prefer the doom to share of dead and gone compeers,
Than parrot be, and live to see *ten times* a hundred years.

RESIGNATION

I'D hate to be a centipede (of legs I've only two),
For if new trousers I should need (as oftentimes I do),
The bill would come to such a lot 'twould tax an Astorbilt,
Or else I'd have to turn a Scot and caper in a kilt.

I'm jolly glad I haven't got a neck like a giraffe.
I'd want to tie it in a knot and shorten it by half.
Or, as I wear my collars high, how laundry men would gloat!
And what a lot of beer I'd buy to lubricate my throat!

I'd hate to be a goldfish, snooping round a crystal globe,
A naughty little bold fish, that disdains chemise or robe.
The public stare I couldn't bear, if naked as a stone,
And when my toilet I prepare, I'd rather be alone.

I'd hate to be an animal, an insect or a fish.
To be the least like bird or beast I've not the slightest wish.
It's best, I find, to be resigned, and stick to Nature's plan:
Content am I to live and die, just—Ordinary MAN.

PRIVACY

Oʜ you who are shy of the popular eye,
(Though most of us seek to survive it),
Just think of the goldfish who wanted to die
Because she could never be private.
There are pebbles and reeds for aquarium needs
Of eel and of pike who are bold fish;
But who gives a thought to a sheltering spot
For the sensitive soul of a goldfish?

So the poor little thing swam round in a ring,
In a globe of a crystalline crudity;
Swam round and swam round, but no refuge she found
From the public display of her nudity;
No weedy retreat for a cloister discreet,
From the eye of the mob to exempt her;
Can you wonder she paled, and her appetite failed,
Till even a fly couldn't tempt her?

I watched with dismay as she faded away;
Each day she grew slimmer and slimmer.
From an amber that burned, to a silver she turned
Then swiftly was dimmer and dimmer.
No longer she gleamed, like a spectre she seemed,
One morning I anxiously sought her:
I only could stare—she no longer was there . . .
She'd simply dissolved in the water.

So when you behold bright fishes of gold,
In globes of immaculate purity;

Just think how they'd be more contented and free
If you gave them a little obscurity.
And you who make laws, get busy because
You can brighten the lives of untold fish,
If its sadness you note, and a measure promote
To Ensure Private Life For The Goldfish.

MATERNITY

THERE once was a Square, such a square little Square,
And he loved a trim Triangle;
But she was a flirt and around her skirt
Vainly she made him dangle.
Oh he wanted to wed and he had no dread
Of domestic woes and wrangles;
For he thought that his fate was to procreate
Cute little Squares and Triangles.

Now it happened one day on that geometric way
There swaggered a big bold Cube,
With a haughty stare and he made that Square
Have the air of a perfect boob;
To his solid spell the Triangle fell,
And she thrilled with love's sweet sickness,
For she took delight in his breadth and height—
But how she adored his thickness!

So that poor little Square just died of despair,
For his love he could not strangle;
While the bold Cube led to the bridal bed
That cute and acute Triangle.
The Square's sad lot she has long forgot,
And his passionate pretensions . . .
For she dotes on her kids— Oh such cute *Pyramids*
In a world of three dimensions.

VIRGINITY

My mother she had children five and four are dead and gone;
While I, least worthy to survive, persist in living on.
She looks at me, I must confess, sometimes with spite and bitter-
ness.

My mother is three-score and ten, while I am forty-three.
You don't know how it hurts me when we go somewhere to tea,
And people tell her on the sly we look like sisters, she and I.

It hurts to see her secret glee; but most, because it's true.
Sometimes I think she thinks that she looks younger of the two.
Oh as I gently take her arm, how I would love to do her harm!

For ever since I came from school she put it in my head,
I was a weakling and a fool, a "born old maid" she said.
"You'll always stay at home," sighed she, "and keep your Mother
company."

Oh pity is a bitter brew; I've drunk it to the lees;
For there is little else to do but do my best to please:
My life has been so little worth I curse the hour she gave me
birth.

I curse the hour she gave me breath, who never wished me wife;
My happiest day will be the death of her who gave me life;
I hate her for the life she gave: I hope to dance upon her grave.

She's wearing roses in her hat; I wince to hear her say:
"Poor Alice this, poor Alice that," she drains my joy away.
It seems to brace her up that she can pity, pity, pity me.

You'll see us walking in the street, with careful step and slow;
And people often say: "How sweet!" as arm in arm we go.
Like chums we never are apart—yet oh the hatred in my heart!

My chest is weak, and I might be (O God!) the first to go.
For her what triumph that would be—she thinks of it, I know.
To outlive all her kith and kin—how she would glow beneath
  her skin!

She says she will not make her Will, until she takes to bed;
She little thinks if thoughts could kill, to-morrow she'd be
  dead. . . .

*"Please come to breakfast, Mother dear; your coffee will be
  cold, I fear."*

SENSIBILITY

I

ONCE, when a boy, *I killed a cat.*
I guess it's just because of that
A cat evokes my tenderness,
And takes so kindly my caress.
For with a rich, resonant purr
It sleeks an arch of ardent fur
So vibrantly against my shin;
And as I tickle tilted chin
And rub the roots of velvet ears
Its tail in undulation rears.
Then tremoring with all its might,
In blissful sensuous delight,
It looks aloft with lambent eyes,
Mystic, Egyptianly wise,
And O so eloquently tries
In every fibre to express
Consummate trust and friendliness.

II

I think the longer that we live
The more do we grow sensitive
Of hurt and harm to man and beast,
And learn to suffer at the least
Surmise of other's suffering;
Till pity, like an eager spring
Wells up, and we are over-fain
To vibrate to the chords of pain.

For look you—after three-score years
I see with anguish nigh to tears
That starveling cat so sudden still
I set my terrier to kill.
Great, golden memories pale away,
But that unto my dying day
Will haunt and haunt me horribly.
Why, even my poor dog felt shame
And shrank away as if the blame
Of that poor mangled mother-cat
Would ever lie at *his* doormat.

III

What's done is done. No power can bring
To living joy a slaughtered thing.
Aye, if of life I gave my own
I could not for my guilt atone.
And though in stress of sea and land
Sweet breath has ended at my hand,
That boyhood killing in my eyes
A thousand must epitomize.
Yet to my twilight steals a thought:
Somehow forgiveness may be bought;
Somewhere I'll live my life again
So finely sensitized to pain,
With heart so rhymed to truth and right
That Truth will be a blaze of light;
And all the evil I have wrought
Will haggardly to home be brought. . . .
Then will I know my hell indeed,
And bleed where I made others bleed,
Till purged by penitence of sin
To Peace (or Heaven) I may win.

Well, anyway, you know the why
We are so pally, cats and I;
So if you have the gift of shame,
O Fellow-sinner, be the same.

INFIDELITY

Three Triangles

TRIANGLE ONE

My husband put some poison in my beer,
And fondly hoped that I would drink it up.
He would get rid of me—no bloody fear,
For when his back was turned I changed the cup.
He took it all, and if he did not die,
It's just because he's heartier than I.

And now I watch and watch him night and day
Dreading that he will try it on again.
I'm getting like a skeleton they say,
And every time I feel the slightest pain
I think: he's got me this time. . . . Oh the beast!
He might have let me starve to death, at least.

But all he thinks of is that shell-pink nurse.
I know as well as well that they're in love.
I'm sure they kiss, and maybe do things worse,
Although she looks as gentle as a dove.
I see their eyes with passion all aglow:
I know they only wait for me to go.

Ah well, I'll go (I have to, anyway),
But they will pay the price of lust and sin.
I've sent a letter to the police to say:
"If I should die it's them have done me in."

And now a lot of veronal I'll take,
And go to sleep, and never, never wake.

But won't I laugh! Aye, even when I'm dead,
To think of them both hanging by the head.

TRIANGLE TWO

MY wife's a fancy bit of stuff, it's true;
But that's no reason she should do me dirt.
Of course I know a girl is tempted to,
With mountain men a-fussin' round her skirt.
A 'andsome woman's bound to 'ave a 'eart,
But that's no reason she should be a tart.

I didn't oughter give me 'ome address
To sergeant when 'e last went on 'is leave;
And now the 'ole shebang's a bloody mess;
I didn't think the missis would deceive.
And 'ere was I, a-riskin' of me life,
And there was 'e, a-sleepin' wiv me wife.

Go' blimy, but this thing 'as got to stop.
Well, next time when we makes a big attack,
As soon as we gets well across the top,
I'll plug 'im (accidental) in the back.
'E'll cop a blinkin' packet in 'is spine,
And that'll be the end of 'im, the swine.

It's easy in the muck-up of a fight;
And all me mates'll think it was the foe.
And 'oo can say it doesn't serve 'im right?
And I'll go 'ome, and none will ever know.

My missis didn't oughter do that sort o' thing,
Seein' as 'ow she wears my weddin' ring.

Well, we'll be just as 'appy as before,
When otherwise she might a' bin a 'ore.

TRIANGLE THREE

It's fun to see Joe fuss around that kid.
I know 'e loves 'er more than all the rest,
Because she's by a lot the prettiest.
'E wouldn't lose 'er for a 'undred quid.
I love 'er too, because she isn't his'n;
But Jim, his brother's, wot they've put in prison.

It's 'ard to 'ave a 'usband wot you 'ate;
So soft that if 'e knowed you'd 'ad a tup,
'E wouldn't 'ave the guts to beat you up.
Now Jim—'e's wot I call a proper mate.
I daren't try no monkey tricks wiv 'im.
'E'd flay me 'ide off (quite right, too) would Jim.

I won't let on to Jim when 'e comes out;
But Joe—each time I see 'im kissin' Nell,
I 'ave to leave the room and laugh like 'ell.
'E'll 'ave the benefit (damn little) of the doubt.
So let 'im kiss our Nellie fit to smother;
There aint no *proof* 'er father is 'is brother.

Well, anyway I've no remorse. You see,
I've kept my frailty in the family.

LAUGHTER

I LAUGH at Life: its antics make for me a giddy game,
Where only foolish fellows take themselves with solemn aim.
I laugh at pomp and vanity, at riches, rank and pride;
At social inanity, at swagger, swank and side.
At poets, pastry-cooks and kings, at folk sublime and small,
Who fuss about a thousand things that matter not at all;
At those who dream of name and fame, at those who scheme for
    pelf. . . .
But best of all the laughing game—is laughing at myself.

Some poet chap has labelled man the noblest work of God:
I see myself a charlatan, a humbug and a fraud.
Yea, 'spite of show and shallow wit, and sentimental drool,
I know myself a hypocrite, a coward and a fool.
And though I kick myself with glee profoundly on the pants,
I'm little worse, it seems to me, than other human ants.
For if you probe your private mind, impervious to shame,
Oh, Gentle Reader, you may find you're much about the same.

Then let us mock with ancient mirth this comic, cosmic plan;
The stars are laughing at the earth; God's greatest joke is man.
For laughter is a buckler bright, and scorn a shining spear;
So let us laugh with all our might at folly, fraud and fear.
Yet on our sorry selves be spent our most sardonic glee.
Oh don't pay life the compliment to take it *seriously*.
For he who can himself despise, be surgeon to the bone,
May win to worth in others' eyes, to wisdom in his own.

LAZINESS

Let laureates sing with a rapturous swing
Of the wonder and glory of work;
Let pulpiteers preach and with passion impeach
The indolent wretches who shirk.
No doubt they are right: in the stress of the fight
It's the slackers who go to the wall;
So though it's my shame I perversely proclaim
It's fine to do nothing at all.

It's fine to recline on the flat of one's spine,
With never a thought in one's head:
It's lovely to lie staring up at the sky
When others are earning their bread.
It's great to feel one with the soil and the sun,
Drowned deep in the grasses so tall;
Oh it's noble to sweat, pounds and dollars to get,
But—it's grand to do nothing at all.

So sing to the praise of the fellows who laze
Instead of lambasting the soil;
The vagabonds gay who lounge by the way,
Conscientious objectors to toil.
But lest you should think, by this spatter of ink,
The Muses still hold me in thrall,
I'll round off my rhyme, and (until the next time)
Work like hell—doing nothing at all.

ACCORDION

Some carol of the banjo, to its measure keeping time;
Of viol or of lute some make a song.
My battered old accordion, you're worthy of a rhyme,
You've been my friend and comforter so long.
Round half the world I've trotted you, a dozen years or more;
You've given heaps of people lots of fun;
You've set a host of happy feet a-tapping on the floor . . .
Alas! your dancing days are nearly done.

I've played you from the palm-belt to the suburbs of the Pole;
From the silver-tipped sierras to the sea.
The gay and gilded cabin and the grimy glory-hole
Have echoed to your impish melody.
I've hushed you in the dug-out when the trench was stiff with
        dead;
I've lulled you by the coral-laced lagoon;
I've packed you on a camel from the dung-fire on the *bled*,
To the hell-for-breakfast Mountains of the Moon.

I've ground you to the shanty men, a-whooping heel and toe,
And the hula-hula graces in the glade.
I've swung you in the igloo to the lousy Esquimau,
And the Haussa at a hundred in the shade.
The nigger on the *levee*, and the Dinka by the Nile
Have shuffled to your insolent appeal.
I've rocked with glee the chimpanzee, and mocked the crocodile,
And shocked the pompous penquin and the seal.

I've set the yokels singing in a little Surrey pub,
Apaches swinging in a Belville bar.

I've played an obligato to the tom-tom's rub-a-dub,
And the throb of Andalusian guitar.
From the Horn to Honolulu, from the Cape to Kalamazoo,
From Wick to Wicklow, Samarkand to Spain,
You've roughed it with my kit-bag like a comrade tried and
    true. . . .
Old pal! We'll never hit the trail again.

Oh I know you're cheap and vulgar, you're an instrumental
    crime.
In drawing-rooms you haven't got a show.
You're a musical abortion, you're the voice of grit and grime,
You're the spokesman of the lowly and the low.
You're a democratic devil, you're the darling of the mob;
You're a wheezy, breezy blasted bit of glee.
You're the headache of the high-brow, you're the horror of the
    snob,
But you're worth your weight in ruddy gold to me.

For you've chided me in weakness and you've cheered me in
    defeat;
You've been an anodyne in hours of pain;
And when the slugging jolts of life have jarred me off my feet,
You've ragged me back into the ring again.
I'll never go to Heaven, for I know I am not fit,
The golden harps of harmony to swell;
But with asbestos bellows, if the devil will permit,
I'll swing you to the fork-tailed imps of Hell.

Yes, I'll hank you, and I'll spank you,
And I'll everlasting yank you
To the cinder-swinging satellites of Hell.

TREES AGAINST THE SKY

PINES against the sky,
Pluming the purple hill;
Pines . . . and I wonder why,
Heart, you quicken and thrill?
Wistful heart of a boy,
Filled with a strange sweet joy,
Lifting to Heaven nigh—
Pines against the sky.

PALMS against the sky,
Flailing the hot, hard blue;
Stark on the beach I lie,
Dreaming horizons new;
Heart of my youth elate,
Scorning a humdrum fate,
Keyed to adventure high—
Palms against the sky.

OAKS against the sky,
Ramparts of leaves high-hurled,
Staunch to stand and defy
All the winds of the world;
Stalwart and proud and free,
Firing the man in me
To try and again to try—
Oaks against the sky.

OLIVES against the sky
Of evening, limpidly bright;

Tranquil and soft and shy,
Dreaming in amber light;
Breathing the peace of life,
Ease after toil and strife. . . .
Hark to their silver sigh!
Olives against the sky.

Cypresses glooming the sky,
Stark at the end of the road;
Failing and faint am I,
Lief to be eased of my load;
There where the stones peer white
In the last of the silvery light,
Quiet and cold I'll lie—
Cypresses etching the sky.

Trees, trees against the sky—
O I have loved them well!
There are pleasures you cannot buy,
Treasures you cannot sell,
And not the smallest of these
Is the gift and glory of trees. . . .
So I gaze and I know now why
It is good to live—and to die. . . .
Trees and the Infinite Sky.

MOON-LOVER

I

THE Moon is like a ping-pong ball;
I lean against the orchard wall,
And see it soar into the void,
A silky sphere of celluloid.

Then fairy fire enkindles it,
Like gossamer by taper lit,
Until it glows above the trees
As mellow as a Cheddar cheese.

And up and up I watch it press
Into appalling loneliness;
Like realms of ice without a stain,
A corpse Moon come to life again.

Ruthless it drowns a sturdy star
That seeks its regal way to bar;
Seeming with conscious power to grow,
And sweeter, purer, gladder glow.

Dreaming serenely up the sky,
Until exultantly on high,
It shimmers with superb delight,
The silver navel of the night.

II

I have a compact to commune
A monthly midnight with the Moon;

Into its face I stare and stare,
And find sweet understanding there.

As quiet as a toad I sit
And tell my tale of days to it;
The tessellated yarn I've spun
In thirty spells of star and sun.

And the Moon listens pensively,
As placid as a lamb to me;
Until I think there's just us two
In silver world of mist and dew.

In all of spangled space, but I
To stare moon-struck into the sky;
Of billion beings I alone
To praise the Moon as still as stone,

And seal a bond between us two,
Closer than mortal ever knew;
For as mute masses I intone
The Moon is mine and mine alone.

III

To know the Moon as few men may,
One must be just a little *fey;*
And for our friendship's sake I'm glad
That I am just a trifle mad,

And one with all the wild, wise things,
The furtive folk of fur and wings,
That hold the Moon within their eyes,
And make it nightly sacrifice.

O I will watch the maiden Moon
Dance on the sea with silver shoon;
But with the Queen Moon I will keep
My tryst when all the world's asleep.

As I have kept by land and sea
That tryst for half a century;
Entranced in sibylline suspense
Beyond a world of common-sense.

Until one night the Moon alone
Will look upon a graven stone. . . .
I wonder will it miss me then,
Its lover more than other men?

Or will my wistful ghost be there,
Down ages dim to stare and stare,
On silver nights without a stir—
The Moon's Eternal Worshipper?

LITTLE PUDDLETON

I

Let others sing of Empire and of pomp beyond the sea,
A song of Little Puddleton is good enough for me,
A song of kindly living, and of coming home to tea.

I seldom read the papers, so I don't know what goes on.
I go to bed at sunset, and I leap alert at dawn,
To gossip with my garden, which I'll have you understand,
Is the neatest and the sweetest little garden in the land;
A span of sunny quietude, with walls so high and stout,
They shut me in from all the world, and shut the whole world
    out,
So that its sad bewilderment seems less than true to me:
As placid as a pool I live, as tranquil as a tree;
And all its glory I would give for glint of linnet's wings;
My cabbages are more to me than continents and kings.
Dominion have I of my own, where feud and faction cease,
A heaven of tranquillity, a paradise of peace.

II

Let continents be bathed in blood and cities leap in flame;
The life of Little Puddleton goes on and on the same;
Its ritual we follow, as we play a pleasant game.

The village worthies sit and smoke their long-stemmed pipes of
    clay,
And cheerily they nod to me, and pass the time of day.

We talk of pigs and clover, and the prospect of the crops,
And the price of eggs and butter—there the conversation drops.
For in a doubt-distracted world I keep the rustic touch:
I think it's better not to think too deeply nor too much;
But just to dream and take delight in all I hear and see,
The tinker in the tavern, with his trollop on his knee;
The ivied church, the anvil clang, the geese upon the green,
The drowsy noon, the hush of eve so holy and serene.
This is my world, then back again with heart of joy I go
To cottage walls of mellow stain, and garden all aglow.

III

For all I've been and all I've seen I have no vain regret.
One comes to Little Puddleton, contented to forget;
Accepting village values, immemorially set.

I did not make this world and so it's not my job to mend;
But I have fought for fifty years and now I near the end;
And I am heart-faint from the fight, and claim the right to rest,
And dare to hope the last of life will prove to be the best.
For here have I four sturdy walls with low and humble thatch,
A smiling little orchard and a big potato patch.
And so with hoe in hand I stand and mock the dubious sky;
Let revolution rock the land, serene, secure am I.
I grow my simple food, I groom my lettuce and my beans;
I feast in colour, form and song, and ask not what it means.
Beauty suffices in itself; then when my strength is spent,
Like simple hind with empty mind, I cultivate content.

Behold then Little Puddleton, the end of all my dreams.
Not much to show for life, I know; yet O how sweet it seems!
For when defeated day goes down in carnage in the West,
How blessed sanctuary is, and peace and love and rest!

BOOKSHELF

I LIKE to think that when I fall,
A rain-drop in Death's shoreless sea,
This shelf of books along the wall,
Beside my bed, will mourn for me.

Regard it. . . . Aye, my taste is queer.
Some of my bards you may disdain.
Shakespeare and Milton are not here;
Shelley and Keats you seek in vain.
Wordsworth, Tennyson, Browning too,
Remarkably are not in view.

Who are they? *Omar* first you see,
With Vine and Rose and Nightingale,
Voicing my pet philosophy
Of Wine and Song. . . . Then *Reading Gaol,*
Where Fate a gruesome pattern makes,
And dawn-light shudders as it wakes.

The *Ancient Mariner* is next,
With eerie and terrific text;
Then Burns, with pawky human touch—
Poor devil! I have loved him much.
And now a gay quartette behold:
Bret Harte and Eugene Field are here;
And Henley, chanting brave and bold,
And Chesterton, in praise of Beer.

Lastly come valiant Singers three;
To whom this strident Day belongs:

Kipling, to whom I bow the knee,
Masefield, with rugged sailor songs. . . .
And to my lyric troupe I add
With grateful heart—*The Shropshire Lad.*

Behold my minstrels, just eleven.
For half my life I've loved them well.
And though I have no hope of Heaven,
And more than Highland fear of Hell,
May I be damned if on this shelf
Ye find a rhyme I make myself.

FIVE FRIVOLOUS SONGS

You Can't Can Love
Lip-stick Liz
The Bread-knife Ballad
The Boola-boola Maid
The Song of a Sardine

[These are included in *Bath-Tub Ballads*, with Music by the author, and published by Messrs. Francis, Day & Hunter, London and Gordon V. Thompson, Toronto.]

YOU CAN'T CAN LOVE

Oh I don't know how fishes feel,
But I can't help thinking it odd
That a gay young flapper of a female Eel
Should fall in love with a Cod.
Yet that's exactly what she did,
And it only goes to prove
That whatever you do you can't put the lid
On that crazy feeling, Love. (*Chorus.*)

.   .   .   .

Now that young Tom Cod was a dreadful rake
And he had no wish to wed;
But he feared that the poor thing's heart would break,
So this is what he said:
"Some fellows prize a woman's eyes,
And some admire her lips;
While some have a taste for a tiny waist,
But me, what I like is—HIPS." (*Chorus.*)

.   .   .   .

"So you see, my dear," said the gay Tom Cod,
"Exactly how I feel.
Oh I hate to be unkind, but I know my mind,
And there ain't no hips on an eel."
"Alas! it's true," said the foolish fish
As she blushed to her finny tips;
"And with might and main, though it gives me pain,
I'll try to develop HIPS." (*Chorus.*)

.   .   .   .

So day and night with all her might
She physical culturized;
But alas and alack! in the middle of her back
No hump she recognized.
And then she knew her love's eclipse
Was fated from the start;
For you never yet saw an eel with HIPS,
So she died of a broken heart. (*Chorus.*)

Chorus after each verse:—

Oh you gotta hand it out to Love, to Love,
You can't can Love;
You'll find it at the bottom of the briny deep
And the blue above.
From the Belgian Hare to the Polar Bear
And the Turtle Dove,
You can look where you please, but from elephants to fleas . . .

Verse 2:

You can look where you like, but from pollywogs to pike . . .

Verse 3:

You can look where you choose, but from crabs to
     kangaroos . . .

Verse 4:

You can look where you please, but from buffaloes to bees . . .
YOU'LL NEVER PUT THE LID ON LOVE.

LIP-STICK LIZ

Oh Lip-stick Liz was in the biz'
That's the oldest known in history;
She had a lot of fancy rags,
Of her form she made no mystery.
She had a man, a fancy man,
His name was Alexander;
And he used to beat her up because
He couldn't understand her.

. . . .

Now Lip-stick Liz she loved her man,
And she couldn't love no other;
So when she saw him with a Broadway blonde
Her rage she could not smother.
Oh she saw them once and she saw them twice,
But the third time nearly crazed her;
So she walked into a hardware store
And she bought a brand-new razor.

. . . .

Now Lip-stick Liz she trailed them two,
For she was tired of weeping;
She trailed them two to a flash hotel,
And there she found them sleeping.
So she gashed them once and she gashed them twice,
Their jug'lar veins to sever;
And the bright blood flowed in a pool between,
And their lives were done forever.

. . . .

Now Lip-stick Liz she went to the police
And says she: "Me hands are gory;
And ye'll put me away in a deep dark cell
When once you've heard me story."
So they've put her away in a deep dark cell
Until her life be over:
And what is the moral of the whole damn show
I wish I could discover.

Chorus after each verse:—

Oh Lip-stick Liz!
What a lousy life this is!
It's a hell of a break
For a girl on the make—
Oh Lip-stick Liz!

THE BREAD-KNIFE BALLAD

I

A LITTLE child was sitting
Upon her mother's knee,
And down her cheeks the bitter tears did flow;
And as I sadly listened
I heard this tender plea;
'Twas uttered in a voice so soft and low:—

Chorus:

Please, Mother, don't stab Father with the bread-knife.
Remember 'twas a gift when you were wed.
But if you *must* stab Father with the Bread-knife,
Please, Mother, use another for the bread.

II

"Not guilty!" said the Jury,
And the Judge said: "Set her free;
But remember, it must not occur again;
And next time you must listen
To your little daughter's plea,"
Then all the Court did join in this refrain:—

Chorus . . .

THE BOOLA-BOOLA MAID

In the wilds of Madagascar dwelt a Boola-boola Maid;
For her hand young men would ask her, but she always was
   afraid.
Oh that Boola-boola Maid she was living in the shade
Of a spreading Yum-yum tree;
And when the day was done, at the setting of the sun
She would sing this melody:—

Chorus:

I don't want no cave-man to caress me;
I don't want no coal-black hands to press me.
All I want is a fellow who wears suspenders;
That'll be the coon to whom this babe surrenders.
For the man I wed must have a proper *trousseau:*
None of your fig-leaf dudes will make me do so;
For it's funny how I feel, but I'm crazy for Socks Appeal,
And my dream is to marry a man with a pair of socks.

While this ditty she was cooing, came a Boola-boola Man,
And he lost no time in wooing, for he punched her on the pan.
Oh that Boola-boola Maid she was terribly afraid,
So he punched her on the eye;
And a woeful Maid was she, as beneath that Yum-yum tree
He heard that maiden cry:—

Chorus as before.

Then with shrieks of ribald laughter, said that Boola-boola Man:
"If it's only socks you're after, I will do the best I can.
Oh I've handed you a pair, and I've plenty more to spare,"

So he socked her on the nose;
And then he laughed with glee as beneath that Yum-yum tree
This lamentation rose:

Chorus once again.

Now the wedding tom-tom's over for this Boola-boola Maid,
And when evening shadows hover, she no longer is afraid.
For she wears a fig-leaf pinny and she rocks a pickaninny
In the shade of the Yum-yum tree;
And she's happy with her He Man though she still dreams of a
    She Man,
As she sings this song with glee:

Chorus, final.

THE SONG OF A SARDINE

A FAT man sat in an orchestra stall, and his cheeks were wet with
    tears,
As he gazed at the prima-donna tall whom he hadn't seen for
    years.
"Oh don't you remember," he murmurs low, "that Spring in
    Montparnasse,
When hand in hand we used to go to our nightly singing class.
Ah me! those days so gay and glad, so full of hope and cheer,
And the farewell supper that we had of tinned sardines and beer;
When you looked so like a little Queen, with your proud and
    haughty air,
That I took from the box the last sardine, and I twined it in your
    hair." (*Chorus.*)

Verse two.

Alas! I am only a stock-broker now, while you are high and
    great;
The laurels of Fame adorn your brow, while on you princes
    wait.
And as I sit so sadly here, and list to your thrilling tones,
You cannot remember, I sadly fear, if my name is Smith or Jones.
Yet oh those days of long ago, when I had scarce a *sou!*
And as my bitter tears down-flow I think again of you.
And once again I seem to see that Maid of sweet sixteen,
Within whose tresses tenderly I twined that bright sardine.
    (*Chorus.*)

Chorus, after each verse:

Oh that sardine in your hair!
I can see it shining there,

720

As I took it from its box,
And I twined it in your locks.
Silver sardine in your hair
Like a jewel rich and rare—
Oh that little silver sardine in your hair!

WARSAW

I WAS in Warsaw when the first bomb fell;
I was in Warsaw when the Terror came—
Havoc and horror, famine, fear and flame,
Blasting from loveliness a living hell.
Barring the station towered a sentinel;
Trainward I battled, blind escape my aim.
ENGLAND! I cried. He kindled at the name:
With lion-leap he haled me. . . . All was well.

ENGLAND! they cried for aid, and cried in vain.
Vain was their valour, emptily they cried.
Bleeding, they saw their City crucified. . . .
O splendid soldier, by the last, lone train,
To-day would you flame forth to fray me place?
Or—would you curse and spit into my face?

September, 1939.

722

ENEMY CONSCRIPT

WHAT are we fighting for,
We fellows who go to war?
Fighting for Freedom's sake!
(You give me the belly-ache.)
Freedom to starve or slave!
Freedom! aye, in the grave.
Fighting for "hearth and home,"
Who haven't an inch of loam?
Hearth? Why even a byre
Can only be ours for hire.
Dying for future Peace?
Killing that killing cease?
To hell with such tripe, I say.
"Sufficient unto the day."

It ain't much fun being dead.
Better to lie in bed,
Cuddle up to the wife,
Making, not taking, life.
To the corpse that stinks in the clay,
Does it matter who wins the day?
What odds if tyrants reign?
They can't put irons on the brain.
One always can eat one's grub,
Smoke and drink in a pub.
There's happiness in a glass,
A pipe and the kiss of a lass.
It's the best we get anyhow,
In the life we are living now.

Who's wanting a hero's fate?
To the dead cheers come too late.
Flesh is softer than steel;
Wounds are weary to heal.
In the maniac hell of the fray
Who is there dares to say?
"Hate will be vanquished by Love;
God's in His Heaven above."

When those who govern us lead
The lads they command to bleed;
When rulers march at the head,
And statesmen fall with the dead;
When Kings leap into the fray,
Fight in the old-time way,
Perish beside their men,
Maybe, O maybe then
War will be part of the past,
Peace will triumph at last.

Meantime such lads as I,
Who wouldn't have harmed a fly,
Have got to get out and kill
Lads whom we bear no ill;
As simple as we, no doubt,
Who seek what it's all about;
Who die in defence of—what?
Homes that they haven't got;
Who perish when all they ask
Is to finish the daily task;
Make bread for the little ones,
Not feed the greed of the guns,
When fields of battle are red,
And diplomats die in bed.

DON'T CHEER

Don't cheer, damn you! Don't cheer!
Silence! Your bitterest tear
Is fulsomely sweet to-day. . . .
Down on your knees and pray.

See, they sing as they go,
Marching row upon row.
Who will be spared to return,
Sombre and starkly stern?
Chaps whom we knew—so strange,
Distant and dark with change;
Silent as those they slew,
Something in them dead too.
Who will return this way,
To sing as they sing to-day.

Send to the glut of the guns
Bravest and best of your sons.
Hurl a million to slaughter,
Blood flowing like Thames water;
Pile up pyramid high
Your dead to the anguished sky;
A monument down all time
Of hate and horror and crime.
Weep, rage, pity, curse, fear—
Anything, but . . . don't cheer.

Sow to the ploughing guns
Seed of your splendid sons.

725

Let your heroic slain
Richly manure the plain.
What will the harvest be?
Unborn of Unborn will see. . . .

Dark is the sky and drear. . . .
For the pity of God don't cheer.
Dark and dread is their way,
Who sing as they march to-day. . . .
Humble your hearts and pray.

L'ENVOI

Once more my sheaf of songs I tie,
And bid them gleefully good-bye,
And feel it will not give me pain,
To never look on them again.
With metronomic measure I
Have beat them out beneath the sky.
And though my facile rhyme I curse,
Sometimes I think they might be worse;
But anyway, as in the past,
I vow that they will be my last.

For I have come to sixty-five,
Content to feel so much alive;
And though grey-haired, I grieve to state
An unrepentant reprobate;
Admiring lads who wench and wine,
But forced, alas! to toe the line;
For I have learnt a thing or two,
As we old coves are bound to do.

I've come to know that storing health
Is better far than storing wealth;
That smug success has little worth
Beside the simple joys of earth;
That Fame is but a bubble brief,
And glory vain beyond belief;
That it is good to eat and drink;
That it is bad to over-think;
That only stupid people claim

To take themselves with serious aim;
That laughter is the Gods' best gift—
So to the Gods our laughter lift;
Aye, though their wrath the Heavens split,
They grant us Scorn, to laugh at it.

And so, frail creatures of a day,
Let's have a good time while we may,
And do the very best we can
To give one to our fellow man;
Knowing that all will end with Death,
Let's joy with every moment's breath;
And lift our heads like blossoms blithe
To meet at last the Swinging Scythe.

FINIS

INDEX TO FIRST LINES

A bunch of the boys were whooping it up 29
A child saw in the morning skies 440
A fat man sat in an orchestra stall, and his cheeks were wet with tears, . 720
Alas! upon some starry height, ... 421
A little child was sitting 717
All day long when the shells sail over 353
A man once aimed that my life be shamed, ... 107
An angel was tired of heaven, as he lounged in the golden street; . . 60
And so when he reached my bed 373
"And when I come to die," he said, ... 236
And when I come to the dim trail-end, ... 284
Another day of toil and strife, ... 454
A pencil, sir; a penny—won't you buy? 474
A pistol shot rings round and round the world; 57
A-singin' " 'Oo's Yer Lady Friend?" we started out from 'Arver, . . 303
As I sat by my baby's bed 540
As I was saying . . . (No, thank you; I never take cream with my tea; 410
At dawn of day the white land lay all gruesome-like and grim, . . 208
'Ave you seen Bill's mug in the Noos to-day? 395
A wild and woeful race he ran 519
Because I have ten thousand pounds I sit upon my stern, . . . 678
Because my overcoat's in pawn, ... 470
Before I drink myself to death, ... 510
Be honest, kindly, simple, true; 244
Beyond the Rocking Bridge it lies, the burg of evil fame, . . . 623
"Black is the sky, but the land is white— 159
Blind Peter Piper used to play 523
Brave Thackeray has trolled of days when he was twenty-one, . . 515
"But it isn't playing the game," he said, ... 295
Can you recall, dear comrade, when we tramped God's land together, - 71
Clorinda met me on the way 472
Come out, O Little Moccasins, and frolic on the snow! 237
Day after day behold me plying 512
"Deny your God!" they ringed me with their spears; 171
Don't cheer, damn you! Don't cheer! 725
Far and near, high and clear, ... 293
Flat as a drum-head stretch the haggard snows; 178
"Flowers, only flowers—bring me dainty posies, ... 326
For oh, when the war will be over 362
From wrath-red dawn to wrath-red dawn 310
"Gather around me, children dear; 540

729

Give me the scorn of the stars and a peak defiant; 408
Give me to live and love in the old, bold fashion; 408
Gold! We leapt from our benches. 144
Gurr! You *cochon!* Stand and fight! 400
"Hae ye heard whit ma auld mither's postit tae me? 306
Hark to a Sourdough story, told at sixty below, ... 645
Hark to the ewe that bore him: 132
Have you ever heard of the Land of Beyond, ... 177
Have you gazed on naked grandeur where there's nothing else to
  gaze on, ... 17
Heaven's mighty sweet, I guess; 636
He dreamed away his hours in school; 532
Heed me, feed me, I am hungry, I am red-tongued with desire; . . 266
He gives me such a bold and curious look, ... 492
He hurried away, young heart of joy, under our Devon sky! . . . 374
Heigh ho! to sleep I vainly try; 438
Here is my Garret up five flights of stairs; 425
Her little head just topped the window-sill; 486
He's the man from Eldorado, and he's just arrived in town, . . . 120
He's yonder, on the terrace of the Café de la Paix, ... 456
He was an old prospector with a vision bleared and dim 150
Ho! we were strong, we were swift, we were brave. 265
"How good God is to me," he said; 526
"Hullo, young Jones! with your tie so gay 580
Humping it here in the dug-out, ... 376
Hurrah! I'm off to Finistère, to Finistère, to Finistère; 530
I count each day a little life, ... 606
I'd hate to be a centipede (of legs I've only two), ... 685
"I do not seek the copper streak, nor yet the yellow dust; . . . 150
I'd rather be a Jester than the Minstrel of the King; 599
I dreamed I saw three demi-gods who in a café sat, ... 480
If you had a friend strong, simple, true, ... 525
If you had the choice of two women to wed, ... 212
If you leave the gloom of London and you seek a glowing land, . . 52
If you're up against a bruiser and you're getting knocked about—Grin. 27
I haled me a woman from the street, ... 37
I have some friends, some worthy friends, ... 537
I just think that dreams are best, ... 226
I know a garden where the lilies gleam, ... 38
I know a mountain thrilling to the stars, ... 217
I laugh at Life; its antics make for me a giddy game, ... 697
I like to think that when I fall, ... 708
I look at no one, me; 498
I looked into the aching womb of night; 415
I'm a homely little bit of tin and bone; 141
I'm crawlin' out in the mangolds to bury wot's left o' Joe—. . . 570
I'm dead. 589

I'm dreaming to-night in the fire-glow, alone in my study tower, . . 195
I'm gatherin' flowers by the wayside to lay on the grave of Bill; . . 339
"I'm going, Billy, old fellow. 568
I'm goin' 'ome to Blighty—ain't I glad to 'ave the chance! . . . 345
I'm holding it down on God's scrap-pile, up on the fag-end of earth; 138
"I'm one of the Arctic brotherhood, I'm an old-time pioneer. . . . 14
I'm one of these haphazard chaps 496
I'm scared of it all, God's truth! so I am; 262
"I'm taking pen in hand this night, and hard it is for me; 270
I'm up on the bally wood-pile at the back of the barracks yard; . . 132
In the little Crimson Manual it's written plain and clear 153
In the moonless, misty night, with my little pipe alight, ... 272
In the wilds of Madagascar dwelt a Boola-boola Maid; 718
I saw three wounded of the war: 582
I sing no idle songs of dalliance days, ... 167
Is it not strange? A year ago to-day, ... 390
I sought Him on the purple seas, ... 538
I sought the trails of South and North, ... 524
I strolled up old Bonanza, where I staked in ninety-eight, . . . 128
It isn't the foe that we fear; 316
I took a contract to bury the body of blasphemous Bill MacKie, . . 103
I took the clock down from the shelf; 219
I tried to refine that neighbor of mine, honest to God, I did. . . . 98
It's a mighty good world, so it is, dear lass, ... 191
It's cruel cold on the water-front, silent and dark and drear; . . . 64
It's easy to fight when everything's right, ... 351
It's fine to have a blow-out in a fancy restaurant, ... 39
"It's getting dark awful sudden. 159
It's good the great green earth to roam, ... 455
It's mighty lonesome-like and drear 242
It's slim and trim and bound in blue; 509
I've been sittin' starin' at 'is muddy pair of boots, ... 328
I've got a little job on 'and, the time is drawin' nigh; 404
I've tinkered at my bits of rhymes 291
I wanted the gold, and I sought it; 3
I was in Warsaw when the first bomb fell; 722
I was once, I declare, a Stone-Age man, ... 168
I watched one day a parrot grey—'twas in a barber shop. . . . 683
I will not wash my face; 135
I wish that I could understand 533
I wonder 'oo and wat 'e was, ... 572
Jack would laugh an' joke all day; 214
Jerry MacMullen, the millionaire, ... 549
Just Home and Love! the words are small 261
Just think! some night the stars will gleam 213
Let laureates sing with a rapturous swing 698
Let others sing of Empire and of pomp beyond the sea, ... 706

Let others sing of gold and gear, the joy of being rich; 489
Light up your pipe again, old chum, and sit awhile with me; . . . 232
Lone amid the café's cheer, ... 432
Me and Ed and a stretcher 311
Men of the High North, the wild sky is blazing; 78
Missis Moriarty called last week, and says she to me, says she: . . 398
Moko, the Educated Ape is here, ... 218
My Father Christmas passed away 205
My glass is filled, my pipe is lit, ... 274
My husband put some poison in my beer, ... 694
My job is done; my rhymes are ranked and ready, ... 417
My leg? It's off at the knee. 320
My mind goes back to Fumin Wood, and how we stuck it out, . . 586
My mother she had children five 689
My rhymes are rough, and often in my rhyming 77
My stretcher is one scarlet stain, ... 389
Never knew Jim, did you? Our boy Jim? 556
No, Bill, I'm not a-spooning out no patriotic tosh 334
Now Eddie Malone got a swell grammyfone to draw all the trade to
    his store; 174
Now Fireman Flynn met Hank the Finn where lights of Lust-land
    glow; 618
Now Kelly was no fighter; 559
Now Sam McGee was from Tennessee, where the cotton blooms and
    blows. 33
Now wouldn't you expect to find a man an awful crank 117
O dear little cabin, I've loved you so long, ... 282
O'er the dark pines she sees the silver moon, ... 44
Of course you've heard of the *Nancy Lee,* and how she sailed away . 444
O God, take the sun from the sky! 336
Oh, have you forgotten those afternoons 507
Oh, how good it is to be 206
Oh I don't know how fishes feel, ... 713
Oh, it is good to drink and sup, ... 536
Oh, it's pleasant sitting here, ... 449
Oh Lip-stick Liz was in the biz' 715
Oh, some of us lolled in the château, ... 379
Oh the wife she tried to tell me that 'twas nothing but the thrumming 300
Oh, weren't they the fine boys! You never saw the beat of them, . . 318
Oh ye whose hearts are resonant, and ring to War's romance, . . . 341
Oh you who are shy of the popular eye, ... 686
Oh you who have daring deeds to tell! 186
Once more my sheaf of songs I tie, ... 727
Once, when a boy, I *killed a cat* 691
One of the Down and Out—that's me. Stare at me well, ay, stare! . . 80
One said: Thy life is thine to make or mar, ... 40
Only a Leather Medal, hanging there on the wall, ... 638

On the ragged edge of the world I'll roam, ... 195

O Tavern of the Golden Snail! 430

O Teddy Bear! with your head awry 517

Out of the night a crash, ... 583

Pines against the sky, ... 701

Poppies, you try to tell me, glowing there in the wheat; 367

Said Hongray de la Glaciere unto his proud Papa: 664

Said President MacConnachie to Treasurer MacCall: 610

Says Bauldy MacGreegor frae Gleska tae Hecky MacCrimmon frae
    Skye: 565

Says I to my Missis: "Ba goom, lass! you've something, I see, on your
    mind." 675

Say! You've struck a heap of trouble— 67

Sez I: My Country calls? Well, let it call. 297

She lay like a saint on her copper couch; 200

She risked her all, they told me, bravely sinking 464

She said: "I am too old to play 607

She was a Philistine spick and span, ... 467

Since all that is was ever bound to be; 394

Singing larks I saw for sale— 648

Smith, great writer of stories, drank; found it immortalised his pen; . 276

So easy 'tis to make a rhyme, ... 452

. . . So I walked among the willows very quietly all night; . . . 299

Some carol of the banjo, to its measure keeping time; 699

"Sow your wild oats in your youth," so we're always told; . . 508

"Tell Annie I'll be home in time 577

That Barret, the painter of pictures, what feeling for color he had! . 562

That boy I took in the car last night, ... 552

The clover was in blossom, an' the year was at the June, ... 229

The cow-moose comes to water, and the beaver's overbold, . . . 258

The cruel war was over—oh, the triumph was so sweet! 54

The Dreamer visioned Life as it might be, ... 271

The humble garret where I dwell 441

The Junior God looked from his place 193

The lonely sunsets flare forlorn xviii

The lone man gazed and gazed upon his gold, ... 252

The man above was a murderer, the man below was a thief; . . . 125

The Moon is like a ping-pong ball; 703

The poppies gleamed like bloody pools through cotton-woolly mist; . 381

The poppies that in Spring I sow, ... 616

*The same old sprint in the morning, boys, to the same old din and
    smut;* 370

The sky is like an envelope, ... 138

The Spirit of the Unborn Babe peered through the window-pane, . . 527

The trails of the world be countless, and most of the trails be tried; . 19

The very skies were black with shame 673

The Wanderlust has lured me to the seven lonely seas, ... 239

The waves have a story to tell me, ... 8
The woes of men beyond my ken 628
The World's all right; serene I sit, ... 244
There are strange things done in the midnight sun 33
There is no hope for such as I on earth, nor yet in Heaven; 68
There lies the trail to Sunnydale, ... 199
There once was a limpet puffed with pride 680
There once was a Square, such a square little Square 688
There was a woman, and she was wise; woefully wise was she; . . . 68
There was Claw-fingered Kitty and Windy Ike living the life of
    shame, ... 91
There were two brothers, John and James, ... 407
There where the mighty mountains bare their fangs unto the moon, . 6
There will be a singing in your heart, ... 251
There's a cry from out the loneliness—oh, listen, Honey, listen! . . 23
There's a drip of honeysuckle in the deep green lane; 330
There's a four-pronged buck a-swinging in the shadow of my cabin, . 46
There's a race of men that don't fit in, ... 42
"There's something in your face, Michael, I've seen it all the day; . 575
There's sunshine in the heart of me, ... 168
They brought the mighty chief to town; 198
They turned him loose; he bowed his head, ... 192
This is the law of the Yukon, and ever she makes it plain: 10
This is the pay-day up at the mines, when the bearded brutes come
    down; 48
This is the song of the parson's son, as he squats in his shack alone, . 14
This is the tale that was told to me by the man with the crystal eye, . 107
This is the yarn he told to me 650
Three gentlemen live close beside me— 494
Three maids there were in meadow bright, ... 655
Three men I saw beside a bar, ... 662
Three score and ten, the psalmist saith, ... 256
To Dawson Town came Percy Brown from London on the Thames. . 630
To-day I opened wide my eyes, ... 643
To-day within a grog-shop near 463
To rest my fagged brain now and then, ... 491
To smite Apollo's lyre I am unable; 601
Tramp, tramp, the grim road, the road from Mons to Wipers . . . 303
'Twas a year ago and the moon was bright 70
'Twas in the bleary middle of the hard-boiled Arctic night, . . . 602
'Twas up in a land long famed for gold, where women were far and
    rare, ... 111
Up in my garret bleak and bare 484
Up into the sky I stare; 479
Walking, walking, oh, the joy of walking! 521
We brought him in from between the lines: we'd better have let him
    lie; 359

We couldn't sit and study for the law; 62
We're taking Marie Toro to her home in Père-La-Chaise; . . . 481
We sleep in the sleep of ages, the bleak, barbarian pines; 21
We talked of yesteryears, of trails and treasure, ... 163
We've bidden good-bye to life in a cage, we're finished with pushing
    a pen; 370
We've finished up the filthy war; 594
We was in a crump-'ole, 'im and me; 364
What are we fighting for, ... 723
What are you doing here, Tom Thorne, on the white top-knot o' the
    world, ... 202
What do they matter, our headlong hates, when we take the toll of
    our Dead? 405
What d'ye think, lad; what d'ye think, ... 579
What was the blackest sight to me 554
When a girl's sixteen, and as poor as she's pretty, ... 346
When a man gits on his uppers in a hard-pan sort of town, ... 50
When Chewed-ear Jenkins got hitched up to Guinneyveer McGee, . 247
When first I left Blighty they gave me a bay'nit 349
When from my fumbling hand the tired pen falls, ... 285
When I have come with happy heart to sixty years and ten, . . . 668
When I played my penny whistle on the braes above Lochgyle . . 622
When I've eat my fill and my belt is snug, ... 376
When the boys come out from Lac Labiche in the lure of the early
    Spring, ... 187
When the long, long day is over, and the Big Boss gives me my pay, . 25
When you're lost in the Wild, and you're scared as a child, ... 228
When your marrer bone seems 'oller, ... 324
"Where are you going, Young Fellow My Lad, ... 332
Within a pub that's off the Strand and handy to the bar, ... 670
Ye who know the Lone Trail fain would follow it, ... 19
You make it in your mess-tin by the brazier's rosy gleam; . . . 369
You may talk o' your lutes and your dulcimers fine, ... 385
You've heard of "Casey at The Bat," 657
You've heard of Julot the *apache*, and Gigolette, his *môme*. . . . 426
You want me to tell you a story, a yarn of the firin' line, ... 356
You who have lived in the land, ... 72
Zut! it's two o'clock 435